AARON BURR

Portrait of an Ambitious Man

HERBERT S. PARMET and MARIE B. HECHT spent four years researching *Aaron Burr: Portrait of an Ambitious Man*. Their next book, *Never Again*, a study of the Roosevelt-Willkie presidential campaign of 1940, is currently in progress.

Aaron Burr by John Vanderlyn, circa 1802.
(COURTESY OF OLIVER BURR JENNINGS)

AARON BURR

PORTRAIT OF
AN AMBITIOUS MAN

BY

Herbert S. Parmet & Marie B. Hecht

THE MACMILLAN COMPANY, NEW YORK

COLLIER-MACMILLAN LTD., LONDON

Library of Congress Catalog Card Number: 67–21421

FIRST PRINTING

The Macmillan Company, New York
Collier-Macmillan Canada Ltd., Toronto, Ontario
Printed in the United States of America

To Frank F. Bergenfeld

To Joan and Wendy

ACKNOWLEDGMENTS

To UNCOVER ALL that was written by and about a man as many-faceted as Aaron Burr is to experience an adventure through the nation's leading repositories, both public and private. It would have been an overwhelming undertaking without the remarkable cooperation that devoted librarians provided wherever we went. Therefore, some trepidation must accompany any attempted enumeration of all who aided this project. In particular, however, we are indebted to the following institutions and individuals for their time and care: the American Antiquarian Society, Worcester, Massachusetts; Edith S. Reiter of the Campus Martius Museum, Marietta, Ohio; the Special Collections section of the Columbia University library; Elizabeth Root of the Hartford Seminary Foundation, Hartford, Connecticut; the helpful and courteous staff of the Historical Society of Pennsylvania; the indispensable facilities of the Library of Congress; the special microfilm services of the Henry E. Huntington Library, San Marino, California; Charlotte Wiggin of the Litchfield Historical Society, Litchfield, Connecticut; Francis Ronalds for his great help and for brightening our visit to the Morristown National Historical Park in New Jersey; the staff of the New York Public Library; Alexander P. Clark of the John Foster Dulles Library, Princeton University; the staff of the University of Virginia's Alderman Library; Howard Gotlieb of Yale University; and A. K. Baragwanath of the Museum of the City of New York. A special word must be reserved for the New-York Historical Society Library, which virtually became our headquarters during the many years of research. Its staff, and particularly Arthur J. Breton of the manuscript division, provided hours of invaluable and gracious assistance. Its director, James J. Heslin, was most helpful in arranging for our use of pictures from their archives. To our editor, Richard Marek of The Macmillan Company, we owe our appreciation for his encouragement and his skilled assistance.

January 26, 1967   H. S. P.
                                                             M. B. H.

CONTENTS

ILLUSTRATIONS

AARON BURR

Portrait of an Ambitious Man

CHAPTER I

The Burrs and the Edwardses

I T was a curious marriage. In May of 1752, Reverend Aaron Burr journeyed to Stockbridge, in the western part of Massachusetts, to visit his friend and fellow divine, Jonathan Edwards. There, he renewed his acquaintance with Sarah, Edwards' third daughter. In the six years since Burr had last seen her, she had matured into a most desirable young lady. And there is little doubt that she pleased the minister, for less than two weeks after returning to his Newark parsonage, Burr sent a young Fellow of the College of New Jersey to fetch the girl and her mother. The two ladies arrived on a Saturday evening, and the following Monday the Reverend Aaron Burr and Miss Sarah Edwards were wed.

The precipitous courtship of the thirty-six year old minister and his twenty-one year old bride rather astounded the gossipy countryside. Burr protested to his dear friend, Reverend Joseph Bellamy, that he was unaffected by "ye Talk," but he apparently thought that some explanation was necessary. "We cannot upon a review see one rash or imprudent step we should alter if it was to do again," wrote Reverend Burr. "We hope none of our Friends will give Themselves any Trouble abt it or ever express themselves concerned about our conduct which we are sure can bear the strictest and most critical examination."[1]

The students at the Latin School which Burr conducted were unused to sharing their teacher and regarded the new Mrs. Burr with a highly suspicious eye. One of them wrote: "As I have yet no manner of Acquaintance with her, I cannot describe to you her Qualifications & properties; however they say she is a very valuable lady; I think her a person of great beauty."[2] Later, however, he wrote glowingly of the Burrs' marital happiness and Sarah's charms, calling her a woman of "very good Sense, of a Genteel & virtuous education, amiable in her person, of great affability & agreeableness in Conversation & a very excellent Economist."[3]

The Burrs set up housekeeping at the Newark parsonage, a vine-covered stone mansion at Broad and William streets. Both of their children were born there: Sarah on May 3, 1754, and a son on February 6, 1756, named after his father. They had illustrious forebears on both sides.

The Burr family had German roots, but five centuries of English life had thoroughly Anglicized them before their arrival in the New World. Colonel Aaron Burr, about two hundred years after his first ancestor, Jehue Burr, had arrived with Winthrop's fleet, received letters from alleged German relatives. He wrote amusingly to his daughter: "You did not know before I told you, and I have not told you yet, huzzy, that you are a Dutchman."[4]

Jehue Burr settled first at Roxbury, Massachusetts, where he was admitted as a freeman in 1632, and then moved west through the frontier wilderness until he and his seven companions emerged on the banks of the Connecticut River. There they built a village called Agawan, later named Springfield. After achieving the dubious distinction of being the first tax collector in the Connecticut Valley, the founder bought an extensive tract of land on both sides of the Housatonic River, at what is now Fairfield. This became the family homestead. Jehue was an active, honored member of the little Connecticut community, often representing it at the General Court.

Reverend Aaron Burr, Jehue's grandson, was born in Fairfield County on January 4, 1715. He was a small, lively, precocious child. While he was at Yale in the summer of 1736, a religious revival swept through New Haven, carrying young Burr with it. In his private journal he made the following entry: "This year God saw fit to open my eyes and show me what a miserable creature I was." He suffered despair until, as he wrote, "It pleased God at length to reveal his son to me as an all sufficient Saviour, and I hope, inclined me to receive him on the terms of the Gospel."[5]

Soon afterward, Burr was licensed for the ministry. He preached first in Greenfield, Massachusetts, and then went to the Jerseys. A year's trial convinced the Reverend and his parishioners that theirs would be a fruitful relationship; and so he was ordained their pastor. "God grant that I may ever keep fresh upon my mind the solemn charge that was then given me," he wrote.[6] The small, elegant man became a distinguished minister and teacher.

Shortly after his arrival in Newark, Reverend Burr founded a Latin School to instruct eight to ten boys in the principles of English and classical languages. The school acquired a widespread and excellent reputation. Its demands became so overwhelming that, coupled with his domestic duties, Reverend Burr's health became seriously impaired. Following strict orders from his physician, he departed for a vacation trip that took him first to Rhode Island to visit friends and then to Boston.

The staid capital of Massachusetts was being rocked by the leader of the "New Lights," the English preacher George Whitefield. He had just completed a triumphal tour through the South and was the guest preacher in Benjamin Colman's church when Burr was present. Whitefield's magnetic voice and dramatic power moved conservative citizens to tears and confessions in open church and caused the more emotional to faint and grovel on the floor. His exquisite pictures of hell and damnation frightened his listeners and, perhaps in some perverse way, made them enjoy their terror.

Burr was at first only mildly interested by Whitefield, but after hearing him hypnotize about ten thousand on the Boston Commons with his eloquence, he decided to speak with him. Before he returned home, Whitefield visited Burr at the parsonage and preached at the First Presbyterian Church, where he was well received. Burr and Whitefield corresponded until the former's death.

After this interlude, the most absorbing task of Burr's life occupied him completely: the founding of the College of New Jersey. The need for an institution of higher learning in the Middle Colonies, both to supply the clerical demand and to allay the dissatisfaction of many with the philosophies of Yale and Harvard, had been felt by the Synod of New York for some time. At first, a charter for a college had been refused by the Anglican authorities, but Governor Jonathan Belcher, newly arrived from England in 1746, was enthusiastic enough to grant their request and to become a patron of the college.

The Charter of the College, published early in 1747, named Reverend Aaron Burr as one of the founders. Reverend Jonathan Dickinson of Elizabeth Town was to be its first president. He was the obvious choice: a leader of the movement, a well known Presbyterian preacher, and a lawyer and doctor as well.

Eight or ten scholars were in residence in private lodgings at Elizabeth Town, taking their classes at the parsonage, when Reverend Dickinson died of pleurisy in October, 1747. Aaron Burr was appointed or elected to inherit the burden, and the students were transferred to Newark.

Reverend Philip Doddridge of London heard the following account of the infant college from Burr:

By ye death of ye great & good man Mr. Dickinson . . . The Case
of ye Students is devolved on Me, which together with ye Care of a
Congregation, makes my work very great and important. . . . I beg
your prayers & Friendship for or. infant College. We labour under
Difficulties at present, both for want of a Fund to support ye Charge
of it and also for Want of Books. We trust God in his Providence
will raise up Benefactors to it, and make it a flourishing Seminary for
Piety & of Learning. . . .[7]

For the remainder of his life, Reverend Burr was dedicated to the
development and improvement of the College of New Jersey, later
known as Princeton. "An House," as Burr described it, must be built
because boarding the students in private lodgings, meeting for classes in
a room next to the jail, had to be a temporary arrangement, especially
since Dickinson's small student body was now expanded to thirty or
forty. Burr expressed the tremendous need for the college, saying,
"There is a great want of a suitable supply for the Gospel ministry,"
and, consequently, many "have entered yt Ministry with too little Furniture for yt. work."[8]

By the time the first commencement took place on November 9, 1748,
President Burr had set up standards for the students. There was to be no
fighting, gaming, drinking, or dicing. Bad company and the frequenting
of taverns or places of public entertainment were forbidden. Second
offenders "shall be expelled the college." All students must be diligent in
their studies and obey their masters or run the risk of expulsion.[9]

Reverend Burr's intellectual achievements as a man well studied in
three classical languages, logic, rhetoric, natural sciences, moral philosophy, *belles lettres*, history, divinity, and politics earned him the accolade
of "an honor to his college and an ornament to the republic of letters."[10] The students, in order to reflect honor on the master, were
expected to participate in a formidable program. To alleviate the
chronic shortage of books and materials that plagued the college, Burr
wrote a Latin Grammar, which was used for a long time.

The first commencement day was most important to Burr because it
marked the beginning of his official term as President. As the morning
sun shone down on the joyous occasion, the academic procession was
headed by the seven graduates, followed by the President and the Governor. They marched from the parsonage to the church as the bells rang
mightily. The program commenced with Reverend Burr's prayer and
the formal reading of the college charter.

In the afternoon, the graduation exercises took place. The President
delivered a handsome and elegant Latin oration that traced the history
of education from ancient times to the College of New Jersey. After

Latin and English orations by the scholars, Bachelor's degrees were awarded. The long day was concluded for the weary President only after the evening meeting with the trustees to discuss and accept the code of laws and plans for future development.

At first, patrons were scarce and some of the prominent citizens were reluctant to send their children to the new college. In time, however, Burr's achievements were recognized as money came in and enrollments increased. The Colony of Connecticut ran a lottery to raise funds to benefit the college. By 1752, it was conceded that a suitable site for the building of a permanent college was needed. Princeton was selected because of its favorable location between New York and Philadelphia. In an effort to raise the necessary funds for buildings, salaries, equipment, and scholarships, Governor Belcher and Reverend Whitefield suggested seeking help from Great Britain. Two trustees traveled to the Mother Country and raised thirty-two hundred pounds, mostly from church collections in England, Scotland, and Ireland.[11]

All this activity netted results. By the end of 1755 a building was going up that contained a hall, library, and rooms to accommodate about one hundred students. "We do everything in the plainest and cheapest manner as far as consistent with Decency and Convenience having no superfluous Ornaments," reported the President. Burr was hoping that he could balance the books favorably and, before long, be able to support a Professor of Divinity, one of many positions he was currently filling himself. Jonathan Edwards, his father-in-law, was his and the trustees' choice for the chair.[12]

The Edwards family had been in America for four generations when Jonathan Edwards was born. The English heritage had been lost in legend. Samuel Hopkins, a friend of the family, told that Richard Edwards, the first of the name known to posterity, had been a London minister whose wife, Anne, had sewn a ruff for Queen Elizabeth. This was a romantic tale, however, for Anne, who died in 1680, would have been an infant in England's golden age. Records reveal that Richard was a minister, but without a regular congregation and served, in addition, as a schoolmaster at the Ratcliffe Free School. After his death during England's terrible plague year of 1625, his widow married a cooper who carried her and his small stepson, William Edwards, to America.[13]

William became a maker of barrels in Hartford, but as that town developed from a frontier settlement to a rising city, the fortunes of the Edwardses also rose. Richard, William's son, prospered, developing the trade into a shipping business. His son, also named Richard, was even farther removed from the tool bench. Having served as town surveyor, constable, and selectman, he was admitted to the bar at the age of sixty and, later, appointed Queen's attorney. His son characterized him as "a stalwart man of noble stature and comely countenance, erect, robust and nimble to an unusual degree, good in argument, pleasant in consultation and well furnished for society."[14]

However, his married life was tragic. Through his wife the trait of insanity was introduced into the family strain. Richard married Elizabeth Tuttle, a violent woman of erratic behavior, given to periodic fits of temper. Just three months after her marriage, she revealed the name of the father of her unborn child to the magistrates. Her new husband paid the fines, hushed up the story, and when the child was born placed it into the Tuttle household. Richard and Elizabeth lived together for twenty-four years and she bore him six children. Finally, despite the Puritan tradition, Richard divorced her. There were other evidences of mental breakdowns in that generation of Tuttles. Elizabeth's brother murdered their sister Sarah with an axe, confessed, and was executed. Another sister killed her son.

Timothy, the only son of Richard and Elizabeth, displayed no sign of the family weakness. On the contrary, he lived a well-ordered existence for eighty-seven years. After receiving a Harvard B. A. and M. A., both on the same day, Timothy became a minister in East Windsor and remained there for the rest of his life. He was logical and hardworking, but his only work of genius was his son, Jonathan. And some attributed the streak of genius to his wife's heritage.

Mrs. Esther Edwards was the daughter of Reverend Solomon Stoddard, the author of a concept called "Stoddardeanism." This allowed professing Christians who were not certain they were in a state of grace to take communion and to participate in certain other privileges. Stoddard was also responsible for the Massachusetts Sumptuary Laws of 1675 that barred extravagant dress as an evil. His wife was the daughter of John Warham, the first minister of the Connecticut colony.

On October 5, 1703, in the East Windsor parsonage, Jonathan Edwards was born. It was still a frontier settlement, for that same year, in nearby Deerfield, his mother's half-sister and two of her children had been killed by Indians. Young Jonathan grew up surrounded by his own large family and his Stoughton cousins. He was an introspective little boy, who, very early, displayed a precocious concern with religion and nature. In the swamps near his house, the small Jonathan erected a booth where he and his companions meditated and prayed, a much admired example of infant piety. Genius was first displayed by his composition of a remarkable essay on the habits of flying spiders.

At thirteen, his boyhood over, Yale received the young man. He did not fit into college life, remaining aloof with his own pursuits. After a struggle between hope and despair, he experienced his conversion. In 1727, he married Sarah Pierrepont of New Haven, whose piety he had noticed when she was only thirteen; thus, another ministerial branch was added to the Edwards tree. The bride's father, James, was the first minister of New Haven and the traditional prime mover of the founding of Yale College. Through her mother, Sarah was related to Thomas Hooker, founder of Hartford. Sarah thus added luster to the Edwards name as well as wit, beauty, and courage.

Jonathan Edwards, perhaps the most famous American theologian, is best known for his sermons of fire and brimstone in which, as the messenger of the Lord, he described the vast liquid mountains that would pour over the damned without mercy, "and the smoke of their torment shall ascend up forever and ever, and they have no rest day or night."[15] God would crush out evil under His feet as the blood of the creatures of iniquity sprinkled His garments and stained his raiment. Edwards' Northhampton congregation trembled as the tall thin figure with the face of an angel stared dreamily into the distance, speaking sorrowfully of the wages of sin. But though he was worshipped, differences with his flock arose because he rejected the liberal policies of "Stoddardeanism." In 1744, a dispute severed him from his parishioners. He published the names of many young people, those of the best families included, who were accused of reading unsuitable books. The fierce objections of the parents widened the rift until, by the end of 1750, a majority of his congregation voted for his dismissal. "I am now thrown upon the wide ocean of the world, and know not what will become of me, and my numerous and chargeable family," the minister wrote to a friend.[16]

His calling was a strange one for an intellectual leader. He went as a missionary to the Indians and the tiny band of white settlers at Stockbridge, a frontier settlement in Massachusetts. Financial disaster had already forced his wife and daughters to augment the family income by selling handmade lace, embroideries, and painted fans to the Boston market. Even in the wilderness, Edwards continued to write theology and answer his critics. And he was not destined to end his life as pastor to Indians because of his daughter's marriage to Reverend Aaron Burr.

Esther Burr found that the addition of little Aaron multiplied her already heavy burden of work at the Newark parsonage. She complained that when she had one child, "my hands were tied but now I am tied hand and foot, how shall I get along when I have got ½ dzn or 10 children I can't devise." There was, however, enough time to write in her *Journal*, started in May, 1755, accounts of the Burrs' home life. The minister's wife was expected to entertain and feed visiting clergymen, trustees of the college, members of the Synod, and other dignitaries. It was tiring and frustrating when, though the meal was prepared and the day was fine, Madame Belcher failed to arrive for dinner. "I don't like it to be served so tho tis by a Governor's Lady—Tis not write is it?" Esther wrote spiritedly.[17]

The slow development of the college buildings at Princeton and the even slower accumulation of the required money concerned her because it worried and aged her beloved husband. She rejoiced upon hearing that the college would be ready for occupancy by August of 1756 and went frequently to admire the progress. When Reverend Burr tried to interest his wife in learning French, she said that she wanted to learn but that a married woman has "something else to care about besides learning French."[18]

Though the French and Indian War was going badly for the British, in the summer of 1756 Esther determined to take her infant son to visit his Edwards grandparents at Stockbridge. The war complicated further what was normally a hazardous and long trip. The voyage by water to New York was delayed because the sloop had to substitute for a troop ship and then there was further delay before leaving the city. Esther reported that she was "quite Sick for the Weather is extream hot and being out all Night before with my little Son I was worried to death."[19] The ship carried them up the Hudson to the Livingston family manor, where her party, which included Esther's brother and one of her sisters, tarried long enough to drink tea. Supplied with a wagon and a servant, they started overland on the first lap of the journey.

The expedition suffered an almost immediate setback when the servant disappeared with the carriage. A wooden cottage that belonged to a large Dutch family gave them refuge. That evening, forty soldiers from Rhode Island descended on the already crowded house but behaved better than Esther had expected. "How many difficulties one meets with in a Journey just so with our Journey throu this life," she observed.[20] No further adventure delayed them until, near the Edwards' home, a tremendous downpour flooded the road and soaked the travelers. Their hired wagon pressed on, however, and they were able to surprise the family "out of their wits."

Esther had planned to stay until the second week in October, but she was frightened by the stories of frontier forts captured, their inhabitants tortured and slain by the Indians. Reverend Edwards refused to listen to her fears, which increased agonizingly when she heard that the enemy had been sighted about thirty miles away. The seventeen soldiers sent to defend Stockbridge were inadequate to protect the fort. Poor Esther declared herself unequal to a "fiery tryal," saying that she was willing to die as God pleases but not to be "buchered."

The Indians did not come and she and little Aaron returned safely to Newark to prepare for the move to Princeton. With seventy students, they migrated in November. Mrs. Burr thanked the Lord that the move was made with "no sorrowful accident . . . to any of our family—Our goods came remarkably safe. I had not a China thing so much as cracked."[21] Reverend Burr conducted the first formal services in Nassau Hall on November 13, basing his sermon on Psalm 119: "The earth, O Lord, is full of Thy mercy: teach me Thy statutes."

Life at Princeton was a contrast to that in the busy town of Newark. The pretty little village now dominated by the college was isolated. "I believe if the French were to take Boston we should not hear of it as soon as they would in London," wrote the President's wife.

Shortly after the removal, an Awakening visited the college. It started in the month of February of 1757, when Lawyer Smith's son, just recovered from an illness, was seized with a sudden concern for his soul. In almost epidemic fashion, others were similarly affected. Reverend Burr was delighted with the constant "Rap, Rap, is the President at home," that disturbed him day and night. He had to send for additional assistants to help in "drawing the nett ashore for it is ready to break with the aboundance of the Fish that are caught in it."[22] Discipline was no longer a problem at the college; studying was done at a furious rate. However, not all of the parents were pleased by the religious fervor. Some, like Lawyer Ogden, withdrew their sons when they heard that the scholars had run mad. But when the final count was taken, it was calculated that the student population had increased.

The transfer to the new location had increased Burr's labors to a point where his delicate frame could no longer withstand the pressure. Although in poor health in the summer of 1757, he visited Jonathan Edwards in Stockbridge and then, on his return, hurried to Elizabeth Town on college business. There he was delayed by the melancholy task of preaching at the funeral of a colleague's wife. Suffering from an intermittent fever, he journeyed to Philadelphia and then returned to Princeton in a state of near collapse. His tasks were still not done because Governor Belcher had died, and President Burr was required to preach the funeral sermon. Although sick with a raging fever, so high that he was irrational during the night, he worked on the sermon and then rode forty miles to Elizabeth Town to deliver it. President Burr's friends noticed and grieved over "the langour of his countenance" and "the failure of his harmonious delivery."[23] Completely debilitated, he returned to Princeton; on September 2, his last illness began.

On that day, Esther Burr terminated her *Journal* with observations on the personalities of her two children:

> Sally . . . is not much of a Baby, affects to be thought a Woman . . . we are about sending her to school, but Mr. Burr is expecting that she will prove a numbhead, but for my part I think her about middling on all accounts — . . . I have taken her to Meeting and she behaves very well and can give a good account of what Papa does there — She can say some of Doct Watts verses by heart and the Lord's Prayer . . . but she is not over apt about the matter. Aaron is a little dirty Noisy Boy very different from Sally almost in everything he begins to talk a little is very Sly and mischievious Has more sprightliness than Sally and most say he is handsomer, but not so good tempered he is very resolute and requires a good Governor to bring him to terms.[24]

Three weeks later, she was a widow. Reverend Burr, on his deathbed, forbade a lavish funeral and directed that the sum that would have been expended be given to the poor. He was buried at Princeton on September 24, in his forty-first year.

Mrs. Burr was comforted only by her children and by the knowledge that her father would come to Princeton as the new president. She rallied all the forces of her religious training to soften her anguish. To her mother, she wrote that she requested "earnestly of the Lord that I may never despise his chastenings, nor faint under his severe stroke . . . I am overcome." Then she begged her parents not to forget "their greatly-afflicted daughter (now a lonely widow) nor her fatherless children."[25]

Shortly after his father's death, little Aaron almost died of a fever. His mother struggled long with her conscience as the baby seemed to be failing. At last, she mastered her misgivings. "God showed me that the child was not my own, but his, and that he had a right to recall what he had lent whenever he thought fit," she wrote to Jonathan Edwards.[26]

The trustees of Princeton regarded Edwards as the perfect choice for the college presidency. He, however, had many misgivings. Not only did he hesitate about leaving his frontier post, but he described his constitution as "vapid, sizy, . . . and a low tide of spirits often occasioning a kind of childish weakness," and confessed his academic limitations to include weaknesses in mathematics and the Greek classics. The trustees ignored his protests.[27]

In January, Edwards preached his farewell sermon to the Indians and then set out with his daughter Lucy for Princeton and new duties. The rest of the family planned to follow in the spring. He arrived on February 16 and was formally inducted into office.

But his reign was destined to be a tragically short one. There had been a serious outbreak of smallpox in the Princeton area, and Edwards volunteered to have himself inoculated to demonstrate his faith in the efficacy of the serum. At first, his progress was excellent. But then, after all danger was thought to have passed, he developed a fever. The pustules in his throat were so large and numerous that he could not take any medicine. Only two daughters, Esther and Lucy, were at his bedside when he died on February 23. He had asked that his funeral "be like unto Mr. Burr, and any additional sum of money that might be expected to be laid out that way I would have dispensed of to charitable uses."[28]

The shock stunned the already bereaved Esther. She had been inoculated at the same time as her father and seemed to have completely recovered. But the fresh blow was too much for her; a fortnight after her father's death, Esther Burr joined him.

After the death of their mother, Sally and Aaron lived in Philadelphia with the family of Dr. William Shippen. In the autumn, Sarah Edwards went to the city to gather up her grandchildren and bring them to live with her. In Philadelphia, she contracted a fatal case of dysentery and died on October 2. She was buried at Princeton, in the cemetery that had lately received the bodies of her son-in-law, her husband, and her daughter. Fortunately for the Burr children, the Shippens were able to provide a good temporary home.

CHAPTER II

Uncle Timothy's Ward

AARON and Sally remained at Philadelphia with the Shippens only until 1759, when their guardianship was assumed by Uncle Timothy Edwards. Just twenty-one himself, Edwards had inherited the responsibility for more relatives than most people support in a lifetime. So when the Burr children moved to the little town of Stockbridge, they found themselves with six others under the age of fifteen. Money drawn from the remainder of the Burr account at Princeton was, fortunately, sufficient to enable Edwards to provide proper care without exhausting his own limited resources.

Edwards was a strict disciplinarian, a rather doctrinaire Puritan with little humor and flexibility. His word was law; his tolerance for youthful exuberance, nil. His weapons are said to have been a firm rod and long "moral exhortations and castigations." At least on two occasions, little Burr staged an open rebellion. Once, at the age of four, he fled from one of his tutors and disappeared for several days; and, six years later, still irrepressible in an age when ten-year-olds were considered ready for real responsibilities, he tried to escape by getting a job as a cabin boy on a vessel bound for the high seas. While working on the quarter-deck one day, he spotted Uncle Timothy in pursuit. Eluding Edwards by climbing to the masthead, he was able to reach a bargain with his pursuer: he would descend and return to his studies only if no punishment were imposed. So the little adventure had not been very expensive.[1]

Only a year after the children had left Philadelphia, they returned to New Jersey, this time to live in Elizabeth Town. Edwards had provided maternal care for his brood by marrying Rhoda Ogden, the daughter of a prominent and controversial politician. Burr now had two new companions, Aaron and Matthias Ogden, Rhoda's brothers. Both were close to Burr's age. At Elizabeth Town, they were his ideal companions for hunting and swimming and boating on the waters between Jersey and Staten Island.

The Burr children were educated with care. Private tutors enabled them to make rapid progress, with Aaron spending long hours at his studies. Sally, with less of an academic appetite, had considerably more enthusiasm for a tutor named Tapping Reeve. Thus, while the Edwards household continued to grow with the arrival of Rhoda and Timothy's own children, Sally went to Connecticut where she then married Reeve, and Aaron went off to Princeton.

His admittance at the age of thirteen had followed a second attempt. Rebuffed two years earlier, largely because of his size and childish appearance, he used the college's curriculum as a guide and spent two years in earnest study. Not only did he want to be accepted, but he sought admission as a junior. His diligence was finally recognized, as was his rather special status as the son of the Reverend Aaron Burr, and he was duly admitted. Nevertheless, collegiate standards had the final say, so the impatient young man had to settle for being a sophomore.

As a student, he often remained with his books as long as eighteen hours a day, even reducing his diet through a belief that heavy meals would lull the ability to concentrate. This regimen, which enabled him to surpass most classmates, he would thereafter uphold as proof of the advantages of light eating and little sleep.[2]

Surviving essays that he wrote during Princeton days display no genius but do provide glimpses into his mind. His puritanical background lends interest to his essay on dancing. "Many indeed are so full of idle scruples, and superstitious fancies that they number it among the deadly sins, and think no person can recommmend [sic] it, who [has] religion really at heart," he wrote, adding that, "as Swift justly Observed reasoning would never make a man correct an ill Opinion which by reasoning he never acquired."[3] Elsewhere, he wrote that "There never was a ready speaker whose language was not generally plain and simple. . . . A laboured style is a labour even to the hearer. A simple style like simple food preserves the appetite, but a profusion of ornament like a profusion of Sweets pall the appetite and becomes disgusting."[4]

Other interests appealed to the student. He joined a literary club, the Cliosophic Society, which enabled him to exchange views with classmates and stimulated an appetite for more reading. Many books were about outstanding military heroes, such as the figure currently in vogue, Frederick the Great. Reading about their lives enhanced vicarious no-

tions of adventure. He also found time to participate with two student
political groups, the Well-Meaning and the Plain-Dealing societies, and
he was apparently the author of a manuscript, now lost, which gave an
account of their demise.

Religion, naturally, was a major concern of every student, but the
course followed by the grandchild of Jonathan Edwards and the son of
Reverend Aaron Burr soon exhibited a fierce independence of spirit,
then an attempted adjustment to accepting the family tradition, and,
finally, a rejection of rigidities. He remained aloof from the great religious revival that attracted so many of his schoolmates in 1771 and 1772.
His own view was that the "awakening," with its hell-fire and damnation exhortations, was a spectacle rather than an expression of true religion. In this, he even won support from Dr. John Witherspoon, the
college president, whose own view was that the revival had engulfed
others in an emotional force that had little to do with rational religion
but was more akin to an ephemeral fanaticism.[6] But Burr had certainly
not discarded religious tenets. One of his closest Princeton relationships
was with the Reverend Samuel Spring, who had studied theology under
Witherspoon and who later became a leader of New England Congrega-
tionalism.

Burr graduated with a Bachelor of Arts degree on September 30,
1772. He did not rank at the top of his class, but fulfilled the prevailing
custom of delivering a commencement oration. Foreshadowing the
future, his topic was "Building Castles in the Air," a theme he later
applied to military, political, and literary pursuits. His delivery was with
an animation and grace that was "excelled by none," except, possibly,
the class valedictorian.[7] Having completed that step, he nevertheless
remained at Princeton long enough to use the college library for further
studies and left the following summer for Connecticut.

Only seventeen years old at that time, Aaron Burr proceeded northward on horseback. At Elizabeth Town, he stopped to visit the Ogdens,
particularly Matt, who had also graduated from the College of New
Jersey, and then went on to Stockbridge. Uncle Timothy had been
living there for the past two years and had turned to business and
farming to support a family of fifteen children. From that Massachusetts
village, Burr went on to Litchfield for a visit with Sally and Tapping
Reeve before joining the theological school conducted by Dr. Joseph
Bellamy in the Connecticut village of Bethlehem.

Burr's choice of Bellamy as a teacher was inevitable. His school was
the most important place in New England for study under the guidance
of an accomplished divine. How better to emulate the wisdom and

godliness of the great man? Bellamy had not only studied under Jonathan Edwards, but had been his good friend. Thus, Aaron Burr, however much he may have lacked the religious zeal of his antecedents, prepared to accept exposure to an ecclesiastical existence.

Bellamy's forte had been his provocative sermons. His greater moderation during recent years, however, had enabled him to criticize students for loud and boisterous preaching. "When I was young I thought it was the thunder that killed people; but when I grew older I found it was the lightning," he liked to say. "So I determined to do what I advise you—thunder less and lighten more."[8] Nevertheless, Bellamy's voice had excited New Englanders, just as it was Bellamy who had been the first Connecticut theologian to start a Sabbath school in his church. This "pioneer of theological education" actively assisted students from 1742 to 1786. His published work, called *True Religion Delineated*, attracted more interest to his educational role, so that when Burr arrived in the fall of 1773, it was the most important place of its kind in New England.

For Burr, the experience was his last serious flirtation with religion. He enjoyed the use of the minister's library and relished the open and lively conversations in the Bellamy home. But, eventually, the prospect of life as a minister depressed him. The higher calling was incompatible with his more adventurous spirit. The confinements and Calvinistic standards of the home became oppressive. More attractive for the young man were the girls of nearby Litchfield, particularly a certain "Miss D." And such activities were inconsistent with long hours of study. His distress intensified during that winter. After returning to the Bellamy home from Litchfield in early 1774, he was greeted by Dr. and Mrs. Bellamy and a household of ministers and students.

Mrs. Bellamy wanted to know whether Miss D. was still at Litchfield, and when Burr replied that she had just left, the response was: "Now the mystery is unravelled. Well, we did not expect you here again this winter."

Bellamy and some of the others then cornered him. "I was mauled most thoroughly for near an Hour," Burr complained to a brief diary he kept for Sally. "What could I do?" he asked; "my tongue was of [so] little use, that I seized it several times and had furious thoughts of biting it of [sic]—and I often wished I had not a drop of blood in my body, unless I could keep it in better regulations."[9]

Then, as he sat with all the ease of a man being tortured, Burr and his love-life—and all the possible cures for such a curious condition— dominated their conversation. It all seemed to last for an eternity. When

Mrs. Bellamy cautioned the gentlemen that they were making him blush, Burr felt that he "could have bit her head off for her kindness with a great deal of pleasure."[10]

Neither Bellamy nor religion turned out to be his love, so his departure at an early date was inevitable. Gradually, letters to Sally began to deprecate Bellamy. Friends heard similar reactions. By late spring, Burr, a fugitive from the world of theology, left Bethlehem and all thoughts of the ministry. He was, he decided, much too sociable for that sort of life, so he joined the Reeves at Litchfield.

They lived on South Street, at the southern edge of the village in a house Reeve had built after their marriage. Burr found that Reeve was intensely devoted to Sally, whose chronic asthmatic condition required much careful attention. Many of her years were spent as a virtual invalid, and Reeve's "tender watching and unwearied care" was commonly known. He even built a large room with a high ceiling so that six giant windows could provide her with enough fresh air. At that same site, Reeve, a large, portly man known for his gentle and dignified manners, founded the Litchfield Law School.

His first student was his brother-in-law, Aaron Burr, who prepared for the bar in the customary manner. He had access to the Reeve library and the benefits of his instruction. He was a serious student and learned quickly. Aaron Burr had, at last, decided upon his future career.

CHAPTER III

The Student Soldier

I N his nineteenth year, Aaron Burr continued to study law with Reeve. He was, as always, a good student and made considerable progress, although he was too attractive and appreciative of feminine charms to spend every hour as a scholar. Matt soon read how Burr warded off attempts to have him marry a certain young lady for her fortune. Not only did Burr include information about mutual acquaintances, but he showed concern for Sally's condition, at one point observing that his sister suffered from "Rheumatism in the stomach."[1] Yet, as gossipy as his correspondence was, it contained little awareness of the growing conflict between the American colonies and Great Britain. Only when a local mob of patriots ransacked the home of suspected loyalists and broke up a court session did he become agitated. And that was in the form of strong criticism of the militant colonials. He called them "sneaks" and left no doubt about what his own position would be should the rabble continue to rampage.[2] But one should not infer that the young student was opposed to the patriotic cause at the time, for, after all, such extremist views were held by only a small segment of the population and Burr, even at that age, was not a violent political partisan.

The tremors that had shaken the colonies were about to jar the complacency of conservative Litchfield. England's attempt to punish the Americans for having dumped East India Company tea into Boston Harbor in December of 1773 had infuriated patriots everywhere. Boston's port had been closed. Self-government had been denied to Massachusetts. A new act enabled the British to quarter troops in private homes. A response to these punitive measures came in September of 1774, when delegates from twelve colonies traveled to Philadelphia to convene the First Continental Congress, which was the first real display of American unity. In March, Connecticut's assembly passed a resolution encouraging contributions to relieve Boston. Then, on the twentieth of April, 1775, word reached Litchfield about the previous day's clashes between the patriots and the Redcoats at Lexington and Concord.

With that news, Burr dropped his moderation and was ready to take up arms. Sally's health had improved so much that his presence, he felt, was no longer vital. He wanted to act. His thoughts turned to the colonial army that was at Cambridge. Writing to Ogden, he suggested that they go off together to enlist in the cause. Ogden, however, replied that he needed more time before he could leave Elizabeth Town. Burr was willing to wait for his friend, but he was too restless to remain in Litchfield.

He went to Ogden's home. While there, he heard more news about the war: that the Continental Congress at Philadelphia had voted to support an army of fifteen thousand men, that six regiments were en route from England to Boston, that New York had voted to raise powder and guns by offering bounties, and that the British had been removed from Crown Point on Lake Champlain.

In mid-July, before proceeding to Cambridge, Burr went to Philadelphia. There, he made several calls. One was to William Bradford, a former Princeton classmate and a future attorney general of the United States. Bradford, writing to James Madison of Virginia, reported that he had "had the pleasure this morning of seeing Aaron Burr who is going to the Camp with one Mr Ogden."[3] That day, Burr also saw Colonel Lewis Morris, a delegate to the Continental Congress. Then he met its president, John Hancock.

When Burr and Ogden reached Cambridge, they carried a letter of introduction from Hancock, presenting them to General Washington in the following manner:

> The earnest desire of several members of Congress, joined to a hearty wish of rendering service to the gentlemen, induce me to take the freedom to introduce to your notice Mr. *Ogden* and Mr. *Burr*, of the *Jerseys*, by whom this will be handed to you. They are gentlemen of reputation, and visit the camp not as spectators, but with a view of joining the Army, and being active during the campaign; I beg you will please to place them in such a department as you shall judge suitable. Your notice of these gentlemen I shall esteem a particular favour. . . .[4]

Burr's visit to Morris had also been fruitful, for the New Yorker had supplied another letter. This one asked for more than mere recognition: immediate rank.

Washington would not grant Morris' request, but it could not be ignored. Morris, pointing to the fine qualities of the two volunteers, asked that they be commissioned. The Commander-in-Chief of the American Army replied in August that officers were designated by the provincial government that had sent the particular regiment; he, therefore, had no control over such promotions. Furthermore, unattached volunteers like Burr and Ogden would cost too much to commission because no colony would subsidize them. Washington then suggested that the Congress ought to consider assuming future control of such designations.[5]

For the two young men, it was, however, a rebuff. With their family connections, Burr and Ogden must have assumed that glowing endorsements from Hancock and Morris would be interpreted as an order, especially by the military commander who had so recently been appointed to his post by the Congress. To a rather brash nineteen year old Aaron Burr, Washington's reaction must have been regarded as a personal snub. It was only the first unfortunate encounter with the future president.

There was only sporadic military activity near Cambridge after Burr's arrival, with seventeen thousand colonials deployed along a semicircle south and west of Boston. The enemy was engaging in the fortification of Bunker's Hill and Roxbury Neck. Burr seems to have been idled by illness most of this time, but tradition says that his real problem was boredom.

The account of his deliverance from this condition has been passed on by Matthew L. Davis, his loyal lieutenant of later years. Burr was said to have been ill and in bed when he overheard a conversation between Ogden and others that referred to a projected expedition. When Ogden was called in to tell his sick friend what it was all about, Burr learned for the first time that a detachment of over a thousand men was preparing to follow Colonel Benedict Arnold through the wilderness of Maine to attack Quebec City. Over Ogden's protests, Burr suddenly abandoned his sickbed and prepared to join the hazardous march.

Although others had recognized the possibilities of such a maneuver, the decision was Washington's. An assault, launched with a simultaneous drive toward Montreal by General Philip Schuyler, would be a diversionary move. By way of the Kennebec River, which can be traversed by going upstream from the Atlantic, the interior of Maine may be reached. Then, by portage across the Chain of Ponds, in the deep wilderness, a party could reach a range called the Height of the Land. Beyond that, Canada. And on the other side of the border, after a descent from the Boundary Mountains, from Lake Megantic the Chaudiere River cascades northward until it pours into the St. Lawrence, spilling into that river just four miles upstream from Quebec City. The hope was that General Guy Carleton could not defend both Montreal and Quebec. To head the expedition, Washington chose thirty-four year old Colonel Arnold.

Burr, with Ogden, at once became part of the company, and nothing could stop them from tasting the adventure. They even had to pay for their own needs, and there is reason to believe that Burr may have helped to finance others as well. Nor could pleas begging him to heed the danger and remain behind do any good once Burr had decided to go along. One friend wrote to warn that he could not survive the campaign. Another, Peter Colt, observed that the circumstances were so foreboding that he could excuse himself without fear of being considered timid. Uncle Timothy even sent a personal messenger all the way to Cambridge with orders to bring Burr home. But the young soldier remained firm; he was ready to march to Quebec.

Arnold's entire detachment consisted of ten companies of musketmen and three of riflemen. The former were divided into two battalions, each with five companies, and under the leadership of Lt. Col. Roger Enos and Major Return J. Meigs. Most of the riflemen were hunters and Indian fighters who had marched for twenty-one days from Virginia with Daniel Morgan.

Others completed the detachment, along with such unattached personnel as Burr and Ogden. Dr. Isaac Senter was, at the age of twenty-two, the outfit's surgeon. The chaplain was Reverend Samuel Spring, Burr's friend from Princeton. Then there was Captain Eleazar Oswald, who served as Arnold's secretary.

The expedition took longer to launch than had been expected. Time was needed for each company to reach its total of effective manpower. Then there was a delay when some of the men insisted on first receiving a month's pay. When they finally did get started, they headed toward Newburyport, the Massachusetts coastal town. From there, transports would carry them to the mouth of the Kennebec.

Burr rejected the opportunity to go to Newburyport by carriage, so on September 13, 1775, he began a forty-five mile march to the port. His arrival furnished him with enough evidence to inform Sally that he was "equal to the undertaking" that lay ahead.[6] On September 19, eleven schooners and sloops were boarded at wharves near the center of the town for the journey to the river.

At the place where Pittston now stands, on the Kennebec, was a little settlement named Gardinerstown. From a boatbuilder there, Arnold had ordered two hundred bateaux. Each boat had to carry six or seven men plus provisions and baggage. Expecting them to be needed for perhaps only two weeks and fully aware of the portages that faced the mission, Arnold had stipulated that they not be heavy. Reuben Colburn, the Gardinerstown boatbuilder, was able to comply readily enough, but the necessary haste resulted in shoddy construction. Not only were many of them too small, but the green pine that formed the sides and bottoms, while heavy, was thin and fragile. The bateaux were used to carry most of the men from that point, as the river had become too shallow for the transports, but Burr chose to travel by carriage for the nine miles to Fort Western.

The Fort turned out to be a fine resting place. Commanding a bluff on the eastern shore of the river, where Augusta now stands, it was a well-built log bastion that was owned by its first and only commander, Captain James Howard. The Howard family proved to be admirable hosts, and Aaron Burr enjoyed "falling on roast chickens and wallowing . . . in a good feather Bed." The family proved to him that gentility and even elegance may flourish in the woods.[7]

But Burr's appearance decried any notion of urbanity. He wore a pair of coarse woolen trousers that covered the tops of his boots, and the same material had been used for his short double-breasted jacket. His short and fringed shirt had been a present from a southern rifleman. About the hat, he wrote that it must have been "meant to help my Deficiency in point of size," for while the headgear itself was small, a large fox tail curled together with a black feather seemed to make him taller. Over his back he carried a blanket, "as that's a thing I never trust from me," he informed Sally. A tomahawk, gun, and bayonet completed his regalia.[8]

Thus dressed, he left the luxury of Fort Western on the morning of September 26, and followed the advance companies of riflemen. As the Kennebec was navigable only for the first forty-five miles, treacherous cascades could only be surmounted by carrying the bateau and provisions to the shore, a task that could occupy most of the day. Each bateau weighed at least four hundred pounds. Such provisions as meat, sugar, flour, salt, yeast, butter, and about one hundred rounds of ammunition for each man, added to much needed tents, blankets, extra clothes and shoes, shovels, axes, kitchen utensils, and medical supplies, brought the total weight being moved upriver to about forty tons. Each portage required loading and unloading. Burr would have to leap into the water just before the rapids, with the rest of the crew; after two handspikes had been passed under the bottom of the boat, four men were able to raise it from the water and place it on the bank. But that was only the expected routine part of the work.

The inevitable hazards appeared. At the Three Mile Falls, dysentery began to plague some of the men. When they reached Ticonic Falls, the first big portage, leaks appeared in several of the inadequately seasoned and constructed bateaux. Provisions were lost or soaked. Rainfall, cold weather, and a swollen river brought additional miseries. Across the Chain of Ponds, bateaux and supplies were carried through desolate and thick woods of cedar and hemlock. At times, the mud was knee deep; other parts of the route were so thick with an undergrowth of roots that passage was impossible. The farther they went, the poorer the drinking water became. Burr reported that it was a sickly yellow, and Senter noted that "no sooner had it got down than it was puked up by many of the poor fellows." A block house had to be built to accommodate the incapacitated. Provisions had also become dangerously scarce.[9] Additional supplies were lost when the Dead River overflowed its banks in mid-October. Many boats were completely destroyed, having been smashed against rocks by storm-driven waters. A depressed Arnold lamented that sick and weakened men added to the "melancholy prospect before us."[10] Then the weather became colder, and several inches of snow covered the ground.

Perhaps the greatest blow to the expedition was the news that Colonel Enos' division had decided to return to Cambridge. Not only was the loss of manpower a major disaster, but they had retreated with supplies others had hoped to share. Caught in the swirling snow of an early northern winter, the men were forced to improvise additional supplies of food. Several dogs were killed, their carcasses stripped and the flesh eaten. Senter witnessed even greater desperation, writing that some of his companions ate shaving soap, shoe leather, and cartridge boxes.

Finally, on November 9, Burr reached the St. Lawrence River. From Point Levi, he could see massive Cape Diamond and the heights of the Plains of Abraham. Between the river and the precipice was the lower town of Quebec City. At that point, he also received the good news that General Richard Montgomery, who had taken over for General Schuyler, was about to dislodge the enemy from Montreal.

Now Montgomery was moving on to Laprairie. At Montreal, General Carleton was on the British brigantine *Gaspe*; but by the time that ship was taken along with the city on the thirteenth of November, Carleton had made his escape to Quebec City. His presence was important to the dwindling morale of the garrison there, which was more than a little awed by the accomplishments of Arnold's men. Having first destroyed all potentially useful boats, the British waited for the Americans to cross the St. Lawrence.

Canoes were collected from the Indians. Scaling ladders were built. The abatement of a storm was awaited. Finally, with the river again calm, the ladders and pikes were carried to the point of embarkation. Burr and Ogden left with Arnold in the first canoe, their oars muffled by cloth wrapped around each paddle. A British patrol vessel was eluded in the darkness, and their canoe landed just above Wolfe's Cove, at almost exactly the same location of General Wolfe's assault in 1759. Returning the canoes with twenty-seven men left on the shore, they promptly established their defenses by forming flank guard wings with six men at each end. The remaining men were drawn together in a body and were prepared, as Ogden observed, "against any number that might have disputed it with us."[11]

Finally, Arnold was able to form the men on the Plains of Abraham. What General Montcalm had done sixteen years earlier they now wanted Carleton to repeat, hoping the British could be lured from the walled city and onto the open field. The men roared "three huzzas," but the enemy's answer was an eighteen-pound shell from within the town that was soon followed by a general shower of ammunition that rose from different parts of Quebec. A hill provided cover for the retreating Americans. Later that day, the enemy set fire to blockhouses near the wall, as well as to some of the homes. Ogden and Burr were helpless as they watched the fleeing occupants: helping them would mean "running in the mouths of their cannon."[12]

On the nineteenth of November, Arnold removed the detachment to Pointe aux Trembles, twenty-four miles up the St. Lawrence. The inadequacy of their arms and the lack of ammunition had convinced the leaders that it would be wiser to raise the siege and move to a point where contact with Montgomery might be more easily established. It was from Pointe aux Trembles that Arnold dispatched Ogden with messages to Montreal.

News of Montgomery's capture of that city had just come. Even more exciting was the hope that the Irish-born general would march down the river and support the little detachment that had defied the wilderness so miraculously only to find itself unprepared to do much about the fortress atop Cape Diamond. Arnold's messages congratulated the General and then noted his own predicament. His retreat to Pointe aux Trembles had resulted from the discovery, he wrote, that the troops had no more than five rounds of ammunition for each man because so many of the cartridges were useless, and almost one hundred guns were unfit for service. "Add to this," he observed, "many of the men invalids, and almost naked and wanting every thing to make them comfortable." Matt Ogden, who had carried the message, was also directed to procure clothing for the suffering little army that was about to face the heart of winter. The inability of Arnold's troops to force Carleton to combat on the Plains had caused the distress, but in a letter to Washington he left no doubt that Montgomery would be able to capture Quebec that winter—with just one condition: that he would have about twenty-five hundred men.[13]

When Burr sat down to write to Uncle Timothy, he was a less confident and somewhat restrained young man. Earlier, he had exuded optimism about being in Quebec soon. Now he merely wrote: "I intend to see the Inside of it if possible."[14] And he told Sally that Litchfield had begun to seem "like some ideal Region in the Moon, some place I have visited in Vision . . . a thousand Raptures."[15]

Burr's mood reflected the frustration and desolation of the men. Having been unable to challenge the fortress, aside from investing the city for nearly a week, was bad enough. The troops were willing, as much "as naked men can be," according to Arnold, but little could be done. It was an army without weapons or ammunition, unable to exploit military opportunities, too weak to resist sustained attacks: a situation frequently duplicated during the war. Their desperate demands constantly harassed a worried Congress. But as the men waited at Pointe aux Trembles and watched for Montgomery, another threat appeared. Four British ships were sighted near the encampment.

Arnold now chose Burr to carry the next message to Montgomery. He was anxious for the "strangely delayed" ammunition and, in addition to reporting that it had not reached him, his letter assured the General that the threat of interception on the St. Lawrence had eased. For Burr, the mission would lead to military rank and fame, as well as provide inspiration for a legend.

Burr's early biographers tell a rather charming story of heroism and cunning. Their hero supposedly left from Lake Megantic, not Pointe aux Trembles, when the detachment was about 120 linear miles from Montreal. Their version meant that Burr separated from Arnold about one month earlier and such a route would have been treacherous. But all possible complications were solved by having the young soldier dress as a French priest; with his knowledge of French and Latin, this seemed entirely possible; with his subsequent reputation for gallantry, everything seemed convenient; and so Burr was portrayed as journeying through a friendly French-Canadian underground that had priests and religious families at convenient intervals. One priest was startled to see the young man expose himself as an American. So enthusiastic was his reaction that he sent Burr to anti-British French Catholic families. Such groups assured the messenger that the *habitants* were only waiting for the Americans to mount an offensive with some force, as they hated both the English and the *seigneurs*. With their guidance, Burr reached an amazed and highly impressed General Montgomery. The thirty-seven year old Irishman immediately made Burr one of his aides-de-camp and gave him the rank of captain.[16]

Burr did get his rank, and Montgomery undoubtedly recognized his ability. A letter of introduction from Arnold had described him as the son of the former president of the college at Princeton, and as "a young gentleman of much life and activity," who had responded to the horrors of the march with "great spirit and resolution."[17]

But the letters he carried prove that he left from Pointe aux Trembles at the end of November; and not only is the priest story without any foundation, but the mission was hardly unusual enough to warrant disguise. Had his friend Matt not travelled the same route only ten days earlier? Numerous others had been going to and fro along the northern shore of the St. Lawrence.

Perhaps even more damaging to the stories about Burr's heroic mission to Montgomery is the realization that he met the General not very far upstream from Pointe aux Trembles. When Burr left Arnold on November 30, the Colonel still awaited the ammunition from the General; but by the very next day, Pointe aux Trembles had received both the supplies and Montgomery. Several witnesses recorded the date of his arrival. They also support General Schuyler's statement that Montgomery's three armed schooners, artillery, ammunition, and provisions had left Montreal on November 25.[18]

The sight of the General stepping into the heavy snow that covered the shore was sufficient to bolster morale. But his cargo was even more attractive. Just before Burr's departure, Ogden had arrived with some of the supplies from merchants, and the ammunition detail returned several hours later. Montgomery, however, arrived with enough clothes to relieve the "naked men" of Arnold's garrison. Having taken them from two British regiments at St. Johns, the Irishman considered them adequate to outfit the company for a year.

On Tuesday, December 5, the combined force returned to resume the siege. Lines were formed on the Plains of Abraham between the suburb of St. Roche and Cape Diamond. As they made preparations to attack, word of panic from within the British garrison convinced them victory would soon follow. The Americans heard from deserters and merchants that the defenders were divided and that Carleton was forced to resort to extraordinary measures to maintain security. Those who had refused to bear arms against the Americans had already been ordered out of the city. Within the next four days, the wives and children of some leading townspeople had also fled, leaving their property behind. Montgomery accepted their flight as a gift from the enemy, noting that many intelligent men thus joined the Americans. They included Mr. Edward Antil, whom Montgomery appointed chief engineer, and Mr. James Price, a Montreal merchant.

When Antil and Price joined the troops, Montgomery and Arnold had their forces camped together on the Plains. Here, Burr had his initial meeting with Captain John Lamb, the "restless genius" leader of an artillery company and New York head of the "Sons of Liberty." Lamb thought that Montgomery's young aide looked "juvenile in the extreme," and his first reaction was to wonder why the General had encumbered his family with a mere boy. But greater familiarity showed that Burr radiated energy and demonstrated such staunch coolness under fire that he was no ordinary man.[19] His audacious behavior was restrained only by the vigorous opposition of Price and Antil, for when a council of war convened on December 16, they convinced Montgomery not to go along with a plan Burr had conceived.

The attack was discussed at the meeting. Little time remained: the New England troops would leave the army after the start of the new year, for their enlistments would then expire. The absence of battering rams to breach the walls would require any siege to last too long, and the frozen ground ruled out trying to dig trenches. Montgomery had to act rapidly, and so Burr offered to lead fifty men to climb the walls with scaling ladders. But the merchants objected. They persuaded Montgomery that only the lower town should be attacked. Over Burr's protests, the council planned four assaults at different places. Price felt that American control of the lower town would induce the inhabitants to surrender the city rather than risk damage to the property. Such a blow would be best made under the cover of a snowstorm, when the fortification would be under a reduced guard. Burr's reaction to these plans was that the men were under an honest but "most fatal delusion."[20]

The attack seemed to be near. The Americans, taking advantage of the frigid weather and working in a heavy snowfall, built ramparts of ice by freezing blocks of snow and water, which led one man to comment: "Who but *Yankoos* would have thought of such a contrivance? Or who but enthusiasts for liberty would carry on a siege at such a season of the year?"[21] High above the Plains of Abraham, falling snowflakes were almost obscured by smoke rising from the city. Houses were being burned to thwart American hopes of finding cover near the walls. Arnold's men were ordered to wear hemlock sprigs in their hats to distinguish themselves from the enemy. The cannonading accelerated, and the ice battery began to weaken, forcing the Americans to pull back.

The cold weather continued, but there was no real snowstorm. Of equal concern was the news that a deserter had alerted the British. Carleton's response was to strengthen the lower town by erecting barricades to replace houses, boarding up windows of the remaining dwellings, and installing cannon at strategic places. Cannon armed the road to the upper town and paving-stones were prepared as weapons. So Montgomery revised his plan. His new strategy involved a twin attack against the lower town, one at Cape Diamond and the other through St. Roche, to the north. Then the men assembled, while bombs continued to fall harmlessly between their position and the city. Brightening skies, however, frustrated their plan to attack on the twenty-seventh of the month. But on Saturday, December 30, with a storm threatening as the wind increased from the northwest, the troops were ordered to form on the Plains at two o'clock the next morning, the last day of 1775.

Only a little more than eight hundred men turned out in the most extreme winter bitterness. As they formed in the darkness, the wind whipped the snow into their eyes and nostrils, and only the warm capotes enabled them to function. The northwest wind brought alternating gusts of hail along with the snow. Drifts threatened the paths. Hopeful that the garrison in Quebec would offer little resistance, underestimating their number, Montgomery prepared to attack with two main thrusts. Arnold would strike the lower town through St. Roche. A force moving along the St. Lawrence, led by Montgomery, would attack from the other end.

Burr walked behind the General and Captain Jacob Cheeseman, who commanded Montgomery's first company of New Yorkers. With him was the first aide, Captain John Macpherson, a wealthy twenty-one year old Philadelphian. All in all, Montgomery led a force of about three hundred men walking in a single column.

Their march through blinding snow led along a gully toward Wolfe's Cove. Advancing one mile to the edge of the precipice above the St. Lawrence was enormously difficult, as the wind piled up the snow. Little noise was made as they struggled in silence to maintain contact with one another. And when they reached Wolfe's Cove, billows of snowflakes filled the great void of the valley and vanquished any sight of the river. Montgomery indeed had his storm!

From the Cove, another two miles lay before the first barrier to the lower city. The path followed the narrow strip of land between the St. Lawrence and the cliff. But this part of the march proved much more treacherous than the route to Wolfe's Cove, as large ice blocks had spilled over from the choked river. Those burdened with ladders found that they were almost insurmountable obstacles. Many climbed as much as twenty feet up the side of the cliff to avoid the chunks, but others suffered painful falls on the ice. Burr kept his eyes on Montgomery. At times, he quickened his pace to keep up with the tall general. When the first barricade was reached, the carpenters went to work sawing down the pickets to let them pass.

The alert excited the town. Churchbells rang. It was about 5 A.M. when the captain of the main guard in Quebec ran down St. Louis Street with the warning: "Turn out! Turn out! Turn out!" The city awoke suddenly. Cannonading could now be heard; shells were coming from the American mortars in the St. Roche area, while the townspeople manned their posts. Fires could be seen burning in the city, and the clouds looked red against the falling flakes.

Some one hundred yards past the first barrier, Burr saw Montgomery begin to struggle with another picket barrier. Again, the carpenters began to cut, and the General himself then tore down half-sawed posts, throwing them aside. Burr followed, with Macpherson and Cheeseman, as Montgomery led them into a road no more than twenty feet wide. Only about fifty men were beyond the second barrier when a blockhouse was passed. But no shots came from it, so they went on. Ahead was a private dwelling. But instead of a home it was now a guardhouse, equipped with four small cannon and with walls that were loopholed for muskets. Inside, John Coffin, a loyalist who had fled from Boston, commanded a small group of Canadians; at the three-pound cannon were sailors. Their matches were ready.

For the rest of his life, Aaron Burr remembered that moment and recalled Montgomery saying, "We shall be in the fort in two minutes," as he neared the house.[22] And that was all. The matches had ignited the three-pounders: a great roar, accompanied by a spray of grapeshot and bullets, blasted those near the little fortress. A ball had entered Montgomery's head. His tall body fell into the snow, along with Macpherson and Cheeseman.[23]

Their deaths panicked the others. Burr and Edward Antil, unhurt and in the middle of sudden chaos, saw the rest of the column retire in disarray. From the rear came the command to retreat. Colonel Donald Campbell, the next ranking officer, had acted to save the survivors from the consequences of their own disorder. But the retreat only imperiled Arnold's force, as the main body could not understand why, by seven A.M., the British were able to employ such a substantial opposing force.

Daniel Morgan complained that Campbell's retreat left them to "shift for ourselves," but Aaron Burr thought Quebec could still be won.[24]

In desperation, with the aid of some of the other officers, he tried to wave the men forward, to collect the disorganized remnants. He motioned them toward the lower town. Captain Richard Platt thought he could have succeeded but for Campbell's order. Having failed to revive the attack, Burr then grabbed Montgomery's body.

It was an impossible task, but working against both the size of the dead officer and the snow, Burr attempted to pull the body to the safety of the American lines. All this happened on the narrow, ice-choked, snow-covered road at the river's edge. But the physical differences made Burr's efforts useless. However, his actions won him immediate recognition from both Arnold and Campbell, whose letters of the next few hours praised the gallantry of the young man who had volunteered to risk the hazards of the campaign against Quebec.[25]

Yet, legends enhanced even these brave efforts. Word circulated in later years that Burr had actually moved the General's huge body, running with it on his shoulders "down the gorge, up to his knees in snow, the enemy only forty paces behind him," according to Reverend Spring's son.[26]

But Private John Joseph Henry noted that Montgomery's body was still near Cheeseman and Macpherson when it was found, at the edge of the river.[27] Moreover, Burr would have moved alongside the St. Lawrence to reach the American lines, not downhill. And, finally, the information that Spring's son supplied so many years later contradicted his father's statement to Senator William Plumer in 1807. As the Senator noted in his diary, "Burr returned back alone & attempted, amidst a shower of musquetry, to bring off on his shoulder, the body . . . But the general being a large man, & Burr small, & the snow deep, prevented him."[28]

Burr emerged from the catastrophe unscathed, much more fortunate than most of the others. In addition to the officers who died when he was at their side, such men as Ogden, Arnold, and Lamb were wounded. Morgan was imprisoned. Neither a casualty, a prisoner, nor a victim of the smallpox that swept through the ranks as the Americans continued to besiege Quebec, he remained with the troops for five more months. He had established a reputation for bravery, patience, and determination. "He was not one of the repining kind," wrote Charles Francis Adams many years later.[29] An eager, immature youth only six months earlier, he was now a respected officer.

When news of the Quebec disaster reached Litchfield in two weeks, it

was withheld from Sally for five days. The Reeves, however, were
fortunate in not knowing that Burr was one of Montgomery's aides, as
they did hear that an aide had died. But the news that Burr was alive was
not only wonderful—it was glorious! From Albany had come word that
Burr had gained honor by his "intrepid conduct."[30]

CHAPTER IV

"*The Most Important Revolution*"

BURR was part of the small force that remained outside the walls of Quebec. His growing awareness that their situation was hopeless made Matt Ogden's letter from New York particularly interesting. Matt wrote that he had been offered an appointment as aide-de-camp to General Washington, but since he preferred a more active post, he would be happy to pass it on to Burr. The position, he added, would make Aaron a major and mean an increase in pay. Although he was fairly certain that the Commander in Chief would accept Burr, Ogden cautioned him not to turn down a sure offer of advancement in Quebec.[1]

Through April, Burr remained at Quebec assisting the new commander, General David Wooster, who had arrived with reinforcements on the Plains of Abraham and Point Levi. Firing from these points at the town failed to accomplish any purpose, proving Captain Burr's assertion that Wooster was uninspired and inadequate.

By the time General John Thomas replaced Wooster, Aaron Burr had left Montreal to rejoin Arnold. Thus, he missed the pathetic conclusion of the siege. When a force of about nine hundred Britishers finally emerged from the town, the tiny American army of 250 dissolved into a complete panic. Riflemen dropped their weapons and the sick and wounded left their hospital beds to stumble feebly into the woods. What could be rescued was loaded into bateaux and steered up the St. Lawrence, while the army, now transformed into a mob of muddy, hungry, tired men, moved west, leaving behind the dead and dying.[2]

Although Burr accompanied Arnold when the army marched from

Montreal to Sorel, he had determined to leave Canada with or without an appointment. Arnold angrily refused to release the young man, at first, but soon saw that he had little choice but to accede.

Still without news from General Washington, Burr went up the Richelieu River to Fort Chambly, where he found that General Thomas lay dying of smallpox, a final sacrifice to the ill-fated expedition. Litchfield was supposed to be Burr's destination,[3] but when he arrived in Albany, he heard about his appointment to Washington's staff and so hurried directly to New York.

New York City, the next target of the British, as Washington properly guessed, had been fortified, first by General Charles Lee and then, after his departure to take over the southern campaign, by William Alexander, the self-styled Lord Stirling.

On April 13, Washington himself entered the city. He was displeased with much that he saw. Though work on the defenses was well begun, the army, he said, was disgracefully undisciplined, riddled with drunkenness and desertion, camp sanitation neglected, protection of civilian property ignored, and the incidence of venereal disease astounding. The General was particularly annoyed to observe that New Yorkers were trading with the enemy on board the British ships of war anchored in the harbor. He wrote, "We are to consider ourselves either in a state of peace or war with *Great Britain*. If the former, why are our ports shut up, our trade destroyed, our property seized, our towns burnt, and our worthy and valuable citizens led into captivity and suffering the most cruel hardships? If the latter my imagination is not fertile enough to suggest a reason in support of the intercourse."[4]

Washington opened his headquarters at the residence of William Smith, but soon moved into Richmond Hill, the estate of Abraham Mortier, located at what is now the intersection of Charlton and Varick streets. The area was then open country, affording a view of the small city of New York and, to the north, beyond the rolling plain, the village of Greenwich. At the foot of the hill, within the grounds of the estate, was a beautiful lake called, at the time, Richmond Hill Pond. Here the General and Martha set up housekeeping with furniture, glassware, and crockery purchased at Continental expense.[5]

Aaron Burr arrived at Richmond Hill late in June. Fresh from the miseries of the Quebec campaign, he expected the beautiful surroundings of his new home would provide the luxury and comfort of a lively city atmosphere. But he was soon disappointed. The tense political situation had almost eliminated social life, and the recently promoted Major Burr found Washington unreceptive, stiff, and somewhat humorless.

In a remarkably brief period of time, Burr's unhappiness with his new post became so acute that he informed John Hancock that he contemplated leaving the service. Washington had already sent Hancock a gloomy description of the life his aides were forced to live, writing: "I give in to no kind of amusement myself; consequently those about me can have none, but are confined from morn to eve, hearing and answering the applications and letters of one and another. . . . If these gentlemen had the same relaxation from duty as other officers have in their common routine, there would not be so much in it, but to have the mind always up on the stretch, scarce ever unbent, and no hours for recreation make a material odds."[6] Small wonder that the active twenty year old was reluctant to stay.

Once more, the obliging President of Congress rescued his old friend's son. He arranged a favorable exchange: Burr would go to General Israel Putnam's staff and Samuel Blachly Webb, Putnam's aide, would join Washington.

General Putnam, one of Rogers' Rangers during the French and Indian War, a tavern-keeper, and selectman from Connecticut, was a fifty-eight year old Major General. He resided at Warren House, a large brick building at the corner of Broadway and the Battery, well located to make the diversions of the town readily available to Burr. During his stay, the attractive young man was made much of by the hearty General, his wife, and his daughters.

But New York was facing a grave situation. On June 25, Major General William Howe arrived from Halifax with a small force followed by more ships and troops, who disembarked on Staten Island. Burr assessed the score as slightly in the patriots' favor in the early summer of seventy-six. The American failure in Canada was balanced by their success in forcing the British from Boston and checking the invasion of the South.

Even in the midst of the anxiety and tension, Burr was able to wheedle a leave. Early in June, he sent his sister the latest family gossip and news of friends that had been gathered from a "6 days rout I took to Jersey and Philadelphia." He added proudly that the "Jersey men turn out in the present emergency like Men really engaged in the cause of Liberty." In the same letter the young Major titillated his sister with the following observation: "A spirit of Matrimony prevails throughout the country—a truly noble spirit & suited to our present Necessities. Who knows but it will reach *even* your Brother—"[7]

Mrs. Reeve's brother already had a reputation for dexterity with the ladies. Among the most attractive of them at the time, it was said, was Margaret Moncrieffe, a fourteen year old temporary war orphan abandoned by her British officer father to the mercies of American friends in

Elizabeth Town. Loathing the dullness and patriotic fervor of that family, as well as a few others whom she tried in rapid succession, she sent a piteous appeal to the gallant old General Putnam, a friend of her father's. He responded at once, stating that Major Moncrieffe was his enemy only on the battlefield, and issued an invitation to Margaret to come to New York. She came and was received cordially by the Putnams; and, inevitably, by Major Burr, who was now a member of the family.

The young lady complained that she had few amusements and much toil at the Putnam household. Her sole relaxation was to flee to the roof where, with her telescope, she viewed the British fleet, an activity which was considered treasonable by no less a person than General Washington. When her father asked for Margaret's return, it was refused, and instead, she was moved to General Thomas Mifflin's house in Kings Bridge.

While there, said the fair Margaret, she met the "*conqueror* of my soul. . . . *My conqueror* was engaged in another cause, he was ambitious to obtain other laurels; he fought to liberate, not to enslave nations—He was a Colonel in the American army and high in the estimation of his country."[8] Soon afterward, Miss Moncrieffe was returned to her father. An engaging note from General Putnam went with her: "*Ginrole* Putnam's compliments to Major Moncrieffe has made him a present of a fine daughter, if he don't *lick* her he must send her back again, and he will provide her with a fine *twig* husband."[9] The Major kept his daughter, and so her American career ended. Later, the girl, known as Mrs. Coghlan, caused quite a stir in the court and fashionable circles of England and France.

Traditionally, Burr has been identified as Margaret's American lover, but the lady's own words contradict this assumption. She states that she met the gentleman at Mifflin's, not Putnam's. Furthermore, her lover was a Colonel, whereas Aaron Burr was a Major. Therefore, though they were both members of the Putnam household in 1776, no romantic attachment can be proved. This is a very good example of the propensity of his chroniclers to link Burr's name with women, particularly notorious ones.

While the early career of Margaret Moncrieffe was unfolding in the Putnam household, matters of deep significance were being resolved for the American people. On July 4, the rebel cause became immortalized in the "Declaration of Independence." The radical element in the thirteen colonies had won, leaving to the others the choice of either casting their lot with the British, who were now "the enemy" to the patriots, or joining the patriots, who were traitors to the British and the loyalists.

The prospect of war in New York became a grave danger to the apprehensive patriots. On the evening of July 9, a mob tore down the equestrian statue of King George III, broke up the lead, and sent it to Litchfield, Connecticut, where the ladies converted it into cartridges.

General Howe, who arrived at Sandy Hook late in June, hoped sincerely to bring peace. However, he could not hurdle the obstacle of the Commander in Chief's title. Consequently, his letter of July 13, which had been directed to George Washington, Esquire, was returned, politely, undelivered.

News from New York was anxiously awaited everywhere. Matt Ogden wrote to Burr from Ticonderoga that there were "twenty different reports, that contradict each other relative to Howe and his fleet."[10] Many, like William Bradford, who had resisted the call to arms, now left their books to engage in the hostilities.

Washington, at his Richmond Hill headquarters, worked to ready his army, probably the largest gathered at any time during the war. Insufficient arms and equipment, short-term soldiers, and a preponderance of unseasoned youngsters handicapped the operation. Burr complained to Uncle Timothy that the British officers "hold us in utmost contempt. Talking of forcing all our lines without firing a gun";[11] but he knew that Washington's fears were warranted. When Burr inspected the troops for Putnam, he found them undisciplined, inadequately armed, and unfit for battle.[12]

The British executed a successful amphibious landing on Long Island the morning of August 23. Before the Americans discovered what had taken place, fifteen thousand redcoats were encamped at Flatbush. When Washington heard the news, he replaced General John Sullivan with Putnam. Burr, of course, went with him.

On August 27, under cover of the night, the English army in three divisions, taking three different roads, surrounded almost all of the patriot out-parties. Lord Stirling's brigade was captured along with its leader. Altogether about a thousand Americans were taken prisoner, including General Sullivan.

The following day, Major Burr reported to generals Mifflin and Putnam that the American army was "in a state of alarm" and "would retreat perhaps after a single fire."[13]

After a council of war held at Philip Livingston's country house, Washington and his generals decided to evacuate the army to New York City immediately. General Alexander MacDougall was put in charge of the effort. At Brooklyn Ferry, the designated embarkation point, ten flat-bottomed boats supplemented by "row-boats, flat-boats, whale-boats, pettiaugers, sloops, and sail-boats were assembled."[14] After a slight delay, at about nine P.M., the first crossings were made. It rained vigorously until about eleven, when the wind shifted from a strong northeaster to a gentle southwesterly breeze, easing the mile trip across the East River. Burr worked at the embarkation point, organizing and despatching the long lines of American troops. By dawn, the task was completed. Except for some heavy equipment that had sunk in the mud, all men and supplies had been transported to the city. The heavy seas kept Admiral Richard Howe, a brother of General Howe, from entering the bay, so it was not until the operation was over that the British discovered the astonishing feat.

The Continentals had no hopes of holding the city, but it was up to Congress to decide whether its destruction should precede evacuation. Washington was reluctant to yield comfortable winter quarters to the British. However, Congress decreed that there should be no damage. Burr concurred with the decision to leave but disapproved of the plan to keep five thousand men in the city, eight thousand stationed in Harlem, and the rest deployed in between.

The British, under General Howe, started their invasion on Sunday, September 15, some forty-eight hours before the task of moving out supplies, the sick, and the wounded could be completed. About twenty thousand Continentals were still south of Harlem Heights, where Washington had composed his strength. Among them were about five hundred commanded by General Putnam, whose task was to guard the fortifications on the north and load the last of the supplies.

Burr, still in the city, had been ordered by Putnam to reconnoiter and bring up stragglers. He found General Gold S. Silliman's brigade, now commanded by General Henry Knox, crowded in an inadequate little fort called Bunker's Hill. It was located midway between Broadway and The Bowery, at what is now Grand Street. When Burr suggested to Knox that he move his men on to Harlem Heights, Knox declared that he had been ordered to that post and was determined to defend it despite lack of water and its vulnerability to attack. The two men quarrelled until Burr, ignoring Knox' authority, addressed the soldiers directly. He told them that, if they remained, nightfall would find them in British dungeons or at the end of ropes. Convinced, the men decided to follow Burr. Riding back and forth among the columns, he led them along the Bloomingdale Road, his dragoons encouraging the Continentals until they joined the main army. There were a few brief skirmishes, but only thirty casualties.[15]

In later years, Burr was very fond of this adventure, and understandably so. After Fort Washington fell to the enemy, a garrison of twenty-five hundred men that had been left in similar circumstances surrendered. And not five hundred survived imprisonment in the notorious British prison ships.

Following the retreat, Washington opposed the British on Harlem Heights. The Americans, outnumbering the enemy slightly, fought aggressively until the British were slowly forced back toward the city. But, not certain about what reinforcements Howe could bring up, the Commander in Chief ordered a retreat. However, the battle restored American confidence and destroyed the myth of British invincibility.

Howe held New York, but it proved to be a less comfortable place than he had anticipated. A fire of unknown origin crippled the city, raging from Fort George to King's College and destroying many fine buildings, such as Trinity Church. The British imprisoned all those in the vicinity who were connected with the American army.[16]

The loss of New York disturbed the patriots greatly. Burr, who was resting at King's Bridge, New York, about two miles from camp, wrote to Aunt Rhoda not to despair, but to be resolute instead of "anticipating improbable calamities."[17]

General Howe had failed to attack the American camp on Harlem Heights because he planned to trap them, instead, by landing his forces to the north, at Throgs Neck. The American generals knew of his plans through deserters but determined, nevertheless, to hold on to Fort Washington. Major Burr agreed with General Lee that this decision was foolish. The fort should be abandoned. They were proved right when, on November 16, it fell with a sickening loss of prisoners and irreplaceable material.[18]

The American army, moving into the winter season, lacked tents and clothing. They were earning their title of "rabble in arms." Burr, at White Plains late in October, wrote to his sister that nights were cold and he wanted any plain metal buttons that were on his "old clothes," his leather drawers, and warmest woolen stockings.[19]

At about this time, an incident occurred that further intensified the ill feeling between Washington and Burr. Colonel Robert Pawling, a fellow officer, related this story, which took place at the Newburgh headquarters.

The General sent for Burr and Pawling. He was at his desk, writing, when they entered. Motioning them to be seated, he continued to write for a few moments and then, excusing himself, left the room. Burr arose and gradually edged toward Washington's desk, glancing at the manuscript. Finally, he stopped to read it. Although the General had been gone less than five minutes, he suddenly returned, surprising Burr in the midst of his surreptitious perusal. Burr was caught, "and there was no escaping the consequences which was a terrific reproof from the Genl."

Pawling added that Burr later "broke out in a furious tirade of curses and maledictions, in which though he did not spare the Genl, he did not spare himself from bitter reproach."[20]

Washington had the opportunity during the war and afterward to block Burr's rise in rank, and, in several instances, to thwart his ambitions. If this was the chief basis for his dislike and distrust, the punishment outweighed the crime.

In later years, Burr often expressed his dislike for Washington and had a poor opinion of him both as a man and as a military leader. William Seward, who later became Lincoln's secretary of state, said that Burr represented Washington as formal, cold, and haughty, "entirely without independence of character, and without talent, and completely under the influence of Alexander Hamilton."[21]

Late November and December saw the great retreat across New Jersey. The tired, ill-equipped Continentals marched day after day to New Brunswick, to Princeton, to Trenton. Lord Cornwallis could easily have stopped them if Howe's orders had not restrained him. Meanwhile Washington escaped across the Delaware.

Alarmed for the safety of Philadelphia, the Commander in Chief ordered lines of defense drawn from the Schuylkill River southward to Delaware. General Putnam, designated to superintend the effort, was assisted by Major Burr.

In the early spring, quartered at Nassau Hall, Princeton, Burr worked at his routine duties while pretending not to mind his failure to attain a berth in a regiment. However, he confessed to Matt (now Colonel Ogden) that many who had been his equals and even his inferiors had surpassed him. But pride restrained him from actively seeking promotion. "I am content to contribute my mite in any station," he wrote rather untruthfully.[22]

When Putnam was ordered to Peekskill, ill health kept Burr at Princeton. By June, however, he was able to rejoin the army and then embark on a special intelligence mission. He was to visit Norwalk, Fairfield, and all the towns in that area to estimate troop and fleet movements. Then he was to return via Litchfield to leave orders for the regiment of General John Nixon's brigade to proceed directly to Albany.

Upon his return from Connecticut, he found a surprise. A letter from General Washington appointed him a Lieutenant Colonel. Instead of reacting with pleasure, Burr wrote an ill-tempered and impudent letter to Washington, which reflected all the frustrations he had contained since the New York campaign. He accepted the appointment but added, "I am, nevertheless, Sir, constrained to observe that the late date of my appointment subjects me to the command of many who were younger in the service, and Junior officers in the last campaign." The letter was not answered.

The belated appointment was to the regiment of Colonel William Malcolm, a middle-aged New York merchant, wealthy and influential, but without military experience. As did other contemporary wealthy gentlemen, he outfitted and financed a regiment, adopted the rank of colonel, and then left the fighting to a second in command.

When Malcolm saw Burr, he was somewhat disappointed by his youthful appearance, fearing that he would not be able to obtain the respect of the men. He soon changed his mind. "You shall have all the honor of disciplining and fighting the regiment, while I will be its father," said Malcolm, and he moved about twenty miles away with his family.[23]

After saying farewell to General Putnam, Burr hastened to Ramapo, New Jersey, and his regiment. He devoted the summer to making soldiers out of the 260 men who composed Malcolm's Regiment. Some of the officers were city boys from wealthy families, most of them with no military experience. Using firm but humane methods, shunning corporal punishment, Burr was able to make his men into models for the army.

The rigors of camp life were relieved somewhat by frequent visits to Theodosia Bartow Prevost at nearby Paramus. The lady lived at the family residence, called *The Hermitage*, with her children, her mother, Anne Bartow de Visme, and her half-sister, Catherine de Visme. Colonel Jacques Marc Prevost, an officer of the British Army, whom she had married in 1763, was stationed in the West Indies.

The Bartows were a prominent local family. Theodosia's grandfather had been one of the pioneers of the Episcopal Church in America and had moved to New Jersey to engage in missionary work. His son, Theodosius, became an important attorney in Shrewsbury, where he married Anne Stillwell. His death, in 1746, preceded the birth of Theodosia, his only child.

The Hermitage belonged to Philip de Visme, Theodosia's stepfather, also a British officer. The house, which still stands, is a stone English-style structure timbered in oak, cypress, and chestnut, built at the end of the seventeenth or at the start of the eighteenth century. Its early history is not known, nor is the origin of its name. Curious features of the house are a number of masonic emblems chiseled on the front facade, probably indicating that it once served as a meeting place for Masons, and a secret room that may have been the storage place for the masonic paraphernalia. The tree-surrounded house stands on the Franklin Turnpike in the modern town of Hohokus.

In spite of the British connections of its owners, *The Hermitage* was a center for society during the Revolution. Ardent Whigs in the area believed that the family should be forced to move behind enemy lines, but not one of them had the courage to carry out this notion.

Theodosia Prevost was a charming young woman of unusual intelligence and learning. She was not a great beauty, as her face had been slightly disfigured by a small scar on her forehead. Nevertheless, in spite of their ten-year age difference, young Burr was completely captivated by her and became a constant visitor.

By September, Malcom's Regiment was stationed at Fort Sidman, just west of Suffern, New York, in an area known as the Clove, a narrow, rocky pass in the highlands that afforded the only entrance to the Ramapo Valley. Burr fortified the pass with earthworks to protect both Washington, in Newburgh, and the nearby Sterling iron mines and forge.

Burr received the news, one autumn day, that the British had crossed the Hudson into New Jersey and were in Hackensack about to advance into the country. Decisively, he ordered his men to march toward them. Then an officer brought a message from General Putnam ordering the public stores to be retired immediately into the mountains. But the Colonel would not be deprived of his adventure. He told the envoy that he could not run away from an enemy and would be completely responsible for his men and the public stores.

His attack on the British, about two miles from Hackensack, was entirely successful. Burr himself had scouted out the enemy while his troops slept, and then set upon them. The local residents were very impressed with the feat and some of them immediately placed themselves under his command.

Meanwhile, General Putnam had despatched General McDougall with nine thousand men to deal with the invasion of the Jerseys. By the time the General caught up with Burr, a week had passed since the Hackensack episode. The two officers compared notes about the shortcomings of the local militia. As Burr reported, they were completely undisciplined and unreliable. "Some joined us last night but are gone," he wrote.[24] News of Burr's raid soon reached headquarters and congratulations trickled back to the young commander.

But Burr was not to be the autocrat of the Post Road for long because orders were received directing him to move on to Pennsylvania. The enemy had been in Philadelphia since September 25, when Congress had fled before them, first to Lancaster and then to York. Howe had played a strange game. Believing, apparently, that his presence in the rebel capital would ignite the Pennsylvania Tories and frighten the patriots, he had abandoned General John Burgoyne and the master plan of a three-pronged attack to cut off New England from the rest of the colonies. By sailing south on July 3, instead of north as planned, Howe made his contribution to the cause of American freedom.

However, Washington was still faced with the present reality: General Howe's formidable army. Putnam had been asked for reinforcements while Washington waited from a position thirty-four miles up the Schuylkill. Burr was ordered to join another brigade, which was en route from White Plains. The regiment was to carry all its baggage but leave the stores behind at the Clove.

The second day of the march to join the Commander in Chief, a letter from General James M. Varnum reached Burr advising him that the enemy had landed at Paulus Hook in great force. He was to halt at the nearest convenient place to protect the Ramapo Valley. He must defend the bridge at Pompton if possible, and if not, retreat to Morristown.

So it was November before Malcolm's Regiment reached the army at Whitemarsh, twenty miles from Philadelphia. There, Sir William Howe made his last attempt to conquer the rebel leader and his ragged Continentals. He planned to surprise Washington's camp, but failed when the Americans were alerted by a vigilant scout. The two opponents set up camp, but for the next few days there were only minor encounters, no real battle. Then Howe, to the disappointment of the Americans, gathered his tents and stole back to Philadelphia to settle down for the winter. At the close of 1777, he had little to show for his efforts, except comfortable winter quarters and, thanks to his brother, the Admiral, the Delaware River open to British shipping. The enemy was not yet defeated, the Pennsylvanians had provided no more than three hundred loyalist troops, and what luxuries could be obtained in the city were only to be had for hard cash. In 1778, General William Howe resigned.

However, while Sir William was feasting and frolicking in Philadelphia during the winter of 1777 and 1778, the patriot army was shivering, starving, and bloodying the snow with its feet not twenty miles away, at Valley Forge. The decision to winter there had been Washington's. He was much criticized because the area was already as bare as if an army of locusts had swarmed through it. General Varnum said: "It is unparallelled in the history of mankind to establish winter quarters in a country wasted, and without a single magazine."[25] But Washington did not want to move into the interior lest Howe forget the existence of his foe.

The condition of the troops was pitiful. They were without breeches, shoes, and stockings; thousands needed blankets. The common diet was flour-and-water paste baked in thin cakes on hot stone called "Fire-cake" by the hungry, half mutinous Continentals. Fresh meat was almost completely lacking; even the salted beef, pork, and herring was scarce and often decayed. There was little water and no springs. A brook, about a half mile from camp, the most accessible source of water, was soon polluted from constant use as a swimming hole and laundry. Disease, of course, resulted. It was probably typhus, or "putrid fever" as it was then called. All through the winter, the disease raged in epidemic proportions, completely out of control. Burr was assigned supervision of the building of "Flying Hospital Huts," which were fifteen feet wide, twenty-five feet long with windows on each side and a chimney at one end. They were roofed with boards or shingles, not dirt; each brigade was to have two hospitals of this type.[26]

Many of the ragged horde of ill-fed, ill-clad, and ill-housed scarecrows that composed the army at Valley Forge could not endure the suffering. Men deserted and failed to re-enlist. Officers handed back their commissions, fifty in one day.[27] One of the few mitigating circumstances was a mild winter. Burr, who had developed a reputation as an excellent disciplinarian, was asked by General McDougall to handle a difficult problem. A detachment of militia had been sent to defend a narrow pass known as the Gulf, situated about eight miles from Valley Forge. Soldiers with a misguided sense of humor had been sending, night after night, false alarms that the enemy was on the march, thereby alerting the sleeping camp.

Burr took over command of the post and instituted a series of reforms that were received with ill-concealed distaste by the capricious personnel. This new regime inspired the detachment to make plans for revenge, plans that included disposing of their new commander.

Once he discovered the plan, Burr went into action. First, he had all cartridges removed from their guns. Then, as the moon shone on the camp through a frosty night, the entire detachment was awakened and formed in the cold for a muster roll call. Armed only with a sharp sabre, the little Colonel inspected the lines of his troops, marching up to each man and looking him straight in the eye as he passed. When he stood before one of the chief mutineers, the guilty soldier stepped from the ranks and aimed his gun at him, shouting, "Now is your time, boys." Resolutely, and with calm determination, Burr raised his sabre and, with one stroke, sliced the arm of the unfortunate mutineer above the elbow so that it dangled by a strip of skin from his shoulder. Summarily, Burr dismissed the men. The soldier's arm was amputated the next day, and threats against Burr ceased along with the false alarms.[28]

In late May, Washington learned that the British were preparing a general movement. He deduced correctly that Philadelphia was to be evacuated and the troops marched across New Jersey to New York. Fear that the French, now entered formally on the rebel side, would blockade the British fleet in the Delaware motivated the withdrawal orders that Sir Henry Clinton, Howe's successor, carried from New York.

To meet the problem, Washington called a council of war to propose that the Americans either follow the track of the British or proceed directly to White Plains. General Charles Lee, lately returned from New York, persuaded the others to accept the White Plains alternative, thus permitting Sir Henry to march to New York unmolested.[29]

Burr received a letter from Colonel Malcolm a few days before the Valley Forge evacuation. He was told that Malcolm had accepted the post of Adjutant General to the Northern army but would still keep his regiment. General Washington, he said, had written to General Horatio Gates that "he cannot conveniently spare you at this time," and so would Burr please recommend three or four officers to go to New York as a recruiting mission.[30] Burr may have been pleased to hear that Washington needed him.

Clinton's army left Philadelphia on June 18; Washington's army left Valley Forge a few days later. Again, Washington questioned his council of war. "Will it be advisable to hazard a general action?" Four days later, the Battle of Monmouth was fought.

The British army was overtaken at Monmouth Courthouse, where they lay in a good defensive position. General Lafayette had been awarded the command of the Americans because he had favored the offensive, but Lee, although opposed to the plan, asserted his seniority over the Frenchman.

Lee's action, on that day, has been subject to much controversy. His preliminary attack, which took place before Washington arrived and the real battle started, has been called "the most confusing in its movements and the most difficult to present or follow in detail of any of the battles of the Revolutionary War."[31] That phase of the battle, however, ended when Lee gave the order to some to retire; some fell back without orders, and a retreat gathered momentum until the mass of sweating, steamy, thirsty soldiers, five thousand strong, were marching back to Englishtown. Lee's supporters reject this version, especially the accusation that the General was quite complacent about the retreat, and insist that the withdrawal was covered by rear-guard actions and had been necessary to save the army from complete annihilation by Clinton.

Washington, in the meantime confident that all was going well, advanced with the main part of the army, whose numbers were only slightly more than those with Lee. Along the road, he met the first evidence of disaster, a fifer, who, upon being asked why he was moving in the wrong direction, answered that the troops were retreating. Washington, exasperated by what he took to be a direct lie, threatened the man with a whipping if he repeated such a thing. But the truth of the fifer's report soon became distressingly evident; exhausted stragglers, a full regiment in retreat, Maxwell's brigade, Ogden's Regiment, all attested to the fact.

Washington, usually well controlled, lost his temper upon meeting Lee and, it was asserted by a number of generals, quite uncharacteristically swore "till the leaves shook in the trees." However, he recovered quickly, stopped the retreat, and organized an attack.

Burr, in command of Malcolm's Regiment, was placed on Washington's left, along with a brigade in Lord Stirling's division, on a rise of ground just west of the westerly ravine. In the midst of the battle, Burr observed a party of the enemy issuing from a coppice south of the main British force. Burr's Regiment, Lt. Col. Rudolph Bunner's Third Pennsylvania Regiment, and others crossed a small bridge over a ravine to check them.

Early biographers have reported that, while Burr's men were crossing the bridge, Washington's aide commanded them to halt by order of the Commander in Chief. Burr pretended that his men were exposed to enemy fire and must continue to cross if they were to reach cover. The aide repeated the order. Burr complied, and consequently, the divided brigade was assailed by enemy fire that mowed down one-third of them while their youthful commander watched helplessly. Somewhat later, Burr's horse was struck by a cannonball just behind the girth of the saddle. The Colonel was thrown to the ground but was not injured.[32] Colonel Bunner, however, was killed by a musket ball and the brigade was withdrawn. They retreated in good order.

A day of heavy fighting had been made even more unbearable by the ninety-six degree heat. That evening, after darkness had forced both sides to retire, the troops remained on the field to resume the battle in the morning. Burr followed his usual practice of visiting his pickets all through the night to make sure that all safety measures had been observed.

When morning came, the American camp was surprised to discover that Clinton's army had slipped away during the night. Overcome by exhaustion, Burr lay down under a tree, his first rest in about forty-eight hours. Waking many hours later, he was very ill with a severe sunstroke that impaired his health for some time and probably predisposed him to the illness that forced his resignation from the army.

The repercussions of the Monmouth battle are well known. General

Charles Lee was arrested and charged with: disobedience to orders, having failed to attack the enemy on the twenty-eighth of June as directed; misbehavior before the enemy, making an unnecessary, disorderly, and shameful retreat; and disrespect to his Commander in Chief, with some letters written subsequent to the battle cited as evidence.

The court-martial, held on August 12, presided over by Lord Stirling, found him guilty and suspended him from his command for one year. Burr, who had supported Lee, partly, no doubt, because of his antipathy toward Washington, received an enlightening letter from him that fall. Lee wrote of his disappointment that Congress had not rescinded "the absurd, shameful sentence of the court-martial." He promised to send Burr a copy of the trial as soon as he could get one. Then he closed with the news that, since he did not know whether his reputation would ever be cleared, "it is my intent . . . to resign my commission, retire to Virginia, and learn to hoe tobacco, which I find is the best school to form a consummate *general*."[33] But he did not enjoy his rural retreat very long, for in 1782, having become "tired of this rascally planet," he died.

A brief but pleasant visit to *The Hermitage* directly after the Battle of Monmouth helped to restore Burr's shattered health, at least for the time being. This was made possible by an order from General Washington temporarily relieving him from active duty.

Sir Henry Clinton's arrival in New York with his troops caused great consternation to the rest of the state. All information that could possibly be obtained relative to the enemy's plans was urgently required. Washington chose Burr to conduct a kind of intelligence service. Because Burr was very successful in obtaining the required information, the Commander in Chief finally commended his efficiency. The General wanted to know, in particular, what expeditions were contemplated by the British stationed in New York, "whether up the North River, Connecticut, or the West Indies?" The British had shifted their emphasis, now that the French had actively engaged in the war, to the high seas and away from their rebellious colonies. New York was being held firmly, but no offensive was projected in the area at that time.

Specific orders were given Burr to send three or four persons to observe the enemy shipping from any convenient heights, such as those at Bergen, Hoboken, or Weehawken. All vital information was to be reported immediately.[34] Washington, who was proceeding slowly with the army toward West Point, arranged to meet Burr in Newark on July 8 to confer with him on the intelligence reports from the city across the river.

Mrs. Prevost invited the American commander to use *The Hermitage* as his headquarters while at Paramus. He and his party stayed there for a few days in the middle of July, resting from the extreme heat and enjoying some leisure. One young officer described the visit as one of talking, walking, dancing, and laughing.[35] After its brief respite, the army continued on the narrow, stony roads to Haverstraw in Orange County.

His stint of espionage work completed, Burr rejoined his regiment. Mid-July, orders were received from Baron de Kalb for Malcolm's Regiment to go to West Point. But Burr received another special assignment. Washington needed him for a sensitive mission that would require the utmost exertion of his "politeness and benevolence."[36]

Fearful that Sir Henry Clinton's presence in New York would stir up Tory sympathy, the New York State legislature had prescribed an oath of allegiance designed to expose loyalists who were hiding behind a facade of neutrality. George Clinton, inaugurated Governor in Kingston, New York, about a year before, had requested that Washington designate an officer to accompany "sundry Persons," guilty of refusing the oath, behind enemy lines.

Colonel Burr received orders the first of August to accomplish the mission. The commissioners for detecting and defeating conspiracies, stationed at Poughkeepsie, sent him a list of those to be exiled. He was to proceed by sloop with his charges from Fishkill, under a flag of truce, "to such place within the enemy's lines as may appear to you to be most proper and convenient."[37]

The sloop with Burr and the gentlemen aboard sailed down the river to New York. The voyage was quite agreeable, except for the request of Mr. William Smith, a wealthy Tory sympathizer, for his "negro men." Burr explained that according to his interpretation of the law, this could not be permitted. However, he did allow Smith one Negro servant for his personal needs. Burr wrote to Governor Clinton that his charges seemed "in high good humour the whole of the passage—I am confident they have not smiled since."[38] New York, where the Tories were unloaded, was under strict military authority.

In the next few months, Burr made this trip a number of times. On one occasion, he conducted Mrs. Prevost and her sister down the Hudson. Lord Stirling had granted them permission to go to New York and return, and the gallant Burr had appended their names to Governor Clinton's safe conduct. It is possible, although there does not seem to be any concrete evidence, that Burr was engaged in continuing the espionage work that he had started in the spring in New Jersey.

The illness contracted by Burr at the Battle of Monmouth continued to distress him. In October he went to Elizabeth Town, hoping that a rest would help, for he felt too sick to continue on active duty at West Point. From there, he wrote to Washington, stating that during the past three months he had taken "every advisable step for my recovery, but have the mortification to find, upon my return to duty, a return of sickness, and that every relapse is more dangerous than the former." Physicians advised that a few months' retirement and nursing would restore him. He therefore asked Washington's permission "to retire from pay and duty till my health will permit . . . provided such permission can be given without subjecting me to any disadvantage in point of my present rank and command." The last "delicacy," as both Burr and Washington referred to the suspension of pay, was received by the General with distaste and a shade of distrust, Burr thought. The answer came back quickly: "It is not customary and it would be unjust," said Washington, to drop pay. He gave Burr leave to retire until his health is "so far re-established as to enable you to do your duty."[39]

Burr, ignoring his physical state, repaired promptly to West Point to rejoin his regiment, insisting that it would be dishonorable to accept pay while absent from duty. In December, Malcolm's Regiment was ordered by McDougall from the Point to Haverstraw. At that place, Burr commanded a brigade composed of Malcolm's Regiment, as well as portions of two others.

Early in the new year, Burr was sent to command the troops on the Westchester lines, a position of great responsibility, for the countryside was the scene of lawlessness and violence. The British headquarters at New York extended their outposts from King's Bridge to West Farms on the Bronx River. American outposts, with headquarters at Peekskill, extended from Mamaroneck on Long Island Sound to Dobbs Ferry on the Hudson River. The area between was a no man's land inhabited by marauders who pretended to belong to whichever side suited their purpose at the moment. They pursued their plundering activities on this neutral hunting ground, unimpeded by either side. Tory sympathizers called themselves "Cowboys," while those favoring the rebels referred to themselves as "Skinners." Their roles were interchangeable, however, depending on the political connections of the day's quarry.[40]

When Colonel Burr arrived to begin his duties, he observed that all the horsemen "were infatuated with the itch for scouting," and that they rode off with merry enthusiasm to pursue this military duty. By the end of the day, with the return of the "scouting party," the unsuspecting new Commander had the answer to the riddle. "I blush to tell you," Burr confessed to General McDougall, "that the party returned loaded with plunder."[41] In their wake, not an hour after their return, came the "piteous applications" from their victims, residents of New Rochelle and Throgs Neck, asking for the return of their goods.

Burr, outraged, instituted drastic camp reforms before the bewildered soldiers were able to divide their spoils. All looting was to stop immediately, whether it be of Tories or patriots. The guards and pickets were introduced to the Burr method: frequent inspections conducted at all hours of the day and night. "Men on Guard are not to put their arms out of their hands at night, pull off their accoutrements or be out of call at any time," the new rules read.[42] And he meant what he said.

Officers were included in the new policies. "The officers are again warned to make themselves immediately acquainted with Orders heretofore issued . . . Repetition of orders is a shameful reflection on any Corps . . . The Commanding Officer is ashamed of the necessity he is under of Enforcing such common points of duty which every Corporal is supposed to be acquainted with much more gentlemen of some Military Experience."[43]

Indifference or disrespect shown to Burr's policy was punished severely. "Every centinel who shall quit his post without firing an Alarm shall receive one hundred lashes on the spot . . ."[44] But, in spite of the consequences, the temptation to plunder enticed the soldiers. Burr ordered such malefactors to be "whipd at the Plundered House" and "to ask pardon of the Injured Party." This last entry, in the unit's orderly book, referred to the Gedney case, which Burr encountered shortly after his arrival in Westchester.

When the Gedneys were plundered during the night, the family was abused and terrorized. The young Gedney boy, managing to sneak past the sentinels, brought the outrage to Burr's attention. "By means never yet disclosed," Burr discovered the identity of the marauders in twenty-four hours. Although, on consulting the register, it was seen that the Gedneys were Tories, the robbers were escorted to their house, forced to restore the booty, and compelled to make arrangements in money for articles that had been destroyed or lost. And, further, by Burr's orders, they were to be flogged ten lashes and forced to apologize for the terror and abuse to old Mr. Gedney. The fear engendered by this disposition of the case discouraged further expeditions of this kind.

However, McDougall had to caution Burr to have some regard for the human frailty of his charges. "I wish you to deal tenderly with them," he said, "as they are brave, and are very sore by the plundering of the Tories." But, at the same time, he was in agreement with Burr's policy of "giving redress to the innocent and helpless."[45]

McDougall was so deluged with complaints, remonstrances, and requests for advice from the energetic Burr that Major Richard Platt, his aide, wrote, "The General's passions like the wind blow high upon every point of the Compass," and begged him to show a little more patience. And then he added, "and you'll have the most respectable command of any officer of your Rank in the Army."[46] But if he punished his men severely for their infractions of discipline, he just as energetically championed their needs. He demanded shoes for them, not French ones that wear out, but good shoe leather, and their ration of rum. He deplored loudly the women "of bad character" who ran back and forth to New York, probably, he thought, carrying information to the enemy. McDougall advised that they should not be permitted to "stroll to New-York without leave. But cause them to be well searched by matrons for papers *immediately* when they are taken; hair, caps, stays and its lining should be well examined."[47]

General McDougall and Platt developed a sincere admiration and affection for the vigorous youth. Years later, Platt summarized Burr's accomplishments while on duty in Westchester: "His humanity and constant regard to the security of the property and persons of the inhabitants from injury and insult, were not less conspicuous than his military skill . . . A country which, for three years before, had been a scene of robbery, cruelty, and murder, became at once the abode of security and peace."[48]

The inhabitants of the area began to endow Burr with supernatural powers and second sight. They said that he could tell a robber by looking at him; this reputation probably caused many an ignorant, frightened culprit to confess from sheer superstitious belief in such occult powers. Furthermore, Burr's Spartan habits of eating and sleeping awed his unsophisticated subordinates. While he was in command, it was alleged, not one soldier deserted and not one was made prisoner.

Burr's activity, however, masked his true condition. He was often ill while in Westchester, and as early as February 25 drafted letters to Washington and McDougall declaring his intention to resign.[49] On March 10, Burr wrote to inform Washington that his health was "unequal to the undertaking." McDougall, he reported, was aware of the situation and had ordered his replacement to take over by March 15, "on which day I purpose to leave this command and the army."[50]

Malcolm's Regiment was destined to go to Minisink to join the expedition against the Indians of the Six Nations. Although Burr's health was very bad, he had returned to Haverstraw to command the regiment until it left for the frontier. He stayed there with McDougall for ten days to discuss the defense of the lines. Finally, on April 3 Washington's reluctant acceptance of Burr's resignation arrived. As soon as all accounts were settled, the young Colonel was to be relieved of his military duties.[51]

Newly released, Burr had no definite plans. He contemplated the possibility of a trip to Europe, but when he found out how long it would take McDougall to arrange a passport from the British general commanding in New York, he discarded the idea. Instead, he planned a series of visits to his family and friends. From Philadelphia, he informed Sally of his intention to go to Boston before visiting her in Litchfield. The Boston trip was to attempt to secure a release for Peter de Visme, Mrs. Prevost's brother, who was being held prisoner there. Burr's efforts to be a "deliverer," however, were not successful.[52] The next month, Washington regretfully refused to intercede in the matter, explaining to the anxious sister that he had never interfered with the disposition of "marine prisoners." So Peter was forced to remain incarcerated.

Early in June, while Burr was visiting McDougall, the British left their winter quarters to strike the first blow of the season in the New York area. Sir Henry Clinton assembled six thousand of his crack troops at King's Bridge, loaded them on seventy sailing ships and 150 flatboats, and then landed them on both sides of the Hudson at Stony Point and at Verplanck Point, just below Peekskill. The feeble Stony Point fort, manned by a handful of Americans, fell at once, and at Verplanck, Fort Lafayette surrendered.

McDougall, stationed in the Highlands, was unable to communicate with Washington in New Jersey because the British had stationed guards at the passes through the chain of mountains to capture all messengers. In spite of his bad health, the danger, and the fact that he was no longer on active duty, Burr undertook the mission. He crossed by ferry from New Windsor and then rode hard all the way to Pompton. The return trip, on which he carried verbal orders from General St. Clair, was accomplished without incident.

The following month, while visiting a friend in New Haven, Burr engaged in his final wartime adventure. To punish the people of Connecticut for their harassment of British shipping and for supplying the Continental army with provisions, Clinton arranged an expedition against them. Twenty-six hundred men disembarked in New Haven harbor and set fire to the town.

Burr was ill in bed when he saw flames light up his bedroom. Though almost too weak to mount a horse, he rode to the heart of town, where he found the militia utterly disorganized and surprised. He then galloped to the Yale College yard where he found the students assembled. There, he made a stirring appeal to the young men, firing them to action and even alerting some of the militia. The small force subsequently managed to worry and detain the British long enough to allow the townspeople to remove their valuables and evacuate the women and children. Years later, Burr recalled that, "There were on the spot officers of higher grade in the militia but all cheerfully submitted to my command."[53] This was his last skirmish.

Burr was now poorer than when he had entered the service. Much of his patrimony had been spent on his soldiers' welfare and equipment. The military life, its danger and its discipline, rather pleased the Colonel, the title he preferred all of his life. But now that he was in enforced retirement, he wanted to seek quiet as far as possible from the noise and bustle of war.

CHAPTER V

A Member of the Bar

BURR was now twenty-three years old. Although he was but five feet six inches tall, his erect military bearing and graceful manner gave him distinction. His best feature was his eyes, which were dark and particularly brilliant. Uninterested in the gentlemanly vices of drinking and gambling, abstemious, almost finicky about food, Burr's weakness was women. It was a vanity, wrote Matthew Davis, that sometimes made him seem ridiculous to his best friends. At this time, while at Litchfield with the Reeves, recuperating from another bout of his illness, he received a letter from a family friend. "Your sweetheart Miss Pope is very unwell [She] had got the fever and ague. Perhaps a short visit from one Colonel might be of service to her. I wont promise for her but I am afraid them rogues eyes of your made a conquest of poor Hannahs heart—. . ."[1]

Unfortunately, the young man was restless and nervous about himself. He admitted that he saw no company, partook of no amusements, and was always grave.[2] Part of his mood was probably attributable to his irritation at having to miss the conclusion of the war. Part of it, no doubt, anxiety about his future. Burr was certain that young Whig lawyers would be greatly in demand after the end of hostilities to replace the pro-British, prewar practitioners. But the completion of his legal studies had to wait for the recovery of his health.

Burr was in Connecticut studying with a Mr. Osmer and, when well enough, taking trips to Paramus for his health and relaxation. Robert Troup, a friend just recently returned to civilian life, was urging Burr to study law with him. Troup acknowledged Osmer's ability but felt that a teacher in New York or New Jersey, where Burr planned to practice, would make more sense. The two never managed to arrange a workable plan, although Burr said that he was sorry to disappoint Troup because he liked him and would have found him "a better antitdote for the spleen than a ton of drugs. I am often a little inclined to *hypo*."[3]

Burr's health continued to be his prime concern. Some friends doubted whether his delicate condition would ever support the rigorous demands of the legal profession. "I am obliged to eat, drink, sleep and study, as it directs," Burr wrote peevishly. He was particularly worried because of the uneven course that the illness took. Just when he seemed demonstrably better, the illness reappeared with renewed vigor.[4]

News about the war from friends actually engaged in it only made Burr petulant. He said that he must be buried in retirement, secure from alarms and remote from the noise of war. Connecticut provided this isolation. However, he was not above sustaining a financial interest in the hostilities by investing in privateers. He had part interest in a sloop, the *Hawk*, with a friend who had informed him that Eastern privateers had been successful against the Quebec fleet and perhaps they, too, would be lucky.[5]

During the summer, Burr tried taking the waters at Ramapo. His uncle, Thaddeus Burr, speculated whether it was their health-giving properties or the proximity of Theodosia that was to help. He teased Aaron about "the lady," and wrote affectionately: "I wont Joke you Anymore about a certain lady. I wish however that your health was established, the Country was at an honourable peace, and you will meet with some fine agreeable Companion."[6] However, Ramapo's waters did not cure Burr. Troup advised him to go south and then on to the West Indies to escape the northern winter cold. William Paterson, perhaps suspecting some psychological element in the ups and downs of the recovery curve, thought that hilarity, cheerfulness, and a serene flow of spirits might improve him.

While Burr was at Paramus during the fall, Mrs. Prevost had an unexpected visitor, the wife of General Benedict Arnold. After his treason plot had been discovered, the General had fled from West Point to the protection of the British frigate *Vulcan*, anchored in the Hudson River. Peggy Shippen Arnold was left in hysterics that were so convincingly loud in her protestation of ignorance of her husband's perfidy that, at Hamilton's request, General Washington ordered that she be allowed to go to her father in Philadelphia.

But Mrs. Prevost, whom Peggy regarded as a Tory sympathizer, was told a different story. As soon as the two ladies were alone, Mrs. Arnold confessed that her theatricals were necessary to save her neck. In reality, she had been disgusted with the shabby treatment that the American command had accorded her husband and she had encouraged his plot.

Long after all the principals were dead, Burr repeated this story, as Theodosia had told it to him, to Matthew L. Davis. The Shippen family, in rebuttal, alleged that Burr told the tale because he had made advances to Peggy when she arrived at *The Hermitage* that day and had been repulsed. Not only does the evidence point to Peggy Arnold's complicity, but British papers have revealed that Mrs. Arnold handled some secret dispatches and that, in 1792, she was paid £350 for her services.[7] Burr actually suppressed the story at the time because of his loyalty to the Shippens, who had cared for him when he was an orphaned child.

By the end of the year, Burr moved about twenty miles from New Brunswick and into the office of Judge William Paterson. Paterson's duties as attorney general of New Jersey did not prevent him from imposing rigid discipline on his law student. Burr appreciated Paterson's serious purpose, but he was impatient to qualify and start his career. He felt that refinement would come in time but at the present, he needed only fundamentals. Paterson understood and remained friendly to Burr when he sought another teacher.

Burr found the answer in the office of Thomas Smith, a New York lawyer who had been forced to suspend his practice because of the war, but who had managed to rescue his excellent library. They both agreed that in six months the young man could be adequately prepared.

Burr moved to Haverstraw, his tutor's home, and subjected himself to a strict regimen of long hours with his books and a severely curtailed social life, relieved only by correspondence with Theo, who was now living in Sharon, Connecticut. Her move from New Jersey had been prompted by mounting Whig persecutions, which even George Washington's protection could not curtail.

Burr was enchanted with Mrs. Prevost and with her two boys. Her unusual elegance set her apart. She read French, which pleased Aaron, who loved to write letters, inaccurately but charmingly, in that language, and was familiar with literature and at home in the world of ideas. Burr thought the boys, young Frederick and John Bartow, sweet-tempered and softhearted.

The Burr-Prevost correspondence was conducted on an amusingly intellectual plane. They discussed education; Burr extolled Lord Chesterfield; the lady admired Rousseau's *Emile*. Chesterfield was a good guide for the worldly life, she said, but for parents who want to form "a happy, respectable member of society, a firm, pleasing support to their declining life," Rousseau's *Emile* should be taken as a model.[8] Their letters often spoke about the Reeve family. Living so close to Litchfield, Theodosia became very friendly with Sally Reeve, who, since the birth of her son, was in almost constant ill health.

The allotted time to complete his studies having been served at Mr. Smith's, Burr determined to present himself in Albany for admission to the bar. He was aware that three years' preparation was the prerequisite for eligibility, but he planned to apply to the Supreme Court to waive the requirement in his case.

As carefully as he would have prepared for a military campaign, Burr plotted his assault on the august bench. He planned to journey to Albany in mid-October, but first, he would line up all potentially valuable allies. General McDougall, who continued to regard Burr with fatherly affection, provided a letter of introduction to General Philip Schuyler in Poughkeepsie. Schuyler, in turn, would provide an introduction to his family and other distinguished persons in the capital.

Burr visited Schuyler, who was later to become his political enemy, and did obtain a letter to present to the court. Arriving in Albany at about the time of the surrender of Yorktown, Burr presented his letters of introduction and credentials to Chief Justice Richard Morris, with a plea for special indulgence because he had studied with Tapping Reeve before the war "long before the existence of the present rule . . . surely no rule would be intended to have such retrospect as to injure one *whose only misfortune is having sacrificed his time, his constitution, and his fortune to his country.*"[9] Until the worthy judges reached a decision, Burr waited in Albany and prepared for the examination.

Theo was now a widow. In October, her husband had died in Jamaica.[10] Now the letters between the two became more affectionate, and it was accepted that they would marry as soon as Burr was established as a lawyer.

Burr was comfortable in his Albany lodgings, in the home of two maiden ladies, but he felt his separation from Theo keenly. He tried to be sensible, promising to devote but a quarter of an hour a day to her letters. In return, she was to give a half hour. "More I forbid, unless on special occasions," he wrote. The children, also, were to write at the given hour, the same one every day. Each was to have his own sheet and write, "if but a single word—Burr, at this half hour, is to be a kind of watchword."[11] The approaching responsibilities not only of marriage but of fatherhood concerned the aspiring lawyer. He advised about the children's education and welfare, admonished Theodosia to be serious, and in her letters, to deal less with sentiment and more in ideas. A

Franklin fireplace was advised for the Prevost home. Burr said that its cost, ten or fifteen dollars, would be twice saved in wood and comfort and was moveable anywhere. Carlos, Burr's slave, traveled back and forth between his master and the Prevosts during the separation, carrying letters and comforts to Theo and the children.

Despite Burr's growing friendship with Robert Yates, an Albany resident and Justice of the Supreme Court, his application to the court was failing to gain acceptance. Finally, he made an eloquent plea before the most distinguished jurors of the day, and was granted the permission. But there would be no lowering of the standards to accommodate him.

Burr passed brilliantly, on a particularly severe examination. On January 19, 1782, he was licensed as an attorney and, three months later, admitted to the bar. He started to practice in Albany and was successful almost at once.

In July, the long delayed wedding took place at *The Hermitage.* Aaron Burr and Theodosia were married under a special license from Governor Robert R. Livingston, by Reverend Benjamin Van Der Linde of the Reformed Dutch Church. The bride was becomingly gowned in gauze, ribbons, and gloves, but the bridegroom, temporarily out of funds, wore his old coat. Theodosia's half sister, Catherine, and her husband, Dr. Joseph Browne, paid all the bills. After the festivities, the new couple stayed in Paramus for a few weeks and then sailed to Albany.

The Burrs and the Prevost children resided in a large roomy house, filled with much joy but without a good servant or money. However, Burr was building up his law practice rapidly. The New York State legislature passed a decree in 1781 that disqualified from practice in the courts all lawyers who could not demonstrate Whig loyalty. This law, in effect until 1786, gave Burr an edge that he exploited. Albany was a bustling small town, the haunt of patroons and the gateway to the fur trade, some of it in illegal intercourse with Canada. It would do until the war ended, and then the Burrs could move south to the more cosmopolitan port of New York. After its long occupation by the enemy, there would be many legal matters to employ the skill of an ambitious, well-connected, enterprising young lawyer: Tory claims, the renewal of business, and the prosperity that must result after the war. But their move was delayed because the British troops in New York, scheduled for spring or early summer removal, remained until late November.

While still in Albany, on June 21, 1783, little Theodosia was born. The infant, reported to have Sally's eyes, was sickly at first but, after a few months, turned into a healthy baby. Theo said Burr was half crazy with pride, which, coupled with his pursuit of the law, "divided his imagination."[12]

The Burr family was already in New York when the Governor and General Washington made their triumphal entry on November 25. Colonel Burr, as a veteran, was entitled to wear a cockade: a black and white riband worn on the left breast and a sprig of laurel in his hat. This was in honor of the Commander in Chief and America's ally, Louis XVI.

It had taken much tactful persuasion to ease Sir Guy Carleton, now the British governor of New York, out of the city. Washington and Clinton had conferred with King George's representatives for months before they had been able to achieve the November evacuation date. They had earned their victory processions. The residue of loyalists still in the city hated to see the British troops leave, and it was not until December 5, just about the time that General Washington took his touching farewell of his officers in Fraunces Tavern, that the British ships finally sailed out of New York Bay.

The establishment of American civil government was quickly followed by the rebuilding of the part of the city that had been burned out in the American evacuation of 1776. In the next few years, the city mushroomed to 3,340 homes. The Burrs lived in a house on Wall Street.

Just as he had expected, Burr's success at the bar was almost immediate. He developed a distinctive and brilliant style, along with the reputation of seldom losing a case. He was "acute, quick, terse, polished, sententious, and sometimes sarcastic in his forensic discussions. He seemed to disdain illustrations and expansion, and confined himself with stringency to the point in the debate."[13] He would pursue his opponent relentlessly until he wore him down and thus achieve the compromise or settlement he sought. Two characteristic sayings were attributed to him: "Now move slow; never negotiate in a hurry," and, *"Never do today what you can as well do tomorrow;* because something may occur to make you regret your premature action."[14] The preparation of evidence was considered his strongest asset. Said Burr: Law is "whatever is boldly asserted and plausibly maintained." He addressed the jury in conversational tones and won them with his elegant manners and familiarity with the details of his case.[15] He was not a legal scholar like Alexander Hamilton, but his cool manner and close reasoning, his spare and severe language, and his skill at confining his argument to a few powerful and prominent points often won cases.[16] Some of his contemporaries considered him overrated, but possibly, his method was far ahead of his time.

The stimulation of his busy and increasingly lucrative law practice along with his concern for his growing family absorbed Burr fully for a time. He assured Theodosia that he would not participate in the scramble for public office that was taking place in New York. But the pressure of his friends and a sense of civic responsibility, combined, no doubt, with a need to be present and involved in the development of the new government, changed his mind. In the spring of 1784, Burr was elected a member of the state legislature.

CHAPTER VI

A New York Politician

THE Burrs had a secure place in early New York's social and political life. The former mistress of *The Hermitage* adjusted easily to the society that included such prominent people as Robert R. Livingston, one of the best known members of that aristocratic family; Melancton Smith, a merchant-lawyer and, from 1785 to 1788, a member of the Continental Congress; and Alexander Hamilton. Hamilton, who was one year younger than Burr, had already served a term in the Congress and was now devoted to his law practice. Nor were the Burrs strangers in such fine homes as the John Jay residence on lower Broadway. Burr was, after all, a leading and brilliant young lawyer.

But politics had begun to complicate his career. Rather than political parties as we now know them, there were primarily factions that were led by an individual, a clique, or a family. These factions composed the main political forces dominating Governor George Clinton's state. One of Burr's earliest biographers observed that while the Clintons held political power and the prolific Livingstons had the advantage of sheer numbers, the "Schuylers had *Hamilton*."[1] General Philip Schuyler had acquired his talented son-in-law through the marriage of his daughter Elizabeth. As for Burr, his early career had been without intense political partisanship.

Logically, Burr should have allied himself with the large and conservative landowners and merchants. His background seemed to offer little choice. There was, as one influence, the traditionalism of his religious heritage. His rigid Calvinistic rearing was poor preparation for belief in the virtues of popular government. Tapping Reeve's Law School, where his stay had been brief but formative, later became noted for its violent Federalism, which placed more faith in aristocratic rule and the virtues of a strong central government; and Reeve himself was so passionately devoted to this belief that he was eventually indicted for seditious libel against Jefferson. Other such influences of Burr's early legal training as William Paterson and Robert Troup were known devotees of Hamilton, who was already regarded as a stubborn Federalist. Yet, in 1787, Robert R. Livingston classified Burr as a "violent whig," thus placing him with the most anti-British and pro-democratic groups, and Matthew L. Davis maintained that it was precisely that radical wing which had elected Burr as a state assemblyman in 1784.[2] Nevertheless, despite such assertions, the first half decade offered few real clues about Burr's future political affiliations. One enemy even charged that Burr had been "an indifferent spectator of passing events" during this period.[3]

The story of the proposed Mechanics' Bill offers a good example of how Burr managed, at this time, to offend a leading source of popular support. The mechanics, as they were then called, were actually the artisans and master craftsmen, the city's carpenters, masons, hatters, tailors, and candlemakers. As a group, they considered themselves exponents of a more democratic interest than the wealthy merchants and the country gentlemen, groups which, according to these tradesmen, were "oligarchic." Since the Chamber of Commerce had won incorporation from the State in 1784, one year later the mechanics saw no reason for not winning similar status and being able to function as a guild to secure their own economic interests. So the Eighth Session of the Assembly received a bill proposing the establishment of the Corporation of the Tradesmen and Mechanics of the City of New York.[4]

The debate was brief but sharp. Did the mechanics have a right to advance themselves as a self-interest group? Was such an act, if sanctioned by the legislature, prejudicial to the best interests of New Yorkers? When the bill was read for the third time, Aaron Burr called for its rejection. He warned that passing such a bill would elevate the mechanics to political power and that the general welfare would suffer. With such an advantage, he argued, they would jeopardize the business of the community, and their ability to set high rates for their labor would deprive immigrant mechanics of an equal opportunity. It was, simply, an attempt to raise the market price. With all other assemblymen from New York City opposing him, Burr's motion was rejected.[5]

But Burr had his own way. All legislation was scrutinized by a Council of Revision that had been established by the State constitution of

1777. Mostly a creation of those who feared excessive executive power in the hands of one man, the Council was an aristocratic body that included the Governor, the Chancellor, and the five members of the state's Supreme Court; they could veto any law they did not want. Quite predictably, they killed the attempt at incorporation. In the Assembly later, Burr and his followers thwarted the legislature's effort to get the necessary two-thirds vote to override the Council. Thus, Burr had clearly aligned himself with the conservatives, and the mechanics then denounced him bitterly. Nothing else about his record during that term had much appeal for such constituents.

Neither did his identification with the anti-slavery movement help his popularity. Slavery was not yet a target for popular opposition, and New York State had, at that time, the largest percentage of slaves in the North. But anti-slavery, while not exactly the objective of a crusade, had been gaining the support of some leading citizens, most of whom were usually identified as Federalists. John Jay and Alexander Hamilton were among the officers of the Society for Promoting the Manumission of Slaves, and in the Assembly, Aaron Burr became a leading advocate of their cause. Adamant against any attempt to compromise, he even opposed those bills that would have brought mere gradual abolition.[6] When he failed to achieve immediate freedom from involuntary servitude, he objected to attempts to deny suffrage rights to former slaves or to ban intermarriage between whites and Negroes.

When his Assembly term expired in 1785, Burr returned to the full-time practice of law. The resulting absence from elective office until 1788 created a gap in his public record and, more than anything else, may explain his avoidance of other significant controversies. It is interesting to note that he left no evidence of a public position during the bitter fight over ratification of the new Constitution that was written in Philadelphia in 1787. The Founding Fathers had, at that momentous session, endeavored to replace the flimsy Articles of Confederation, which had merely brought the states together within a "firm league of friendship," with a federal system that would increase the relative authority of the central government. Whether New York would accept this change was to be determined by a special convention at Poughkeepsie during the summer of 1788. And although Burr was merely a private citizen at the time, he had actually been an anti-Federalist candidate for the Assembly in April of that year. If he did harbor an opinion, he was curiously discreet.

For the Poughkeepsie convention, there was a special election of delegates. Governor Clinton's hostility toward the Constitution helped to

arrange matters neatly in behalf of the anti-Federalists. Although rigid
suffrage restrictions for all other elections for state offices confined voting to the wealthy and the propertied, elements that generally favored
ratification, the choice of representatives to this gathering was open to
all free white male citizens over the age of twenty-one. The Federalists
would be, therefore, placed at a disadvantage, which was Clinton's purpose. And Burr's name appeared in the newspapers as a Clintonian
candidate to represent New York City.

Yet, it would be wrong to conclude that his opposition to ratification
was known, or that it was assumed because he had been elected to the
Assembly as an opponent of the Hamiltonians. Actually, he eventually
declined to compete in the special election. Had he been an open supporter of the Constitution, his position would have antagonized the
Governor and the state's small farmers, but it would have pleased the
wealthy merchants and lawyers of New York City and Albany. Since the
required number of states had already voted to ratify the Constitution
before the New York convention could complete its session, the delegates at Poughkeepsie succumbed to the inevitable; even then, they
approved it by the slender margin of thirty to twenty-seven. Burr wrote
that he considered it a "fortunate event and the only one which could
have preserved peace." He also alluded to the convention's awareness of
the previous votes of approval by Virginia and New Hampshire, which
had already provided more than the minimum needed for approval.
Then he added: "I think it became both politic and necessary that we
should adopt it."[7] This comment to a friend was a clear statement of the
obvious. Whether Burr's attitude was purely expedient is questionable;
but, for one of the "violent whigs," a group so strongly opposed to
surrendering the virtual autonomy of the states, his tone was remarkably
moderate.

Actually, he must have been in substantial agreement with the need
for a stronger central government. The nation had to fulfill foreign and
domestic commitments. With the states often acting in opposition to
their neighbors, a unifying force was needed. The creation of an executive branch would provide some direction for the new country. New
York, along with other sovereign states, would have to yield some
powers. While Burr undoubtedly recognized the need for a stronger
government, he probably preferred some amendments to protect the
rights of the states. He must have had this in mind when he predicted
that the Constitution would not last fifty years. Much later, he recalled
this gloomy forecast and acknowledged the Constitution's continued
viability. Nevertheless, he still thought the "crash will *come*, but not
quite as soon."[8]

Life with Burr was often complex and frustrating for Theodosia, for his involvements and activities were frequently burdensome. She did not, for example, always have patience for her husband's young wards. Such children usually belonged to his clients and were often the products of unhappy circumstances. For many years, his home catered to a procession of such children until other arrangements could be made for each one.

One waif made Mrs. Burr lose her usual charity. While Burr was gone on one of his many trips, she wrote to urge him to settle the disposition of a little girl named Margaret. "The child of such a mother," she complained, "is not worth retaining, but rather a lucky riddance."[9] There was little she could do until her husband resolved the matter, but it is relevant to note that nowhere in all of Burr's papers is there even a hint that he could ever share such a sentiment.

His frequent absences from home and Theodosia's chronic illness were far greater impediments to the marriage. His trips seemed interminable. Theo sent him effusive and impassionate letters that were reminiscent of the highly emotional writings of Esther Burr. Rarely well, she needed her husband's constant attention. Bartow took care of his stepfather's office during some of these absences, so at least one son remained with her; but neither he nor baby Theodosia could compensate for her missing husband. Referring to a home filled with wards as well as her own children, she wrote to her husband: "If I pass thro' a day without being heart-sick with the noise & different little calls from one triffle to another I think myself fortunate."[10] When he was gone for a particularly long time, she once wrote: "Even little Theo gives up her place on mamma's lap to tell dear papa—'come home.'" The little girl was then less than two years old. And then she added, rather wistfully, "It is the last time of my life I submit to your absence, except from necessity to the calls of your profession."[11]

Yet Burr had always been solicitous toward Theodosia. Just before the birth of Sally, their second daughter, in 1785, he worried about his wife's running up and down stairs and cautioned her against overexertion. "How do you live, sleep, and amuse yourself?" he asked. He urged long walks and little sleep and, most characteristically, advanced the virtues of a simple diet.[12]

Little Theodosia had already begun to respond to her father's attention. She was two years old when her mother noted that "the most engaging child you ever saw . . . frequently talks of, and calls on, dear papa."[13] The mere mention of her absent father's name was enough to make the child melancholy, she wrote.

Their youngest daughter, Sally, was a sick baby. Burr suspected trouble when Theodosia's letters failed to mention the child's progress. Blame for any setback, he felt, could be attributed to her meat diet, which he regarded particularly dangerous during the fever-ridden late summer months. At such times, Burr wrote, "animal diet is unfriendly. I beg you to watch the effects of this whim with great attention."[14] No remedies helped.

All hoped ended in February of 1789, when, before her fourth birthday, Sally died. "The late melancholy event in our family," Burr told one of his stepsons, had made it "particularly disagreeable and improper . . . to leave home at this juncture."[15] Mrs. Burr's anguish exceeded any she had ever known, for, as she wrote, "a tender, affectionate friend just opening into life with every unfolding virtue, guileless, innocent, sincere, beautiful . . . passed gently from me to the regions of bliss . . . Yes my Sally is there, & gone but a little before me—." And she added: "But a little & I shall meet her—where sorrow dare not intrude . . ."[16]

Burr's reputation as a lawyer continued to gain. His adherence to Chesterfieldian mannerisms, his war record, and his pedigree had already brought some distinction. But even more important was his obvious skill and learning. His list of volumes in his library and of books he intended to purchase showed a heavy interest in ancient history, particularly the works of Pliny the Elder, Suetonius, Livy, and Tacitus. Such contemporary histories as Gibbon's *The Decline and Fall of the Roman Empire* were also familiar to him. Other works included *Don Quixote*, which his wife had begun to read and then discovered, to her annoyance, that Burr had misplaced the third volume. He also guided her reading, at one point suggesting that "Abbé Mably's little book on the Constitution of the United States" was far superior in French than in any translation. Other interests included accounts of voyages and theological works. Many law books were sent to him by an agent in Ireland, volumes following lists that were forwarded across the Atlantic. From the New-York Society Library, which was housed in Federal Hall, Burr also borrowed many additional books during these years.

In politics, Burr succeeded for a more practical reason: he was an expert in the art of political maneuvering.

Since 1777, George Clinton, the king of New York politics, had occupied the executive seat as the state's first governor. A vigorous patriot, his successful measures against both the frontier Indians and the Tories had won great popularity from the yeoman farmers. They had also approved his denial of tariffs to the Congress and his opposition to the Constitution. Clinton's marriage to Cornelia Tappan had given him the helpful ties of the Wynkoop family. In 1789, the Federalist problem was how to defeat him.

Burr, so often suspected for Federalism at heart, that year joined with Clinton's enemies and aided Alexander Hamilton. The two men were certainly well acquainted by that time. Hamilton had met Burr during the battle for Manhattan in 1776. His marriage to Elizabeth Schuyler had given him the society and financial advantages of General Schuyler's family, and he had moved to the leadership of the Federalist cause in New York at a time when Burr was still reticent about his own politics. When Burr gained the loyalty of a group of followers, Hamilton called them "Burr's Myrmidons."[17] Whether or not Hamilton's implication was accurate, it was plain from almost the start that the two gifted lawyers were natural rivals.

But, in 1789, they worked together. Governor Clinton could not, Hamilton reasoned, be stopped by an out-and-out Federalist. Even the success at Poughkeepsie had not hidden the anti-Federal strength. Victory would be more likely with a moderate candidate who appealed to all factions. So Burr and Hamilton united to support Judge Robert Yates, a man who would uphold the new Constitution and still be supported by a sizeable number of Whigs. The two young lawyers served in Yates' behalf on a committee of correspondence, a defection from anti-Federalism that was later used to prove Burr's political infidelity. Yet, for Burr, his support was mere loyalty to a good friend, one who had been valuable in helping him clear the barrier that had threatened to delay his admission to the bar. Yates' subsequent showing was strong, but not enough to topple the invincible Clinton.

The Governor was too wise to harbor grudges. Determined to consolidate strength in preparation for the next election, he wasted little time. The resignation of the Attorney General enabled Clinton to appoint Burr to that state-wide office. Burr's talents were evidently valued, as were his "Myrmidons," or "Tenth Legion," as his daughter would later call them. Clinton's move was also designed to enlist Burr and his followers and to pit him against Hamilton. The Governor had, however, thereby helped to further another political force.

The Livingston family was also a great power. The prolific and wealthy New Yorkers had been identified with the Federalist ideals of Hamilton. But Clinton had been astute and realized that the lack of Livingston appointees to high offices, and the complete neglect of minor members of the family, was disenchanting the clan with Washington's administration.[18] Establishing Burr as the attorney general was an important part of the Governor's plan. He had placed his man in a position of sufficient prestige to be recognized by the legislature, which then elected federal senators, and would surely elect Burr. Once Burr was elected, Clinton could recognize the Livingstons by appointing Morgan Lewis, the Chancellor's brother-in-law, as the new attorney general.

In 1791, everything went as planned. The Federalists, as expected, supported Hamilton's father-in-law, General Philip Schuyler, for the Senate. Burr's name was advanced by an Orange County assemblyman, and he was then able to defeat Schuyler when the Senate concurred with the Assembly. But even Burr, viewing the circumstances of his own election, commented that there "was uncommon animosity & eagerness in the opposition."[19]

It was hard to say whether the Federalists were more disturbed by Schuyler's defeat or by Burr's victory. Robert Troup, Burr's old friend, commented that the "twistings, combinations, and maneuvers to accomplish this object are incredible. . . . As to myself, I believe I shall withdraw from politics for the present. I am disgusted to my heart."[20] "This is the fruit of the Chancellor's Coalition with the Governor," wrote another friend of Hamilton, "the Die is Cast and I fear too much that your Predictions will be Verified!"[21]

Schuyler's defeat and Burr's victory was a setback to Hamilton's bid for political power. The arch-Federalist's early distrust of Burr now became an overwhelming, passionate, and often irrational hatred of a rival whose motives he had learned to suspect. And Burr had no trouble assessing Hamilton's reaction. "I have reason to believe that my election will be unpleasing to several Persons now in Philada.," he wrote to Sedgwick. Hamilton, who had been President Washington's Secretary of the Treasury since 1789, was then at the temporary national capital.

However appetizing the triumph may have been for Burr, and as valuable as the conquest was in his drive for political prominence, it only meant additional hardships for his wife. With Congress in Philadelphia, Burr was home even less often then ever; and Theodosia's health remained very poor. On April 2, 1793, Burr noted that her condition, although better than in recent months, "continues to be wavering & precarious."[22] She had begun to choke frequently. Every three or four weeks, fits of vomiting and nausea seemed to overwhelm her so seriously that Burr feared for her life.

He sought whatever medical advice he could get. Local doctors, including Theo's brother-in-law, Dr. Joseph Browne, gave their opinions and prescriptions. But in no case, as Burr wrote, "with *any sensible good effect.*" Finally, he turned to one of Philadephia's best known men, Dr. Benjamin Rush. He tried hard to describe the illness, acknowledging the

difficulty of making an accurate judgment without the patient's presence and venturing to guess that his wife's discomfort "assumes all the
appearance of a nephritic complaint."[23] Her choking had not lessened,
and perhaps was even increasing. Nor was her condition reacting to any
particular type of diet. In December, Dr. Rush advised giving her hemlock, which Burr assured Theodosia would have the "narcotic powers of
opium, superadded to other qualities. When the dose is too great, it may
be discovered by a vertigo or giddiness; and that he has known it to
work wonderful cures."[24] More and more, he relied upon Dr. Rush, to
whom pills prescribed by others were sent for approval.

It was during April or May of 1794 that a desperate, lonely, and pain-
wracked Theodosia wrote to the Reeves at Litchfield: "My dear friends
where are you in all my distress, that you do not come to see how I
suffer—come & pray you my sufferings are not to be committed to . . .
Perhaps I may see you, perhaps not—I have wrote to you many times,
but I never heard from you do come, if Sally cannot—come—Reeve
come I pray you, come I beg you, come . . . to your wretched."[25]
There is no evidence of any response, or that one could have been made
in time.

Burr was in Philadelphia on May 19, 1794, when a messenger brought
the news that Theodosia Prevost Burr had died the day before. He had
been caught unprepared because the previous word had been encouraging. As he explained to Uncle Pierpont Edwards, "so sudden & unexpected was her death that no immediate danger was apprehended until
the morning that she was relieved from all her earthly cares."[26]

A widower at the age of thirty-eight, Senator Burr was left with his
eleven year old Theodosia and a zest for politics. As was characteristic
of him, he could do nothing less than influence the course of both.

CHAPTER VII

Dangerous Factionalism

O N Monday, October 24, 1791, Senator Burr was seated as a member of the Second Congress. The man who was suspected by some of belonging to neither party, of shifting from one group to the other, arrived at a time when the controversies over Hamilton's fiscal program and the reaction to the "liberty, fraternity, and equality" revolution in France had already separated men into groups that were beginning to resemble political parties. The anti-Federalists braced to resist what they claimed was an aristocratic attempt to pervert the Constitution by destroying republican aspirations. Federalists viewed with growing contempt those who would undermine the interests of property and weaken the national government, especially since the opposition contained so many of those who had fought against the Constitution in 1787 and 1788. The dangers of the "spirit of party," which Washington would later cite, had already begun. Even the "father of the Constitution," James Madison, had turned against Hamilton's federalism; and, within the President's cabinet, Jefferson was already countering the Federalist enlargement of the central government. Hamilton, stung by the election of Burr over Philip Schuyler for the Senate, had begun what would seem to be a career devoted to checking the rapid rise of the junior Senator from New York. And Burr was now completely committed to a life of politics.[1]

Having been used by Clinton and Livingston to stop Schuyler, and thus classified as an anti-Federalist, Burr's views substantiated his republicanism. Only two weeks after his election, he expressed reservations about Hamilton's proposal for a Bank of the United States. Referring to the bill that became law later that month, Burr warned against its hasty passage without careful deliberation. He pointed out that "a charter granted cannot be revoked & this appears to me to be one of those Cases in which delay can be productive of no evil—." While hedging about flatly opposing the measure, since he had not examined it carefully, he noted that the speculators and brokers were excited by its possibilities. He referred to David Hume's essay "On Money," in which there "are some ingenious thoughts respecting the Utility of Banks." Burr seems to have shared Hume's concern that, in the long run, an unnatural increase in the supply of money would create an inflationary market. Such a condition could hurt the interests of a trading nation.[2] Burr was also an early admirer of Philip Freneau's infant paper, the *National Gazette*, an anti-Federalist journal designed to counter John Fenno's *Gazette of the United States*.[3] Furthermore, Colonel Robert Troup suspected that Burr was in league with Jefferson and Madison in an attempt to unify the Northern and Southern anti-Federalists.

Troup's observations were not farfetched. Burr's election did represent an important Northern victory for the anti-Federalists and his success in the election had catapulted him to national prominence. Anti-Federalists, then beginning to organize their resistance, had to enlist all resources as they opposed the Administration, and Burr's name was linked to this attempt.

Such political aims were associated with Jefferson's celebrated botany trip of May, 1791. On the seventeenth day of that month, Jefferson left from Philadelphia to start a 920 mile journey through New York State and New England. First, he went to New York City, which he reached on May 18 or 19. Madison had been in the city for several months, and meeting Jefferson, he accompanied the Secretary of State along an itinerary that included Lake George and then parts of Vermont and Connecticut. Crossing Long Island Sound, they continued along the north shore of Long Island and then back to New York City. It was a holiday trip; for Madison, a matter of "health, recreation, and curiosity," but for Jefferson largely a scientific expedition for the study of "botanical objects" and the annoying Hessian fly.[4] Others, however, felt that Jefferson and Madison must have had a more practical purpose.

Troup's letter to Hamilton of June 15, 1791, sparked the speculation. "There was," wrote Burr's former friend, "every appearance of a passionate courtship between the Chancellor [Livingston], Burr, Jefferson & Madison when the latter were in town." Echoing Cato's advice to the Roman Senate, Troup supposed that their design toward Hamilton was strictly "*delenda est Carthago*," "Carthage must be destroyed."[5] Later, John Church Hamilton, son of the Federalist leader, reiterated that there had been "frequent interviews with Chancellor Livingston and Burr," before seeing Clinton in Albany.[6] Madison's biographer states that the Congressman had met with Burr several times to unite him with Chancellor Robert R. Livingston, "who was still brooding over Hamilton's rejection of him for the Senate seat given to King."[7]

But Troup's observation is the only inkling of such a meeting. Madison could have seen Burr and Livingston in New York, or when travelling with Jefferson they may have lingered at Clermont, where the Chancellor was holding a court.[8] Burr was in New York that spring, not leaving home until June 12.[9] However, the forging of a Northern-Southern political alliance through a series of conferences is not revealed by the writings of any of the five participants. Jefferson wrote only nonpolitical letters about the trip and his stay in New York had lasted only two days.[10] According to Jefferson, Madison's health did profit from the journey; but, unfortunately, the description of the trip that Ambrose Madison received from his brother has been lost. That Burr's letters contain no hint of what occurred is not surprising. Burr was cautious whenever he wrote, and any sessions that may have been held were neither for the benefit of prying post-riders nor for Troup to substantiate his suspicions. In the absence of anything concrete to enforce Troup's comments, there is the distinct possibility that the trip had no more significance than was claimed by Jefferson and Madison. Jefferson was interested in the plant life of New England and in the Hessian fly nuisance, and Madison was in need of relaxation and sunshine.

Federalists were worried about Burr. Troup was no fool. Even if he exaggerated, he was an articulate observer, but his efforts to assure Hamilton were not convincing. After raising the spectre of anti-Federalists tumbling "the fabric of the government in ruins to the ground," he denied having the "smallest uneasiness" about their success. "You are too well seated in the hearts of the citizens of the northern & middle states to be hunted down by them," he wrote to Hamilton.[11] Others had Burr involved in an axis with Clinton and Livingston, now joined by Jefferson and Madison, to agree to support Clinton as their vice-presidential candidate against Adams in 1792. Burr's own ambitions refute the theory that he had agreed to promote the interests of the man who had made him a major politician.

Weary and ill, Burr finally arrived at Philadelphia on the Sunday before the opening of Congress. Accommodations were scarce in the city, but he found a room at a boarding house run by a Mrs. Roberts. Though modest, it would do until he could find decent quarters. He had many invitations to dine with the important people of Philadelphia, but his mood was unreceptive. Or, possibly, he refused to appear in society with the inadequate clothing he had brought from New York. Brooks, his servant, was overdue with the bulk of the wardrobe. Burr's wife was still alive, and so he requested "a waistcoat, white and brown, such as you designed. You know I am never pleased except with your taste."[12]

The following week, he found tolerable winter quarters in a quiet, orderly, well-furnished house owned by two widows. Not accustomed to having boarders, they made an exception for Burr, who was pleased. "The old lady is deaf," he reported, "and upon my first coming to take possession of my lodgings, she with great civility requested that I would never attempt to speak to her, for fear of injuring my lungs without being able to make her hear."[13]

One of the first major problems that Burr faced in the Senate was the Indian crisis in the Northwest Territory. Warfare had been reopened by the Indians above the Ohio River because of dissatisfaction with the treaties made by their chiefs. Travelers and frontiersmen had been the victims of plunder and destruction and looked to the federal government for assistance.

At a joint session of Congress, October 25, 1791, which Burr attended, Washington asked for enlarged powers to restore security to the troubled area by inflicting penalties on those of both races who infringed on treaties and endangered peace. Following the speech, Vice President John Adams assigned Burr and two others to a three-man committee to draft a reply. It was a masterfully innocuous answer that they sent to Washington.

But just a few days later, General Arthur St. Clair's army was ambushed and slaughtered not far from Fort Wayne. Men, women, and children were mutilated, burned at the stake, and hacked to death. The massacre was achieved despite the superior size of the American force.

By December, the horrible news reached Congress. Burr wrote to his wife that the details of the massacre as related by the surviving General St. Clair "engrossed my thoughts for some days past. No public event since the war has given me equal anxiety."[14] Later, he told Pierpont Edwards, "We are much agitated and divided by an Indian War and much at a loss to know how to dispose of it, can you advise us?"

There were some rumors, which Burr denied, that he would be given a command in the Indian War. He did, however, vote with the majority to permit the President emergency powers to employ Indians in the West to help end the menace of the frontier. Privately, the Senator was critical of the white man's lack of good intentions toward the redskins. He suggested that Mohawk Chief Joseph Brant might be able to approach the Miami tribes and negotiate successfully for both sides.[15]

As a freshman senator, Burr's role was mostly routine. He was placed on a committee with Connecticut's Roger Sherman and John Rutherfurd of New Jersey to "report a bill determining the time of choosing the Electors of President and Vice President, and the day in which they shall give their votes, and prescribing the mode of transmitting the votes to the seat of Government."[16] Burr's committee, chaired by Rutherfurd, reported back a bill that not only led to the present date for choosing presidential electors but also prescribed a line of succession to the highest office that lasted until 1886. Their recommendations, which passed the Senate by a fifteen to twelve vote on February 17, 1792, and four days later, the House, established the president pro tempore of the Senate and the speaker of the House of Representatives as next in line after the vice president.[17] The only significant item that Burr opposed during that first winter in Philadelphia was the proposed appointment of Gouverneur Morris as Minister to France.

Morris' nomination was controversial, for he was an undoubted aristocrat who made few concessions to democratic notions. Monroe called him a "monarchy man" and complained that he went to Europe to "sell lands and certificates."[18] Others cited the failure of his special mission to London in 1790 to settle the question of a commercial treaty and the continued occupation, by the British, of Western posts on American soil. Joining not only Monroe, but many New Englanders, Burr voted against Morris' confirmation. Rufus King, his Senate colleague from New York, quoted Burr as complaining about Morris' unfortunate behavior toward the English ministers. So badly had Morris conducted himself, said Burr, that the English "were offended & refused, after an abrupt breaking up of an interview, to renew it."[19] Morris had, indeed, made himself *persona non grata* to the British government.[20] But Burr's position was the minority view and Morris went to France.

Burr had other and more personal matters on his mind at this time. One was his claim against the government for a three months payment that he had failed to receive during his final days in the army. Because he had anticipated that such a petition from a senator might be regarded as suspect (it was a few weeks after his election, and long before he went to Philadelphia to assume his duties), he requested Massachusetts Senator Theodore Sedgwick to press the claim in his behalf. Figuring that the government now owed him four or five thousand dollars, including accumulated interest, he stressed that he "did more duty than a score of others who have rcd all the Emoluments." Then he wrote, "It touches my pride to petition for anything," but noted that his impending departure from his lucrative practice made the money seem more attractive than ever. "There have doubtless been some principles adopted upon these subjects," he wrote; and then, referring to the Secretary of the Treasury, he added, "Hamilton will tell you candidly what they are—but you probably know as well as he does—Do nothing which will have the least appearance of indelicacy."[21] Burr thus began the process of collecting depositions to substantiate his claim, a fruitless attempt that Aaron Ogden was still pursuing for him forty-three years later.[22]

Another determination was to write a military history of the Revolution. Maintaining an astonishing schedule, he woke up at daybreak, sometimes as early as five A.M., and busily transcribed historical material from government records. While he wrote, a servant brought his breakfast from a neighboring cafe, another tended his fire, while a confidential clerk helped him search and copy. Burr continued to work until ten A.M. on weekdays, but was able to devote his Sundays almost entirely to his project. Finally, he had collected several boxes of material.[23] Burr's attempt to examine the papers pertaining to the late surrender by the British of the Western posts was, however, thwarted by Jefferson in the following winter. The Secretary of State informed him that "it has been concluded to be improper to communicate the correspondence of *existing ministers*. He hopes this will, with Colo. Burr, be his sufficient apology."[24] An order from President Washington forbade his examination of any further records, frustrating the completion of his work. Although an early biographer of Burr asserts that "if the searcher of the records had been a Senator approved and trusted by the Secretary of the Treasury, he would not have been denied access to them—at least, not in a peremptory manner," such a conclusion must remain highly speculative and probably implausible. There is certainly no reason to believe that Jefferson's denial of Burr's right to inspect letters was the consequence of Hamilton's influence over both the President and the Secretary of State.

While Burr was in Philadelphia, his New York friends were preparing for that state's gubernatorial election of April, 1792. For Burr, election as governor was a most attractive prospect. Both his salary and patronage power would increase. Although Burr and his friends could hardly expect any cooperation from the incumbent, Clinton, his candidacy had other potential sources of support. The dissidents among the anti-Federalists, for example, might be expected to desert the Governor to get behind Burr as a more likely winner. But more important were the Federalists. His reputation as a man with no firm party ties, a man with many Federalist friends, heightened his appeal to those with little confidence in the possible dethronement of Clinton by an established Federalist.

Serious obstacles, however, existed in that quarter, too. Philip Schuyler, whom Burr had recently defeated, could hardly be expected to help him secure Federalist support. The man whose ambitions were most stymied by Burr's victory in 1791, Hamilton, defeated in his bid for power in the state, would certainly be a formidable power to overcome. And more important than any of these considerations was the possible candidacy of Robert Yates. As the loser in a close election three years earlier, this friend of Burr had the first claim on the Federalist nomination. There was little that the Burrites would or could do as long as he remained available.

But early in February, prospects brightened. Yates declined to run. Even before his official announcement on February 9, the decision was known. Federalist Isaac Ledyard informed Hamilton that not only was there considerable pro-Burr sentiment in New York, but that Burr might also attract those "ancient friends" of Judge Yates.[25] This opportunity was precisely what was needed by the small band of seventeen Burrites who had met in New York to promote the Senator's candidacy. When Yates finally revealed his intentions at a meeting in New York, the Albany *Gazette* complained that his rejection of the nomination came despite repeated overtures "by many of our northern friends, as well as a number of respectable citizens of New York, but he remains inflexible."[26] "The Plot is now Come out," Henry Livingston wrote to General Samuel Webb, adding the news that Burr had subsequently "declared himself a candidate."[27]

Friends of both Burr and Hamilton appealed for the Treasury Secretary's support of Burr. Ledyard tried to assure Hamilton that Burr had "expressed a sincere regard for the safety and well-being" of the Union. "With respect to yourself," he added, "he expresses an entire confidence in the widsom and integrity of your designs, and a real personal friendship, and which he does not seem to suppose you doubt of, or that you ever will, unless it may arise from meddling interveners."[28] Hamilton was also told that there would be "zealous support from Yates," who was, as Ledyard had pointed out, still under Burr's "personal dominion." Furthermore, there was the warning that Federalist failure to support Burr against Clinton would place them in behalf of the "interest of the old incumbent." Burr's success, without Hamilton's support, would enable Burr to use his influence against Hamilton, whereas Burr's election as governor would remove him from the Senate, where he was an active opponent. But failure despite Hamilton's aid would force Burr to moderate his conduct because of the obligation that he would then have incurred. His defeat without that support would, on the other hand, return him to the Senate, where he could display even more vehemence against the Administration.[29]

Despite this reasoning, Hamilton remained firm. Any other course would have been inconsistent, for the Secretary regarded Burr as a "pestilent politician," without restraints to his ambition and with few political convictions other than his own self-interest. Many years later, his son, John Church Hamilton, observed that his father "preferred to increase an hostility which he knew would be unrelenting, rather than risk the interests of the State."[30] Hamilton had thus rejected the type of pro-Burr argument that the Albany *Gazette* carried from "Plain Farmer," who urged Burr as a moderate with appeal to followers of both parties because "*he did not belong to either party.*"[31] Hamilton solved the dilemma of whom to support by persuading Chief Justice John Jay to leave the Supreme Court for the governorship. When a large gathering of merchants met at Farmer's Hall in New York City's Hanover Square, Jay won their unanimous support. On February 13, he agreed to become the candidate.

Two days later, a meeting of Clintonians at Corré's Hotel chose Clinton and Pierre Van Cortlandt again as candidates for governor and lieutenant governor. The New York *Journal & Patriotic Register* reported that the electioneering had already begun; and the paper noted with unappreciated timeliness, "It has been shrewdly remarked, that we are to have no *scandal* on this occasion—should it turn out so, it ought to be faithfully recorded."[32] Also announced was the fact that Clinton, Jay, and Burr were all being offered as candidates.

Burr, with the Senate in Philadelphia in the midst of work on the electoral bill, was the only one of the three candidates absent, but that alone was not fatal, for his supporters were certainly active. Nevertheless the obstacle posed by the presence of two major candidates, each with fanatical party support, was too great. The Federalists were following Hamilton's leadership, even though such people as Ledyard did express their disappointment at the Secretary's rejection of the Burr overture. Going along with the most likely source of power, the Yates people fell into line behind Jay. Finally, in early March, came newspaper announcements that Burr had removed himself as a candidate.[33] Most of Burr's people then went to work for Clinton.

Some of his friends, however, continued to oppose another term for the Governor. Particularly active behind Burr in Ulster County had been Peter Van Gaasbeek, a prominent merchant and leading political figure of Kingston. Van Gaasbeek, who was one of Burr's chief creditors and a close friend, had led a group that considered Burr the most likely man to stop Clinton. It was with obvious regret, therefore, that they received the news of Burr's withdrawal. Still pursuing their major objective, Van Gaasbeek and his group then endorsed Jay. Only the desire to change the administrations, Van Gaasbeek informed Burr in March, would enable Jay to get a substantial vote. Many hesitated about accepting their new candidate because of his connection with the Society for Promoting the Manumission of Slaves. "We have had to encounter many difficulties on that score," noted the Kingstonian. Then, while expressing optimism about their eventual ability to elect Jay, Van Gaasbeek consoled Burr with the statement that, had he remained the candidate, "I would have pledged myself that three fourths if not four fifths of the County would have been in your favor. I sincerely believe the ensuing will be the warmest and most spirited Election that ever has been in Ulster."[34]

Partisan fury exhausted every means of promoting both candidates, with Jay the natural target of those who denounced the privileges of wealth and class. Clinton was charged with having betrayed his people by forming an alliance with the Livingstons and with using extensive patronage powers to keep the state firmly under his control. The class division was sharp. All the traditional rivalries between the small farmers and the proprietors of large estates, between the wealthy merchants and lawyers and, on the other hand, the mechanics and shopkeepers, now reached an intense level. But the greatest furor followed the balloting.

If the votes had been validated from all counties, Jay would have been declared the winner; but support for the contention that returns from Otsego, Tioga, and Clinton counties were illegal would deprive the Federalist candidate of enough ballots to give Clinton the victory by a plurality of 108 votes. In Otsego alone, Jay's actual majority was estimated at four hundred, and he probably had an additional margin of two hundred in Tioga County. But according to the state constitution, all ballots had to be delivered by the election inspectors to the sheriffs of the respective counties. The sheriffs were then required to place the returns in a box and deliver them to the Secretary of State, who was then responsible for placing them before a canvassing committee, a body of twelve legislators, six chosen by each house. The canvassers had the final authority for counting and then announcing the winners. But the committee, which then included such men as Melancton Smith, David Gelston, and Peter Van Cortlandt, Jr., voted by seven to four to reject the returns from the three counties, thus giving Clinton a victory that was as questionable as it was slender.[35]

The reasons were purely technical. Richard R. Smith, who, although his term had expired, continued to retain the office of sheriff of Otsego because his successor had yet to be sworn in, received the ballots and then conveyed them by a specially deputized person to the Secretary. In Tioga, the sheriff had given the ballots to a deputy, whose subsequent illness forced him to submit them by his clerk. The sheriff of Clinton County had transmitted his votes by a man who had not been deputized.[36] All three cases had provoked considerable discussion among the canvassers, who then decided to submit the controversy to New York's two senators, Rufus King and Aaron Burr.

It was clearly a matter of whether the technicalities involved were important enough to invalidate the suffrage rights of three counties. Acceptance of the votes would undoubtedly determine the election, as whatever plurality Clinton may have received from Clinton County would have been insufficient to overcome Jay's victory in the other two counties, even with the Governor's 108 majority throughout the rest of the state. Such obvious political prudence could certainly dictate that the votes ought to be counted. But Burr's situation was complicated by the fact that the anti-Federalists had sent him to the Senate in the first place and a conflict between that commitment and his reluctance to alienate whatever Federalist support he held. Until Hamilton had blocked him only a few months before, he had sought backing from the aristocratic party for the governorship. Any decision in such a heatedly partisan controversy would separate him from friends in the other party. And implicit in the entire issue was the question of whether justice would be done or the law would be observed.[37]

King advised them to count the returns. The expiration of the one-year term of Otsego's sheriff, Mr. Smith, did not deprive him of the authority to act, according to King. State law simply prohibited any canvasser from serving four successive terms, and he had been appointed in 1791. Since no other sheriff had been sworn in, King maintained that "R. R. Smith was then lawful sheriff of Otsego." He took the position that "such acts as tend to the public utility, and such as he would be compellable to perform, such as are essential to preserve the rights of third persons, and without which they might be lost or destroyed, when done by an officer *de facto*, are valid."[38] The inability of the Tioga deputy to complete his duty had been an "act of God," which left him with no choice but to send his clerk with the ballots. In such cases, said King, there must be a liberal construction of the election law to preserve the right of suffrage. Furthermore, King saw no reason why the lack of formal deputization for a man who acted as "merely the sheriff's servant" should justify the invalidation of Clinton County's votes.[39]

Hamilton could certainly agree with King's pro-Jay sentiments. Little would have pleased him more than the defeat of Clinton, and on July 25 he informed King that he had a similar view of the election. But Hamilton cautioned against doing anything to change the seven to four vote of the canvassers. Some had mentioned the possibility of calling a convention to settle the issue, and there was even talk of force. Hamilton, in a prudent and statesman-like opinion, cautioned against any temporary expediency that would upset the constitutional authority of the canvassers. It would, he wrote, have "too much the appearance of reversing the sentence of a Court by a legislative decree." And, he warned, "The precedent may suit us to-day, but to-morrow, we may rue its abuse."[40]

Burr had been tossed a dilemma and he turned to others for assistance. King's willingness to provide an opinion had forced him to do the same. Virtually all respected contacts were solicited. Theodore Sedgwick, for example, informed Governor Caleb Strong of Massachusetts that Burr had visited him earlier at Stockbridge and that Sedgwick had been urged to obtain Strong's opinion. "He is very anxious that you should not deny his request," he wrote, "and says that he has a right on the score of friendship to demand of your opinion."[41] Burr spent several hours in a discussion of the matter with Pierpont Edwards, and through Tapping Reeve he obtained additional views from Jonathan Trumbull and others in New England.[42] Opinions were also gathered from James Monroe, who was in France at the time, Attorney-General Edmund Randolph of Virginia, and Jonathan Sergeant, who had been Treasurer of Princeton during Burr's college days. In an effort to vindicate himself of charges that his opinion must necessarily be a product of anti-Federalist bias, Burr told his Federalist friend, Jacob De Lamater, that it would "be the extreme of weakness in me to expect friendship from Mr. Clinton. I have too many reasons to believe that he regards me with jealousy and malevolence."[43]

There is no evidence that Burr consulted with Jefferson. But the Virginian's opinion, as expressed in a letter to Madison, ought to be read alongside Hamilton's view that Clinton should take office because upholding the constitutional power of the canvassers was, if nothing else, enlightened self-interest. Jefferson observed that, "It does not seem possible to defend Clinton as a just or disinterested man if he does not decline the Office of which there is no symptom; and I really apprehend that the cause of republicanism will suffer and its votaries be thrown into schism by embarking it in support of this man."[44] Thus, each of the opposing intellectual leaders sensed the harmful consequences of having his own party claim victory. Both giants had the wisdom to take the long-range view.

Burr's position was not only a political one, although there seems to be little doubt that politics had become his major motivation. The Senator was also a lawyer, and it was for his legal ability that his reputation had soared. Good politics could shatter a fine legal reputation, and vice versa. There was only one thing Burr could do: gather advice and information, and then deliver a strong legal opinion. And this he did.

He decided that the technicalities of the law should be upheld, and therefore sustained the claims of his party. His decision adopted a scholarly tone by delving back into English history, where he noted that provisions had been made for the authority of the incumbent sheriffs to continue under special circumstances. Statutes enabled them to fulfill their official functions unless they had been officially discharged from office. But, Burr maintained, English statutes were no longer the laws of the State of New York and nothing had been substituted to cover this contingency: Mr. Smith, therefore, had had no authority to act as sheriff in Otsego. There was no reason why his successor could not have been sworn in to discharge his duties even earlier, had his attendance been "really desired." How, then, could the ballots of Otsego be counted? Burr's opinion also invalidated the Tioga ballots, for there was no possible way of upholding the notion, "by any fiction or construction," that the deputy's clerk was the same as the sheriff actually delivering the ballots. Only in Clinton County, where no written deputation had been executed, were the returns valid, wrote Burr, maintaining that "verbal and written deputation by a sheriff are, in law, considered as of equal validity, particularly when it is to perform a single ministerial act."[45] And Clinton was the only one of the three disputed counties that had not given Jay a majority of the votes.

Burr's opinion aroused all who were ready to believe that the Senator was a diabolical politician worthy of no one's trust. Josiah Hoffman complained that "Burr was not exercised in vain—He acted a principal part in the drama—or rather remained behind the scenes, *slyly* instructing each man in his *party*—The tragedy now commences, and his character surely will be one of the *victims* in the catastrophe." Hoffman then went on to maintain that Burr "will prostitute talents, honesty & integrity for the purposes of revenge, or for the prosperity of a party."[46] Robert Troup, who had complained to Jay that the canvassers were, by consulting Burr, merely seeking additional support for their views, later wrote that "we all consider Burr's opinion as such a shameful prostitution of his talents, and as so decisive a proof of the real infamy of his character, that we are determined to rip him up. We have long been wishing to see him upon paper, and we are now gratified with the most favorable exhibition he could have made."[47] The issue was clearly drawn along party lines, and Federalist fears were justified by the State Assembly's decision, in a vote of thirty-five to twenty-two, to sustain the ruling of the canvassers. Jay had to bow to Clinton.[48]

The real responsibility for what had happened in Otsego County should be attributed to Judge William Cooper, the father of the novelist. Judge Cooper had failed to deliver the commission to the new sheriff, which would have formally relieved Smith of his responsibilities. But even that was not unusual. A subsequent investigation revealed that there had been seventy cases, all involving sheriffs in New York's counties between 1777 and 1792, in which the functions of the office had been continued by the incumbents after their commissions had expired. In one case, such a sheriff had even been empowered to execute a criminal.[49] The investigation also showed that in the same year as the election dispute, the sheriffs of Kings, Queens, and Washington counties, whose terms of office had ended, also had not received new commissions in time for them to deliver ballots, rendering them no more legitimate than those from Clinton, Otsego and Tioga.[50]

That the election of 1792 had confronted Burr with a difficult problem was largely because of his own efforts to acquire political support. As early as the autumn of 1791, Burr had journeyed up the Hudson River and then, below Albany, had headed eastward into Massachusetts, where his destination was the Berkshire town of Stockbridge. There, in a season brightened by the tawny leaves of the mountain woodlands, he consulted with Theodore Sedgwick. The New Englander, ten years older than Burr, represented his state in the House as a holdover from the First Congress. As a latecomer to the idea of independence during the Revolution, and as a vigorous supporter of the new Constitution, Sedgwick could never be regarded as anything but a loyal Federalist. This made him no different from many of Burr's other friends. But the letters of the two men and, in particular, their use of a cypher, suggest that the Senator was paying more than a mere professional or courtesy visit to the Congressman. Sedgwick, no doubt, served as Burr's contact man for more than just opinions concerning the canvassers' dispute. Just as the Stockbridge politicians would later be used to reach other New Englanders, Burr was busily cultivating strength that autumn for future uses.[51] One year later, he emerged as a candidate for the vice presidency.

There was, at that time, no official vice-presidential candidate. Neither that office nor the presidency were designated by the voters. Voting was done by the electors chosen by the states. The Constitution said that each member of the Electoral College would be able to cast two ballots. The only restriction was that one vote had to be for a candidate from a state other than his own. The procedure was designed to leave a substantial number of final decisions up to the House of Representatives, where each state would have an equal voice. Two things seemed to make that outcome likely: the requirement that election by the electors could only be obtained by a clear majority of all the votes cast, and the absence of a two-party system. The lack of formal political parties seemed to guarantee wide distribution of the electoral votes, as in 1789, when a dozen men shared the 138 ballots that were actually cast. A clear majority would then be unlikely. Logically, the man with the second highest total would become the vice president, as he would be a true second choice, a runner-up, a candidate of stature, one whose presidential potentialities had impressed many of his countrymen. The vice president could not, and did not, consider himself a member of the administration. Indeed, he could be a leader of the opposition. A vital part of this system was that the electors could not indicate whether one particular man was being supported for the presidency and the other for the vice presidency.

How to cast that second electoral vote *against* John Adams became the object of maneuvering that assumed, for the first time, the characteristics of a real party effort. An important man in uniting the opponents of all regions, now referring to themselves as Republicans, or Democratic-Republicans, was John Beckley, the first clerk of the House of Representatives. Beckley displayed much of the rising partisan fervor as early as September 2, 1792, when he wrote to Madison that domestic issues had become a "contest between the Treasury department and the people." He noted the rising opposition to the Whiskey Tax that was erupting in Western Pennsylvania and predicted that it would bring "much further disquietude" to Hamilton. Hopefully, he felt that the Republican interests would be able to exert "a decided weight" in the next Congress. This, he added, ought to be particularly true if Clinton's claim to victory in New York's disputed election was sustained.[52] Beckley, the Virginian, was thus working to forge a community of interests among the Northern and Southern opponents of the Administration.

But as Beckley watched the New York situation unfold, he could see—as did many others—that Burr, the man who had failed so recently to obtain the governorship, had placed himself in contention for the vice presidency. As a senator, Burr must certainly have been considered as a leader of the New York Republicans. Governor Clinton was, of course, his major competitor. Both men were still deeply involved in the disputed election when Beckley journeyed to New York in September. When the clerk reached Burr, he delivered a letter from Dr. Benjamin Rush. "Your friends everywhere look to you to take an active part in removing the monarchical rubbish of our government," Burr's distinguished friend had written. "It is time to *speak out*—or we are un-done."[53]

Others, considerably less friendly, had already seen Burr's efforts in his own behalf. On September 17, his colleague in the Senate, Rufus King, informed Hamilton that Burr was working hard at building up support. Moreoever, warned King, there was little doubt that his purpose is "well understood by our Antis."[54] Alexander Dallas, who was serving as the Secretary of the Commonwealth of Pennsylvania, was in New York and told King that Burr would have support for the vice presidency in Dallas' state, and Pierpont Edwards' mission was to duplicate that backing in Connecticut. King, seeing the combined efforts of the Republicans, feared that Adams' vote might be reduced enough to persuade him to decline the high office for a second term. "Should they succeed in degrading Mr. Adams," he warned, "much would be apprehended in respect to the measures which have received the sanction of government."[55] But the most vitriolic attack came from Hamilton. While the Secretary was convinced that Burr's movements were merely diversionary efforts for Clinton, the very possibility that Burr might succeed brought out Hamilton's almost psychopathic hatred of his New York rival. A Clinton victory would be bad enough, Hamilton told a friend after he had read Rufus King's letter, but at least the Governor is honest. Burr, however, "is unprincipled, both as a public and a private man." He cares not about anything but climbing "*per fas aut nefas* to the highest government post. Embarrassed, as I understand, in his circumstances, with an extravagant family, bold, enterprising, and intriguing, I am mistaken if it be not his object to play the game of confusion, and I feel it to be a religious duty to oppose his career."[56] One week later, he expressed his fears more succinctly:

> Mr. Burr's integrity as an individual is not unimpeached. As a public man, he is one of the worst sort—a friend to nothing but as it suits his interest and ambition . . . 'Tis evident that he aims at putting himself at the head of what he calls the 'popular party,' as affording the best tools for an ambitious man to work with. Secretly turning liberty into ridicule, he knows as well as most men how to make use of that name. In a word, if we have an embryo Caesar in the United States, 'tis Burr.[57]

But the Burr candidacy remained alive. Many thought Clinton had committed a fatal error by accepting the questionable victory in the recent state elections, and by early October Clinton indicated that he was not a truly interested candidate.[58] And, quite suddenly and without any warning, Burr found himself the recipient of a gubernatorial appointment. Reminiscent of Clinton's other maneuvers that had removed possible competitors, on October 2 Burr was nominated as a judge of the Supreme Court of New York and as a member of the Council of Appointment. Since both the nomination and its confirmation by the Council were made without his consent, Burr promptly declined the honor.[59]

The next day, John Nicholson informed Madison that the Republican leaders at Philadelphia had considered the circumstances of the shady New York election and what appeared to be Clinton's reluctant candidacy for the vice presidency and had agreed to support Burr, "whose talents, abilities and firmness of character are . . . fully equal."[60] Furthermore, Burr was the more likely of the two to get additional support from the Middle and the Eastern states, where his efforts had been exerted. Now the decision seemed to rest with the Southern states. Their support for either man would make the difference, Nicholson wrote, noting that the preference for Burr at Philadelphia could easily shift to Clinton if that seemed more promising. And Clinton, while saying he desired to decline in Burr's favor, did not "absolutely refuse to serve if elected."[61]

Having excited some curiosity during a stay in Philadelphia in September, Burr was in New York as the maneuvering reached the decisive stage that October. To Nicholson at Philadelphia, Burr dispatched that ardent Republican merchant, Clintonian, and skilled debater, Melancton Smith. This former Revolutionary War soldier and member of the Continental Congress was introduced by Burr as "the representative of the republicans of this State and the Man of the first influence in that Interest—The most entire Confidence may be placed in him as to Men and Measures—any arrangements he may make with you will be entirely Satisfactory to those in this State with whom you wish to unite. . . ."[62] Thus was an effort begun to secure intersectional support for Burr's candidacy. Those at Philadelphia now understood the purpose of his September visit. Oliver Wolcott, Jr., Hamilton's ranking aide in the Treasury Department and eventual successor, wrote to his father in Litchfield that prospects were good for Burr to have considerable support.[63] Hamilton's increasing anxiety had probably touched off Wolcott's pessimism, for the Secretary no longer seemed sanguine about his theory that Burr was merely conducting a diversionary tactic for Clinton. Hamilton now told Charles C. Pinckney of South Carolina that Burr "has no other principles than *to mount, at all events*, to the full honors of the State, and to as much more as circumstances will permit— a man in private life not unblemished."[64]

While Smith was thus arousing concern among Federalists in Philadelphia, he and Marinus Willett sent a messenger to Virginia with a letter addressed to Madison and Monroe. Monroe read that Burr was being offered as a substitute for Clinton as the favorite of Republican electors. But it was Monroe's adverse reaction to the proposal, together with the concurrence of Madison, Jefferson, and other Virginians such as Patrick Henry, that apparently dashed Burr's brief hopes. For Monroe, writing from his home at Albemarle, had considered the possibility but reached the conclusion that even if the thirty-six year old Burr might not be too young, his political rise had been too swift to enable conscientious men to agree that he was already eligible for so high an office. Since success could only result from a union of Republicans throughout the different states, he noted, such an effort should be made for a "person of more advanced life and longer standing in publick trust . . . particularly one who in consequence of such service had given unequivocal proofs of what his principles really were." Monroe then added, "To place this gent'n, or any other of his standing in the chair of the present incumbent, wo'd not be well thought of in America."[65] On October 19, Monroe and Madison sent a joint reply to Smith and Willett to state that Clinton was better known and more likely to get the greater number of electoral votes in opposition to the Federalists.[66]

But a decision was made even before the Virginians responded. The insider on the scene was John Beckley, who had returned from New York, which he noted was "specially deserted" during that unhealthful season, and had attended an overdue meeting of the Pennsylvania and New York Republicans. They met in Philadelphia on the evening of October 16, with Smith representing the New Yorkers. According to Beckley, their purpose was "to conclude *finally* & *definitely* as to the choice of a V. P." By unanimous agreement, they decided "to exert every endeavor for Mr. Clinton, & to drop all thoughts of Mr. Burr." And, in addition, Beckley told Madison, Burr had assured him that he was completely behind the Republican attempt to remove Adams from the vice presidency and to replace him with Clinton.[67] What agreement facilitated this outcome may never be known, but Burr later maintained that he had withdrawn with the hope of certain Southern commitments for the 1796 election.[68]

What should be noted at this point is Beckley's observation of Hamilton's opposition. He noted the appearance of additional Hamilton newspaper letters under the signature of "Catalus," and then added, quite prophetically: "His efforts direct & indirect are . . . extraordinary— perhaps his inflexible pursuit of the object, has betrayed him into means, which may eventually *betray him*, and *sufficiently* expose the position & corrupt interference by the T-y departm." Moreover, Hamilton's private indiscretions during the summer of 1791, yet to be publicized, were known to Beckley, who now revealed that he had "a clue to something far beyond mere suspicion on this ground, which prudence forbids a present disclosure of."[69] Five years later, Beckley's published revelations would involve Burr in an episode between Hamilton and Monroe.

Much has been made of Burr's reticence about politics in his letters. Not only are written expressions hard to find, and his thinking often very difficult to fathom, but the use of cyphers to veil such references from interested parties often obscures what little is available. But one letter that is not completely mysterious, and which serves as an example of his method, was written to Jacob De Lamater. Burr was in New York, and two weeks had passed since that night in Philadelphia when Clinton had emerged as the man to get the second electoral vote of each Republican. So Burr wrote:

> Your letter by Mr. Addison was particularly kind, after my long *supposed* silence. We may make use of *both keys or ciphers*, and if some of the persons or things are designated by different characters, no inconvenience will arise; if there should, we will correct it.
>
> V is to be the candidate, as my former letter will have told you. He has the wishes of 9 for his success, for reasons which will be obvious to you. Do you think that 8 would be induced from any motive to vote for him?[70]

When the electors finally balloted, all 132 gave their first ballots to Washington. The second votes were divided, but Adams could not be stopped. He received seventy-seven to Clinton's fifty. The five remaining ones were split, with Jefferson getting four from Kentucky and Aaron Burr one from a South Carolina elector.

The election marked an important step in the establishment of a two-party system in America. Unanimity had prevailed toward Washington's candidacy; but the earlier harsh opponents of loyalism, the "violent whigs," the upholders of the Articles of Confederation, and the enemies of what appeared to be an aristocracy too often contemptuous and suspicious of the birth of liberty in France, while remaining strangely tolerant toward the British, had now evolved from a mere cluster of factions that had orbited around individual leaders. Attempts to coordinate the national efforts of the Republicans, which had resulted in Burr's rejection by the Southerners, now gave them the structure of a political party.

Burr, however highly he was regarded by many of his friends—and he was now at the peak of his popularity—was still suspected of an inordinate devotion to Federalist principles. It is, perhaps, rather ironic that the man for whom Hamilton had developed such a passionate hatred was still regarded as an unknown quantity by so many of his own party. A Virginia Republican, while seeing Burr and Hamilton as the "two most efficient actors on the political theatre of our country," nevertheless regretted that Burr's name was not on the Federalist side. He "must have essentially acted in concert" with Hamilton, anyway, reasoned the Virginian. Furthermore, an observation of Burr's conduct had revealed to the suspicious Republican traits "of character which sooner or later will give us much trouble. He has an unequalled talent of attaching men to his views, and forming combinations of which he is always the centre." The emergence of Burr as a future leader of a "popular party in the northern states" would not have surprised this man, who concluded that such a party would "subvert the influence of the southern states," for "the cause of republicanism in this country is connected with the political ascendancy" of those states.[71] That Burr had too many Federalist friends and too many reservations about Republican causes were evidences of moderation that he would have to overcome before winning the approbation of the broad base of the new national party.

CHAPTER VIII

The Squire of Richmond Hill

THE Burrs had been living at Richmond Hill, which had served as Washington's New York headquarters in 1776 and, until the national capital moved to Philadelphia, as the John Adams residence. Abigail Adams had fallen in love with the place. When she and her husband left, Burr took over their lease. A lover of good living, he quickly moved an array of expensive furnishings into the mansion and provided his sick wife with splendor. Their spectacular dinner parties attracted New York's finest society.

No less attractive than his country home was Burr himself, particularly to women. Numerous letters prove that the man who lived as a widower for nearly four decades after Theodosia's death did not exist as a celibate. He was short and his build was slight, but his presence was nevertheless dignified and commanding. His speech sparkled with wit and was clear and melodious, one acquaintance commenting that "honey trickles from his tongue." Women were attracted by his interest in them almost as much as for his own charms. As they spoke, he stared with absorption, listening with attention and devotion.[1]

Although both his youthful exploits and his adventures after Mrs. Burr's death have often been described, nothing has been known about a romance that dated back to the years of his marriage. That one was with a girl named Rebecca Smith, called "one of the most admired beauties that ever adorned the drawing-rooms of Philadelphia." Sixteen years younger than Burr, Rebecca was the daughter of the Reverend William Smith, the first provost of the University of Pennsylvania and a protégée of Benjamin Franklin. Rebecca's portrait by Gilbert Stuart immortalizes her beauty.

Exactly when Burr met her is not clear. But in 1814, when Rebecca nostalgically recalled the past, she reminded him that it was more "than 23 years since I called you friend."[2] In the spring of 1791, Burr had been away from home on an extended trip, one that had exasperated Mrs. Burr; but Rebecca's recollection was possibly inaccurate and they may have met during one of his earlier business trips to Philadelphia. Adding to the confusion is her statement of 1817 that he had loved her for almost thirty years. That would date their relationship back to 1787, some seven years before Theodosia's death, when Rebecca was only fifteen.[3]

Nevertheless, after she had renewed their acquaintance, she reminded him that he had been "the love of my youth."[4] Even later, she wrote that "in bloom of youth—generally thought of as unthinking, romantic & visionary & without *common sense*, I had the wisdom to select you for my friend." Then she declared that "my heart has never for an instant been estranged from you."[5]

The early phase of the romance had ended in 1792, when Rebecca began her unhappy marriage to Samuel Blodgett, Jr. Blodgett, more than fourteen years older than his bride, had made a fortune in the East India Company. Burr's opportunities to see Rebecca after that were limited, as the Blodgetts moved to Washington, where Blodgett was interested in the planning and layout of the future capital city. There, his use of lotteries to promote the sale of Washington real estate brought financial ruin that ended with his imprisonment for debt, and Rebecca was left to care for their four small children. Blodgett died in the spring of 1814; by then the family had returned to Philadelphia, where, four months after the funeral, Rebecca resumed her friendship with Burr.

It was Burr who then became the executor of Blodgett's estate and to whom the widow turned for assistance, legal and otherwise.[6] For many years, Burr was a visitor at the home of the widow Blodgett, who resided on Lancaster Turnpike above High Street, which is now Philadelphia's Market Street.

But Burr's most important girl was little Theodosia. Six days after his wife's death, he informed Uncle Timothy that his "much affected and distressed" eleven year old had borne the stroke "with more reason and firmness than could have been expected from her years."[7] It was with little exaggeration that he later asked: "for what else, for whom else do I live?"

Theodosia had become his fulfillment of not only what a daughter should be, but of the intellectual goals that he, far ahead of his time, knew women could reach. He had first seen such possibilities in his own wife. Mrs. Burr had read widely, and little more than a year before her death, he declared that she had first inspired his respect for the feminine intellect.

That his own ideas were sound became abundantly clear after he had read an English book called *A Vindication of the Rights of Women*. Its author was the environmentalist, Mary Wollstonecraft, who later became the wife of the political writer William Godwin and whose daughter married Percy Bysshe Shelley. Miss Wollstonecraft had written that if women are not prepared by education to become the companions of men, they "will stop the process of knowledge, for truth must be common to all or it will be inefficacious with respect to its influence or general practice." Great controversies resulted from her advocacy of coeducation and state responsibility for the cultivation of both men and women.

Writing to his wife from Philadelphia, Burr could hardly contain his enthusiasm for the thesis. He had spent all night with the book. Not only was it of interest because of Miss Wollstonecraft's sex, but he found that it expressed the legitimate claims of those interested in educating females. "Your sex had in *her* an able advocate," he assured Mrs. Burr. After all, Burr himself had blamed the inadequacies of feminine training on the "errors of education, of prejudice, and of habit."[8] Only one week earlier, he had expressed his designs for little Theodosia by writing:

> If I could foresee that Theo. would become a *mere* fashionable woman, with all the attendant frivolity and vacuity of mind, adorned with whatever grace and allurement, I would earnestly pray God to take her forthwith hence. But I yet hope, by her, to convince the world what neither sex appears to believe—that women have souls![9]

They called the little girl "Miss Prissy," and she filled the house with fun and pranks. Small, but plump and rosy-cheeked, she was, nevertheless, weak after her sick infancy. Yet, there was much reason to hope for future success. Not only was she becoming an attractive young girl, but with a father devoted to the education of women and, especially, to the creation of two fine examples within his own family, Theodosia could hardly fail to reach far beyond the erudition of her contemporaries. He had also enrolled his wife in the enforcement of an arduous regimen that would drive Theodosia toward that goal.

Fortunately, there was enough money. Into a household already crowded with Burr's stepchildren and servants came an array of tutors. A Mr. Shepherd taught writing and arithmetic and Mr. St. Aivre gave violin lessons. The languages—French, Latin, and Greek—were taught by Messrs. Chevalier, Gurney, and Leshlie. Others offered instruction in horseback riding, skating, and playing the harpsichord, as well as in each of the arts. Having been forced to sustain greater pressure than any modern educator would prescribe, the child thus became the model for Burr's pedagogical views and an affirmation of Mary Wollstonecraft's beliefs.

He saw to it that she followed a rigid routine, one that required her to find time for Greek, a daily lesson in Terence, and the translation of forty lines from Virgil. "The Greek will I hope advance rapidly," he wrote from Philadelphia; "remember that it is to be your principal occupation."[10]

But it was French that she would later be able to use with distinction. To prove her diligence and progress to her absent father, and also to show the efficacy of her tutors, she mailed him many of the translations, which he had requested. Once, he even offered money as a reward for more lessons. This, he informed his daughter, would be in addition to "the pay which you receive in having pleased and gratified me."[11]

His dedication to her training often bore the marks of an unrelenting pedagogue. His concern for what he had considered her first duty, the continuation of studies, was shown by his evaluation of her letters. "If the whole performance was your own," he once wrote, "which I am inclined to hope and believe, it indicates an improvement in style, in knowledge of the French, and in your handwriting. I have therefore not only read it several times, but shown it to several persons with pride and pleasure."[12] Letters that failed to pass his scrutiny became examples for future improvement. In early 1794, he revealed that his pleasure at receiving letters "written with tolerable spirit and correctness" was so great that he needed two or three readings to discover its errors. Once he overcame his initial joy and pride, he began to analyze her work. His reply then included all the necessary observations for the improvement of her grammar, style, and spelling. His letter of January 7 included such corrections as he compiled in the following list:

recieved for received
wis*sed* for wis*hed*
exeed for e*x*ceed
acurate for accurate
laudnam for laud*n*um
exteme for ext*r*eme
*i*ntirely for *e*ntirely[13]

He asked her to use the same words in her next letter.

Much of this correspondence also involved the keeping of a journal. Not only would it be a fine exercise for her literary training, but he thought that her dedication of ten minutes every evening for entries would also become a source for reports about her activities. He even sent a sample of what such a journal should contain. Then he pursued the matter carefully, hardly ever letting her forget about the new mission. Never one to drop an undertaking, he once asked her to remember that "occupation will infallibly expel the fiend ennui, and that solitude is the bug-bear of fools."[14]

There are indications that Mrs. Burr did not always approve of the pressure. How much dissent resulted from the sick woman's own agonies and what portion reflected the burden of enforcement that had been given to her is difficult to assess. While suffering physical anguish, she must have felt the competition with Theodosia for her husband's attention. Then, too, while the absent father could dictate the regimen, his wife was left with the task of supervising and enforcing the satisfaction of both the girl's educational needs and Burr's concepts. Burr sensed that the liaison had become impaired when he wrote with concern about getting no recent word about the progress of nine-year-old Theodosia. In reply, Mrs. Burr observed tartly that, "Theo. never can or will make the progress we would wish her while she has so many avocations."[15] At the same time, she expressed her own impatience to go to the country, adding that what Theo really needed, at that point, was to play with other children, for she should "be at liberty for a few weeks, to range and gain in health a good foundation for more application at our return, when I hope to have her alone." Then, showing annoyance at having to provide, in addition to her other duties, accommodations for the children of her former brother-in-law while he traveled to England, she added: "I will have her alone. I cannot live so great a slave, and she shall not suffer. My time shall not be an unwilling sacrifice to others; it shall be hers." She thereby assured Burr that Theodosia was not being neglected. But, asserting some independence, she stated that she would not "use severity; and without it, at present, I can obtain nothing; 'tis a bad habit, which she never deserves when I have her to myself." Despairingly, she added: "What a provoking thing that I, who never go out, who never dress beyond a decent style at home, should not have a leisure moment to read a newspaper." And why, she wanted to know, would it be impossible for Burr—"your lordship"—to return home?[16] Yet, to conclude that Mrs. Burr was in open rebellion would be an overstatement, for she loved her husband and did not question the role of a good wife and mother.

Mrs. Burr's little rebellion had been prudent. She finally did escape from the city and reached Pelham, where Frederick had a place. There, little time was lost, for she continued to guide Theodosia's studies.

Moreover, she attempted to appease Burr and to justify her own actions by citing the desperate need to leave town during July. "The heat and drought exceed all recollection," she wrote. Referring to the threat of yellow fever, the scourge of the late summer and early autumn months, she told Burr that "the town is extreme unhealthy," and that they were fortunate to be at Pelham. "There is always air—never hot enough to incommode one. I am certain the child would have suffered in town; she was much reduced; her voice and breasts were weak." This act of self-justification shows that she had learned how to appeal to her husband.[17]

If Burr was the child's taskmaster, he was also the solicitous father. Theodosia's maturing love and affection for him grew in direct proportion to his interest in her development. It is little wonder, then, that Mrs. Burr had to hit out to plead her own cause. While she found it so difficult to get Burr home from one of his trips, and felt that his efforts to return were half-hearted, she could observe his affection for Theodosia. She read all about Burr's search through a Westchester shop for a French book suited for his "intelligent, well-informed" nine-year-old girl. At last, he bought a "work of fancy," and one that, fortunately, was also "replete with instruction and amusement." He longed for the pleasure of placing the two volumes in her little hands.[18] Once, when trying to recover from a severe headache as he sat in his Philadelphia room with both feet in warm water, his head "wrapped in vinegar and drinking chamomile tea," the only thing that seemed to bring pleasure was his wife's account of Theodosia's growth. "I am charmed with your account of Theodosia," he managed to write. "Kiss her a hundred times for me."[19] It was only natural that this relationship became more significant after Mrs. Burr's death.

It was, of course, time for both Bartow and Frederick to assist with the burdens, but Mrs. Burr's oldest children had their own careers to consider. Bartow had been studying law, in addition to his assiduous work in Burr's New York office. On the first anniversary of his mother's death, he was in France as the secretary to James Monroe, the American ambassador in Paris. Frederick, married and living in Pelham, could not be of much help. Fortunately, the slaves—Peggy, Alexis, and Tom—were faithful and devoted to Burr and Theodosia. In addition to the numerous servants, Burr hired a French governess, Madame de Senat, who would both cultivate their manners and further refine their French.

Not long after Theodosia Prevost Burr had died, another child came to live at Richmond Hill. She was Natalie de Lage, whose father was a French rear admiral and whose mother was a maid of honor to Marie Antoinette. When the monarchy was overthrown, the child was separated from her mother and came to the United States with her nurse.

She was a pretty, dark-haired girl, one or two years older than Theodosia, and the story of her flight from France excited Burr's imagination. Furthermore, a child with her pedigree and knowledge of French would be an ideal playmate for Theodosia. And Richmond Hill gained from her beauty and warmth.

Burr arrived in Philadelphia in mid-November of 1794 with Theodosia. John Adams, noting the buoyant, confident New Yorker taking his Senate seat, thought he was "as fat as a duck and as ruddy as a roost cock," almost as though it had been Burr and not Senator William Maclay who had referred to Adams as "His Rotundity." While others whispered that profitable speculations had delayed him, Burr's spirits were certainly brightened by Theodosia's presence. "To be sure," she wrote to Bartow, "I was a pretty good traveller a coming here."[20]

Now a national political figure, Burr had already made several good friends. One of them was the widowed daughter of Mrs. John Payne, at whose house Burr boarded. Dorothea, as she was named, but always known as Dolley, had lost her husband, John Todd, in Philadelphia's terrible yellow fever epidemic of 1793. Widowed at the age of twenty-five, with a son less than two years old, she had named Burr as the baby's sole guardian to provide care and education. Surprisingly, only two years later, Burr was already informing Dolley's mother that little John Todd was "perusing his Studies with success—He will want for nothing whilst under my care."[21] And it was in the spring of 1794 that Burr, "her trusted friend and adviser," figured in a note to one of Dolley's friends. Dolley needed a chaperone before she could receive James Madison, the Virginia Congressman. "Thou must come to me. Aaron Burr says that the great little Madison has asked to be brought to see me this evening," she wrote.[22] "Little Madison" had received his favor from Senator Burr, and on September 15, 1794, he married Dolley Todd.

At about this time, Burr became the patron of a twenty-year-old art student. The lad, John Vanderlyn, later to become a major painter, was born in Kingston, New York, at the time when young Aaron Burr was following Benedict Arnold through the Maine wilderness. Burr's patronage proved vital to Vanderlyn's career.

However much Burr may have enjoyed assisting such deserving people as John Vanderlyn and Natalie de Lage, Theodosia remained his greatest concern. One of their separations, and an absence that caused him endless anxiety, came during the fall of 1795. After a brief summer visit with his daughter, Burr left on a journey that was to take him to Thomas Jefferson's home by mid-October. Yet it was an apprehensive Burr who traveled south.

Yellow fever had appeared in New York City, but there seemed to be no reason for unusual concern, and so he had been able to leave without fear for Theodosia's safety. The first incident had been on the brig *Zephyr*, which had arrived in July from the West Indies. A boy had died aboard the ship as it docked. Later, at Fitch's Wharf, where Dover Street met the East River, a ship from Liverpool had reported an outbreak among its crew. Then it attacked a family on Water Street near Dover, finally spreading through Water Street, which paralleled the river. By late August, around the time of Burr's departure, it was confined to that one area, with the exception of a single case in John Street near Burling Slip. Burr's office at 30 Partition Street, near the corner of the present Fulton and Church streets, was much closer to the Hudson River side and, at that time, near the outskirts of the town, but most cases had been in the thickly populated, low-lying section along the East River. Furthermore, Theodosia could always retreat from her quarters at Partition Street, in the rooms adjacent to the office, and go up to Richmond Hill. She could even go to Frederick's place at Pelham. Besides, on August 28, the city's Committee of Health issued an optimistic report that, although the fever had claimed twenty victims during the preceding four days, there were already signs of improvement.[23]

But the epidemic intensified after Burr left. On the last day of August, fearing contagion, and recalling Philadelphia's yellow fever horror of 1793, Pennsylvania's governor prohibited all traffic between Philadelphia and New York. Burr, having reached Bristol, Pennsylvania, was then detained. Still there three days later, despite his need to get to Philadelphia, he received a letter from a colonel requesting permission to rescue his own family from the contaminated area by moving them into Richmond Hill. "I could not therefore refuse," Burr explained. Then he warned Theodosia to gather together Anthony and Peggy and leave Partition Street.

Throughout September the fever spread, leaving the Water Street district and moving along the East River up to the Seventh Ward. The northeastern quarter of the city became deserted. At least twenty thousand fled from homes to take temporary refuge in the nearby countryside. Outbreaks were reported in even higher sections at the city's center.

By the time Burr finally reached Washington, en route to Monticello, word came that the fever had appeared in Partition Street. Yet a letter that Theodosia had sent six days earlier was filled, as he observed, with "more wit and sprightliness than you ever wrote in the same compass." After advising her to proofread all letters before sealing them, he voiced his distress at finding that she was still in town. He directed her to leave, preferably for Frederick's; but not without taking along "a good parcel of books."24

The next few days were thoroughly unpleasant for him. Anxiety about Theodosia nagged as he looked for mail saying that she had, finally, left the city. His last letter had been written on a Monday, but he had become ill the next day and was "performing quarantine by authority not to be questioned or controverted," and so he confined himself to his room. By Wednesday, one side of his face was inflamed, his eyes were red and puffy, and buzzing filled his ears. Still ill by Saturday, he began the first installment of a three-day letter. Part two, written on Sunday, revealed his agitation. "It is now ten days since I have heard from you," he reminded her, adding that the prevailing situation had made the interval a very long one. Left "in a city infected with a mortal and contagious fever, I hope, nay, I persuade myself that you observed my wishes by escaping from it to Pelham." He hoped that such news would end his constant worry.25

His condition made the ordeal even more unbearable. Forced into idleness, he could think of little else. Fortunately, he was ignorant about the real magnitude of the outbreak, which was serious enough to have been responsible for the death of seventy-one people at Bellevue Hospital during the month of September. Only the advent of the first frost could relieve the situation. Although Dr. Richard Bayley of the New-York Hospital did blame the putrid pools of water that had collected in the lower areas of the city, there was no water supply to combat the dirt; but even as such doctors as Bayley swatted the numerous mosquitoes and cursed the pests, they were convinced that the stagnant water containing garbage emitted "noxious vapors" that accounted for the "peculiarity of the state of the air." That, they felt, was the real cause.26

Monday brought some hope to the sick Burr. A letter from Theodosia reveals that she had, finally, left Partition Street. But instead of finding shelter at Frederick's country home, she had gone to her uncle, Dr. Joseph Browne. She had, in fact, been obedient enough to go to her brother's place, but the loneliness of Pelham had convinced her to leave for the Brownes, where she at least had the companionship of her cousins. After her departure from New York, she estimated that the daily death rate had soared beyond thirty.27

Burr then continued his journey. He reached Monticello and visited with Jefferson for one day before starting northward. By the time he returned to New York in early November, the autumnal cold had spared the city from further devastation. Theodosia was well, except for a cold and sore throat.

CHAPTER IX

Political Frustrations

ORMAL political ties were still very tenuous in 1792. Newspapers rarely assigned party labels to the names of candidates, and perhaps the best way to categorize most public office-holders was to study how they voted on a number of key issues. Even the choice of electors from New York, which was done by a November session of both houses of the legislature in 1792, showed no solid line-up behind one or another set of candidates for the privilege of choosing the next President and Vice President. Yet, by that year, there were some signs that political divisions were emerging: organized efforts had been made to support a candidate for the nation's second highest office. The opponents of Hamiltonian federalism had arisen. Among them, there was conviction that those termed "aristocrats" were plotting for nothing less than the restoration of everything English: monarchy, society, economic classes. All of this, they felt, would soon pervert the Constitution and destroy the glorious achievement of 1776. Hamilton's designs seemed quite plain, even diabolical, and Washington was clearly under his influence. As for Aaron Burr, his Senate career inevitably brought him closer to the position of the zealous anti-Federalists who opposed such evils. While many of his friends were Federalists who felt he was imbued with at least a touch of their convictions, his senatorial battles supported the Republican cause. Some myth-makers have even portrayed him as the founder and a leader of Tammany Hall.

Tammany is now popularly regarded as the most partisan of partisan political organizations. This description may not be accurate, but it is important to note that Tammany's original objective was somewhat different. At first, it was really a fraternal society that served as an outlet for those opposed to such "presumptuously organized foreign National Societies" as St. Andrew's, St. George's, and St. Patrick's, which held views regarded as "deep and dark as the holy Inquisition," as though they were satellites of foreign despots eager to poison the new American version of democracy.[1] In reality, then, Tammany started as a nativistic group; the membership considered itself truly patriotic, and as one of the founders later explained, they were determined to "counteract the growing evil of the day."[2] Tammanyites were, at that time, Federalists as well as anti-Federalists.

Claiming Burr as an originator of the group not only minimizes the accomplishments of others, notably William Mooney, but also advances the proposition that Burr manipulated both Mooney and the Society for his own ends. There is, however, no evidence that Burr had anything to do with either the organization or its founder during the Society's early years; and the membership list that is still available shows that he never actually joined them.[3] Tammany remained essentially a fraternal and patriotic benevolent organization for about half a decade.[4]

Tammany's movement toward partisanship was gradual. With an early membership of moderates bound by a patriotic desire to protect the achievements of the Whigs, the Society nevertheless began to respond to the political conflicts of the time. As such, it reflected the growing two-party cleavage of the entire nation. Most members were enthusiasts of the French Revolution, and they celebrated on July 14 in commemoration of Bastille Day. Invited guests were representative Frenchmen of New York. While Federalist members could only wince, others criticized Secretary of State Hamilton's policy of funding state, foreign, and domestic debts, which brought windfalls to those who speculated in government certificates, and condemned his enthusiasm for a Bank of the United States. All such ideas were regarded as hostile to republicanism. In the fall of 1793, the membership listened to Mrs. Ann Julia Hatton's poems championing the anti-Federalist cause. This good lady, described as the "Poetess Laureate of Tammany," wrote an opera called *Tammany, or the Indian Chief*, which contained such bold expressions of the ideals of liberty and equality that its production caused a sensation in March of 1794.[5] Many of the more ardent Democratic-Republicans also joined the New York Democratic Society when the city got its first local "Jacobin" club—as the Federalists preferred to call it—in 1794.[6]

Democratic-Republican societies had begun to sprout in the new nation in 1793. Before the year had ended, eleven "Jacobin" clubs were in existence.[7] Critics saw little difference between them and the French benevolent and patriotic societies that had appeared in some of the major American cities. As sympathetic as these groups may have appeared toward the French Revolution and the cause of popular government, they concerned themselves mostly with domestic issues.[8] These political divisions were furthered by each conflict between the Administration and its critics. When the French Minister to the United States, Edmund Genêt, boldly defied President Washington by sponsoring the sailing of French privateers to attack British shipping within the safety of American waters, Hamilton's attempt to embarrass the pro-French anti-Federalists had helped to promote partisan conflicts.[9] Only two weeks after Genêt had arrived in America, in April of 1793, Washington had declared his government's neutrality in the war between France and England. This gave new impetus to the formation of the "Jacobin" clubs.

Burr's anti-Administration position now became more explicit. He was for a constitutional amendment to bar from Congressional membership those who held offices or stock in the Bank of the United States. He also voted to compel the Administration to reveal the diplomatic exchanges between France and the American ambassador, Gouverneur Morris. Political divisions had hardened to the extent that Burr was one of twelve senators who stood together on both partisan issues.[10]

Much more significant was the effort to unseat Albert Gallatin of Pennsylvania. Born in Geneva in 1761, the independent-minded young man had arrived during the American Revolution to sell tea. The son of an aristocratic family, he had sacrificed the possibilities of becoming politically prominent in his native city-state or of entering one of the professions. In America, the man who later became famous for his career in public finance was a complete failure as a land speculator, or even as a farmer. But western Pennsylvania, where he finally settled, eventually became Gallatin's political stronghold. As did so many others in the agricultural West, he advocated the Republican cause. Even in the short time he sat in the Senate, between December 2, 1793, and February 28, 1794, he angered Alexander Hamilton by a motion that would have required the issuance of a detailed accounting of the government's finances. The effort to unseat him became an early outstanding example of party politics.

Burr was given a leading role in the defense of the Pennsylvanian. He was convinced that Gallatin was being victimized by a purely Federalist political maneuver, an attempt to apply to the naturalized American a constitutional interpretation which, had it been used earlier, would have disqualified all members of the first Senate that had met in 1789.

Citizenship in the United States for nine years was required by the

Constitution; but national citizenship had existed only since 1781, with the adoption of the Articles of Confederation. Prior to that date, Americans were only citizens of each state. So the members of the First Congress could hardly have held their seats, legally, without an interpretation that made the provision applicable to those who had been naturalized after the ratification of the Constitution in 1788. And Gallatin had taken his oath as a citizen of Virginia in 1785. There was little doubt, then, according to Burr and the other Republicans, that Gallatin was being victimized by an *ex post facto* interpretation.

Gallatin had hurt his own cause by a blunder. At a party caucus, he made an indiscreet comment about the possibility of his own ineligibility. Without that statement, there probably would have been no challenge. He took his oath of office as a Senator on December 2, 1793, and immediately afterward Vice President Adams read a petition from nineteen citizens of York, Pennsylvania, challenging his seat. Adams must have recognized the legitimacy of Gallatin's election, for, as President of the Senate, he promised to support the Pennsylvanian in case of a tie vote.[11]

To Burr went the major responsibility for Gallatin's defense. The petition from York had first been studied by a committee headed by John Rutherfurd of New Jersey. After a debate of several days on their report, the Senate voted on January 13 to refer the matter to a new committee, to which Gallatin might present evidence for consideration. Gallatin knew that the outlook was ominous, as the committee consisted of four Federalists and three Republicans. Their meetings revealed Gallatin's own expression about his ineligibility; but the defendant then denied that the charges were sufficient to cost him his seat. The report that reached the Senate floor from the committee on February 20 stated that Gallatin had offered insufficient reasons for not presenting evidence of his citizenship and that "it is now incumbent on Mr. Gallatin to show that he has become a citizen of the United States and when."[12] The debate lasted seven days. Rufus King, Burr's colleague from New York, took the lead in presenting the case against Gallatin, and so John Taylor of Virginia sent a note to Burr suggesting that he reply to King, "*first*, because you desired it; *second*, all depends upon it; no one else *can* do it, and the audience will expect it."[13] Jammed galleries heard Burr's words. The rule that excluded the public from Senate deliberations was waived, and the crowds listened to the carefully measured tones and prose of the New Yorker's defense.[14]

But his effort was in vain. Just before the balloting, which was held on February 28, Senator Benjamin Hawkins of North Carolina suddenly left Philadelphia. Gallatin had expected support from him. Also, the senior Senator from Pennsylvania, Robert Morris, who had vowed neutrality after having originally introduced the York petition, now joined in the anti-Gallatin vote. Vice President Adams never had a chance to cast a ballot. Gallatin lost by a vote of fourteen to twelve.

Gallatin always believed that he had been the real winner. As had happened after Clinton's dubious victory in New York's gubernatorial election of 1792, such a flagrant maneuver provoked popular resentment, feelings strong enough to return him to political life. He had many personal affairs to attend to, anyway, during his temporary retirement. Only four months earlier, he had taken Hannah Nicholson as his second wife. A woman of many social connections, she had several relatives in Congress and was a daughter of Commodore James Nicholson of New York, a man who was an influential Republican. It was thus useful for Burr to win the gratitude and friendship of both Albert Gallatin and his father-in-law.

Despite Burr's vigorous defense of Gallatin's cause, other Republicans continued to question Burr's fidelity to their party. Even his opposition to the Administration's conduct of foreign affairs helped little. Yet, in 1794 and 1796, Burr served as one of the outstanding critics of Administration attempts to arrange a commercial treaty with Great Britain.

When President Washington submitted the name of Chief Justice John Jay to the Senate for approval of his appointment as an envoy extraordinary to England, Burr again went to battle. He did not oppose the attempt to negotiate with the mother country, as neither Federalists nor Republicans desired the continuation of the King's troops in outposts on American soil along the Canadian border. The Treaty of Paris of 1783, which had ended that battle for independence, had provided for the British evacuation of such holdings. All seven fortresses should have been abandoned with "all convenient speed," but the Englishmen had lingered on with little intention of yielding military protection of the fur trade.[15]

Their commerce flowed on the waters of the Great Lakes and to the sea through the St. Lawrence River. To Americans, the foreign presence was an obnoxious reminder of the new nation's weakness. There was not enough strength to force British fulfillment of the treaty, and the intervening years had also failed to bring a commercial agreement for trade between the two nations. The pumping of imposts into the American ports, and its subsequent enrichment of a needy Treasury Department, required the arrival of tariff-paying foreign goods. Since more business was done with England than with any other country, a severe price would have to be paid for jeopardizing relations with the British. After the French had declared war against England on February

1, 1793, Washington's Proclamation of Neutrality in April was an attempt to avoid trouble. Nevertheless, not only were the Americans being harassed on the frontier, as the fortresses also helped to mobilize the Indians against spreading white settlements, but the Orders in Council of June 8 and November 6 enabled His Majesty's navy to seize cargoes from American ships engaged in the valuable trade with the French West Indies, in particular, and even with France herself. To remedy this situation was all to the good as far as Burr was concerned, and he was sympathetic with those who felt that Jay was too pro-British. Burr and James Monroe then led the fight for the appointment of either Madison or Jefferson.[16]

Three days after the President's nomination was received, Burr countered with a resolution. Why not, it asked, use our present minister to Great Britain? Thomas Pinckney of South Carolina was already in London. His services could be employed "at much less expense, than by an envoy extraordinary," under an appointment that "is at present inexpedient and unnecessary." Moreover, Burr questioned the propriety of using someone of Jay's position because, "to permit judges of the Supreme Court to hold, at the same time, any other office or employment emanating from, and holden at the pleasure of, the executive, is contrary to the spirit of the constitution; and, as tending to expose them to the influence of the executive, is mischievous and impolitic."[17] Although Burr's effort was defeated by a vote of seventeen to ten, the Senator's opposition had been firm. He was one of the minority of eight out of twenty-six senators to vote against the final confirmation of Jay.

Another diplomat whom Burr had opposed earlier, Gouverneur Morris, now had to be replaced. The French, accusing him of being a monarchist and an enemy of their revolution, had asked for his recall. As the French had so recently complied with the American request to remove Genêt, there was little else Washington could do. The known Federalist coolness toward the new French government meant that, as Monroe put it, "a republican character" would have to be chosen as a replacement.[18]

Several men were discussed. Chancellor Robert R. Livingston of New York was regarded as an experienced hand, especially since he had handled the nation's foreign affairs before the adoption of the Constitution. Burr's name was also advanced. Neither man was urged "in preference to the other," wrote Monroe, but "only for consideration."[19] As the weeks went by, Monroe's information was that the Senator's candidacy appeared to be continuing "under circumstances very favorable to his success," but a judicious appraisal of Burr's chances would have been less optimistic. Washington would have had to overcome his own personal objections before appointing Burr. The recollection of some incidents may have finally persuaded the President against him: that day at the Newburgh headquarters when Burr was embarrassed in the act of reading papers from the General's desk; the circumstances of Burr's resignation from military service. Foremost, however, was probably the preponderance of invectives against Burr that the President must have absorbed from his determined Secretary of the Treasury, Hamilton.

Livingston, however, did not want to leave the Chancery Court and thus rejected the opportunity. Edmund Randolph, who had succeeded Jefferson as head of the State Department, then paid a morning call to Monroe to ask whether he would accept the legation to France. Randolph's explanation was that the President's determination to send a Republican did not include Burr. The official reason was that Washington did not want to give the impression that only New Yorkers were being sought. Monroe, assured that Burr was out of the question, thus became Minister to France. It was not a complete loss for Burr's family, however, as the Virginian soon called John Bartow Prevost to Paris as his secretary.[20]

Remaining at home brought what seemed like a new opportunity for Burr: his next real chance for the governorship. Since George Clinton had led New York for so many years, a change was imminent in 1795. Clinton was certainly not too old at fifty-four to hold office again, but illness had been plaguing him. Inflammatory rheumatism had become severe enough to force him to inform Lieutenant Governor Pierre Van Cortlandt and the Speaker of the House that he would be unable to attend that year's legislative session in Poughkeepsie, and a written message was delivered instead of Clinton's annual speech. Undoubtedly, too, he was reluctant to face what seemed like certain defeat. His physical condition provided a graceful excuse to exit, and with both parties searching for candidates, it was not surprising that Burr's name was advanced.

Again, support came from both Federalists and Republicans; in each case, a minority pressed for his candidacy. When Burr's political associations are examined, they contrast with his partisanship in the Senate. It was not only a matter of guilt by association that damned Burr in the eyes of many, but also his willingness to support the Federalists, as he had done in the Yates-Clinton election of 1789, and, in turn, to receive their help. In an era when political parties were in their infancy, Burr seemed unable to label either party as evil or virtuous. Rather than conclude from this that he refused to represent any particular viewpoint, it would be more accurate to say that he regarded basic differences as insufficient to keep either alignment from helping him achieve the first function of every politician: enough votes to be elected. For, while so much has been made of the traditional differences between the Federalists and the Democratic-Republican cause as epitomized by the Hamilton-Jefferson clash, little has been said about the essential agreements that did exist. By the 1790's both parties were for the Constitution, however much they may have argued about its interpretation. Neither wanted to return to Great Britain. Neither attacked the sanctity of private property. Both wanted a viable government capable of maintaining the institutions that, after all, were a continuation of the pre-Revolutionary society. Even the class distinctions that have been cited so often, designating the Federalists as "aristocrats," cannot obscure the important overlapping that did exist. The Livingstons, after all, had become Republicans; and they were among the mightiest of landowners. Neither Jefferson nor Madison were what anyone would consider as yeoman farmers; and Republican ranks included a minority of the wealthy city merchants. In short, the broad-base support so characteristic of American political parties had already become evident. In this light, Burr's position is not so shocking. If enough Federalists would coalesce around his candidacy in 1795, as in that frustrated attempt of 1792, then even if he lacked strength within his own party, he might yet win the governorship.

Hamilton refused his party's offers of support, for he wanted Federalists to nominate Jay. And so Egbert Benson, a lawyer active within his party in New York City, wrote that Jay's candidacy "had been so decreed from the beginning." All this was unknown to Jay, who was in England trying to secure a treaty. Should the result of such efforts be unpopular or controversial, as was likely because of the popular enthusiasm for the French cause, its publication could be delayed until after the April election for governor. Only its premature appearance would jeopardize Jay's position, but Hamilton was prepared to gamble.[21] The belief that Jay had been cheated out of certain victory in 1792 was sure to sweep him into office this time.

That August, Burr had been visiting with upstate friends, the Thomas L. Witbecks, using their Albany County home at Watervliet for side-trips to adjacent parts of the state. By November of 1794, Federalist State Senator Stephen Van Rensselaer informed Joseph Ogden Hoffman, a staunch Federalist lawyer of New York and an original member of Tammany, that "Burr is the avowed Candidate for the Government."[22] Hoffman gave this information to Senator Rufus King with the additional report that Peter Van Gaasbeek of Kingston was "one of his *engaged Partisans*."

Hoffman and King were determined to defeat Burr. At the close of

1794, they heard that Albany Federalists, aided by Hamilton's father-in-law, General Schuyler, had backed Jay. Rensselaer had agreed to run with Burr as candidate for lieutenant governor. Now, support for Jay had to be won in New York City. The importance of that backing was stressed in a letter to Hoffman warning "that immediate attention should be paid to our friends in Ulster, in Dutchess in particular, as Mr. Burr's Creatures are indefatigable thro' the whole State."[23]

Burr's workers continued to press hard. Undoubtedly inspired by Clinton's official declaration of nonavailability, which the Governor released on January 22, Van Gaasbeek called for an early meeting to announce the candidacy of Burr and Van Rensselaer.[24] The "Antis" had already held several meetings in an attempt to choose a candidate, and they had trouble selecting from among Robert Yates, Burr, and Chancellor Livingston. Finally, at a caucus that consisted of forty leading Republicans from various parts of the state, they settled for Yates.

The efforts of the Burrites had been inadequate. Only six votes supported them, and all of these came from within New York City.[25] Even then, after William Floyd of Long Island's Suffolk County had been chosen to be Yates' lieutenant governor, there was some expectation that Yates would refuse.[26] But the Chief Justice of the State Supreme Court, who had accepted the Federalist nomination in 1789, was also ready to obtain any designation possible to reach the state's highest office. Burr then realistically dropped all hopes of being nominated.[27] Lingering efforts by Van Gaasbeek in Burr's behalf also failed, until the Kingstonian, who had been elected as a member of the Third Congress, finally informed Rufus King that he would again deliver his pro-Burr committee to Jay's side.[28]

Another Burr effort had collapsed. Hamilton's choice, John Jay, was the man to oppose Yates. Although Burr was in Philadelphia and there is no record of any direct activity to promote his own chances, there is little doubt that his partisans worked with his blessing. Surely, his ardor for the governorship had not cooled.

Jay's ability to defeat Yates in 1795 depended upon a race against publication of the new treaty that Jay had negotiated with England. The election at the end of April gave him about 53 percent of the votes, and on July 2 the substance of the treaty was made public in New York. As had been feared, there was bitter popular reaction. Hamilton and Jay were hung in effigy, and Hamilton was hooted down at a public meeting on Broad Street in New York.[29] A wave of protest divided the new nation as nothing else had done since the ratification of the Constitution.

When the President called the Senate into a special session that summer to consider the treaty, Burr was present. On June 8, Vice President Adams ordered that its exact contents, as delivered by Washington, should remain secret during their debate. What the legislators then heard was unpalatable. The new treaty of commerce had failed to include provisions for the protection of neutral American shipping, and had even legalized specific restrictions. Concessions were made to British interests in pursuing their war against France and in protecting the commerce of the West Indies, for which the Americans won agreement to establish a mixed commission to settle claims based on damage to American shipping.[30] But at the same time, no provisions were made for the return of slaves or indemnification for them, as had been provided by the Peace Treaty of 1783. Just as the Americans had failed to fulfill their obligation to pay debts owed to British merchants, the slave provision had been ignored. The only tangible gain was the promise that the British would finally evacuate their posts along the American frontier by June 1, 1796, and even that was a questionable victory. After all, such compliance would only bring the English up to date with the obligations under the 1783 treaty. In essence, then, Jay's Treaty was a way to avoid a war with England—a war for which the new nation had no desire and little strength.

The treaty that Burr now opposed was largely Hamilton's own creation. Sympathetic toward England with an awareness that she was America's most important customer, Hamilton had also become the major contact for the British minister to Washington, George Hammond. At one occasion, just before Jay sailed for London, Hamilton indicated his acceptance of the principles of the British Orders in Council that "foodstuffs can be contraband, and the neutral flag does not always cover enemy goods."[31] His acquiescence to the Orders, except for extreme interpretations that had been enunciated by the local vice-admiralty courts of the West Indian colonies, undermined any real chance that the subsequent negotiator, Jay, could have had to force their relinquishment.[32] And so Hamilton, who had promoted the treaty, was also instrumental in shaping its language. Burr and other Democratic-Republicans, eager to publicize its obnoxious provisions, were unable to override Vice President Adams' order that their deliberations proceed in secrecy.[33] But Burr fought on.

Before many days had passed, Albert Gallatin wrote from Philadelphia that he was "told that Burr made a most excellent speech" against the treaty.[34] On June 18, Burr had requested an audience with the President, but whether or not it was granted is not known. Although outnumbered, he led the attack with determination. Hamilton sent a letter to Senator King about a rumor that had reached New York that the treaty had been rejected. He noted that the "anxiety . . . about the result, is extreme. The common opinion among men of business of all descriptions is, that a disagreement to the treaty would greatly shock and stagnate pecuniary plans and operations in general."[35] Burr's greatest attack, the one that reached Gallatin's ears, was still to come. On June 22, he introduced a motion to delay further consideration of the agreement.

Burr catalogued his objections. Calling for a renegotiation with Great Britain, he itemized the Republican criticisms. He wanted to expunge those articles that, by providing for the shelter and refuge of armed vessels, were an obvious affront to France because they had compromised American neutrality. Going contrary to earlier assurances Hamilton had given to Hammond, now embodied in Article Two, Burr wanted to eliminate the concessions to British fur-traders and settlers granting them a continuation of their rights even after the evacuation of the frontier posts. As far as Canadian territory was concerned, Burr asked for changes that would give American citizens "the use of all rivers, ports, and places within the Territories of His Britannic Majesty in North America, in the same manner as his subjects may have of those of the United States." As a concession to the South, in particular, which had obtained no concessions by the treaty, renegotiations should achieve the payment for "the value of the negroes and other property carried away, contrary to the 7th article of the Treaty of 1783." And the mixed commission that was provided to determine the spoliation payment should also assess the British government for the *"loss and damage sustained by the United States by the detention of the posts."* He also wanted a more liberal statement in the controversial twelfth article concerning goods not indigenous to the West Indies that might be sent there in American ships, which would aid Northern mercantile interests. Also repugnant to Burr was Article Fifteen, which he rightly viewed as not only offensive to France but a restriction of American sovereignty, because it restrained the United States from establishing reciprocal agreements with other nations, namely France. Finally, he wanted a modification of the twenty-first article that would have permitted "citizens of either party" to accept "commissions in the Army or Navy of any foreign power."[36]

There can be no doubt that Burr's ideas would have served the best interests of the United States. But the new nation was, quite simply, in no position to achieve a better settlement. Recognition of this reality doomed his proposed modifications. While the treaty gained little that had not been promised earlier, and, in addition, antagonized the French,

Washington had asked for its ratification only after deciding that avoiding a war with Great Britain and obtaining a commercial treaty were worthwhile objectives. On June 24, the Senate finally gave its approval and closed the extended debate.

The controversy was one of the most dramatic events in the evolution of the two-party system, as the Federalists and the Democratic-Republicans had differed sharply over the issue. The public protests were directed at all Federalists, and it is probably true that Jay would not have been elected had the treaty been released before the April balloting. The hardening of party lines that resulted drove the last remaining Federalists from New York's Tammany Society.

Soon after the close of the special session, Burr left Philadelphia and returned to his home on Partition Street. He was then able to attend to his legal practice and to transact negotiations with his land agent. After a welcome stay with Theodosia, which coincided with the earlier phase of the yellow fever outbreak in 1795, he made an important trip to Virginia. His destination was Monticello, the home of Thomas Jefferson.

Jefferson was enjoying his second retirement. He had looked forward to domestic tranquility and the pleasures of a rural life; the matters that occupied his attention were chiefly the construction of his beautiful mountaintop home and agricultural problems. Since early January of 1794, when he had left Philadelphia after his tenure as Secretary of State, he had been removed from any direct involvement in political affairs. Actually, his Virginia neighbor, Madison, had led the partisan battles during this period. Burr, too, particularly after his fight against Jay's Treaty, was cast as a leader of the anti-Administration forces.

While the subject of Burr's discussion with Jefferson on that October day is unknown, speculation suggests that the treaty must have held their attention. His visit was later used in an attempt to tie the philosopher-statesman-scientist-architect to the Northerner, for publicizing such an association would serve the purpose of local Federalists by discrediting Jefferson's loyalty to his own state. Indeed, precisely such an attempt was made by one Leven Powell, the only Federalist that Virginians would choose as an elector in 1796. While acknowledging Burr's "considerable talents," Powell charged that his one-day session with Jefferson was used to plan "the rash and violent measures brought forward in the last session of Congress." Reinforcing this was an assertion that Monticello was, at the same time, being used as a rendezvous for considerable plotting, and that the discussions were followed by letters from Jefferson to other Southerners "urging them to persevere in the line of conduct agreed to."[37] Two of Jefferson's neighbors promptly counterattacked with a denial that Jefferson had received any such gathering of politicians other than Mr. Burr.[38]

Jefferson was silent about the coming elections, so that whether or not he and Burr discussed the outlook for 1796 is highly speculative. Each state still chose its electors according to its own particular method and there was no official agreement on candidates by a national political party. Such partisan lines were not completely firm and conventions in the modern sense were unknown until over three decades later. As was the case among the Republicans in 1792, when Virginians had helped to destroy Burr's support for the vice presidency, selections resulted from a general agreement among the few party leaders. But the election of 1796, following the bitterly partisan fight over the ratification of Jay's Treaty, was another major step in the formation of political alignments.

Washington's retirement was virtually certain. To Monroe in Paris, Burr wrote in September that "the best informed of either party are firmly persuaded that he will not be a candidate."[39] Actually, as early as March the President had revealed his decision to retire. Adams now became the logical successor for the Administration. The party leader, Hamilton, then supported Thomas Pinckney for the vice presidency. Not only was Pinckney a South Carolinian, which balanced Adams' Massachusetts background, but the favorable treaty with Spain that had just been negotiated by Pinckney to secure the use of the Mississippi River and the port of New Orleans for American shipping was bound to make him popular with the South and the West.[40]

So great was the esteem for Pinckney, in fact, that many Federalists preferred him to Adams. He was regarded as less pro-British and more moderate than the "monarchistic" New Englander. Robert Goodloe Harper, a representative from South Carolina, noted that his candidacy was even winning over some Republicans. Hamilton also sought to have Pinckney come in first, ahead of the rather independent Adams.[41]

But there was another possible candidate: Aaron Burr. At least one Federalist, Jonathan Dayton, a congressman from New Jersey and a lifelong friend of Burr, sent two letters to Theodore Sedgwick. The first one suggested that an Adams victory was unlikely and that Burr's candidacy would be preferable to a victory by either Jefferson or Pinckney. Knowing that Burr was counting on Southern support for 1796, Dayton wrote that, in addition, he "will find some friends also in the middle as well as in the Eastern" states.[42] The next day, even more excited about the prospect of Federalist support for Burr, Dayton wrote: "Every moment's reflection serves only to impress me more with the importance of fixing upon some plan of cooperation to defeat the designs of Mr. J's friends." Should Adams not succeed, "is it not desirable to have at the helm a man who is personally known to, as well as esteemed & respected by us both? I assure you that I think it possible for you & me with a little aid from a few others to effect this."[43]

Dayton's audacity astonished Theodore Sedgwick. The Massachusetts Senator rejected the idea on two counts: First, he denied the inevitability of Adams' defeat, pointing out that the Vice President would get the first vote of a sufficient number of electors to install him as President. Then, turning to Burr, Sedgwick cited the tenuous relationship between Burr and his own party. The Republicans know that "he is not one of them," he wrote, "and of course they will never support but always effect to support him." He cited Monroe's selection over Burr as minister to France as evidence of poor Republican backing. Then, as though to clinch his point, Sedgwick wrote: "They doubtless respect Burr's talents, but they dread his independence of *them*."[44]

Sedgwick lost no time in forwarding Dayton's two letters to Hamilton. He added no comments except to caution against "a breach of confidence" for Dayton's sake. Hamilton's contempt for the documents was clear. With distaste, he wrote on Sedgwick's note: "concerns Dayton's intrigue for Burr."[45] Thus, Dayton's effort was squashed.

If Burr had urged his Federalist friend from New Jersey to "intrigue" in his behalf, he was, nevertheless, busily trying hard for Republican support. Harder than any other anti-Federalist, with the exception of the industrious John Beckley in Philadelphia, Burr campaigned during the early autumn of 1796. All in all, he spent six weeks going through the New England states of Connecticut, Rhode Island, Massachusetts, and Vermont. Reporting this to James Madison, Beckley added, "I doubt his efforts any more directed to himself than anybody else. You well know him. . . ."[46] In Boston, Burr helped to set up Sam Adams as a presidential elector and spent several October days conferring with such Republicans as Jonathan L. Austin, William Jarvis, and his good friend Dr. Eustis.[47] When he returned to New York, he wrote to Pierpont Edwards in New Haven, asking him to "favor me with one line respecting your hopes from the Electors of Connec. & R. I.—The Jefferson Ticket will have a large Majority in Penna unless the Votes of the three Western Counties [where the Whiskey Rebellion had been fiercest] should have been *stolen or fraudulently suppressed*, which there is some reason to apprehend—."[48]

For their vice-presidential nomination, the Republicans were less unified than in their determination that Jefferson was to be the man to head the party's drive to oust the "aristocrats." William Loughton Smith, a congressional Hamiltonian from South Carolina, had noted the

unresolved Republican situation when he informed Senator Izard of his
state that Chancellor Livingston, Senator John Langdon of New Hampshire, and Senator Pierce Butler of South Carolina were possibilities
along with Burr. The objections to Burr, Smith added, were mainly the
belief that he was "unsettled in his politics and are afraid he will go over
to the other side."[49] As late as November 8, Smith, writing from Philadelphia, was still telling Izard that the Republicans "are not perfectly
agreed among themselves as to the Vice President."[50] Little is known
about what was done to advance Langdon's interests; but Butler was
enthusiastic about his own chances and there was, as usual, considerable
support for Livingston from New Jersey, where some members of the
numerous Livingston family were active. New Yorkers also boosted the
Chancellor.

But Burr was the favorite. In Pennsylvania, most Republicans of
stature, including Albert Gallatin, were for him along with "the whole
body of Republicans" from that state.[51] On June 26, Philadelphia was
the site of a caucus of Republicans from the various states. Much to the
distress of Pierce Butler, who consequently walked out of the meeting,
they agreed to run Jefferson and Burr.[52] Nevertheless, the intraparty
hostility continued to haunt Burr. Oliver Wolcott, Jr. later wrote to
his father in Litchfield that the Antis "do not expect that Col. Burr will
succeed, and they secretly wish that Mr. Adams may be elected to his
present station."[53]

While he waited for word about the electors, Burr lingered in New
York. Any desire to leave for Philadelphia and the opening of the
Second Session of the Fourth Congress, which convened on December
5, was suppressed because of his desire to be with Theodosia and Natalie. Their presence and attention relieved the mounting disappointments.
Burr, showing concern over the political situation in virtually every
letter written during this period and aching to remain in New York
with his girls, was clearly distraught.

The next few months were bitter. Throughout December came news
of the voting by the electors in the states. As the trend became clear,
Hamilton informed Rufus King that the "event will not a little mortify
Burr."[54] By the time Burr brought himself to leave Theodosia and
return to his duties in Philadelphia, all the votes were known. John
Adams had won the highest office with seventy-one votes and Jefferson's sixty-eight meant that he would be the next Vice President. Then
came Pinckney with fifty-nine, which placed him third. Burr trailed the
top three with just thirty votes. Not only was he far behind Jonathan
Dayton's most cherished dreams, but more than half of the Jefferson
electors had turned to another man for their second ballot. Virginia, in

particular, from which he had hoped for good news, torpedoed whatever chances he may have had. Their electors had given him but one vote while twenty had gone to Jefferson. Similarly, he got nothing from Georgia and South Carolina, although Jefferson was the unanimous first-place candidate of those Southern states. And he had failed to get a single vote from all of New England and his own New York, where Federalist electors had been chosen. Just Pennsylvania's thirteen votes that were added to scattered fragments from the South and the two Western states of Kentucky and Tennessee comprised his thirty.

The Adams victory had also defeated the last-minute efforts of the French to promote the Republican cause. France decided to act through her anger at American acceptance of Jay's Treaty. Foreign Minister Adet, representing the French Directory in Philadelphia, had fulfilled his orders from Paris by early November decrees that attempted to swing the election to Jefferson. In a Philadelphia newspaper, he announced the French intention to deal with American shipping by applying to her navigation the type of interference sanctioned for the English by the treaty and praising Jefferson as the candidate whose republicanism was most palatable to France.[55] While none of the leading Republicans had connived with Adet or even welcomed such potentially embarrassing foreign interference, the outlook for future relations with France had obviously become ominous. But Burr's own relations with Adet and his government were even more interesting.

CHAPTER X

The Enterprising Aaron Burr

B URR returned to his Senate seat on Tuesday, January 12, 1797. Then he traveled to New York before the end of the month, only to journey back to the capital in time to hear Vice President Adams announce the results of the past election; but his remaining days in Philadelphia were destined to be few. The New York legislature had been restored to its usual Federalist control. In March, its members voted for Philip Schuyler to succeed Burr, and the ex-Senator returned home after completing one full term.

He was now free to devote himself to private interests. Today's law-yers often enter business ventures, or they may utilize their capital more impersonally by investing in the stock markets. But in Aaron Burr's day, land purchase was the usual form of speculation. Burr had been involved in such dealing in an official way in 1791, when, as his state's Attorney General, he served as one of the five land commissioners who had sold three and one half million acres of state lands to one Alexander Macomb at a price considerably less than others were charged for comparable holdings. An investigation later failed to prove any improprieties. But Burr, who had not been present during the months when the deal was being negotiated, was nevertheless suspected by some of clandestine participation in the unsavory-sounding scheme; and even those who accepted his innocence cited his absence as proof of how little time he devoted to his public office.[1] Whether he acted as a public official or as a private lawyer, land always remained the most important source of his major speculations.

Such deals were common, with or without ready cash. Usually short

of money, Burr borrowed sums that often reached five figures, a considerable amount in a day when one could barely earn $3,000 a year as a
member of the President's cabinet. Not surprising was the citation of
such debts by derogators like Hamilton as further examples of Burr's
improprieties. Yet it should be remembered that lavish borrowing from
individuals was necessary when fortunes were made and lost quickly;
when banks were scarce, unreliable, and often partial; and when financing carried no government guarantees.

Land transactions involved Burr in negotiations with operators like
John Nicholson, Timothy Green, and Oliver Phelps. A Welshman,
Nicholson joined with the Holland Land Company and other investors
in the purchase of vast tracts of land to the north and west of the
Allegheny River in Pennsylvania. Burr bought one hundred shares of its
stock. Other land purchases were scouted for Burr by Green. Originally
from Massachusetts and with numerous connections in South Carolina,
Green often served as Burr's agent for such ventures. In 1794, when
Burr was busy with affairs of government, Green spent the summer
months journeying through the western part of New York State. There,
he inspected Genesee River lands, which Burr purchased two years
later.[2] Other transactions associated Burr with Phelps, one of the outstanding land developers of his day. It was through Phelps that Burr
obtained large tracts in western New York.

He bought one hundred thousand acres from Holland Land Company
holdings. This deal resulted from desperation, for his finances were in
bad shape at the time he left the Senate and he had been unable to raise
money by selling his Pennsylvania Population Company stock. Creditors
like Peter Van Gaasbeek were pressing him. Always the gambler hoping
to recoup his losses, Burr had to borrow from others for the purchase
and arranged for payment of the lands at twelve shillings an acre.

To protect his contract against default, he had to turn over to
Theophile Cazenove, the Holland Company agent, a bond for twenty
thousand dollars as security. This was issued in the name of Thomas L.
Witbeck of Albany. He also mortgaged his Pennsylvania Population
Company holdings. All financial obligations could be met, he hoped, by
selling his lands at a huge profit. It had seemed like a good gamble; but
his timing was unfortunate. The land market had fallen sharply by the
end of 1796 and he was left with no way to meet his payment that was
due in 1797, which subjected him to the heavy penalties that had been
written into his contract.

Financial difficulties were one matter, but his ventures had other overtones. In the fall of 1797, British Foreign Minister Lord Grenville received a warning from his envoy to the United States, Robert Liston.

Writing from Philadelphia, Liston reported that an American Anglophile "has confidentially informed me that he suspects there exists a project for the purchase of extensive territory in Upper Canada of which the leading though not the ostensible members are men of high-flying democratick sentiments who would rejoice to see an independent Republick, established in Canada in the room of the present Colonial and Monarchical Government." Only two promoters were mentioned; one of them was Aaron Burr.[3]

Liston had cause for alarm. The situation he had been watching for a long time was replete with threats against British North America. Of interest to the French government, desiring to recover Canada, was the possibility of fomenting a revolt among French-Canadians. "Citizen" Genêt, one of Adet's more notable predecessors as minister to the United States, had included among his undiplomatic maneuvers the sending of American agents into Lower Canada. Operating in what is now the Province of Quebec, they attempted to stir dissension. When Adet later represented his government at Philadelphia, he endorsed such designs, hoping that Canada could become "an indispensable appendage" to the French Republic. He even distributed a pamphlet among the French-Canadians that boasted of the advantages of a republican government over British rule.[4] Liston, an experienced diplomat who was very much aware of such activities, had written a confidential letter to the lieutenant-governor of Lower Canada in November of 1796. The document told about Adet's desire to seize Canada for France and warned about the presence of agents in the Province.[5] There was also an alert against a possible invasion which, with strong support in Vermont, would be led by Canadian citizens and American adventurers.

A French-dominated Canada was the last thing desired by the Federalist administration of the United States, but American citizens were nevertheless involved. The lands were cheap and attractive. Large tracts were covered with fine white pine that could be floated down the many rivers to the Great Lakes and from there to the timber mills. One American, a Rhode Islander named David McLane, was arrested in Quebec for seditious activities and then hanged, drawn, and quartered. Others, like Ethan Allen and his brothers, rebuffed by the British when they tried to further Vermont's interests by establishing commercial ties with Canada, plotted the acquisition of Canadian territory. In 1796, Ira Allen had purchased arms in France for the ostensible purpose of supplying the Vermont militia. Suspecting that his real design was to promote a revolution among the French inhabitants of Lower Canada, a British warship captured his equipment.[6] Finally, in response to advertisements placed in the United States by the governor of Upper Canada, now Ontario, thousands of American speculators poured into the northern country after 1796 and purchased some of the best tracts. Only expediently pledging their loyalty to the Crown and taking an oath of allegiance, they were in concert with others working from American territory to plot the conquest of Canada.[7] From Albany during the summer of 1797, Comte de Volney, a Gallic scholar and author, took charge. He later returned to France to "concert measures for the operation." The military plot called for a force of six thousand French-Canadian soldiers to land at Kamouraska. There would also be an invasion from the west. To make such a diversionary move against Upper Canada while French troops were arriving from the east, a General Collot had been enlisting recruits from among the Indians.[8]

Thus, Liston was receptive to warnings about Burr. He also advised Grenville of "others of the same stamp, who have the character of being disinclined to Great Britain, and enemies to every form of regal power." An additional alert was sent to Peter Russell, the President of Upper Canada.

Burr, among his many other enterprises, was involved in Canadian lands. Throughout his last year in the Senate, he made heavy purchases, financed by loans from numerous individuals, including David Gelston, the New York politician, Witbeck, and especially John Lamb. From Lamb, the revolutionary leader of New York's Sons of Liberty and Burr's fellow campaigner at Quebec, he borrowed what was an astonishing sum for those days. In 1796, at the height of his commitment in Holland Company property, he received almost twenty-three thousand dollars from the sixty-one year old soldier.[9] Most of this sum went for land along the south shore of Lake Ontario, the Genesee River region, and in Onondaga and Ontario counties; but his interests also reached the north shore of the great lake. On September 5, he notified Witbeck that Timothy Green was "on his way to upper Canada, from which place he will draw on you for a sum not exceeding Six hundred Dollars and at not less than Twenty Days, which bill I beg you to honor of my account—."[10]

Other events showed Burr's proximity to Canadian affairs. Captain Joseph Brant's Mohawk Indians were, at that time, ripe for French overtures. Although they had remained loyal to the Crown during the American Revolution and had moved north of the Canadian border, their dissatisfaction with English rule had grown during the postwar years. A grant of lands in Upper Canada, on the peninsula between lakes Huron, Erie, and Ontario, had failed to mitigate their distress, for Brant soon discovered that the British had failed to give them a clear title to the territory. This thwarted his plan to engage in the profitable business of selling acreage to the white settlers. But the government's claim to pre-emptive rights rendered such ideas futile.[11] It was at this time that Burr invited Brant to Philadelphia.

There, on February 27, 1797, the Senator entertained the famous Indian. In a letter to a friend, the next day, Burr described the Captain as the "king of the Mohawks," and wrote about his opulent existence.[12] He also sent a note to Theodosia. She and Natalie were, he informed the girls, about to be honored by the presence of Brant at Richmond Hill. "He is a man of education—speaks and writes the English perfectly —and has seen much of Europe and America," Burr wrote. "Receive him with respect and hospitality."[13] Theodosia fulfilled her responsibility and, in her father's absence, arranged a fine, well-attended dinner party for the Indian, who was passing through New York en route to New England. From Massachusetts he went to Albany.

But what Burr did not mention in his two letters was the subject of the discussions with Brant. The English restrictions had, of course, prevented Burr from even attempting to buy land from Brant, but the fifty-five year old Indian had not undertaken his mission for frivolous matters. Both the difficulties of travel and Brant's determination to aid the Mohawk interests exclude that possibility. His expedition could have hardly avoided touching the Canadian situation, particularly since he arrived at Albany while Volney was plotting the contemplated thrust against British North America.[14] Moreover, when the Indian dined with Burr at Philadelphia, they were joined by the same Volney, in addition to such eminent individuals as Adet and Talleyrand, who would shortly assume the post of minister of foreign affairs for the French Directory.[15] Adet, in addition, had only recently been Burr's guest at Richmond Hill, where the French minister's portrait had been painted by John Vanderlyn. Therefore, while Brant's biographer explains that the gentlemen at Philadelphia spent an evening that "was not only agreeable, but highly intellectual entertainment," their real concern was quite plain.[16]

Furthermore, within the next two months, Volney, before undertaking his function at Albany, spent time with Burr in New York, at almost precisely the time when the Colonel was writing to John Lamb about "the amt. of the note for the Canada Purchase."[17] Two days later, Burr gave Volney a letter of introduction to William Eustis, asking his friend to "contribute, which no man can so effectually do as you, to render his residence in Boston agreeable."[18]

"The men pointed out are Mr. Burr of New York, Mr. Boudinot of New Jersey," wrote Liston to Grenville, and then urged that such threats should be met "by confining any speculators that may make their appearance to the rules laid down for the settlement of the province."

Burr's precise role in this affair may never be known, but his correspondence with fellow land-speculator Oliver Phelps suggests further that Liston's information merited careful attention. Only to Phelps was Burr free to mention his project, for the Massachusetts merchant had once listened to his plan. On December 16, 1797, while the designs against Canada were brewing, Burr reminded Phelps that, "We once talked . . . of some projects which I should like to discuss more fully with you." The far from private postal system only permitted Burr enough freedom to add that, "It is probable that I shall go to Europe in the Spring, though I do not wish that this should at present be spoken of—."[19] One week later, he divulged to Phelps what he was to repeat to his intimate friend but never to anyone else. "I have a large sum of money in Paris," he wrote.[20] Supposedly in the throes of severe financial difficulties, he twice suggested to Phelps that "the most agreeable kind of accommodation" for certain debts could be met by drawing "a bill on Paris."[21] John Bartow Prevost was then in the French capital as Monroe's secretary, but when his own debts were due, Prevost did not hesitate to pay for them with drafts drawn in his stepfather's name. He was certainly not the source of Burr's Parisian funds.[22]

The "Paris" referred to, then, in the midst of the endeavors of Messrs. Adet and Volney, and their meeting with Burr and Brant in Philadelphia, points toward the French Directory. What passed between Burr and the American representatives of this short-lived French government was more than fraternal toasts and good wine. Colonel Burr, who would soon startle suspicious Republicans by his vigorous espousal of defensive measures during the undeclared war between his own country and France, was, nevertheless, participating in a plot to drive the British from North America. The grandiose scheme of its assorted sponsors fizzled out because of inadequate military support, and the eventual disposition of the Parisian funds remains a mystery; but even if most of it had been available to Burr, extreme caution and discretion would have inhibited its use. A substantial part of the money must also have been appropriated for land purchases in Upper Canada.

While precise motives may never be determined, some things do seem clear. Burr's earlier stated faith in the direction of France's new republic was not unlike the optimism of many Republicans, including Jefferson. In this view, the British had been the main violators of American rights, with their infringement of Yankee shipping and persistent occupation of frontier posts that had only recently been discontinued. It had been Burr's proposed resolution that had attempted to force a rewriting of

Jay's Treaty to open Canadian waterways to American commerce, a measure certain to have enhanced the value of contiguous lands.[23] The Allens of Vermont had similar motives. Just as the Vermonters wanted to improve profits by more direct commercial ties with the Great Lakes–St. Lawrence River inland water route, which was the natural outlet for the northern frontier of that day, Americans interested in this territory would not have exactly minded the replacement of the Crown with a government that, in exchange for such assistance, might be more congenial to their desires. It should be recalled that the Allens had attempted to negotiate with the British before their adoption of more militant measures. In Burr, the French recognized not only a friend, not only a speculator with his own interests at stake, but also a man of influence, ability, and daring, who could provide momentum to the American-based plan of Adet's operations.

If Burr's land ventures had become involved in international intrigue, the scheme could only be deduced, and even then in a superficial way. One wonders who was Liston's "friend to Great Britain" informant and how much of the story seeped through to Hamilton, who may have been thinking of this and other matters when, four years later, he revealed to Gouverneur Morris "that Mr. Burr is now in frequent and close conference with a Frenchman, who is suspected of being an agent of the French government, and it is not to be doubted that he will be the firm ally of Buonaparte."[24] To John Rutledge, Hamilton made a perceptive observation about the possible activities of a financially embarrassed Burr. "He must therefore . . . have recourse to unworthy expedients. These may be a *bargain* and *sale* with some foreign power or combinations with the public agents in projects of gain by means of the public monies perhaps and probably to enlarge the sphere—a *war*."[25] But whatever Hamilton may have known or suspected about these transactions, Burr's activities with the Holland Company were made transparent and led to charges of impropriety that dwarfed the Macomb scandal of 1791.

Burr's connection with Cazenove and the Holland Company, while open to criticism as being improper for a legislator, differed little from the maneuverings of Schuyler and his famous son-in-law. As things turned out, the major distinction concerned their needs in relation to the Company. Both wanted cash: Schuyler, for his Western Inland Lock Navigation Company, his dream of a future canal system which the legislature had chartered under his guidance in 1792; and Burr, the sale of lands for profit and avoidance of the penalty imposed by his contract.

The Holland Company, which had been started by Dutch bankers, had bought up more than five million acres in central and western New York since 1792. For such large holdings, many buyers were needed. The shattering of the land bubble in 1796 left both Burr and the Company in bad straits. At the same time, Cazenove wanted to open a new market. European immigrants represented that potential source, but only in Pennsylvania were such lands open for settlement by aliens. Not only the Holland Company agent, but other land holders and interests, such as Charles Williamson, who managed the Pulteney Lands for Englishmen, needed such assistance.

Cazenove thus went to work. He had already raised large sums in America by speculating on the depreciated government securities after Hamilton's intention to urge the central government's assumption of state debts was known. Equipped with the necessary cash, he was able to buy a sizeable quantity of the soon-to-be profitable paper.[26] Now, in his attempt to enable aliens to own land, he employed Hamilton's services. The former cabinet member was thus charged with the mission of securing from the legislature a law that would permit aliens to hold New York lands. He worked with the youthful Samuel Jones and their efforts resulted in the passage of a 1796 law that gave aliens a seven-year period of land tenure.[27]

It was inadequate, failing to fulfill the Company's expectations, which was nothing less than *carte blanche* for aliens to purchase and hold lands on the same basis as American citizens. Only such an open door would attract buyers. Hence, the involvement of Philip Schuyler and his Canal Company.

The canal project needed money. Cazenove could provide additional capital. What was more logical than for Schuyler, still a state senator, to acquire funds from the Holland Company in exchange for helping to push through the legislature a more liberal alien land bill? What emerged on March 17, 1797, was a magnificent example of log-rolling. A new law permitted aliens to hold land for twenty years. Also incorporated was the condition that the Canal Company would be given a $250,000 loan or its equivalent in stock.[28]

Nevertheless, it all fell short of Cazenove's best interests. The shattering of the land bubble rendered the price too high and made the payment expensive in return for a mere twenty-year tenure. Anything less than no restrictions at all would be insufficient to really open the field to a large new market. With what was an obvious identity of interests, Cazenove turned to Burr.

Burr's need for money was aggravated by John Lamb's pressure for repayment of the loans. Lamb was in a most distressing situation. At the Customs House, under his jurisdiction as Collector of the Port of New

York, death had deprived him of the services of his son-in-law, Charles Tillinghast. To replace Tillinghast as assistant collector, he had gambled on the good faith of an Englishman who had previously been in jail for debt. Lamb's generosity in paying the man's obligations had secured his freedom. Others had vouched for his integrity and ability. After being in charge of Tillinghast's department, however, the Englishman suddenly announced that the death of a wealthy relative had provided an inheritance that enabled him to retire. But his departure was followed by the discovery of a large deficiency of Customs House funds. Further investigation swelled the size of the loss, and although not even Lamb's enemies condemned him as guilty, his property and holdings were mortgaged to restore the funds. That Burr reacted with sympathy to his friend's need is clear.[29] He even proposed that Lamb take over the house and property at Richmond Hill on very favorable terms, but his creditor did not want to jeopardize Burr's position with others who were after him for money. He added, however, that at "the same time I must intreat you to provide in some other way for the balance due me."[30] Three weeks later, after strong northeastern winds had forced his Albany-bound boat to return to New York "& abandon the Journey," Burr revealed to Lamb that he had attempted the trip with "but 20 dollars which I took to bear my expenses."[31] A few days later, Lamb resigned as Collector of the Port of New York. Doing everything possible to repay his distressed friend, Burr nearly cleared his obligations by early June. "The trouble & anxiety which has attended these transactions, which I hope to apologize to you for any apparent inattention to you—In truth I could not see you with pleasure while these matters were unsettled—"[32]

Two days later, Burr sold the furnishings of Richmond Hill to Sir John Temple, the English Consul General. Temple's $3,500 bought all the fine contents of the mansion. He also leased the house from Burr for his family. How Burr felt without the use of Richmond Hill and with Theodosia spending much of her time at Mrs. Allen's home in New Jersey he revealed to Pierpont Edwards the following year when he described himself as "a kind of Bachelor" in his quarters at 55 William Street, which was near the corner of Pine.[33] Cazenove's timing was good.

The agent was also shrewd. Burr's new role as a member of the Assembly was of potential value to the Holland Company. Soon after returning from his expired Senate term, Burr was nominated by New York City Republicans to serve again in the state legislature. A New York City revolt against continued Federalist domination prompted their support of a coalition ticket of thirteen assemblymen to represent the state's most populous center. Five Republicans were included, but not Burr. The five were the only winners who had Federalist support, while all Republican-backed candidates, including Burr, won by a majority of 875 votes, a marked departure from past city elections.[34] That the Federalists had avoided an endorsement of Burr was surely an example of Hamilton's handiwork, but the Republican popular vote gain of twenty-three percent over the previous year helped to assure Burr's election. Thus, the changed situation meant that Schuyler, who had earlier represented Cazenove's interests in the state legislature, now held Burr's former seat in Philadelphia. And Burr could hardly fail to be an influential personage at Albany.

Burr, like every land speculator, shared the Holland Company's desire to open the market to new customers. He sent Timothy Green to Europe late in 1797 to find new outlets. Desperately, after early optimism had begun to fade, Burr instructed his agent that if "you cannot succeed in Britain, you must try France."[35] Broadening his efforts, he had also supported the quest by contributing to those who had commissioned James Wadsworth of Geneseo to look for buyers in England.[36] How much simpler things would be for the Messrs. Green and Wadsworth, and how the value of their investments would soar, if the twenty-year alien land holding restriction were liberalized!

For the Holland Company, the judicious use of money—legal expenses, the stockholders were told—could be put to work through Burr. Such would be the price of guiding the new law through the legislature. Allocated was the sum of ten thousand dollars, of which three thousand went to Josiah Ogden Hoffman, the state's Attorney General, one thousand to Thomas Morris, the state Senator from the Western District, and one thousand to a Mr. L., who was discreet enough to withhold giving a receipt and demanded secrecy. What remained, $5,500, was for Aaron Burr. But Burr's money was a loan, payable in two years, and not an outright gift.[37]

On New Year's Day of 1798, Burr was in Albany with Theodosia for the opening of the next legislative session. From the capital, Burr wrote to John Lamb, whose good friends were trying to salvage what was left of his reputation and property. "I reproach myself exceedingly for having left New York before the business was finally settled," he wrote, and offered to return home and superintend the liquidation of his own property to win Lamb's exoneration. "That your peace of mind should be disturbed or personal safety endangered by an act of friendship and generosity to me is the most humiliating event of my life—and I shall be most wretched until I hear the course the business has taken."[38] But Lamb was to lose all his holdings, and the disaster exacerbated his deteriorating health. The old patriot died a little more than two years later.

That legislative session was a busy one for Burr. He was appointed to a committee for the elimination of imprisonment for debt. As during his earlier membership in the legislature, he played an active role in promoting a bill to end slavery in the state. On February 7, he voted with the majority to pass "An act for the gradual abolition of slavery," which was the beginning of a successful attempt to end the "peculiar institution" in the Empire State.[39] At this time, the legislature received a flood of petitions calling for favorable action on a bill entitled "An act to enable certain persons to purchase and hold real estates within this State." Burr's failure, on February 10, to prevent the rejection of a bill entitled "An act to encourage emigration to this State," which was lost by a vote of forty-nine to forty-one, left him undaunted.[40] It merely indicated the difficulty of the coming fight.

The powerful opposition to the Holland Company's desired legislation now came from the Schuyler-Hamilton interests, for the canal people worked to block any new alien law. Such legislation, they feared, would thwart any hope of getting the quarter of a million dollars for their pet project. Allying themselves with other opponents of liberal land laws for aliens, these interests rallied patriotically to safeguard American citizens from the evils of foreign capital.[41] Word from Holland that the Dutch company would absolutely refuse to make the loan anyway, and Burr's assurances that the new bill was ambiguous and hazy and that it would nonetheless continue the Company's financial obligation to the Western Inland Lock Navigation Company, began to reduce the opposition and gain new supporters for the cause. Strangling amendments were defeated. Senator Thomas Morris, who hoped to become a Holland Company manager, had already pushed the bill through the upper chamber. "We have passed a law allowing aliens to hold lands in this State," Burr was able to write to Oliver Phelps on April 4, for an unrestricted landholding law for aliens and their heirs had been passed two days earlier.[42]

Nevertheless, Cazenove kept after Burr to fulfill his contract. Witbeck, meanwhile, had become "uneasy for his credit, and teased me to take up his bond by giving other security," Burr later revealed, because "his credit at the bank and elsewhere became affected by it" when word of the transaction spread throughout Albany.[43] That Cazenove then accepted a transfer to an equal bond by Burr's stepson, Frederick Prevost, now a solvent gentleman, was no gift to Burr, as one bond was as good as the other. Not only did Cazenove continue to hold this protection, but he also kept the mortgage on Burr's twenty thousand acres of Pennsylvania Population Company lands. As Cazenove continued to demand payment for the New York lands, in December, 1798, Burr was ready to cancel the contract by returning the property. But Cazenove's persistence finally resulted in Burr's forfeiture of not only his Holland Company lands but also the Pennsylvania acreage. In exchange, Prevost's bond was dropped and Burr was absolved from repaying the $3,450 he still owed from the original $5,500 loan.[44]

That the entire transaction acquired political overtones is not surprising, nor is the resulting clash with a member of the Hamilton clan. In 1797, Burr himself had helped to prevent a duel between James Monroe and Hamilton over the latter's widely publicized illicit relations with Mrs. Maria Reynolds. In 1791, when still in Washington's cabinet, Hamilton had an affair with the lady, the wife of a swindler and blackmailer, James Reynolds. Monroe's reluctance to clear Hamilton of Reynolds' charges of malfeasance as Secretary of the Treasury, rather than adultery, and Hamilton's belief that Monroe had furnished the exposé for James T. Callender's scurrilous history, which contained "singular and authentic papers respecting Mr. Alexander Hamilton," led to preparations for a duel. Monroe requested Burr to be his second. Burr, however, helped to prevent the clash. "If you . . . really believe, as I do, and think you must, that H. is innocent of the charge of any concern in speculation with Reynolds," he advised Monroe, "it is my opinion that it will be an act of magnanimity & justice to say so in a joint certificate." And then he added: "Resentment is more dignified when justice is rendered to its object."[45] To conclude the matter, Monroe assigned Burr the job of drafting a final agreement.[46]

Through Hamilton's acquaintance with Cazenove, accounts of Burr's transaction reached John Barker Church. Church, who had married Angelica Schuyler, another of the General's daughters, was Hamilton's loyal brother-in-law. Word reached Burr during the late part of the summer of 1799 that Church was responsible for circulating rumors that the Holland Company had bribed Burr to support the Alien Lands Act. In accordance with the prevailing code of honor, Burr challenged him to a duel.

They met at Hoboken, on the Jersey shore opposite New York City. Using pistols, each fired one round without effect, except for a ball that tore through Burr's coat. While "the seconds were preparing to load a second time," Robert Troup informed Rufus King, "Church declared he had been indiscreet and was sorry for it, and thus the affair ended." Then Troup added: "Church wanted proof of the charge—but it has long been believed."[47]

Just as were many other imputations, real or imagined, this was accepted by Burr's detractors. Hamilton later reminded Rutledge of the strong suspicions that Burr had "corruptly served the views of the Holland Company in the capacity of a member of our legislature and understood to have been guilty of several breaches of probity in his pecuniary transactions."[48] He then observed that Burr "is of a temper bold enough to think no enterprise too hazardous and sanguine enough to think none too difficult."[49]

Our forefathers were far from generous toward one another; by their standards modern politicians seem extraordinarily charitable. But even according to their view, Burr was outstandingly controversial. Yet the existing papers showing his Holland Company transactions indicate that he was less culpable than several others, including Schuyler and Hamilton, who had worked out a very convenient deal between the Company and their own canal interests. What is less excusable was Burr's close legislative involvement in behalf of interests in which he had a direct stake, and what may justly be deplored was his complicity in a project to establish as our northern neighbor a power regarded as hostile to the United States by those who were charged with conducting internal and external affairs.

CHAPTER XI

Of Fevers and Water Pipes

A T the age of forty-one, Aaron Burr had reached a significant
position within the Democratic-Republican hierarchy. Although
not a leader in the modern sense, with state-wide control over
patronage, he was a figure of experience, skill, and prestige, a politician
with a viable organization in New York City. Whatever doubts existed
about his political convictions, and qualms heard about scruples, it was
to him that ambitious Republicans looked for future success in the
rapidly growing state.

The city's expanding commerce and population continued to
strengthen its political power. More directly, New York City came to
hold the balance of power between the state's two parties and the twelve
electoral votes that were at stake every four years. Despite the presence
in Albany of a Federalist governor, the first to follow the long Clinton
reign, Republican victories in city elections had become sufficiently
possible to threaten the continuation of Federalist supremacy. Success
for the new party in 1797 was especially sweet when the Federalists had
been compelled to support a coalition ticket as the only way to back
some winners. Such vigor, however tenuous, had enabled Burr to move
to the state legislature after the end of his single term as a United States
senator.

The growth of Tammany as a partisan organization, a process born
amid the news about the Whiskey Rebellion and then Jay's Treaty,
paralleled this new strength. A glance at the membership list showing
those who joined during its first decade reveals a virtual directory of
New York's active anti-Federalists, particularly after the start of its

partisan phase. John Swartwout, a politician and merchant whose name was to become almost synonymous with the word "Burrite," had been one of the earliest members. Not much later, one hundred and sixteen names down the list, was the signature of John Bartow Prevost, Burr's stepson. Other Burr acquaintances and close associates were such Republicans as his brother-in-law, Dr. Joseph Browne, Melancton Smith, Edward and Brockholst Livingston, Morgan Lewis, and James Nicholson.[1] Particularly well known as a Burrite, after this period, was Matthew L. Davis, a politician and journalist, who followed Philip Freneau as the editor of the *Time Piece and Literary Companion*. A Sachem in 1799 and 1800, Davis eventually became so devoted a friend that Burr left his papers to him. His tribute to forty years with Burr was his destruction of "delicate" letters and the authorship of a laudatory two-volume work of biography and correspondence.

The conspicuous absentee from this list was, of course, Burr himself. But with the membership of both his stepson and brother-in-law, as well as Davis and Swartwout, Burr's interests were not neglected. That he never did join the organization that became the heart of the Democratic-Republican surge in New York City seems strange and can only be explained by conjecture. It is tempting to believe the theory that his absence reflected an aristocratic rejection of association with an organization that was dominated by mechanics. Over half of Tammany's officials during 1795–1800 were from this group.[2] But this was not strong enough a repellent for two Livingstons and Morgan Lewis; Commodore James Nicholson, Gallatin's father-in-law; or even Bartow. Burr's non-membership can more plausibly be attributed to his avoiding what would have been a dogmatic political commitment. With such representation in their camp, anyway, he could either mobilize their resources or pursue an independent course. At the moment, however, as the ex-senator whose 1796 electoral vote bid had suffered the defections of Virginians and other Southerners, he was the wounded party.

Jefferson would later confide to his *Anas* that his earliest acquaintance with Senator Burr had "very soon inspired me with distrust," and he "habitually cautioned Mr. Madison against trusting him too much."[3] Yet, when he sent Burr a long letter in the spring of 1797, it consisted of an intimate and cogent discussion of foreign affairs that displayed full awareness of Burr's necessarily high standing in the party. Certain was the recognition by the Vice President of Burr's importance in New York. It was neither the first nor the last instance of a politician recognizing an ally through political expediency, as Jefferson now evidently felt was warranted to soften the blow Burr had so recently received from Virginians.[4] Burr, obviously flattered by the gesture, replied almost immediately. "The moment requires free communication among those who adhere to the principles of our revolution," he answered.[5] Moreover, Jefferson had stated his hope of seeing Burr in Philadelphia, and it was a desire that was not lost on the Colonel.

When the former minister to France, James Monroe, arrived at the capital less than one week later, on June 27, Burr was there. Along with Jefferson and Gallatin, he received a two-hour briefing from the re-called Monroe about the Administration's relations with France. The deteriorating relations with the Directory had been making news. Ear-lier that month, a "friend in Phil." had written to inform Burr that "We are raising in Senate 4 Batt. of artillery, 4 Troops of horse, compleating our frigates and buying nine others." And Burr had then observed to Eustis that perhaps fiery Congressional speeches, particularly the one by Robert Goodloe Harper of South Carolina, could force the Directory to accede to American "Magnanimity and Justice."[6] A few days later, President Adams signed a bill to allocate one hundred and fifteen thou-sand dollars to fortify ports and harbors. The conference of top-ranking Republicans could not have ignored the implications of deteriorating relations with France.

Between the ratification of the English treaty and the establishment of the Napoleonic regime, policy toward French violations of American neutrality influenced domestic and foreign affairs. Monroe had been recalled for his inability to satisfy either government. The more violent Federalists were demanding a tougher anti-French policy, as over three hundred and forty American vessels had been seized by French priva-teers within eighteen months, and American property losses to the Directory had exceeded fifty-five million dollars. In every action but the impressment of seamen, the French had been emulating England's policy toward America. Preparations for a special American mission to the Directory by John Marshall, Elbridge Gerry, and Charles Cotesworth Pinckney, the new ambassador to France, were already under way that July when Burr returned to New York and Theodosia and Natalie. He later went with his family to Albany, where the fight for the Alien Lands Bill took place.

Republican hopes were then jolted, in the spring of 1798, with the receipt of dispatches from the three envoys to France. They arrived in Philadelphia on March 4. Although the President revealed their exist-ence to Congress the next day, their substance was not disclosed until April 3. Outraged legislators, with bitter reactions coming from both parties, heard how Talleyrand had insulted Marshall, Pinckney, and Gerry by making negotiations with the Directory contingent upon the prior payment of a bribe; to which the righteous Pinckney was romantically reported to have exclaimed: "No! No! Not a sixpence!" The request had been made by three of Talleyrand's unofficial agents, the "X, Y, and Z" of the episode. Not only did they want a quarter of a million dollars for Talleyrand, but also an American loan to France and an indemnity for Adams' hostile speech to Congress that was made during May of 1797. Adamant in their rejection of the overture, despite what had been Gerry's singular attempt to break the deadlock, the Americans gave up. The affront seemed like a confirmation of Federalist suspicions toward French designs and signaled the real start of an undeclared war. For when Adams revealed their dispatches to Congress, he noted that they could not succeed "on terms compatible with the safety, the honor, or the essential interests of the nation" and urged Congress to prepare for war.[7] Jeffersonian attempts to minimize the affair were futile. War seemed inevitable.

Burr was re-elected to the Assembly that April, less than four weeks after Adams had spoken to Congress. His party affiliation was not evidence of any lack of enthusiasm for war preparations. It was Burr who reported his committee's findings that the Governor should estimate the cost of "putting the city and port of New-York in a respectable state of defence."[8] Two weeks later, another effort by Burr to fortify New York was a call for the purchase of more heavy cannon, or at least to do whatever was necessary to provide a better defensive plan for the port.[9] Although his resolution for such unlimited expenditures was defeated, the other members from the city had supported him. In every instance during the Albany debates, Burr urged a maximum effort, and it was a stand that harmonized with the main concern of New Yorkers. Hugh Gaine, the printer, noted in his journal that the town was "full of the News from Philadelphia about France and America."[10]

Although the XYZ disclosures had jarred the Republicans and had helped to re-elect Governor Jay, who received fifty-four percent of the votes in competition with Robert R. Livingston, the outcome was largely a confirmation of confidence in Jay rather than a great Federalist success. Republicans like De Witt Clinton and David Gelston were elected to the state Senate, and the city's Republican assemblymen won with fifty-two percent of the votes. Their percentage had thus dropped thirteen points since 1797, but the victory, along with several upstate successes, showed their viability in the state. Furthermore, now elected with Burr, in addition to John Swartwout, was John Bartow Prevost.

Young Theodosia, thrilled by the success of her stepbrother, later wrote to tell him that, "We do not take Albany papers but if when you make a speech you will write to me on what day that great event took place I will go to the office for a newspaper & read it from beginning to end, although I should feel tired & sleepy in the middle of it, from not understanding it I mean."[11] That was just one month before he was to marry Frances Ann Smith, the daughter of Dr. Samuel Stanhope Smith, President of Princeton College; and so Theodosia's letter added, "If you hear from F. write me how she is for I really feel that I can love her, too; when is she to be my sister? I will be bridesmaid; if I should go to Princeton on foot & alone for it."[12]

The impending war was the main concern that year. Debates raged about the wisdom of imposing an embargo upon shipping or constructing stronger fortifications. Just before the polls had opened in New York, a discussion to settle the question at a crowded meeting had erupted in a fight. *Greenleaf's Journal & Patriotic Register* praised the opponents of arming as the "true Americans—no Englishmen; no Frenchmen; they will defend their country against all invaders, as citizen-soldiers, upon the genuine principles of the rights of man!"[13]

Congress, however, sought to pay for defensive measures by adopting a direct federal property tax. Of the two million dollars levied upon the states, New York's share was $181,680, to be obtained from buildings and lands. If the upstate farmers, mostly old Clintonians, were chagrined, they could be comforted by the burden that had befallen New York City's "Quality Row" Federalists, for the tax was a graduated one. The agricultural sections, however, were burdened with taxes that would not be collected from the great landed proprietors but from their tenants, a good reason for many of the landless farmers to oppose Federalists.

The Jay administration then imposed a general property tax for New York State. Going into effect in 1799, and prompted by borrowing from private banks to meet current expenses, including the state's share of fortifications, the tax further damaged Federalist popularity.[14] In everything that was done to promote preparations for war, Burr was identified as a vigorous supporter.

Some Republicans interpreted his stand as a capitulation to Federalist-generated war fervor. Certainly, his position was consistent with the need for Republican assemblymen from the city to avoid charges of neglecting the defenses of their city, the chief port. As Burr was their most prominent member, his leadership is not surprising, however inconsistent it may have appeared to the critics of his friendship toward France. The Republican polemicist, James Cheetham, having turned against Burr and victimized him with bitter diatribes, was to charge that Burr's new militancy was merely a Hamiltonian-like bid for high rank in the growing military build-up.[15]

There was competition for military leadership, and Burr was a contender. His name appeared on a list with other Republicans that President Adams had forwarded to General Washington. Again he was vetoed. Secretary of State Timothy Pickering told Oliver Wolcott, Jr., that Adams' "strange ideas" concerning the general and staff officers would not enable Burr to become a quartermaster general. The reason was simply that Washington could not confide in him.[16] But at the local level, it was Hamilton, now named as a major-general, who worked with Burr.

Their growing political and personal antagonism did not interfere. Since their mutual support for Yates, legal matters had often brought them together. Now, both zealous to protect the home front from anticipated French assaults, they served with Colonel Ebenezer Stevens on a citizens' committee for the defense of New York Harbor. Hamilton had even suggested Burr's appointment as superintendent of the fortifications. Burr would, he felt, accept the assignment "if an *adequate compensation* be annexed." Continuing to comment on the qualifications of his rival, Hamilton added, "I know not what collateral objections may have arisen from recent conduct of that Gentleman; but independent of these I should favour his agency in the business."[17] But it was Hamilton who was finally chosen.

The war scare had been mounting. News reached the city in mid-July that a French privateer had captured a Captain Smith of Boston. The Captain's ship had been seized en route to Martinique, and patriotic New Yorkers fumed at the report of the mass butchering of the crew. A few days later, a fistfight on the Battery involved President Adams' secretary, Samuel Malcolm, who had been indiscreet enough to sing the Federalist song "Hail Columbia!" within earshot of dockworkers who preferred tunes that were more congenial to the French Republic.

Burr was in Albany that August for the opening of the Assembly's twenty-second session. His quarters were at Mrs. Vischer's boardinghouse, far upriver from the port that was getting so much attention. Very much involved in expediting the construction of further fortifications, he suggested to Colonel Stevens that a letter from General Hamilton "might be useful" to bring some dissenting upstate members into line behind their measures.[18] On August 10, he reported for the committee and noted their feeling that such construction "is an object of the utmost importance to the honor and welfare of the State," and called for adequate appropriations without delay.[19] Three days later, Prevost delivered his first address, supporting these efforts. Bartow stressed that the expense of the necessary security "is a secondary consideration, and we cannot doubt but that our fellow citizens will cheerfully submit to such taxes."[20]

Yet, Burr was careful to maintain distinctions that Federalists rarely cared to make. When Assembly Speaker Dirck Ten Broeck attempted to single out the "open violence of the French Directory" in the bill to provide for the defenses, Burr countered with a motion to strike the words in favor of the phrase "all foreign nations." With the support of his fellow city assemblymen, Burr won his point by a comfortable margin.[21] As the chairman of the committee to examine the state's mode of taxation, Burr also reported that the prevailing system was inequitable and argued for "a system of taxation on just and equal principles, but with all possible diligence to be projected and adopted." His report led to the passage of a resolution ordering the Comptroller to submit a plan for a uniform system of taxation.[22] He was the leader of a responsible minority cooperating for the common good, but nevertheless spoke for the opposition party. That month, when John Tayler and James Watson were candidates for the United States Senate seat vacated by John Sloss Hobart, the Federalists won by selecting Watson in a party line vote.[23]

Burr wrote to Ebenezer Stevens complaining about the agonizingly slow struggle to win military appropriations. He regarded the battle as "infinitely fatiguing & laborious to me; yet I do not despair of accomplishing something which shall gratify my fellow citizens."[24] Nevertheless, charges that he had deserted the Republican cause or assumed the role merely to enhance his own chances of securing a command from Washington, as Cheetham later wrote, were unfair. Military precautions were nonpartisan, at least in providing direct protection for New York City.

That summer, the Federalists moved to further the exploitation of the war scare by consolidating their strength with an ill-concealed attempt to equate the Republicans with subversive interests. In July, their Congressional majority passed a series of measures that President Adams signed and supported, while even Hamilton feared they were excessive. Known collectively as the Alien and Sedition Acts, they actually consisted of four separate measures.

All were carefully designed to weaken the "Jacobin" opposition to the virtuous upholders of the Constitution. The Alien Enemies Act empowered the President to imprison subversive foreigners in time of a declared war, while the Alien Act legalized their deportation as dangerous characters. Particularly transparent was the Naturalization Act. Aimed at reducing the political potential of the normally Republican immigrants, it delayed their period of naturalization by expanding the residency requirement from five to fourteen years. Jefferson regarded the bill as a direct threat to the political life of Geneva-born Albert Gallatin, while Robert Goodloe Harper, speaking for the extreme Federalists, urged that only birth should qualify one for citizenship. Even more partisan than these three laws was the Sedition Act, passed on July 14, 1798. This forbade the publication of "any false, scandalous and malicious writing" that sought to malign the government or its leaders. The acts were similar to repressive measures enacted by England just a few years earlier, but the most frightening aspect was their enforcement.

As actively as he had sought to enforce the city's defenses, defying suspicions of an alleged Federalist taint, Aaron Burr was equally energetic in opposing the new laws. His political acumen responded with a sure legislative position and, simultaneously, the deft utilization of all possible resources to defeat the sponsors of the Alien and Sedition Acts. This effort was the prelude for the election of 1800.

There was a long list of Republican newspapermen, printers, and editors whose silence was a goal of the Sedition Act. Fearing the political power of the opposition press, ready to suspect dissension as unpatriotic, the Federalists were quick to use their new weapons. Even before the Sedition Act was passed, the *Time Piece*, a Republican semiweekly with close links to Burr, was singled out as an example of why the law was necessary.

The *Time Piece*, published in New York City, had powerful anti-Administration credentials; and, by coincidence, its existence dated from nine days after Adams was inaugurated. Its first editor was Philip Freneau, whose *National Gazette* had been admired by Burr, one of its earlier subscribers. When Freneau relinquished his control to retire from journalism in March of 1798, Matthew L. Davis became the editor. Davis, in turn, sold the enterprise to Dr. James Smith and John Daly Burk. This final change of management came while the Alien and Sedition Acts were pending in Congress.

Burk was no stranger to Burr. Best remembered as a playwright and for a four-volume history of Virginia, Burk was an outspoken Irishman who had escaped from his native country while still a Trinity College student, after trying to rescue a condemned political prisoner. He brought his republicanism to the western shores of the Atlantic and soon afterward published a newspaper in Boston. The paper lasted only about six months, but Burk was more successful as the author of an historical play called *Bunker Hill, or the Death of General Warren*. First produced in New York in 1797, it became a perennial Fourth of July favorite for half a century thereafter, its battle scene a unique innovation for the dramatic stage. Its publication carried an appreciative dedication to the man Burk felt "indebted for the subject of my drama," Aaron Burr. Departing from his "system" of avoiding this form of tribute, Burk remembered "with what courage and patriotism" Burr had "stepped forward to fight the battles of your country."[25]

Burk's alleged crime was his attack on President Adams. The President's handling of the letter from Elbridge Gerry revealing Gerry's extended and solitary efforts to negotiate with the French, after the frustrated Marshall and Pinckney had given up, was the subject of Burk's vehement criticism. The editor implied that Adams had altered portions of the letter "to promote certain ends in this country."[26] Earlier comments by Burk had already aroused the Administration. By the time Secretary of State Timothy Pickering had alerted Richard Harison, the federal district attorney in New York, about the possibility of punishing the alien, Burk had already been arrested with his partner, Dr. Smith—eight days before the actual passage of the Sedition Act.[27]

Both proprietors were brought before District Judge John Sloss Hobart. Burk was charged under the common law with seditious libel and Smith with only libel. Supporting Burk and contributing the two thousand dollar bail were such Republicans as Colonel Henry Rutgers, Peter R. Livingston, and Burr. Smith had wealthy relatives to pay his share of the bail. Burk and Smith were then released pending a trial before Supreme Court Justice William Paterson.

Burr's involvement continued, his connection with Burk well established. Robert Troup told Rufus King that Burr had enabled the Irishman to get the money to buy the *Time Piece* and later alleged that Judge Hobart had refused to take Burr alone as a surety.[28] When the *General Advertiser* attempted to prove the seditious behavior of Republicans by quoting Congressman Edward Livingston's letters to Burk, the paper cited what it thought was Livingston's praise for the "man whose dedicatory incense having tickled the nostrils of a certain Colonel [Burr], is in return, by him, patronized and supported."[29] After Burk and Smith had severed their partnership following Smith's charge that the Irishman had been guilty of excessive criticism, the paper collapsed, silenced by the Federalist weapon. Recognizing the probable consequences of a trial, Burk turned to Burr to expedite his proposition.

He wanted the Colonel to arrange for an agreement that would permit the case to be dismissed in exchange for his own voluntary departure from the country. In December, Burr relayed this to Harison, who secured the consent of President Adams. But Burk, who had escaped from Ireland disguised as a woman, remained in the United States under an alias and moved to Petersburg, Virginia, while awaiting the expiration of the Alien and Sedition Acts. He was never tried. Thus ended Burr's effort for an individual victim; but the incident merely heralded his more significant fight against a law that harassed, fined, and imprisoned only Republican editors and also jailed such notables as Vermont Congressman Matthew Lyon and a radical from England, Thomas Cooper. Altogether, ten anti-Federalists were jailed and fined. "This disease of the imagination will pass over," wrote Thomas Jefferson, "because the patients are essentially republican."[30]

The Republican medication was Jefferson's own Kentucky Resolutions and Madison's counterpart that came from the Virginia legislature. Both denied the right of the federal government to impose such measures. As expressed by the Virginia Resolutions of 1798, it was "a power not delegated by the Constitution, but, on the contrary, expressly and positively forbidden by one of the amendments thereto,—a power which more than any other, ought to produce universal alarm, freely examining public characters and measures, and free communication among the people thereon, which has ever been justly deemed the only effectual guardian of every other right." They thus charged the Federalists with an unconstitutional assumption of power. Alexander Hamilton, who had expressed misgivings about the laws, nevertheless reacted by viewing the resolutions as "an attempt to change the government," and he told Jonathan Dayton that opposition had grown bolder and "more open and more enterprising in its projects" than ever before.[31]

Others took an even more extreme position, trying to limit all elective federal office-holding to native-born Americans. Before 1798 had ended, the Massachusetts Resolutions called for a constitutional amendment to this effect, and other states endorsed that view.

Burr fought the Massachusetts Resolutions and the Alien and Sedition Acts. In January of 1799, as an assemblyman from a seaport becoming crowded with immigrants—targets of the Federalist measures—Burr stated that "natives have been exclusively the subjects of corruption."[32] He repeated this statement when the Resolutions came before the Assembly after their endorsement by the Senate. The *Commercial Advertiser* noted that Burr's charge that the amendment was "retrospective, and therefore unconstitutional" had really begun his political career.[33] But no legitimate distinction can be made between this attitude, which successfully turned back the proposed endorsement, and his opposition to the Alien and Sedition Acts through efforts to endorse the Virginia and Kentucky Resolutions. This was despite his feeling that, "in the honest love of liberty, [they] had gone A LITTLE TOO FAR."[34]

He was behind every attempt to win legislative approval for Jefferson's position. He voted in behalf of a motion which stated that the "alien and sedition laws are unconstitutional, impolitic and contrary to the dearest interests of freemen, and consequently that they will without the solicitation of this House immediately repeal the same." But it failed to carry, the vote being fifty-eight to thirty-four. Along with John Bartow Prevost, Burr then backed John Swartwout's motion to deny to the Constitution the authority to permit the passage of such legislation. Again, the Federalist majority overcame the challenge, this time by a fifty-two to forty-one vote. When Swartwout subsequently tried to have the Alien Act labeled unconstitutional by the Assembly, Burr and his followers were defeated by a larger margin. Burr himself had failed, during the course of the same day, to win approval for a statement reserving the right for citizens of the state "to express their opinions respecting any act of the Congress of the United States or any other public measure." The day was a complete disaster for the Republicans, whose position anticipated by nearly a century a Supreme Court decision terming the Sedition Act unconstitutional, as the Federalist majority finally adopted the view of Chenango County Assemblyman Nathaniel King that it was "unwarrantable" for the state legislatures to assume the authority to declare acts of Congress unconstitutional.[35]

Politically, however, it had not been a total loss. Burr had placed himself and Republican followers squarely against positions that were repugnant to the Irish and other new Americans who were swelling his city's population, sending the total number over sixty-five thousand by 1800, or nearly double the figure of just one decade earlier. Burr's success in winning a leverage of political support from the newcomers, whose allegiance was increasingly to the leaders of the Democratic-Republican Party, was undoubtedly the rationale for the *Commercial Advertiser's* observation about the launching of his "political career." But their support could not be fully realized without the repeal of the Naturalization Act and a much greater liberalization of the state's suffrage restrictions.

The shocking Federalist laws had just begun to be felt in the City of New York, with Burk's *Time Piece* already doomed to total silence, and progress was being made in the construction of fortifications to defend the port from the feared war, when the dreaded pestilence of late summer returned with its deadly fever in 1798. Fortunately for Burr and Theodosia, they had left the city on August 2 for a trip that took them throughout the state as far west as Niagara Falls and they did not return until November 7, but it was an epidemic that played a significant role in Burr's career. Those who remained in town as yellow fever struck contributed to a constantly mounting list of victims, which included the much respected Republican merchant Melancton Smith, who became the first fatality when the fever appeared in July. On the seventeenth of August, Hugh Gaine recorded the death of seven persons.[36]

After felling Smith, the fever attacked several of his neighbors; then, almost simultaneously, it appeared at Burling Slip on the East River. Inland, at Ryder's Alley, which still follows its L-shaped course from Gold to Fulton streets and which, in 1798, contained the homes of some of the "most respectable citizens," the fever struck at every residence. Almost every household there lost one or more people.[37] By the twenty-fifth of August, the daily death rate had reached ten, so the Common Council ordered the placement of the public hearse at the disposal of the commissioners of health.[38] As during Philadelphia's horrible epidemic of 1793 and New York's of 1795, the cry "Bring out your dead! Bring out your dead!" was a familiar appeal. That summer, Philadelphia, Boston, and several other towns were also affected.

By late August, the fever was the only concern of New Yorkers, and the ordinary routines of city life had been changed. The Common Council granted special permission enabling butchers to sell meat at their homes rather than defy the sickness from vulnerable stalls. The New York *Spectator* announced that a half-sheet edition of the newspaper would have to suffice for the duration of the epidemic. Almost everybody sought to leave the sick area and flee to the country, although, as in the havoc along Ryder's Alley, this outbreak seemed most severe in some of the more affluent neighborhoods.

By the end of the month, people were hurrying to get away, determined to remain in safety until the first frost. The average daily death rate of forty-five during September included fifty-eight on one day and hastened the exodus. Business stagnated. Merchants moved to temporary makeshift country locations to fulfill the needs of displaced citizens. Only along Broadway and the upper parts of the town was there commercial activity. There were probably over two thousand deaths during the outbreak.[39]

Yellow fever seemed to envelop its victims in a "general languor and heaviness," almost like a stupor, according to the careful observations of Dr. Alexander Hosack. Its onset was marked by "a sense of cold and shivering—acute pain in the head, especially above the eyes," he had written in 1797. With back pains that frequently extended down the extremities, "the skin was hot, dry, and much flushed," and the eyes were covered with water. A rapid pulse, nausea, vomiting, and diarrhea also signaled an infection. As the fever raged, the urine became turbid or yellow, "as if tinged with bile."[40] How to counter the disease was a complete mystery.[41]

The physicians grasped frantically for new cures. Hundreds of victims were reportedly relieved with castor oil and sweating teas. Bleeding the patients no longer seemed efficacious. Nearly every doctor contracted the fever; the Mayor's brother was among those who died. Others finally fled to the country.

"Our city is in the deepest mourning!" wrote Robert Troup to Ambassador Rufus King on October 2. "At least two thirds of our fellow citizens are now in the country. We have lost many, very many valuable men." And then, after estimating that over fourteen hundred had died, he added a hopeful note: "The weather is now getting cool and the fever is consequently beginning to abate. Nothing but frost—and a severe frost too—will restore us to our usual health."[42]

They knew what would end the pestilence. They recognized its symptoms. But the cause remained unknown. Ignoring the presence of mosquitoes as just another phenomenon of the season, they could agree with Dr. Richard Bayley's condemnation of the collections of putrid water. Troup himself recalled that a heat wave had been accompanied by "the longest shower ever remembered here; and this by filling cellars, choking drains, &c. put our whole mass of filth into a state of violent fermentation." Foul vapors came from the lingering pools of water, and the aroma had combined with the stench from "a large quantity of beef stored in different places in the neighborhood of Burling Slip, and which bad packing and extreme heat rendered putrid."[43] The poor drinking water was also blamed, pointing once more to the intolerable absence of a city water system.

While the epidemic was still at its height, the *Commercial Advertiser* carried a denunciation of the city's failure to provide a supply of healthful water:

> The Collect behind the Tea-water Pump is a shocking hole, where all impure things center together and engender the worst of unwholesome productions; foul with excrement, frogspawn, and reptiles, that delicate pump is supplied. The water has grown worse manifestly within a few years. It is time to look out for some other supply and discontinue the use of a water growing less and less wholesome every day. . . . Take the matter into consideration, and resolve every man for himself, to leave no stone unturned to have this grand object of watering carried thro.[44]

The correspondent concluded by predicting annual plagues until a solution appeared. Frequent return of the fever seemed to support his position; and the lethargic response to the obvious need justified his strong words. The solution had, after all, been delayed for many years.

Attempts had predated the Revolutionary War. When the English occupied the city in 1776, the project for a water works system that had been started by Christopher Colles was abandoned. The end of foreign rule brought new proposals before the Common Council, while individuals like Chancellor Livingston had attempted to place such endeavors in private hands. Second thoughts about the rejection of such plans in favor of a municipal system, however, delayed action. Private enterprise was commonly regarded as the wrong approach to the project. Yet the inability or unwillingness of the city to finance its own system deferred action, even while several other proposals were received.

An interested party was Dr. Joseph Browne. Burr's brother-in-law had submitted a plan, in response to solicitations by the Common Council, in 1796. After continued inaction, and only one month before the start of the 1798 epidemic, it was Browne, a physician, scientist, and engineer, who presented a paper entitled "Memoir of the Utility and Means of Furnishing the City with Water From the River Bronx." Browne's plan called for tapping the waters of the Bronx River by constructing dams across both that stream and the Harlem River. From there, a series of pumps and pipes would be used to divert a flow into a reservoir at a high point on the hilly northern part of Manhattan Island. By stressing his belief in the association of the prevailing pathetic water situation and the recurrences of yellow fever, Browne's point was timely. However, his memoir had called for the capitalization of two hundred thousand dollars for construction and private operation of the system. But however tardy the Council had been in activating a municipal company, it was not prepared to concede that it should not be a public project.[45]

A special committee report to the Council in December, after the epidemic, rejected the idea of private ownership. It stated that only the "Prospect of considerable Gain," which would be at the city's expense, would interest investors.[46] Browne's engineering plans, however, were regarded "with some few variations, the most eligible that can be adopted."[47] When the Joint Health Committee Report reached the Council in January, the drainage of stagnant water was an important recommendation; and the report urged "a plentiful supply of fresh water as one of the most powerful, and earnestly recommend that some plan for its introduction into this city, be carried into execution as soon as possible."[48]

None of these papers, including Browne's, carried Burr's name. His three-month absence had occurred between the presentation of Browne's memoir and the December committee reply. But there is no doubt that the physician's interest, while genuine and not merely expedient, was also the enterprise of brother-in-law Burr. His efforts of the subsequent months to overcome the Council's opposition to a private company testified to Burr's involvement. In all the aforementioned transactions, the Assemblyman had been an interested party; now his open intervention was necessary to achieve the real objective.

Doubts about several parts of Browne's paper were heard. Many thought that his cost estimate was unrealistically low. There were also differences over the proposed method for conveying the water, and whether or not the Bronx River was the best source. Most people pointed to the readily available water in the Collect, a spring-fed pond located in the then upper part of the city. They insisted that it could be cleansed of the dead animals and other putrid garbage and thus be made wholesome and pure.

To survey the Bronx River and deliver an expert's report, the Council hired William Weston, an English engineer. Having come to the United States to work on canals in Pennsylvania and New York, Weston was no stranger to Philip Schuyler of the Western Inland Lock Navigation Company; so before the Englishman arrived in the city Schuyler introduced him to Hamilton, who was in Albany. Hamilton's subsequent estimate that the project would cost one million dollars, rather than Browne's much lower amount, resulted from this conference.

But Weston's recommendations were close to Browne's. He rejected the use of the Collect, citing the experiences of European cities and predicting that growth of the city would spill refuse into the springs and then contaminate the pond even after a thorough cleaning. He called the Bronx River the best source, but urged that a larger number of gallons be set for the city's daily requirement. Modifying Browne's more elaborate plan for conveying the water, he made the rather novel proposal to include a filtration system to purify the water in the reservoir.

The Council, finally ready to begin, agreed to ask the state legislature for the necessary legal authority and all possible financial support for a municipal system. Approval would have wrecked Burr's plans. Fortunately for him, the Council request went to a committee of the thirteen city assemblymen that had been established to report on "the means proper and necessary to be adopted for the prevention of pestilential diseases in this state."[49] And Burr, as the leader of the Republican dominated group, was the chairman.

Burr used his resources to advocate a private company. The Council's insistence on a municipal works was unique for those days, and Burr worked to establish doubt about its ability to control such a large enterprise. Failure of government projects elsewhere, such as on an upstate road construction program, furnished supporting evidence. Finally, on

February 16, the committee granted Burr a ten-day leave to sound out the real attitude of the Common Council toward a private company.[50]

Again, Burr and Hamilton joined efforts. Burr included the influential Federalist in his committee of six important individuals to appeal to the Council in behalf of a private company. The other Federalists were the president of the Chamber of Commerce and the president of the Bank of New York. Republicans in the group, besides Burr, were John Broome, a war hero, prominent merchant, and former Chamber of Commerce president, and Peter H. Wendover, president of the Mechanics Society and later a sachem of Tammany. Hamilton's willingness to join demonstrated his belief in the importance of a water supply company, but most persuasive may have been the inclusion of his brother-in-law, John B. Church. Church had been appointed as a director of the water company that Aaron Burr was now seeking to establish, the Manhattan Company. Burr's reputation for moderation and his social and family background had made it easier for the other Federalists to join.

The committee of six first appeared at Mayor Varick's office on February 22. They told him that doubt about the Council's request for municipal water works powers had made the requested consent "problematical."[51] When the Mayor reported the visit to the Council, he was requested to secure a signature for the committee's memorandum and a detailed accounting of their objections. Burr's triumph was in securing a strong endorsement by signature from Hamilton.

Hamilton wrote on February 26 to inform Varick that he had "no objection to authenticate them by my Signature—and I freely add that the changes in the Plan . . . which they suggest have the full concurrence of my Opinion."[52] Hamilton's memorandum was particularly persuasive with the Federalist majority on the Council. His reputation for financial acuity was secure. He could hardly be ignored when he estimated that the city could only supply a small part of the one million dollars that would be needed. "To raise what may be wanted by taxes to carry out the enterprise with vigour might be found so burthensome of the Citizens as to occasion the operation to languish." He also outlined a proposal for a private company, deviating from Burr's original idea to have the city own one-fifth of its stock by suggesting that it purchase one-third. Burr disliked this plan, which was a way of giving the city tighter control over the private company, but he was pleased when the Council agreed on February 28 to grant the request of his special committee.[53]

Burr was well on his way to success. He had already selected a twelve-member board of directors for his Manhattan Company, which was organized to supply the city with fresh water. All members were of greater financial means than himself. Three Federalists were included, and the nine Republicans were representative of the three major factions within their party—the Clintons, the Livingstons, and the Burrites. The wealth of the Republicans reduced their distinction from Federalists to a matter of political labels. Six were founders of or held shares in the Tontine Coffee House, an exclusive center for the leading merchants. Moreover, it was Burr who had sold a large portion of the company's stock before selecting the directors. Swartwout bought two thousand shares, as did Chancellor Livingston, and De Witt Clinton owned one thousand: enough Federalists purchased lesser amounts to help get the company started. Despite such financing, Burr was careful to maintain Republican control.[54]

He needed to fulfill one more goal before introducing a bill to charter the Manhattan Company as the supplier of water. He sought to prevent the legislature from making duties from auction sales available to the city. Such revenue would enable the Council to purchase one-third of the stock, as Hamilton had suggested; its rejection would also enforce his argument that the Company needed special financial powers because the state could not be expected to support either a municipal or a private water company in New York City.[55]

Finally introduced that March was a bill that proposed a highly favorable charter. Water could be brought in from a wide area around the city and the company would have complete control over rate-setting. Its water would not be required for fire-fighting without a fee, and satisfactory street repairs were not mandated to follow the installation of pipe lines. But the company was committed to "furnish and continue a supply of pure and wholesome water" for all willing purchasers within ten years after its incorporation or face dissolution. Near the end of the bill, there was the section that Burr had maneuvered to get. It read:

> *And be it further enacted,* That it shall and may be lawful for the said company to employ all such surplus capital as may belong or accrue to the said company in the purchase of public or other stock, or in any other monied transactions not inconsistent with the constitution and laws of this state or of the United States, for the sole benefit of the said Company.[56]

James Fairlie of New York presented the bill in behalf of Burr's committee. The Assembly's final passage came shortly after the legislators convened at nine the next morning. A few days later, after overcoming the only opponent within the Council of Revision, Judge John Lansing, who objected to the freedom granted for the use of surplus capital, the Manhattan Company was chartered. Its capitalization was two million dollars. Opponents would soon charge that Burr had rushed the bill through before its contents could be scrutinized. Subscribers to the *Commercial Advertiser* soon read charges that the Manhattan Company bill, "with unheard of privileges and undefined powers," had passed "without its ever being *read in the House*," a travesty despite Burr's claim that its nature was private "and only respected a supply of water for New York, and moved that it be read by its *title only*! Thus was passed an act as important, and I assert more dangerous and ruinous to the City than any that ever passed the Legislature."[57] Robert Troup reported to Rufus King that bringing water to the city was only the "ostensible object" of the Company, "but its real object is to furnish new projects and means for speculation." More specifically, Troup noted the rumors that surplus capital would be used to start a new bank.[58]

The rumors were true. The Bank of Manhattan had been born. Nothing was said about a bank when the directors held their first meeting on April 15; they merely announced an opening sale of subscriptions for the following Monday. Purchasers would be welcome at the Tontine City Tavern on Broadway and be asked to pay $2.50 for each share. On the same day, the Common Council approved the purchase of two thousand shares for the city. Talk about a bank irritated Federalists while attracting their money as a potentially good investment, one that would have been less attractive if bound as a public utility. Robert Troup bought twenty-five shares on the first day. By September, after making a definite decision in May "that so much of the surplus capital of the company as may be deemed necessary, be employed in discounting paper securities, and that . . . an office of discount and deposit be established," the doors were opened for banking at what is now 40 Wall Street.[59]

One may wonder which man surprised Federalists more during that year, President Adams in February with his sudden decision to send William Vans Murray to reopen negotiations with the French—in defiance of his own cabinet and party—or Burr's bank. Banking was subjected to so much political partisanship in those days that the existence of only two banks, the local branch of the Bank of the United States and Hamilton's Bank of New York, both Federalist controlled, had disadvantaged Republicans. Bank policies favored political sympathizers. That financing enterprises, especially for political purposes, was almost impossible when banks were controlled by the opposition had long been understood. It was one reason for the traditional Republican suspicion of banks. Federalists might now blame Burr for securing the charter, but their own financial ambitions had contributed to his success. Burr, who had been considering banking for many years, had taken an important step to prepare his party for a fight to win the election of 1800.

The Manhattan directors were clearly aware of the need to implement a water system to fulfill the requirement of the charter and to refute charges that banking was their only goal. "Socrates" asked in the *Commercial Advertiser*: "Is the Manhattan Company instituted for the purpose of bringing water into the city or of banking and speculation?"[60] From London, Rufus King wanted to know whether the company's objective was "Commercial, political, or religious, tho on recollection of names it is plain it cannot be the last."[61] Browne warned Burr about the difficulties involved in conveying the water to as much as one half of the city as early as the summer and fall, but added his expectation "that enough will be done to satisfy the Public and particularly the Legislature that the Institution is not a speculating Job."[62]

Work began. Wooden pipes were constructed by boring a hole lengthwise through logs, and these were fastened together by fitting the tapered end of one through the widened hole of the next one. Water finally began to flow, despite such problems as sand choking the pumps and impeding the system almost hourly, through the underground pipes that ran for almost a mile below the city streets. So eager was the company to counter the impression that water was not its main interest that some of the directors, including Burr, paid personal visits to the site of pipe installations. Although its ultimate promise was never fulfilled, the project appeared hopeful and the Manhattan stock went up. "The water works of the Manhattan Company go on with great rapidity," reported Troup in December. "I have now a plentiful & constant supply of better water than our tea water by a conductor which brings it into my cellar near the kitchen. The stock of the company is on the rise. The company does a great deal of discounting business—and is gaining ground in public esteem."[63]

But the short run effect damaged Burr and his fellow Republicans at the polls that April. The election took place just four weeks after the charter had been granted. Criticism of his maneuver, coupled with intimations of an illegitimate involvement with the Holland Company, helped the Federalists. Republicans were charged with abandoning their hostility toward banks, which had been the popular attitude, and of employing unscrupulous methods. Federalist literature, circulating just before the election, claimed that banking was indeed the real objective of the Manhattan Company. The New York *Gazette and General Advertiser* charged Burr and his friends with "scandalous duplicity."[64] Their entire ticket from the city, headed by Burr, was defeated by nine hundred votes. For the Federalists, it was the biggest victory since 1796.

CHAPTER XII

Jefferson's Running Mate

OWEVER badly the Republicans and Burr had lost in 1799, and however much it had delayed their attempt to wrest the state from Federalist control, winning in 1800 would more than undo the damage. For 1800 was a presidential election year; and New York State was bound to play a major role in determining the outcome of the electoral vote. In 1796, Adams could not have won without that state's twelve votes, and the alternating fortunes of the two parties made New York's ultimate choice for 1800 more of a toss-up than in any state with similar power.

Burr was ready to lead. With his customary energy and attention to detail, he organized the assault. Shortly after the start of the new year, he made a "flying-trip" to Philadelphia to see Jefferson. His mission was to instill the Vice President with confidence in New York's coming adherence to the Democratic-Republicans and with faith in his own ability to achieve that goal. For, as Burr told him, enough Republicans would be chosen to the state legislature during the annual April elections to insure the party's ability to pick the twelve electors. Their choice would be made at the November session of the legislature. Jefferson, immediately telling Monroe about Burr's visit, reported that the energetic New Yorker had stressed that winning all twelve votes from his state required effective leadership. Otherwise, the Republicans would remain "disjointed, & will lose every question."[1]

Their good fortune could be assured with a gain of three or four Republican seats in the state Senate and, even more important, by electing an entire slate of thirteen Assembly candidates from New York

City. Such office-seekers ran on a joint, county-wide ticket offered by their party; and, although their individual totals varied somewhat during the annual elections, it was becoming normal for them to succeed or fail together. Thus, a Republican or a Federalist victory would actually mean a total difference of twenty-six assemblymen choosing the electors. No wonder Jefferson told Monroe that "all will depend on the city election."[2]

It was also clear that Jefferson would be the Republican presidential candidate, which really meant that the Vice President would get one of the two votes cast by each Republican elector. Accordingly, Burr's close friend, Matthew L. Davis, wrote to Albert Gallatin: "I believe it is pretty generally understood that Mr. Jefferson is contemplated for President."[3]

A victory in New York could make Jefferson the President. If Burr's visit had been prompted by a desire to win Jefferson's confidence, it should not be assumed that it was deceptively optimistic, for the outlook in New York had improved. It had become easier to depict Federalists as sinister plotters who were trying to twist their Constitution into a weapon for absolute rule or to return the Atlantic's western shores to George III. The aristocrats had, after all, been unyielding when John Swartwout had risen in the Assembly and, in the name of democracy, had urged a subdivision of the state's four senatorial districts, a maneuver that would have created twelve sections from which to choose electors.[4] But the Federalists, to no one's surprise, were not ready to yield any portion of their electoral votes and fought against the reform —just like "royalists." In Virginia, where the Federalists were then in the minority, *they* were the ones to advance a district election.

Another boost to Republican hopes in New York stemmed from the fiasco surrounding Jedediah Peck. Peck was a curious man. A semi-literate itinerant surveyor, religious fanatic, farmer, and, later in his career, a pioneer of New York's system of free public education, Peck was both an assemblyman and a Court of Common Pleas judge from Cooperstown in Otsego County. His political identification had been as a Federalist. But he had strayed from his party to support Burrite Swartwout's electoral vote reform in February of 1799. For this, Peck soon found himself both stripped of his judgeship and opposed for re-election by William Cooper and the Otsego Federalists. But his popular appeal was enough to re-elect him in April of 1799 for still another year.

When the Federalist majority in Congress enacted the Alien and Sedition Acts that summer, Peck became the outstanding example of dissent within his own party. In Otsego County, he boldly circulated a petition of protest. For his action, William Cooper, Cooperstown's Federalist Congressman and the father of the novelist, secured Peck's arrest.[5] The prisoner was then removed from the lovely little village on the shore of Otsego Lake and taken to New York to be tried for sedition.

It was the best publicity the anti-Federalists could have had. Peck's trip was a triumphant journey, a dramatization of the pernicious enforcement of the Alien and Sedition Acts. Republicans charged that he had been "taken from his bed at midnight, manacled, and dragged from his home," all because of his courageous petition.[6] Jabez Hammond, a contemporary politician and historian, observed that:

> A hundred missionaries in the cause of democracy, stationed between New-York and Cooperstown, could not have done so much for the republican cause as this journey of Judge Peck. . . . It was nothing less than the public exhibition of a suffering martyr for the freedom of speech and the press, and the right of petitioning, to the view of the citizens of the various places through which the marshal travelled with his prisoner.[7]

But the Federalists soon realized their blunder and dropped the trial at the last moment. Burr then shrewdly sought a firm identification of Peck with his Republican Party. What better way to keep the western counties from voting for Federalists? The next politically inspired attempt to force a change in the state's method of choosing electors, in April of 1800, was led by Burr's new agent, Jedediah Peck. Again, it was blocked.[8]

Other events continued to brighten their prospects. With the Peck fiasco and the harassment of anti-Administration printers in and near the city, the Alien and Sedition Acts had provided an effective issue. So had property taxes and the mobilization of a peacetime army. Those who labeled the French crisis as a Federalist conspiracy were freer to do so after Adams had startled his own party by moving to negotiate a treaty with the French. This act provoked anguished protests from the President's own cabinet, and the subsequent dispatch of a new three-man commission to end the undeclared war exposed the Hamiltonians to criticism for having tried to pervert the Constitution. The battle that raged in the partisan newspapers was over which party could be entrusted with the nation's liberties—the "aristocrats" and the "monarchists" who had fathered and implemented the Constitution, or the Republican "mobocracy" that included so many of its earlier opponents.

Political developments were continuous, as states held elections at different times, but the increasing partisanship was somewhat subdued with the arrival from Mt. Vernon that December of the news that

General Washington had died. Republicans and Federalists eulogized the great man. Even Tammany held a procession to honor the first President, and the city participated in the national mourning. On January 8, the Park Theatre dedicated its program to his memory, and the subsequent anniversary of his birthday became a day of tribute. But the history of their personal relations obviated any feeling of deep sorrow from Burr. Troup observed that Burr avoided the ceremonies and public displays.[9]

That winter was a busy one for Burr. The trial of one Levi Weeks, who was charged with the murder of a prostitute named Gulielma Sands, whose body had turned up in a Manhattan Company well, consumed a lot of time. With Hamilton as his partner, Burr won Weeks' freedom. But to handle Hamilton, politically, Burr laid careful plans. Jefferson had noted that, "we may say that if the *city* election of NYork is in favor of the Republican ticket, the issue will be republican."[10] And he depended upon Burr to justify the optimism. Burr, who had already prepared his ticket, was withholding its release until the Federalists had first published theirs.[11]

The Federalists had trouble choosing their candidates. Of the thirteen men who had been elected on their 1799 ticket, only Nicholas Evertson and John Bogert agreed to run again. Matthew L. Davis, revealing to Gallatin the presence of Republican spies at the Federalist meeting, told how Hamilton's difficulties had been aggravated by their rejection of the honor.[12] Responsible for this attitude was their opposition to Hamilton's plan to win the presidency for Charles Pinckney instead of for John Adams.[13] Not surprisingly, what resulted was a mediocre ticket. Davis lampooned their obscurity by referring to Bogert merely as a "baker," while he listed Gabriel Furman as "nothing," John Croleus as a "potter," Isaac Burr as a "grocer," James Tyler as a "shoemaker," and Abraham Russel as a "mason."[14] Evertson, one of the two incumbents, was not a "party regular." Not only had he been associated with both parties from time to time, but he had also served as Grand Sachem of Tammany in 1797.[15] Davis had supplied Albert Gallatin with an accurate estimation of the ticket, which had loyalty to Hamilton as its only strength.

Burr watched and waited patiently. Behind him were the financial resources of the Manhattan Company. As "Philander" put it, "A necessary competition has annihilated the despotism of banking monopoly. This happy circumstance has strengthened the republican interest, at the expense of their opponents."[16] He also had a ticket that was much more than a match for Hamilton's collection. Not only did it contain more celebrated names, but its design was the unification of all leading Republican interests. Added to this feature was its inclusion of known Revolutionary War heroes, men with enough voter popularity.

Half a century later, a Tammanyite participant in much of the planning recalled that Burr first began by writing down eleven names, including his own. But the thought that lingering resentment over the Manhattan Company affair would draw Federalist fire and jeopardize any ticket with Burr's name changed his mind. With the aid of Peter Townsend of Chester, Burr became a candidate from Orange County.[17] There was no residency requirement for assemblymen, and Orange was miles away from the furor over the new bank.

But the names that remained on the list were substantial. At its head was none other than George Clinton. Now retired and over the age of sixty, the former governor nevertheless represented a powerful interest among the state's Republicans. In addition, there were Brockholst Livingston and General Horatio Gates. When all three had refused to run, a committee of four men, including Burr and Davis, was organized to apply more pressure.

Livingston and Gates were relatively easy to persuade. First, Livingston warned that some candidates would refuse to serve. But Burr, determined to affix this important family name to his edifice, replied, "Mr. Livingston, you and I can agree at one: I will agree to serve my country on this occasion, and I am sure that you will not refuse." And Livingston answered: "No; if the rest will serve."[18] With Gates, a personal friend, Burr used the "most mild and persuasive language," and the General then made his acceptance contingent upon Clinton's candidacy.[19]

The key man was rather weary. Uppermost in his mind was the very recent death of his wife. A peaceful rural life in Ulster County was most inviting, and supporting Jefferson did not appeal to the volatile warrior.

The committee then besieged Clinton. Three times they tried; the third day they convened at Burr's house, where Clinton met the group by appointment. He told them that if Burr were the presidential candidate instead of Jefferson, he would have no hesitation. But he could never endorse Jefferson. Nevertheless, he finally consented to have his name placed on the ticket as one of the thirteen Republican assembly candidates from the city. But he reserved "to himself the right [which he subsequently exercised] of stating in conversation that his name was used without his authority or permission."[20] And he vowed to avoid active campaigning, as that might seem like support for Jefferson.[21]

Burr, then, had a ticket that dwarfed Hamilton's. He had not only
united the major factions of his party but had secured attractive names.
Livingston, Clinton, and Gates were well known figures, but Burr was
able to add other notables. Samuel Osgood was the holder of a good war
record and had also served in Washington's original cabinet. Henry
Rutgers owned a good portion of the city's land and his Revolutionary
War days had been succeeded by membership in the state legislature.
Also included were John Broome, the faithful Swartwout, and Philip
Arcularius, a well-known lawyer with experience as a member of the
Common Council. Only after Hamilton had released the Federalist
names did Burr reveal his list, which was then confirmed by a nominat-
ing caucus. This procedure was carefully planned by Burr:

> As soon as the room begins to fill up, I will nominate Daniel Smith
> as chairman, and put the question quickly. Daniel being in the chair,
> you must nominate one member, I will nominate one . . . and other
> . . . and, in this way, we will get them nominated. We must then
> have some inspiring speeches, close the meeting, and retire. We
> must then have a caucus and invite some of our most active and
> patriotic Democrats, both young and old, appoint meetings in the
> different wards, select speakers to address each, and keep up frequent
> meetings at Tammany Hall until the election.[22]

Thus, Tammany was put to work, functioning as a smooth, modern
political machine under the guidance of nonmember Burr. "If we carry
this election," Davis wrote to Gallatin, "it may be ascribed principally
to Colonel Burr's management and perseverence."[23] Meetings were held
at Tammany Hall, with speeches about the importance of the election.
Tammany subdivided the city into small, workable districts. Each was
supervised by a special committee that was directed to draw up lists of
voting inclinations of each resident. Ward meetings then evaluated their
reports and planned further strategy.[24] A finance committee prepared a
list of wealthy Republicans to determine which people would contribute money and which would prefer to work rather than part with
some of their assets. It was a task that required the recording of personal
idiosyncrasies to obtain the maximum advantage from each man and an
estimate of what would be required to get him to vote. Davis has told
how after one wealthy but "parsimonious" individual had been assessed
for one hundred dollars, Burr knowingly discounted the possibility of
his further assistance. When a rather wealthy but lazy gentleman was
assessed one hundred dollars, Burr directed that the amount be doubled
and that no labor should be expected. "He will pay you the two hundred

dollars and thank you for letting him off so easy," Davis recalled Burr as having said, adding *"that the knowledge and use of men consisted in placing each in his appropriate position."*[25]

For additional financing, the role of the Manhattan Company cannot be ignored. Although little direct evidence is available, even to justify the stories that its money helped to purchase land to qualify additional Republicans as voters, its existence was a factor.[26] Davis, for example, expressed relief that the bank would not be an election issue, but assumed that "the Manhattan Company will in all probability operate much in our favor."[27]

The partisan press treated the coming election as a showdown between alien philosophies, as though losing would surrender American institutions to a monstrous force designing the subversion of the Constitution and, hence, whatever safeguards remained. The Federalist *Daily Advertiser*, sounding the alarm, warned of the possible sacrifice of all patriotic plans "at the altar of Jefferson's *illuminated* philosophy." A Jacobin victory would ruin merchant shipping and destroy the navy. "The music of the hammer along our wharves and the hum of busy industry will not be heard," was the prediction, while the "temple of the most High will be profaned by the impious orgies of the Goddess of Reason, personated as in France by some common prostitute."[29] Apprehensive, once the polls had opened on the twenty-ninth of April, the Republican *American-Citizen* warned that their party was opposed by the "weight of property" and that the result was "doubtful on the side of liberty."[29]

The election was a total effort for Burr. For two months, he had kept open house at his own home. Refreshments were available on the table, and there were extra mattresses for the committees that worked endlessly. There, they received reports from the network of subcommittees. When the polls opened, Burr went from ward to ward, visiting each polling place. Meeting Hamilton, who appeared on horseback, Burr treated the crowds to their debates. On May 1, Burr remained at the seventh ward, the most populous and crucial, for ten hours. John Dawson informed Monroe that to "his [Burr's] exertions we owe much —he attended the place of voting within the city for 24 hours, without sleeping or eating."[30] The seventh ward, which Burr regarded as the key to the election, had the most voters. But after Republican successes there in 1797 and 1798, fifty-seven percent of its residents, largely workers with a sprinkling of wealthier country residents along its northern fringes, had supported the Federalists.

The polls closed on the evening of May 1, and the results were known by the next night. Each Republican had won by an average plurality of

450 votes. Even the Republican congressional candidate, Dr. Samuel L. Mitchill, had been elected, and the victorious tide had carried along three state senate candidates from the city and surrounding counties, which comprised the Southern District.[31] Only the requirement that limited senatorial and gubernatorial votes to the largest property-holders kept the Republicans from carrying the city proper for these offices as well. And Burr was elected to represent Orange County in the Assembly.

The city victory had been a great triumph. Burr's leadership was undisputed. He had marshaled all the fragments of the party, presented the voters with attractive candidates, and masterminded a campaign that was modern in concept, showing the way for future urban politicians. Perhaps he had learned something from John Beckley's conduct of the Pennsylvania elections of 1796, but he had also added unmistakable touches of his own. Shrewd use of people and skill at organization were obvious assets. Even the fact that his party's victory had been state-wide, giving them a majority in the legislature without counting the city, had been at least partly attributable to Burr's management. Jedediah Peck, who had been embraced by Burr after his arrest, led all other candidates to win re-election from Otsego County. As a result, the Assembly contained an anti-Administration majority of sixty-four to thirty-nine, and the Federalist majority of six in the Senate could not keep New York from delivering twelve votes to Jefferson in November.

"The Victory is complete," the exuberant Burr wrote to Jefferson, "and the manner of it highly honorable."[32] Davis notified Gallatin that, "The management and industry of Colonel Burr has effected all that the friends of civil liberty could possibly desire."[33] And Hamilton informed Governor Jay that even the returns from Long Island and Westchester were depressing for Federalists.[34] But Hamilton had not given up.

Ready to use any means to stop Burr, he suggested a drastic measure to Governor Jay. For it was a crisis that needed extraordinary methods, and it would be foolish to sacrifice the "interests of society by a strict adherence to ordinary rules," he wrote. He then urged Jay to convene the lame-duck Federalist-controlled legislature to pass a law removing the election of electors from the Assembly and Senate and placing the choice in the hands of the people by districts. That would almost surely cut into the twelve electors about to be selected by the new Republican majority in November, and it was reminiscent of the motion Burr and Peck had advocated when they had represented the minority. But such a move after the April elections, for immediate implementation, was like changing the rules in mid-game to benefit one side. Jay, fortunately, found it distasteful and buried Hamilton's suggestion with the endorsement: "proposing a measure for party purposes, which I think it would not become me to support."[35]

Burr's supporters could now give their full attention to influencing the party's choice of a vice-presidential candidate; and their own preference was certainly not surprising. Burr had been disappointed twice before. He was now ready. Who had done more to insure victory? How logical and proper it would also be for the Virginian at the head of his party to have a Northerner with him for the second highest office! Davis lost no time in raising the point with Gallatin, citing the general expectation that New York would furnish the candidate. And then it could only be Chancellor Livingston, George Clinton, or Burr.

Davis pointed out the limitations of the first two men. He cited doubts about Livingston's decisiveness, particularly carping at the "timidity" of his opposition to Jay's Treaty, as well as general suspicions about the republicanism of the Livingston family. As for Clinton, wrote Davis, he "grows old and infirm," and had even been reluctant as an Assembly candidate. The Tammanyite, newspaper editor, and friend of Burr then reached his inevitable conclusion: "Colonel Burr is therefore the most eligible character," he stated. "If he is elected to the office of V. P., it would awaken so much of the zeal and pride of our friends in this State as to secure us a Republican governor at the next election." His rejection, however, would "chagrin and disappoint" the organization. "I feel very anxious," he added.[36]

That Burr wanted the designation is clear. This time little would be left to chance, as he recalled former obstacles. "Burr says he has no confidence in the Virginians," Maria Gallatin informed her husband; "they once deceived him, and they are not to be trusted." The day before his wife's words were written, Gallatin himself had wondered about the choice between Clinton and Burr. He had already delegated to his father-in-law, Commodore Nicholson, the task of sounding out "the wishes of the New York Republicans."[37]

Nicholson made his first stop at the home of George Clinton. The former governor was reluctant. He emphasized the years of past devotion to public service and pointed out that his wife's death had left him with family responsibilities that demanded attention. He also feared that, having been elected as an Assemblyman with the power to vote for twelve electors, his own candidacy for the vice presidency would be most impolitic. There were also other candidates, like Livingston and Burr, who might do as well or even better. After listening patiently, Nicholson then managed to win Clinton's reluctant consent by pointing out that the success of the Republican cause was dependent upon the presence of his name. Once elected, he could even resign if necessary. "After much Conversation on the subject," Clinton later recalled, "I finally agreed that in answering Mr. Gallatin's letter he might mention that tho I was averse to ingage in public Life yet rather than that any danger should occur to the Ellection of President (which I could not however believe would be the case) I would so far consent as that my Name might be used without any contradiction on my part."[38] Nicholson then left, drafted his reply to Gallatin, and returned the next day to show it to Clinton. The old politician gave it his approval, and then Nicholson departed.

He went to Burr's residence. Finding Burr home alone, he exhibited Gallatin's letter and the reply about to be sent to Philadelphia. Burr's agitation was obvious. The Colonel talked about his mistreatment by the Southerners and stated that he would be wiser to attempt the "certainty of being elected" governor rather than risk the chance by trying for the vice presidency. His words had convinced neither himself nor Nicholson. Burr then left the room.

The Commodore was then confronted by Swartwout and Davis, who were shown the letters and told what had happened. "One of them declared with a determined voice that Col. Burr should accept and that he was obliged to do so upon principles which he had urged at the late election" that called for the subordination of all personal considerations for the good of the party, Nicholson stated less than four years later. Swartwout and Davis then disappeared and returned with Burr. After further conversation, "Col. Burr with apparent reluctance consented."[39] Nicholson then changed his letter in favor of Burr "as the most suitable person and perhaps the only man," stated that Clinton had declined, and then won final approval from Burr. When informed about the switch, Clinton voiced his relief at having been released.[40]

The Philadelphia meeting was a unanimous endorsement of Burr for second place.[41] It was to be his third and easily his most serious effort to reach that high office. Gambling on winning, he thus set aside gubernatorial ambitions.

Burr spent the early part of that summer of 1800 at home with Theodosia. As it turned out, there would be no more such summers, for she had met a gentleman from South Carolina, a member of one of its wealthiest and most influential planter families. His father was the largest slave-holder in the state and had been a personal and political friend of Jefferson; and so his son, Joseph Alston, was a good Republican. Now a young man of twenty-one, a member of the South Carolina bar and a political novice, he had been introduced to Theodosia during a northern visit. As the year progressed, Burr had little doubt that his daughter was in love with the young man, who would soon remove the lady of Burr's household.

For the late summer, or the "fever months," Burr planned a visit to New England, particularly Rhode Island, where he hoped to get an assessment from Governor Arthur Fenner, a Republican. But young Alston was to precede Burr, so the Colonel gave him a letter of introduction to Dr. William Eustis; but first he wrote the following:

> Joseph Alston, a young man of very respectable family & fortune from S. Carolina will hand you a letter from me (of mere introduction). . . . I beg your particular attention to him—but more—I beg you to analyze and anatomize him soul & heart & body, so that you may answer me all questions which I may put to you on that head when we shall meet in Providence—Mr. A. will probably attend you to Providence for I have told him that I should expect to meet you there— . . .
> P. S.: Mr. A *is republican.*[42]

Even before Burr had left, Hamilton was warning Federalists about him. He wrote to James Bayard, Delaware's only Congressman, that Burr "is intriguing with all his might in New Jersey, Rhode Island, and Vermont," attempting to consolidate anti-Federalist support in the same region of his 1796 fall campaign. His election, wrote Hamilton, would bring an attempt "to reform the Government *a la Bonaparte*. He is as unprincipled and dangerous a man as any country can boast—as true a Catiline as ever met in midnight conclave."[43] But Hamilton was dismayed to find other Federalists regarding the elevation of Burr instead of Jefferson as a possible mitigation of the impending disaster that would be brought by the defeat of Adams. George Cabot of Massachusetts felt that Burr's moderation would be more palatable than Jefferson's "Jacobinism," for while power and property could satisfy Burr, the Virginian "must see the roots of our society pulled up and a new course of cultivation substituted."[44] Jefferson could thus be defeated by enough Federalist electors voting for Burr.

Burr's New England trip was prompted by the need to acquire enough electoral support to secure himself against defections elsewhere, which could place either Adams or Pinckney as the Vice President. While those Northern states seemed clearly Federalist, Hamilton himself had recognized that uncertainties in Rhode Island might enable Governor Fenner to "promote the interest of Jefferson."[45] When Burr saw Fenner in Providence, the Governor told him of his plan to run as an elector; therefore, he might be able to vote for Jefferson and Adams.

That would place the former in the President's office and elect Burr as the next vice president. The plan promised to avoid what many soon began to fear was a real possibility—a tie between the two Republicans. Hamilton's notions of possible Republican success in Rhode Island must have resulted from the respect for Governor Fenner's ability to be chosen as an elector in what was a predominantly Federalist state. So Burr was hopeful of securing the additional support for Jefferson without dropping anticipated strength in other states, and safeguard himself while protecting Jefferson's victory. On his return to New York, he informed Chancellor Livingston that, "In R. Island, where Electors are to be chosen by the people, a Jefferson ticket is formed and will at least receive respectable support."[46] Two weeks later, he added that it was a "moral certainty that Jefferson will have all the votes of Rhode Island."[47] He later repeated that as a distinct possibility in letters to John Taylor of Virginia and to his uncle, Pierpont Edwards.[48] It is little wonder, then, that on August 6 Hamilton again stated the possibility of Burr's success with Governor Fenner.[49]

With such hopes, it is not surprising that Burr should have exerted efforts to keep the Southerners from casting their second ballot for some one else, as they had four years earlier. He then utilized the services of young Alston, who was en route home to South Carolina, to give Madison a letter from David Gelston, the New York political friend of Burr. The letter stressed the strong assurances that Rhode Island would give the Republicans three votes. "We depend on the integrity of Virginia & the southern states as we shall be faithful & honest in New York," it said, quite pointedly.[50] Burr sent his own letter to Madison on the following day, and repeated the probable good news from Rhode Island.[51] Madison, accepting these assurances, asked Monroe to guard against "a division of the Republican votes."[52] With Alston, whom he described as "intelligent, sound in his principles, and polished in his manners," Madison passed the good news on to Jefferson. Alston reached the Vice President with not only Madison's letter but with a letter of introduction from Burr.

It all seemed to be going smoothly. That October, Burr had exposed Hamilton's maneuver to place Pinckney in Adams' place at the head of the Federalist ticket. Hamilton had attempted to influence the South Carolina vote by circulating a pamphlet called *A Letter From Alexander Hamilton, Concerning the Public Conduct and Character of John Adams*. Somehow, by means not clear, Burr secured a copy of this polemic and promoted an unauthorized publication of extracts. This forced Hamilton to reveal the entire document and ignited a bitter dispute among the Federalists.[53] Burr had succeeded in driving a wedge into the defensive opponents by publicizing their desire to tamper with the electoral machinery. Now, in late 1800, as they waited for the reports from the various states, the possibility of a tie began to grow. Realizing this, Madison assured Monroe that Jefferson would win even in the event of a tie because of the support he would get in the House of Representatives. Madison had been visited by George William Erving, a wealthy Bostonian, who had gone south with warnings that "Mr. Jefferson's election ought to be secured against accident," which might create another winner. For some reason, Erving failed to discuss the matter with Madison and so the Virginian, with Burr's assurances in mind, remained confident.[54]

Jefferson was less sanguine. He noted that the Republicans had done poorly in the Charleston city elections, losing eleven out of fifteen places, cited the uncertainties caused by "local & personal interests and prejudices," and cast doubt on the validity of Governor Fenner's assurances.[55] And the returns were spotty. The Charleston weakness was in contrast to successes in New York, where the legislature met on November 6 and, predictably, chose twelve Republican electors. In Virginia, the town of Frederick gave the anti-Federalists a three to one victory. But Pennsylvania looked bad and Rhode Island was uncertain, at best. Jefferson's fears were real.

So were Burr's. Only the day before the Virginia electors had voted, Madison received Gelston's latest effort to head off a possible move by the Virginians to ignore the assurances about Rhode Island. To protect Jefferson's lead over Burr, the New Yorkers had heard, there was a renewed possibility that Virginia would deprive Burr of one or two votes. "I am not willing to believe it possible that such measures can be contemplated," he wrote, adding that "integrity and honour we rely upon in Virginia." And then, this time without mentioning any specific names, he wrote, "We are well aware from good information that three States, two at least, will give Mr. J. 3 or more votes, more than Mr. B. will have."[56] It was this statement that made any further reduction from Burr's column seem too risky and, consequently, solidified all of Virginia's votes for Jefferson and Burr. Madison later added the following to Gelston's letter: "A confidence that this would be the case induced Virginia to give an unanimous tho reluctant vote for B. as well as J."[57] Twenty-three years later, Madison recalled that Gelston had sent a false assurance "that the votes of another [state] would be different from what they proved to be."[58]

Fading confidence in the Rhode Island outcome had indeed induced the Burrites to fire blank ammunition in a desperate effort to return the same protection. Gelston's apprehension had been triggered by word of different calculations of the probable Rhode Island vote. His most recent letter contrasted with his and Burr's earlier reliance on Rhode Island as the one state that could implement the necessary difference between the two candidates. Only Governor Fenner's personal entry as an elector could have had any chance of bringing in Jeffersonian support from that state, and this, Burr later explained, was lost when the Governor, for some "plausible reasons," withdrew his name from the Rhode Island Republican ticket.[59]

On November 18, only three days before Gelston's letter, Burr's fear of what was happening in Rhode Island was shown in a letter to Pierpont Edwards. He noted that rumors "tend to alarm us sometime for R. Island & S. C.—We have no certain account of either—as to R. I. we expect to hear from you—."[60] When Virginia then gave both Burr and Jefferson twenty-one votes, the possibility of a tie became real.

Eyes turned toward an eight electoral vote state, South Carolina. The darkened outlook from Rhode Island had increased the importance of those Southern votes. While Robert Troup was sure of a Federalist majority, Burr thought its electors would all be for Pinckney and Jefferson.[61] Such votes would clinch the presidency for Jefferson. But then, from Columbia, South Carolina, came word from Philip Freneau. After tabulating the votes won by each elector, and thus showing the selection of eight Republicans, the writer added: "The vote tomorrow I understand will be Thomas Jefferson 8. Aaron Burr 7. Geo. Clinton 1. You will easily discover why the one Vote is varied."[62] The information had to be convincing enough for Jefferson to have reacted by offering Chancellor Livingston the job of Secretary of the Navy in his forthcoming administration.

December, then, was crucial. Complicating matters during the early part of the month had been an injury to Theodosia's foot and ankle. There was also talk about her marrying Alston, who was sending her letters about the "propriety of early marriages, in spite of the authority of even Aristotle," and attempting to dispel her prejudices against living in South Carolina.[63] With his daughter, Burr remained in New York until he had to join the legislature at Albany. Political matters, however, dominated those weeks.

Jefferson, considering everything settled in his favor, was now in a generous mood. On the fifteenth, he wrote from Washington City to discuss the probable outcome and assured Burr that he would be at least four or five votes ahead of Adams despite the necessary reductions to prevent a tie and regretted that Burr's aid would not be available for the new administration. Such was the position of the vice president in those days—not even a member of the administration. "It leaves a chasm in my arrangement," were his charitable words, "which cannot be adequately filled up."[64] He hoped to see Burr at the new capital on March 4.

The next day, Burr received letters from Wade Hampton and Timothy Green. Both had originated from Columbia on December 2, the same day Freneau's South Carolina report had been sent. They also told of the Republicans' triumph and of the probable casting of one ballot for Clinton to avoid a tie. But the same mail also brought a letter from Maryland Congressman Samuel Smith. Smith, a wealthy Baltimore merchant and a convert to Jeffersonian republicanism, was a close friend of the Vice President.

Burr's reply to Smith, written with the intelligence that a tie was improbable, was a forthright rejection of his possible complicity in any Federalist maneuver to upset the wishes of his own party. He thus wrote:

> It is highly improbable that I shall have an equal number of votes with Mr. Jefferson; but if such should be the result, every man who knows me ought to know that I should utterly disclaim all competition— Be assured that the federal party can entertain no wish for such an exchange, as to my friends, they would dishonor my views and insult my feelings by harbouring a suspicion that I could submit to be instrumental in counteracting the wishes & expectations of the U. S. and I now constitute you my proxy to declare these sentiments if the occasion shall require.[65]

The next day, another letter came from Smith, discussing Jefferson's probable cabinet and soliciting Burr's views. Burr responded with a strong endorsement of Albert Gallatin for the Treasury Department, dismissing objections to the Pennsylvanian as "frivolous and absurd." "I shall go to Albany about the middle or last of January to attend the legislature as a member for Orange County," Burr also reported. "It will scarcely be possible for me to join you at the inauguration, and yet of all things I should like to partake of the joy and brighten the chain."[66]

But the South Carolina reports had been erroneous. Their electoral vote had given an equal number to Jefferson and Burr. With the other states going the same way, a tie seemed assured. Now Jefferson told Madison of the imminence of an "absolute parity between the two republican candidates" and lamented those Federalists who "openly declare they will prevent an election, and will name a President of the Senate, *pro tem*."[67]

Considering that the Republicans controlled enough Congressional delegations to win in the House of Representatives, the Federalists now had three possible alternatives. They could, most easily, do as Hamilton now clearly preferred: satisfy the obvious Republican desires and resolve the deadlock in favor of Jefferson. "If there is a man in this world I ought to hate, it is Jefferson," wrote Hamilton. "But the public good must be paramount to every private consideration."[68] He supported this view with some well-reasoned but often bitter diatribes against Federalist support for Burr. It was naive to suggest, he cautioned, that "Mr. Burr can be won to the federal views," for the Republican inducements will always be stronger. Furthermore, Burr's insatiable appetite and his personal fiscal irresponsibility must necessarily lead him to "corrupt expedients" and the use of "unprincipled men"; he will use "the rogues of all parties to overrule the good men of all parties," for "his career proves that he has formed himself upon the model of Catiline, and he is too cold blooded, and too determined a conspirator ever to change his plan." A Jeffersonian administration, unlike a Federalist-supported President Burr, must bear the "whole responsibility of bad measures."[69] To Sedgwick, to John Rutledge, to any Federalist of influence, Hamilton kept up his anti-Burr barrage. In all of these statements, it is clear that he regarded Jefferson as the man most trustworthy and least likely to place personal ambitions above the best interests of the country. Perhaps an equally persuasive argument was the advantage of Federalist disassociation from the new administration, which would leave them free to act as a true opposition party.

There was a second alternative. Congressman John Dawson warned Madison that a Federalist plan to support Burr would hinge on their desire to prevent an election by keeping either man from getting a majority.[70] Some Federalists did contemplate a plan that would have effectively frustrated the electoral system by using their power in the House to keep either man from getting the necessary nine states. Since the Constitution had stipulated that each state would get one vote when voting for President in the House, the affirmative votes of nine states were needed for a majority. A bill might then be passed by the Federalists to enable the Senate to choose a President "under certain circumstances." The choice might then be Supreme Court Justice Samuel Chase, a violent Federalist, or either the Secretary of State or the Senate President Pro Tem. This move would have been, according to Jefferson, "a *stretch* of the constitution."[71] When Gouverneur Morris mentioned this plan to Hamilton, he reported that the Federalists had even begun to "cast about for the person" to fill the office. But he called it "a wild measure" and noted that it was already being dropped from active consideration.[72] Surely, too, the Federalists were aware that any such usurpation of the presidency, as the Republicans regarded the real meaning of the plan, would be met by armed resistance. The *American-Citizen* warned that bloodshed might be the consequence of such maneuvering.[73] Rumors of preparations to offer military aid against attempts to "stretch" the Constitution persisted into the new year, along with Republican reports that, despite what Morris had written to Hamilton, notions of a Congressional solution were being kept alive. Accustomed as they were to viewing each Federalist move as a conspiracy, Republican exaggerations of this threat were not surprising.

But the most likely possibility was the Federalist impulse to support Burr as the most acceptable of the two candidates. Samuel Sewall reported that many in Washington thought "that Burr must be voted for by the federalists as being the least of two evils," and, for himself, expressed the view that Burr's occupancy of the first office would install a man with "less enthusiasm and philosophy" than Jefferson and free of the "nonsense of democratic plans, in which the friends of Jefferson if not himself, are completely involved." Furthermore, Sewall reported, by supporting Burr the Federalists "may retain a necessary influence upon the Admin. and the election itself will divide their adversaries."[74] Uriah Tracy saw Burr as "a cunning man. If he cannot outwit all the Jeffersonians I do not know the man."[75] Burr's supporters also included, quite naturally, Jonathan Dayton; but, more significantly, what began to appear to be a majority of the Federalists now talked of defying Hamilton and backing the Colonel.[76] Theodore Sedgwick must have dismayed Hamilton with his observation that however unworthy Burr may be, "the evidence of his unworthiness is neither so extensively known nor so conclusive as that of the other man."[77] Burr's reputation for moderation was a compelling factor that increased his appeal for those who could only view with horror the prospect of Jefferson as president. Anybody but the man who had authored so scathing an attack against the Administration in the letter that Jefferson had written to Philip Mazzei in 1796! Such sentiment saw Burr's election as a far better choice.

On the twenty-third of December, in recognition of this attitude, Burr reaffirmed his loyalty to Jefferson. "It is the unanimous determination of the republicans of every grade to support your administration with unremitted zeal," he wrote. Then he added a strong vow of loyalty: "As to myself, I will cheerfully abandon the office of V. P. if it shall be thought that I can be more useful in any active station. In fact, my whole time and attention shall be unceasingly employed to render your administration grateful and honorable to our country and to yourself. To this I am impelled, as well by the highest sense of duty as by the most devoted personal attachment."[78]

The latest states to report electoral votes confirmed the certainty of a tie, and Burr soon received direct advice from a staunch Federalist, Robert Goodloe Harper of South Carolina. Harper noted the inevitable

Republican overtures for Burr to announce his declension in favor of Jefferson; but he advised the New Yorker to be more discreet, to "take no step whatever, by which the choice of the House of Representatives can be impeded or embarrassed." Even more significantly, Harper advised Burr to, "Keep the game perfectly in your own hand."[79] It would also be more prudent, he added, for Burr to forego a written reply and not to answer "any other that may be written to you by a Federal man."

Thereafter, with the approaching official announcement of a tie, and the certainty of a vote in the House, Burr did just that. He made no move to solicit Federalist support. Jefferson told his daughter that the Federalists had hoped they "could debauch Col. B.," but they had been embarrassed by his "honorable and decisive" conduct.[80] Samuel Smith later told his son that none of Burr's correspondence or conversation *"with me would warrant the charge made against him of having intrigued with the Federal party for his Election."*[81] A Federalist, William Cooper, maintained that had "Burr done anything for himself, he would long ere this have been president."[82] Nor did Burr make a move to discourage such assistance. Samuel Smith, who had solicited Burr's letter of December 16, a letter that had done much to relieve Republican anxieties, was now rebuffed in his attempt to get a final clear-cut disavowal. Burr, in Trenton at the end of December, wrote to Smith on the twenty-ninth as follows:

> At the moment of leaving town I received a great number of letters on the subject of the election and I perceive a degree of Jealousy and distrust and irritation by no means pleasing or flattering— The letters are however generally answered by those which I have written you; but one gentleman (of our friends) has asked me whether if I were chosen president, I would . . . resign— The question was unnecessary, unreasonable and impertinent, and I therefore made no reply. If I had made any I should have told that as at present advised, I should not— What do you think of such a question? I was made a Candidate against my advice and against my will; God knows, never contemplating or willing the result which has appeared—and now I am insulted by those who used my name for having suffered it to be used—This is what we call going on principle and not men—I presume however that before this time you are satisfied that no such terrible event is, or ever was to be apprehended; and that no such intention was ever entertained by those who laugh at your absurd claims—[83]

Burr had also indicated his intention of remaining at Trenton until January 3, but then would travel on to Philadelphia for a meeting with

Smith. Meanwhile, on the second day of the new year, the counting of ballots confirmed what had been expected: Jefferson and Burr each had seventy-three votes. Adams and Pinckney were left behind with only sixty-five and sixty-four, respectively. The Federalist calculations that sufficient support for Burr was present in the House to keep Jefferson from winning the needed total of nine states increased the importance of Smith's mission. Bayard told his fellow Delaware politician and Republican, Caesar A. Rodney, that, "Your friend Jefferson cannot be elected against the will of the federal party; and tho the course which will be taken is not absolutely decided upon, yet the inclination is much in favor of Burr."[84] Timothy Pickering had much the same message for Rufus King.[85] Smith, then, kept his appointment with Burr in Philadelphia. The Congressman was a lodger at the same Washington rooming house used by Jefferson and was undoubtedly serving as his agent. Smith met Burr, in a supposedly secret session, with Colonel Benjamin Hitchborn. What he heard from the New Yorker was most revealing.

The account that Jefferson later recorded in his *Anas* corresponds in every substantive detail with a letter written by Gabriel Christie of Maryland. At the same meeting, Burr was asked what would happen if the Federalists persisted in their support of him; and he replied, "We must have a President, and a constitutional one, in some way."

"How is it to be done?" Hitchborn asked. "Mr. Jefferson's friends will not quit him; and his enemies are not strong enough to carry another."

"Why," replied Burr, "Our friends must join the federalists, and give the President."

At breakfast the next day, Burr repeated his theme. "We cannot be without a President. Our friends must join the federal vote."

"But," Hitchborn pointed out, "we shall then be without a Vice President; who is to be our Vice President?"

Burr replied: "Mr. Jefferson."[86]

The outlook was most confused. Burr used no agents to solicit Federal support, nor did he soften his resistance to pleas that he remove his own candidacy. As long as Bayard of Delaware, who alone would decide his state's vote in the House, cared to vote for Burr, finding a ninth state to seal Jefferson's victory seemed to be impossible. Another Republican, Albert Gallatin, saw the danger in the Federalist maneuver as one of mere pretense of voting for Burr while really trying to "defeat the election," pointing out that no choice was possible as long as this plan remained in effect. Should a real attempt to usurp the office of the president be made by the Federalists, he feared the outbreak of violence. Only his calculation that the Republicans could depend upon strong physical resistance quelled his fears of a civil war. "My opinion is, however, decided that we must consider the election as completed," he added, "and under no possible circumstance consent to a new election."[87] By the end of the month, Gallatin seemed somewhat more nervous and suggested that only an attempt to usurp the government could explain the Federalist plot to prevent an election. Yet, in a letter to his wife, he softened this conjecture by pointing out that only a small minority of Federalists could be so irrational. Gallatin's conviction about the need for settling the election constitutionally was, therefore, similar to Burr's.

Gallatin, heir apparent to the Secretary of the Treasury, and Burr, tied with Jefferson for first place, each had an obviously close interest in the outcome. If Gallatin could not have a Jefferson victory, the second best result would be to somehow keep the presidency in Republican hands: some Republican. To Burr, seeing the opposition to Jefferson among Federalists, it had become evident that only *he* could unify them behind a legitimately chosen chief executive. Throwing his support openly behind Jefferson would make the Virginian no more palatable if usurpation was the aim, for the opposition party could continue to prevent an election. It could, moreover, destroy whatever confidence he had among Federalists. At best, from Burr's point of view, he would lose the chance to ride at the head of a Federalist-Republican coalition and become the third president of the United States. But he had to first act with discretion, move with care, and watch his timing. No overt move could be made until the arrival of a propitious moment. For the coming crucial days, he would be occupied at Albany, anyway, serving with the legislature and, above all, attending his daughter's wedding.

Theodosia Burr, in her eighteenth year, married Joseph Alston in Albany on the second of February, 1801. The service was conducted by the Reverend John Johnston at the Dutch Reformed Church. The next day, Burr saw his only child leave with her husband for New York, where they planned to spend a brief honeymoon at Richmond Hill before continuing down to South Carolina. He had thus given away his most cherished possession.

For the most part, his attendance at the legislature, far from the scene of decision at Washington, was consistent with watchful waiting while the battle raged. The newspaper debates revolved about the relative merits of the two candidates, with a number of Federalist writers agreeing with Hamilton's opposition to their party's apparent support for Burr. The Washington *Federalist* asked how the Jeffersonians could justify their reluctance to elect Burr, while "Hobson" told *Gazette and General Advertiser* readers that Burr's selection would create a third party rather than unify the existing ones. Burr, he pointed out, would retain power by "forming a Faction among the dregs—the refuse of both parties."[88] In Washington, the talk among Republicans, in particular, centered on the alleged usurpation and the probable course of the balloting by the state delegations. On February 1, Jefferson wrote to tell Burr of Federalist plots to "sow tares between us, that they might divide us and our friends."[89]

Meanwhile, from Washington, New York Congressman Edward Livingston was writing to tell Matthew L. Davis of Jefferson's imminent election. He figured that eight states were certain—New York, New Jersey, Pennsylvania, Virginia, North Carolina, Tennessee, Kentucky, and Georgia. Two, Vermont and Maryland, were divided and could therefore cast no vote. This prediction was then based on an expected change from one member of a divided state, which would then become Mr. Jefferson's ninth. Others, following this lead, might even give Jefferson as many as ten or eleven of the sixteen states.[90]

It is likely that Livingston communicated this information to Burr at Albany at about the same time, for Davis must have been in New York when he received the letter. Livingston's optimism about Jefferson's chances was not, however, unanimous. Albert Gallatin, more fearful about usurpation than he had indicated earlier to his wife and sensing that, in any case, chances for a Republican administration might be lost, sat down on the third of February and wrote to his good political companion, the man who had once defended his eligibility to serve as a senator, Aaron Burr.

Gallatin's letter was delivered at Albany on Thursday, February 12, one day after the House had begun to vote and the deadlock was already confirmed. Burr read the letter carefully, then summoned to his quarters Peter Townsend and John Swartwout. With these two confidants, he discussed Gallatin's surprising suggestion. Gallatin, Jefferson's trusted friend, had pointed out that the final outcome of the balloting was in the hands of three Congressmen: Smith of Maryland, James Linn of New Jersey, and Livingston of New York. These men were actually friendly to Burr and would certainly prefer his election to usurpation or continued deadlock. Through their votes, Burr's victory was possible. But, Gallatin was later recorded by Townsend as having pointed out, Burr must be on the spot himself in order "to secure them." In other words, hasten to Washington immediately.[91] Burr could then exert the necessary influence to decide the election in his favor and Gallatin would, of course, find his hopes still in Republican hands with his own elevation as secretary of the treasury as certain under Burr as under Jefferson. Neither

Jefferson nor anyone else has ever suspected Gallatin's role; the prudent Burr quite naturally destroyed the letter.

Both Townsend and Swartwout were rather smitten by the suggestion and advised Burr, according to a New York merchant's subsequent transcription of Townsend's statement, to "get into the first conveyance you can procure—lose not a moment—hasten to Washington and secure the prize—" Burr agreed. Both men then left the room to return to the legislature. When they came back some time later, they found that Burr's baggage was packed. He was ready to leave. "But at the critical moment his heart failed him," Townsend later recalled to merchant Benjamin Betterton Howell; "he remained at Albany and wrote letters."[92]

Two letters are known. His reply to Gallatin expressed surprise at the intelligence, which had contradicted Burr's most reliable sources. In language so couched as to conceal Gallatin's message, but nevertheless with enough clarity to provide a direct reply, Burr used Livingston's information—which was by no means the prevailing belief—to say that he had been "assured that all was settled & that no doubt remained but that J. would have 10 or 11 Votes on the first Trial." He thus, upon reflection, had retreated from the Townsend-Swartwout counsel that he do as Gallatin had suggested. Making clear that he disagreed with the proposal to seize the mantle of power in Washington, but only because he thought Jefferson would win a majority of the states, he still left room for another possibility. "In case of usurpation, by law," he told Gallatin, "by P. of Senate pro. tem. or in any other way, my opinion is definitely made up and it is known to S. S. [Samuel Smith] and E. L. [Edward Livingston]." In other words, he was ready to make an overt move only if the situation was desperate enough to threaten the Constitution and his party. In that case, he notified Gallatin, he could be reached in New York after the twenty-first of February and did not expect to reach Washington until just before the inauguration, or, he assured Gallatin, "sooner if the intelligence Which I may receive at N. Y. shall be such as to require my earlier presence—"[93] It is interesting to speculate what Burr might have done at that moment if he had known that a deadlock had already occurred.

It was probably his most important letter. He had succeeded, through circumspect behavior, in preserving his position as the alternative to dangerous indecision, a power Burr could not have kept had he made an overt and possibly futile endorsement of Jefferson. A premature move would tip his hand and destroy party harmony, but his arrival at the new national capital as the one man who could obtain enough support from each party might yet prevent a civil war. It was, for Burr, undoubtedly the position of an opportunist, but one that was also germane to the bitter national struggle. "Your expectations respecting the election correspond with my wishes & my uniform belief," he wrote to Livingston four days later.[94]

As he sat in that Albany room, his baggage still packed, he was conscious of another need. And that was to protect his standing with Jefferson, particularly in case Livingston's forecast proved accurate. His second letter of that day assured the Republican leader that, "I set down as calumny every tale calculated to disturb our harmony." The fears of his friends had been calmed. After all, he was the "depository of all their cases and anxieties." He closed by urging Jefferson "to believe in the very great respect & esteem" with which he was held.[95]

Livingston had been close to the mark, but it was far from that simple. Even while Burr was contemplating Gallatin's letter, several ballots had already been completed. Starting on Wednesday, February 11, they revealed the deadlock. The divided delegations of Maryland and Vermont, and the pro-Burr vote of Delaware's only representative, Federalist James Bayard, had limited Jefferson to just eight states. Although six had been given to Burr, Jefferson still needed one more, so they resumed balloting. The House had made continuous efforts until three o'clock on Thursday morning, completing twenty-seven ballots before adjourning for a nine-hour break. Despite the snowstorm that had hit Washington the day before, Representative James Nicholson, ill with a high fever, had insisted on being present for each ballot. A bed was provided to accommodate him. He was still in the House on Saturday afternoon, when the completion of thirty-three ballots failed to show a change.[96]

The city of Washington had become a center of tension. Rumors of a resort to arms swept through the capital. One account that created a stir said that Republicans were already arming in Philadelphia.[97] John Beckley explained that this "calumny" was founded on the removal by Federalists of several hundred stands of arms and eighteen pieces of cannon into the public arsenals. The crowds that began to pour into Washington from different parts of the Union were fully aware that usurpation would be resisted by force. Little was needed to spark wild rumors among the excitement seekers, who crowded every rooming house in the city. More than fifty persons were reportedly sleeping on the floors of one such establishment. Blankets served as beds and greatcoats became blankets.

Then the solid division began to yield. On Sunday, Samuel Smith assured Bayard of Jefferson's views on the subject of the public credit, the maintenance of the naval system, and the retention of subordinate public officers despite their political views.[99] Smith had previously sounded out Jefferson, without the future president *"having the remotest idea of my object."*[100] Bayard, seeing the impossibility of persuading the Republicans to shift to Burr, told other Federalists that he would change his vote. His party's fears of the consequences of legislative usurpation led to a caucus. Its result became known on February 17.

The Burr supporters from Vermont and Maryland cast blank ballots, giving their states to Jefferson, who was now elected by the choice of ten states. Bayard, unable to bring himself to actually vote for Jefferson, also responded with a blank, as did the delegation from South Carolina. Burr, then, had four. Just as the Republicans had originally planned: President Jefferson and Vice President Burr, on the thirty-sixth ballot. But not without a near disaster.[101] The affair pointed up a constitutional defect that was later corrected by the Twelfth Amendment, which required electors to vote specifically for presidential and vice-presidential candidates.

The exciting news traveled rapidly from Washington. Two days later, it reached Baltimore. On the twenty-first, the New York *American-Citizen* voiced the excitement of Republicans by heralding the prevention of "a counter revolution." Tammany's celebration was conducted in a brilliantly illuminated Wigwam, as sixteen special lamps, one for each state, glowed through the windows. Brother Martling had prepared a handsome collation. It was a Democratic-Republican triumph; its resolution was mainly a victory for the Constitution. Up north, in Epping, New Hampshire, a state legislator named William Plumer observed to Henry Dearborn: "I neither love or fear names—tis measures that ought to influence us, either to approve or condemn the doings of any administration. It would be happy for our Country if the reign of party would yield to that of reason & propriety."[102]

And so it had. Not because Hamilton had been particularly influential in his effort to stop Burr, but because the Republicans had refused to yield from their purpose and had, therefore, kept the Federalists from pushing too far. Burr was now Vice President-elect. Not properly understood, even to this day, it has been interpreted as an example of yet another intrigue.

CHAPTER XIII

Man Without a Party

THE Capitol overlooked the budding federal city from Jenkins Hill. Even unfinished, it dominated the north shore of the Potomac. On the muddy terrain that had been reserved for the new city, buildings were widely scattered. Every now and then, however, one could see long rows of brick houses: the products of numerous speculators. Indeed, New Jersey Avenue boardinghouses were already leasing rooms to congressmen. Despite this activity, the course of the main thoroughfare, Pennsylvania Avenue, was still "marked by a tangle of elder bushes, swamp grasses, and tree stumps."[1] One could still see houses without roofs and buildings that had been abandoned before completion. Somewhat more encouraging was the sight of brick-covered structures like the one built for the Treasury Department. At the center of the incipient city, the Capitol itself had been constructed with white stone from a Virginia quarry; in its midst, where the South Wing now stands, was a temporary brick structure that was so poorly ventilated and so precariously supported by exterior props that it was known as the "Oven." Since 1800 it had been serving as the chamber of the House of Representatives but, as Theodosia Burr Alston was soon to observe, the new federal census had shown the need for a larger forum. Only the North Wing was ready for business; and it was in this Senate chamber that Aaron Burr had taken the oath to become the third vice president of the United States.

It was noon of the same day, March 4, 1801, when Burr sat with the Chief Justice of the Supreme Court, John Marshall, and with President-elect Thomas Jefferson. The Virginians were, of course, political opponents. Swearing in Jefferson was a painful assignment for Marshall.

Waiting for the swearing-in and anticipating the Inaugural Address, the new Vice President looked forward to political tranquility. From Philadelphia, one week earlier, he had written to Gallatin concerning the charges in circulation about his conduct during the recent campaign. "They are now," he had observed, "of little consequence & those who had believed them will doubtless blush at their own weakness—."[2] It was natural, or at least it should have been, that his industry and skill should now be rewarded. His friends were sure that Jefferson could not have won without Burr's work. So was he. There was no reason to suspect, therefore, that the journey to the nation's second highest office would be anything but triumphal.

Burr had reached the capital in time to receive a host of foreign visitors at his Georgetown quarters. That settlement of some five thousand, which had been incorporated in 1789, was three miles upstream from the capital. A road rutted from the constant flow of carriages made its use hardly bearable. But Georgetown was a better place for dignified residences and possessed a more stately atmosphere than the capital. Its substantial brick houses and well kept gardens savored of English life. In choosing to live there, Burr agreed with many congressmen. Representative Roger Griswold of Connecticut, for example, had voiced a common attitude when he had called Washington "a city in ruins," and one that was "both melancholy and ludicrous."[3]

Now in the Senate chamber, Burr could see about a thousand people assembling. Then, the Chief Justice rose and administered the oath to Mr. Jefferson. The new President was most conspicuous. He was over six feet two inches tall and had reddish hair. His frame and frontier complexion caused a foreign visitor to observe that his figure was "like that of a tall, large-boned farmer."[4] His voice, in contrast, was weak and barely audible in the hushed chamber.

The message contained everything a new president should say. Harmony was particularly urgent for one who had been victimized by many years of intense political rivalry, and for a man who had had to endure challenges of his own loyalty and religious convictions. So he assured the country that he was not a wild Jacobin, nor were his political companions mere Francophiles.

"Let us, then, fellow-citizens," he said, "unite with one heart and one mind. Let us restore to social intercourse that harmony and affection without which liberty and even life itself are but dreary things." Then, as his audience listened in silence, he reminded them that "every difference of opinion is not a difference of principle. We have called by different names brethren of the same principle"; and, looking out at the large assemblage, he added: "We are all Republicans, we are all Federalists."

This much quoted sentiment brought disquiet to the band of politicians who, having finally taken control of the federal government, now expected the spoils of victory. And Burr compared it with an exhortation that the "energies of the men ought to be principally employed in the multiplication of the human race." In this type of sentiment, he assured his son-in-law, ladies find much to applaud and men "promise an ardent and active co-operation." It is from such a profound position that one can go on to say that "we are all republicans, we are all federalists." And, Burr concluded: "I hope the fair of your state will equally testify their applause of this sentiment; and I enjoin it on you to manifest your patriotism and your attachment to the administration by 'exerting your energies' in the manner indicated."[5]

As Jefferson's administration progressed, and the months went by, it became evident that Burr's first year as Vice President had demonstrated his political vulnerability both in New York and nationally. With an eminent political office, his power to accommodate loyal followers should have been considerable. Burr had sent his own list of candidates for federal offices to the President. As the undisputed Republican spokesman from his state, the Vice President included the names of David Gelston, John Swartwout, Theodorus Bailey, Matthew L. Davis, and Edward Livingston. All were selected to replace Federalist incumbents, and each man was designated for a specific post: Collector of the Revenue, Marshal, Supervisor of the Internal Revenue and Inspector, Naval Officer of the Port of New York, and District Attorney.[6]

The Vice President seemed almost casual about pressing the matter. However, he took particular care to designate which positions would be most appropriate for each nominee and then advanced their interests in several letters to such contacts as Samuel Smith, who had been appointed Secretary of the Navy, and Albert Gallatin. At one point, he was moved to remind Smith that such requests were not "official letters to be filed in the Navy office for the benefit of present clerks & future Ministers!"[7]

Most of the activity was carried out from New York, where he learned about Theodosia's safe arrival at the Alston home. Theo, who had established a close relationship with Frances Ann Prevost, seemed excited as she wrote to her sister-in-law about the warm reception given by the Alstons. So hospitable had everyone been that she questioned Northern notions about the alleged reserve and coldness of Carolina women. Burr, pleased and relieved to hear about her safe arrival, now looked forward to joining Theo and planned to sail southward by April 20, although he noted that "One obstacle interposes; that you can conjecture."[8] His daughter was, as always, the recipient of Burr's most intimate accounts of sexual adventures, and so there is little doubt that she knew what he meant by the word "obstacle." Even when still in Washington, one week after the inauguration, he did not dismiss as unlikely the possibility of matrimony. Yet, considering that his projected date of departure from New York would have removed him before the annual spring election, a reasonable conclusion is that he did not, at that time, anticipate any direct involvement in local political battles. Such a personal consideration as romance must have received substantial weight. Nevertheless, the journey was abandoned, "for reasons which I cannot now detail," he informed Eustis.[9] He complained to Theo that "The pain of my own disappointment leaves me no room for any sympathy with yours." He had had to forego sailing on the brig *Echo* that was due to leave for South Carolina that same morning, April 29. But, cryptically, he added that even if the "insurmountable object" were removed, "it would yet, for other reasons, be barely possible for me to go at this time."[10]

What he meant by the words "at this time" is not hard to understand, for it was the end of April; in New York, that brought the annual elections for all assemblymen and, in 1801, also for the governorship. Burr had no choice but to remain in the city to work for the party, which hoped it could win again with George Clinton. Clinton had not been governor since he had refused to run again in 1795. He had then reversed his own intentions in 1800 by permitting his name to be placed on Burr's assembly ticket and, afterward, had stepped aside for Burr to get the vice presidency.

As the Republican Party had evolved from the factions clustering around a handful of personalities, the most essential political consideration for one of Burr's ambition and station lay in preserving powerful support. Thus, one might regard the retention of a group of loyal followers—Burr's "Myrmidons," or the "little band," or the "Burrites" —and the reality of what a later era would view ominously as a political machine. This Burr had created. And people like Davis, Swartwout, Gelston, and now William Peter Van Ness and others, had formed its nucleus, plotted its maneuvers, and exerted every effort in its leader's interests. For his concerns were also theirs. His success would result from their contributions; and their future help depended upon what he could do for them. To do this, he needed patronage opportunities that were available from the nation and the state administration. Bountiful crops could be expected when both were controlled by the proper political party. Burr must have been pleased, then, to learn that even before April 1, two of his friends had been given appointments. Swartwout was made Marshal and Edward Livingston became the District Attorney for New York City. Burr, who had included both designations in his recommendations to the President, lost no time telling Samuel Smith about receiving the news, "with the most lively Joy." Then, with an eye to the near future, he suggested that the intentions demonstrated by Jefferson "will operate beneficially on our approaching election."[11] The appointments were bound to be a partisan stimulant. Burr appreciated their timeliness and figured that they were worth some five hundred additional votes.[12] As a result, he found himself fully committed to push George Clinton's comeback attempt to regain the governorship and to help win the return of another slate of Republican assemblymen from New York City.

He pursued this effort optimistically, exuding confidence in a substantial Republican victory. Chancellor Robert R. Livingston, recently appointed as minister to France by Jefferson, was told that Clinton's majority would fall somewhere between eight and eleven hundred votes.[13] Gallatin was assured that the "result of our approaching elections in this City will show that the late changes in office have had a happy effect."[14] One of the additional "late changes" had been the appointment of Daniel Ludlow, the Manhattan Company's first president, as a navy agent. Not only was his elevation an additional bolster to Republican hopes for more patronage, but Ludlow's large family would now be able to back the party's cause with enthusiasm. The desire to repeat the Republican triumph of 1800 threatened to overwhelm the best Federalist efforts, notwithstanding the feverish campaigning of Alexander Hamilton, whom Burr said was working "day and night with the most intemperate and outrageous zeal."[15] By the opening of the polls for the three days starting with April 28, there seemed to be little that Hamilton and all his cohorts could do. Burr, confined to the scene of the battle against his desires, found his glowing reports vindicated by the resulting Republican sweep that carried Clinton back to Albany.

Even allowing Burr credit for a substantial role in the campaign, however—and evidence of exactly what he did do is lacking—Burr had remained in New York for other reasons. Handbills, suddenly appearing that April, were aimed directly at him. He was charged with having connived to steal the election from Jefferson; but, even more seriously, with having intrigued for the active support of Federalists against the best interests of his own party. Thus, the accusation was thrown at him not only in his own city but by literature sent to other parts of the country.[16] The charges were circulated by those seeking to remove Burr's power in the state. Their real object was made clear by a man now working to advance Clinton, Samuel Osgood, the former Postmaster General and one of the well-known candidates on Burr's assembly ticket of 1800. Osgood complained about the recent appointments granted to Swartwout, Livingston, and Ludlow. In a letter to James Madison on April 24, when Burr was still entertaining visions of visiting Theodosia, Osgood charged him with duplicity. He said that there was "strong Evidence that the three Gentlemen appointed in this City are entirely devoted to the Vice President; and had it been in their Power, we have Reason to believe, that Mr. Jefferson would not have been President." He went on to recommend that future appointments in New York should be channeled through George Clinton.[17] Osgood's letter was written only one day before Burr informed Eustis that something had arisen to delay his projected trip. Furthermore, his final announcement to the Boston physician about the impossibility of seeing Theodosia came on the evening after the first day of balloting.[18] The election campaign had certainly run its course by that time; and had politicking caused his distress, he could have sailed for South Carolina on the vessel that left the next morning. But the attack had to be countered, and Burr chose to remain in New York.

"I could not resist the solicitations which were made to me on that head," Burr finally acknowledged after Eustis had determined the real reason. "The handbills were numerous, of various descriptions, uniform however in Virulent and indecent abuse and since my former letter I discover that to Villify A. B. was deemed of so much consequence, that packages of them were sent to Various parts of the country. . . . I always presume that my friends will treat as false, everything said of me, which ought not to be true," continued the Vice President. "These papers were exhibited as being characteristic of the party by which they were issued."[19]

Also opposing Burr from within the Republican Party was the Governor's thirty-two year old nephew, De Witt Clinton. This young man had graduated from Columbia College in 1786 at the head of his class and had been introduced to politics as his uncle's private secretary. In 1797, he was elected to the Assembly and, since the following year, had been a state senator. The younger Clinton was considered by Alexander Hamilton as a dangerously ambitious man. But Clinton and Hamilton had one thing in common: both wanted to get rid of Burr.

Burr's troubles were only beginning. The spring attacks commenced a twofold drive to destroy his patronage power. That it was launched with the full support of George and De Witt Clinton, taking advantage of a bludgeon capable of removing their opponent, there could be little doubt. Their victory in the state elections of 1801 had elevated their strength. On May 17, President Jefferson, having absorbed more allegations about Burr's conduct, wrote to George Clinton about filling patronage jobs. He addressed Clinton as the man experienced in "the most difficult & most irksome" responsibility of making appointments to office, for advice about filling the positions of collector, naval officer and supervisor. All were being held by Federalists. Replacements had also been suggested by Burr, Jefferson admitted. Yet, despite Burr's distinct nomination of Theodorus Bailey as the supervisor and Davis as naval officer, Jefferson's letter reversed their designations. The President did, however, acknowledge the claims that Bailey's temperament was unsuited for the position of naval officer and that Davis, on the other hand, was not of sufficient stature to fill the other post.[20]

These events coincided with the actual liquidation of Burr's patronage powers. The election of Jefferson had, first of all, enabled the Republicans to right themselves with the Livingston family. Numerous cousins and in-laws were appointed to various offices. Both Jefferson, at the seat of government in Washington, and Clinton in New York favored them at the expense of Burr.[21]

Matthew L. Davis became a leading victim. The frustrations experienced by this loyal Burrite amounted to the most stunning repudiation of his chief's power. In letter after letter to Gallatin, Smith, and Jefferson, Burr had clarified his view that Davis should replace Richard Rogers, a Federalist holdover, as naval officer of New York rather than be given the job of supervising the internal revenue for the district. Burr had, in taking his position, considered Davis' youth as a handicap for the fiscal post.

The matter was bound to emerge as a leading manifestation of the bitterness that had already separated the Vice President from the President. Davis, who was the only man for whom Burr had made a vigorous fight, was eager for the appointment. In daily expectation of its fruition, he had bypassed other job offers. He was only twenty-eight years old, but youth had been no disadvantage for many others. Burr, relying on Gallatin as his most trusted friend within the administration, hopefully directed a growing indignation toward the new head of the Treasury Department, all in Davis' behalf. On June 28, Burr complained that ever since Edward Livingston had revealed the contemplated appointment, reports had begun to circulate about "secret machinations against Davis." He reasserted Davis' qualifications to become the New York naval officer, while, at the same time, he implied that the victim of the machinations had simply become the butt of anti-Burr agitation within the state's Democratic-Republican Party. It was, in short, a continuation of the efforts that had appeared during April to destroy Burr as a political force; and, Burr warned, "Davis is too important to be trifled with."[22]

Burr was not exaggerating. Davis certainly had become a scapegoat, and the lethal weapon was being applied by De Witt Clinton. That year, the Governor's nephew had been elected to a place on the Council of Appointment. This victory was to give him powers over patronage that even exceeded those held by George Clinton. For the younger Clinton, together with his brother-in-law Ambrose Spencer and dutiful Republican Robert Roseboom, comprised a trio on the Council that could not be stopped by the Governor's lone vote. While still in office, Governor John Jay had lashed back at the denial of the executive authority to make appointments. He even cited George Clinton's clashes with the Council. But when a vote was taken in April, the legislature refused to resolve the issue. Instead, it recommended the calling of a convention for October to amend the state's constitution.

During his first summer without Theodosia, caught amidst the swirls of local political machinations, Aaron Burr gradually fell into even deeper distress. Unhappily for him, Natalie was to return to France. But before she left, Burr had arranged for John Vanderlyn, just back from six years in Paris, to paint her portrait. Shortly afterward, she sailed for Le Havre with Robert R. Livingston and his family.

Nor did Theo remain at home. She ventured away from the malarial lowlands of South Carolina's Tidewater. Accompanied by some of the Alstons, she left by water on a northwestern journey that took her through the wilderness of New York State and, eventually, to Niagara Falls. From there, she paused in Canada long enough to visit with Joseph Brant. The Mohawk chief sent Burr a glowing account of their meeting. "You made two, perhaps more conquests on your Northern tour—King Brandt [sic] and the stage-driver; both of whom have been profuse in their eulogies," Burr later reported to his daughter. "Brandt has written me two letters on the subject. It would have been quite in style if he had scalped your husband and made you Queen of the Mohawks."[23] The Alstons visited Montreal and Quebec and then Halifax, from where they sailed for New York. Burr then did have a chance to spend some days with both Theo and Natalie, whose final departure occurred within one week after Theo had resumed the southward leg of her journey.

At this time, while Burr was pressing loyally for Davis, Bartow was named to succeed Richard Harison as Recorder. This followed a letter from Burr to George Clinton concerning his stepson's loyalty to republicanism.[24] William Peter Van Ness, another Burr nominee, was appointed as a public notary. So it cannot be stated, as has been done, that Burr's people were completely ignored by the new state administration.[25] Burr's difficulty, however, soon became more apparent, for not only was Davis still being bypassed by Jefferson, but a Clintonian, Samuel Osgood, was made supervisor instead of Theodorus Bailey. Increasing the damage to Burr's prestige was the subsequent appointment of such loyal Clintonians as Richard Riker, Tunis Wortman, and Sylvanus Miller to offices in New York City, which, of all places, Burr had a right to consider as his territory.

De Witt Clinton was still unacquainted with Jefferson, but the state senator who had held so much power via his control over the Council of Appointment had other means of access to the Administration. One of them was Mr. Madison, now the Secretary of State. In early September, more than one month before the date designated by the state legislature for the holding of a new constitutional convention, Clinton observed to Madison that the promotion being engineered for Matthew L. Davis "has appeared in a very extraordinary light to many reflecting men of the republican party." By "reflecting men" he meant, of course, anti-Burrites. Alluding to Burr, he wrote that "when viewed in connection with other appointments recommended *by the same person who is now so extremely anxious for Davis* and the ambitious plans of that person which have hitherto been unfolded and are now daily unfolding, would in my opinion render this appointment very injurious to the republican interest of this State."[26] His advice was to delay making any appointment, even though it would continue the tenure of Rogers as naval officer, until "a suitable successor" could be found. De Witt Clinton had thus reached into the upper echelons of the Administration. By deciding which to honor, in the case of Davis and in the future, the Administration could help to determine which New York faction would prevail.

Davis pursued his own cause. In September, after having been received with sympathy in Washington by Albert Gallatin, the Burrite saw Jefferson at Monticello. He carried a letter of introduction from Gallatin that called him "a man of talent, particularly quickness and correctness, suited for the office, of strict integrity, untainted reputation, and pure Republican principles."[27] After some petty talk, the New Yorker had to leave Virginia with the story that nothing would be decided until Jefferson had had a chance to meet with his cabinet.[28] The President's response was a clear indication of Burr's standing with the Administration. Furthermore, the job as naval officer finally went to another Republican: Samuel Osgood. Davis had obviously been the wrong man's choice.

After the rebuff, matters became even worse. In October, Burr was in Albany as a delegate from Orange County for the special convention that had been called to amend the state's constitution. When the session began, a unanimous vote celebrated the presence of the Vice President by electing him to serve as president of the convention. Its purpose was, first of all, to place a limit on the number of senators and assemblymen who might be chosen in the expanding state and, of greater significance to Burr, to resolve the conflict that had arisen between the Council of Appointment and the state's governors. That question was the ability of the Council to control appointments. The twenty-third article of the constitution of 1777 had, in providing a council of four senators, stipulated that the governor's appointments would be subject to their "advice and consent." Furthermore, as its presiding officer, he could vote only to break a tie. This part was clear; but unclear was the Council's authority to nominate individuals. Such power, in the hands of the four senators, would undermine the governor's authority and enhance the strength of whatever party or faction could rule the Council. Therein lay the power to name district attorneys, mayors, sheriffs, county treasurers, and numerous other officials. It was, in short, juicy bait for political leaders. And the 1801 convention merely ratified this point.

A powerful Council meant a strong De Witt Clinton. One might then wonder at the apparent ineptitude of Burr for having permitted this result. Yet Burr was a victim of a bipartisan move to confirm a point that had been advanced earlier by both parties, and the resulting vote was as predictable as it was overwhelming. Neither Burr nor any other individual could have stopped it. Whichever party commanded a majority in the legislature would also control all state appointments, and the Council was subsequently able to control over fifteen thousand jobs.[29] That the Burrites would be excluded from state patronage to so great a degree was not surprising.

Late that October, Burr returned to New York. For the next few weeks, he was occupied with efforts to sell Richmond Hill and the surrounding property. As usual, he needed more cash to pay his debts. Using the New York merchant William Edgar as his agent, the negotiations proceeded throughout November, shortly after Theo had returned to South Carolina. On the fifth, he wrote to inform her that the deal would probably be consummated within the next ten days for $140,000, "which, though not half the worth, is enough and more."[30] Four men were interested in buying the property, and there was trouble achieving a settlement with each one. There was some attempt to claim that the asking price was much too high, and Burr reacted angrily. He offered to have the estate appraised and to accept ten percent less than its true value. Finally, the entire sale fell through, "partly by whim and partly by accident," Burr explained to Theodosia. "I go to Philadelphia in two or three days; but shall return and not set off for Washington till near Christmas."[31]

Burr's trip was put off until early in the new year. Although consultations with Eustis had finally convinced him to discontinue the active practice of law while serving in so high an elective office, his days were filled with attention to other matters. He sent supplies, as well as a cook and a maid, to Theo. He was an interested reader of the accounts of the death of Hamilton's son Philip in a duel with Captain George I. Eacker after a dispute which, as Burr correctly guessed, had resulted from political differences. The Jersey dueling grounds at Weehawken was the scene of the actual exchange, which had followed young Hamilton's derision of Eacker for the militant Republican's oration denouncing the Federalist administrations.

When Burr arrived on January 12, 1802, to join the Seventh Congress, he was already six weeks late, a delay that at least one congressman thought was "no doubt a political maneuver."[32] But however suspicious others were about his intentions, no observer could deny his skill. He sat at the head of the Senate as a resolute but judicious officer, who was in firm command of the proceedings. A talent for precision and a lawyer's ability to seize the essence of debates were real assets.

By the start of the new year, the Senate was involved in a major party debate. Before the Federalists had relinquished power to the Republicans in early 1801, they had passed the National Judiciary Act, which seemed to Republicans like a diabolical plot to maintain Federalist control over the nation's court system. While the measure had reduced the size of the Supreme Court from six to five, a fine opportunity for outgoing President John Adams to appoint Federalists to judgeships had been created by its establishment of a system of six new circuit courts. Sixteen new appointees were needed to staff them. There was much to justify this need because the circuit-riding responsibilities had encumbered the Supreme Court justices, and, furthermore, enactment of the bill had been brewing long before the date of its actual passage.[33] Not only was the act a plum for Federalist job-seekers, but its enlargement of a branch of the central government was consistent with that party's principles. Few were surprised, then, that the Republican-dominated Seventh Congress should have attempted to repeal the obnoxious legislation.

With Burr in the capital city, the big question was whether he would support the Administration and help to execute the repeal. Word had been spreading about the Vice President's negative attitude toward Jefferson and his policies, in addition to the allegations that had already assigned him a devious role during the election of 1800.

Then Burr was given the opportunity to vote. When a vote taken on whether the Judiciary Bill repeal should be read for a third time—which was necessary before final passage—ended in a tie, Burr voted in the affirmative. He thus broke the deadlock and encouraged the Republicans. But their optimistic expectations were destroyed the next day when Burr, this time voting to break a tie on Jonathan Dayton's motion to delay the bill by referring it to a select committee, voted "yea" —directly contrary to Republican hopes. He told the senators that he wanted "to ameliorate the provisions of the bill" so that it would become more acceptable. Moreover, he made clear that his action was in the belief that recommittal would not kill the bill. As he had predicted, it was finally signed into law on March 31.[34]

Burr's role had provoked a furor. To Barnabas Bidwell, he expressed doubts not about its constitutionality; that he granted. But instead, "whether it would be *constitutionally moral*, if I may use the expression, and, if so, whether it would be *politic* and expedient, are questions on which I could wish to be further advised."[35] In his letter to Joseph Alston the next day, it was "the equity and expediency of depriving the twenty-six judges of office and pay" that bothered him.[36] Although his position won the support of such Republicans as Alexander J. Dallas of Pennsylvania, who also considered the move "impolitic and inexpedient," other Republicans felt that he had attempted to sabotage their plan.[37] They had hoped for an easy victory. Instead, they were now certain that the Vice President was interested in wooing the Federalists as part of his opposition to the Administration.[38]

There is much, however, that may be said in defense of Burr's vote. As President of the Senate, he had a moral duty to acquiesce to the strong desire for a committee appraisal of the legislation. His confidence that the return of the absent Senator Stephen R. Bradley of Vermont would provide the additional vote to discharge and pass the repeal had permitted an act of statesmanship. Moreover, his reservations about liquidating the new and short-lived judgeships were also understandable. Yet, what is hard to discern, unless one grants that he was making overtures to the Federalists, was his defiance of the Republicans while he was already being lashed for political infidelity. Burr's vote on the Judiciary Act repeal, then, did not inspire the Republican opposition to him: it merely fed the existing rancor. And more trouble was now developing in New York.

The newspaper partnership of James Cheetham and David Denniston, of the staunchly partisan New York *American-Citizen*, had already unleashed its intentions of ending all support for Burr, and in behalf of the Clintonians, it now turned upon him. Cheetham, a former hatter from

Manchester, had left England during the radical riots of 1798. It was
with Burr's help that, in May of 1801, he was able to take over half
ownership of Denniston's paper, which had come out two months earlier as the successor to John Greenleaf's *Argus*. Denniston was a poorly
educated farmer with but one important qualification: his cousin was De
Witt Clinton. Editorial leadership fell, naturally, into the hands of
Cheetham and his vitriolic pen. Truth and accuracy was hardly as important to this journalistic team as aiding its benefactor. Even by the
end of 1801, before Burr's role in the Judiciary Bill fight, their future
role as Clintonian polemicists had become clear. The objective was, of
course, to place Burr on the defensive, break his ties with the Administration, and clear the way for Clintonian domination of New York
politics.

Cheetham's letter to the President of December 10, 1801, revealed the
outlines of the coming attack. He told Jefferson that Burr had plotted to
secure the appointment of one particular elector in 1800 who would
fulfill an arrangement that called for voting for only one of the two
Republican candidates. The successful withholding of a Jefferson vote
could have made the difference and thus decided the presidency for the
Colonel. Only a strategic demand to have each elector expose the ballots
about to be deposited had, according to Cheetham, thwarted the plot.
Burr's trip to Rhode Island of September, 1800, when he had visited
Governor Fenner, was also called an attempt to arrange the electoral vote
in his own behalf. Timothy Green's mission to South Carolina, undertaken while that state's vote was in doubt, was also part of the plan,
Cheetham charged. Cheetham then accused Burr of open criticism of
the Administration because of his disappointment over the dearth of
appointments. The objective was "to bring the present administration
into disrepute, and thereby to place Mr. Burr in the Presidential Chair."
And Cheetham's inevitable conclusion was: "Extraordinary enterprises,
whose known objects are Dishonorable and unjust, call for Commen-
surate means of counteraction."[39]

Already under way, however, even while Cheetham was announcing
this purpose to the President, was an affair that the journalist would
soon exploit. Burr had, at this time, recently returned from a business
trip to Philadelphia. Every expectation was that he would soon leave for
Washington and the opening of the Seventh Congress. But once in New
York, Burr read about what one John Wood, a linguist, printer, and
historian who had come to the United States from Scotland in 1800,
had written in the guise of a "History of the Administration of John
Adams." Burr had, in fact, helped to supply Wood with some biograph-
ical material. But when the Vice President read the finished product,

he was stunned to see a denunciation of the Adams administration that was so extravagantly exaggerated that its publication could only win sympathetic support for the irresponsibly abused Federalists. Adams' regime was called a "hydra of despotism" and his presidency was denounced as years of "tyranny and corruption." The year of the passage of the Alien and Sedition Acts, 1798, was described as an American "reign of terror."[40] To Theodosia, Burr wrote that the work's five hundred pages consisted of principally low scurrility and ill-told private anecdotes."[41] For the next month, Burr, largely through William Peter Van Ness as his agent, tried to negotiate for its suppression. It was clearly better to have no anti-Federalist history than one of that calibre.

Then began the intricate negotiations between Burr, his agent Van Ness, Wood, and its printers, the New York firm of Barlass and Ward. The book was ready for sale in December of 1801; 1250 copies were in crates and ready for shipment. A copy had also been sent overseas for a London edition. Another one was in the hands of Clintonian Tunis Wortman, and its mere return was no guarantee that it had not been duplicated. Wood's contract had given Barlass and Ward full control over the book. Thus, when Burr had persuaded the author of the need to intervene, Wood offered to replace the manuscript within ten days "on condition that the present edition be entirely suppressed. *Should it not be suppressed*," he warned, "*you will be prosecuted for the libels it contains*."[42] Meanwhile, Van Ness acted without Burr's knowledge and offered Barlass and Ward one thousand dollars for all printed copies. Furthermore, Van Ness' fear that Wortman's copy had been duplicated prompted his request for a bond from the publishers that would protect him for an unauthorized publication. At the same time, they needed to work rapidly to prevent the appearance of a British edition. What followed was a series of offers to cover expenses, threats to sue for libel, plans to present Barlass and Ward with a Burr-approved substitute edition, a hurried message to England via the December 12 sailing of the brig *Recovery* to kill the British edition, and, after Wood had been maneuvered into revealing Burr's role, their agreement to suppress the book. When Burr left for Washington, the matter was still being negotiated. Van Ness wrote that Swartwout and Davis had considered the possible consequences and were suggesting that publication of the work in its present form might be preferable. They feared Clintonian charges that Burr had acted to prevent criticism of Federalists. The plan to substitute a new edition, they felt, might only enable the opposition to allege that the critical material was subsequently introduced for political reasons. Furthermore, they pointed out that publication of the work would bring sympathy for the attempt at suppression.[43]

Nevertheless, Burr's plan was fulfilled. He paid a thousand dollars for what turned out to be a very temporary thing. Subsequent events vindicated Swartwout and Davis.

In May, the 1250 copies were transferred from Ward's shop to Van Ness' home. Almost all were then burned.[44] But Cheetham and the pro-Jeffersonian editor of the Philadelphia *Aurora*, William Duane, had acted before the transfer to Van Ness and had managed to secure a copy.[45]

Burr's reputation in the city had already been attacked by the Clintonians through their leading propagandist, Cheetham. Even though the main blows were yet to come, the damage to his standing in his party was already evident. At Washington, Burr had become isolated from the heart of Republican power. He was too impotent to have any control over legislation that he opposed, such as the abolition of internal taxation. In early April, William Peter Van Ness received a letter from his congressman brother, John, which observed not only Burr's reluctance to display his weakness by pressing for any additional patronage powers but that "his influence & weight with the administration is in my opinion not such as I could wish."[46] On the eve of the spring elections of 1802, Cheetham printed an editorial that denied the allegation made in the Federalist New York *Evening Post* that the Republicans had chosen a slate of "Burrites" who were not really loyal to the party.[47] Robert Troup mentioned Cheetham by implication when he informed Rufus King that the "Clintonian and democratic printer in this City during the winter has blackguarded Burr without reserve." But Troup also hoped that Clinton's "violence" had "excited a powerful public sentiment against the administration." If the gist of the pro-Administration animosity toward Burr came from suspicions that he had courted Federalists, there was little to suggest that any of them were, in turn, rushing to accept him. Those who would do so, suggested the *American-Citizen*, were Federalist papers like the *Evening Post* and the *Daily Advertiser*, which would seek to attract Burrite printing revenue by fulfilling the Vice President's notion of a "union of all honest men."[48]

That line had become another handy bludgeon. It referred to Burr's comment at a Federalist dinner in honor of Washington's birthday. Burr, whose coolness to the departed hero was well known, had declined an invitation to attend. The dinner, held in the capital city, went on as planned without the honorary presence of the Vice President. But shortly after the meal had ended, Burr entered. The celebrants were in the midst of praising the departed leader and Burr, having been ushered to a seat at the head table, was asked to make a toast. Rising with his glass and facing the Federalist group, he toasted to "The union of all honest men!"[49]

He left the room soon afterward. What he had said was not very different from the President's own Inaugural Address sentiment. Yet, coming as it did, it could only be interpreted as a slap at the Administration for having abandoned him to the political vultures that were already nibbling at his remains and as an invitation for Federalist support. A number of Federalists, and very possibly a majority, actually did interpret his comment as an attempt to enlist their aid. Robert Troup, as usual cognizant of Burr's activities, reported Hamilton's belief that there was "a cabal going on at Washington between Burr and some of the federalists," and he also noted that such activities had "created heart burnings with some of Burr's party."[50] Two weeks later, when Burr attended a Republican festivity in celebration of the Administration's first year in office, he was toasted with three cheers but soon withdrew.

Still, his pregnant daughter commanded the Vice President's attention. The day after his appearance at the Federalist dinner, he toyed with the prospect of becoming a grandfather. "If you will have *Pet* or *Peet, Peter, Peter Yates, Peter Alston, Petrus Burr* (or by any other name he may be known) taught to write a good hand, and make me a present of him, I will subscribe myself your very much obliged and humble servant."[51] By early March he was contemplating plans to travel to South Carolina before May, when the child was due. He would, of course, have been happier to have had Theodosia nearby. Perhaps, then, he was being more than whimsical when he wrote to Alston that her situation, "so far from being an objection, ought, in my mind, to be an additional and strong motive. With her Northern constitution," he explained, "she will bring you some puny brat that will never last the summer out; but, in your mountains, one might expect to see it climb a precipice at three weeks old."[52] And Theodosia herself, wistfully longing for New York, told Frances Prevost that it would be wonderful to see their "*two sons* playing together." With her usual charm, she added: "if a daughter my only wish is that she may be the Frances of her day."[53] By mid-April, Theodosia was cheered to learn that her father would soon be on his way. He was able to leave the capital city on April 19 and eleven days later reached Georgetown, South Carolina, where he planned to spend three weeks. "Unfortunately, the stage was full—not even a seat vacant for the vice-president," he wrote to Theo.[54] On May 22, with her father present, Theodosia's son was born. He was named Aaron Burr Alston.[55]

His birth had hurt her physically. Her illness was regarded as a temporary disability, one that Alston did not take too seriously, although she was suffering from a prolapsed uterus.[56] A few weeks after the child was born, Theo traveled north with the infant, her in-laws, and Burr to escape from the heat and fevers of the Carolina Tidewater. After leaving Alston, who had agreed to the separation for the child's health, the party traveled up the coast by boat past Cape Hatteras to New York. They reached the city on May 29.

In Burr's absence, and with the spring elections of 1802 over, the most serious anti-Burr attacks began. Troup, who refused to let himself be fooled by the announced reasons for Burr's trip to Carolina, already called the Clintonians much more influential in New York than the Burrites. He told Rufus King that they hated Burr "as much as the Jacobins in France hate Bonaparte."[57] On May 26, their opposition became public. It was thoroughly consistent with Cheetham's advance word to Jefferson. The *American-Citizen* carried the preface of what Cheetham called *A Narrative of the Suppression by Col. Burr of the History of the Administration of John Adams, Late President of the United States, Written by John Wood*, which was only a partial title. Cheetham's name was not mentioned; but its author was identified as "one who from his *connection with the parties*, had an opportunity of knowing the very minutiae of every step taken in the suppression."[58] In the complete version of the *Narrative*, which was then published, Burr was charged with having suppressed Wood's book because it had offended the Federalists. With the publication of the *Narrative*, the Clintonians had thus assailed whatever political prestige Aaron Burr still held. And they were not finished.

Six days after the attack had begun, a purloined edition of Wood's *History* went on sale. The timing was magnificent. William Coleman's *Evening Post*, a Hamiltonian organ which had nevertheless attacked Cheetham's *Narrative*, simultaneously reprinted an account from the North Carolina *Minerva* that told of new evidence of Burr's Federalist affinities as expressed when he had visited the home of an aristocratic family at Lumberton, South Carolina.[59] His old friend Troup, who had just sent Rufus King a copy of Wood's book, labeled as "an infamous falsehood" all suggestions that Burr had conspired with Federalists. Troup was, in fact, quite indignant at the accusation that those of his own party had conducted any business with Aaron Burr. Nevertheless, he conceded that "we have reason to think that Burr has been caballing with some of our friends to the southward." He was, of course, referring to Charles Cotesworth Pinckney of South Carolina, whose elevation to replace Jefferson in the next election was charged by

Cheetham as having been the real purpose of Burr's recent trip to the South. The successful execution of such a maneuver, Cheetham had held, would guarantee Burr's retention of the vice presidency. But Troup regarded Burr as "a gone man, and . . . all his cunning, enterprise, and industry will not save him." He also seconded Cheetham's view of Burr's character.[60] "Habituated to intrigue," Cheetham had written, "and distinguished by the *secrecy and celerity* of his movements, it is problematical whether even his confidential friends could bring home to him a single act of his of moment."[61] All this was followed by the July publication of another assault by the *American-Citizen* publisher, this one called *A View of the Political Conduct of Colonel Burr.* Added to a harsh portrait of Burr as a political swindler was the charge that he had intrigued to win the nation's highest office during the last presidential election.

De Witt Clinton's direction of it all was quite obvious. General John Armstrong had resigned from the U. S. Senate in February, and the state legislature had subsequently voted on a joint ballot to elevate the Governor's nephew to his office. Burr's friends then charged, in the midst of the Cheetham-created furor, that the Clintonians had connived to secure Armstrong's resignation. While such claims were without any evidence, they accentuated the bitterness. Cheetham's newest pamphlet was a venomous document, accusing Burr of having been an expedient member of neither party or of both parties, of having shown more interest in personal ambition than in principles, and of disregarding the obvious Republican intent to select Jefferson as the party's presidential candidate. Hardly anything was omitted from the impressive list of charges. Even Burr's most recent role during the judiciary debate was cited, with Cheetham's conclusion that "it is certain that Mr. Burr acted in concert with the federalists."[62] That Burr's friends should have reacted to all this, while the Vice President remained silent, was the result of continuing loyalty from his closest followers.

John Swartwout stood by Burr. It was Swartwout, now a marshal, who accused Clinton of trying to destroy Burr because his own insatiable ambitions needed the destruction of such a formidable rival.[63] When Clinton called Swartwout "a liar, a scoundrel and a villain," the Marshal demanded an apology. Clinton refused; and so on the last day of July the two men took to the Weehawken dueling ground. Clinton displayed his marksmanship and Swartwout his determination. Despite repeated offers to end the firing, Swartwout persisted long enough to receive two rounds of ammunition in his left leg. But his wounds were in vain as Clinton refused to apologize. "I am sorry I have hurt you so much," Clinton reportedly told the fallen man; then, turning to the seconds, he added: "I don't want to hurt him; but I wish I had the *principal* here. I will meet him when he pleases."[64] It was a statement that Burr interpreted as an indirect acknowledgment that Clinton was "an agent in the calumnies against me."[65]

Meanwhile, Burr did not reply. He seemed more preoccupied with the "bustle of moving" as he prepared to have Theo and her infant move from his city residence into Richmond Hill. No doubt his greatest concern at this time was over her illness, the seriousness of which she omitted from her letters to Alston.

Instead of accounts of her own discomfort, Theo worried about Alston's ability to manage in her absence and so described herself as a gay young lady enjoying all the splendors of Northern society. But such accounts made her behavior seem frivolous to him. No responsible nineteen-year-old mother, her husband wrote, would regard so lightly the seriousness of caring for an infant so far from home. South Carolina women, he asserted, would consider such a state as "very delicate" and would know better than to be "very gay or to mix much in company." He was clearly unhappy when he read of her "numerous engagements."[66] And he was even more annoyed when Theo went to Ballston Spa, north of Albany. Unaware of her need to seek comfort from the mineral waters at that place, Alston sent a petulant letter about the immorality of "a lady's going to any watering place."[67] He advised that Lebanon Springs was a more respectable resort, if she had to go at all.

Lebanon was east of the Hudson River and near the Massachusetts border, but when Theo did go there Alston felt no better. So removed was he from any knowledge of her illness that, from the agony of his loneliness and possessiveness, he wrote: "I suppose you are perfectly gay at Lebanon! parties and balls in constant succession; where, no doubt, you appear one of the most favorite belles."[68]

His attitude had made further deception impossible. One explanation was as painful as the other, and so Theo revealed her true condition. He received the letter sixteen days later, and his reply was one of shock and contrition: "My prescription is not intuitive; at such a distance from you, I could only judge from appearances."[69] After Theo returned to New York City, where she was mostly bedridden and under her father's supervision at Richmond Hill, tender and solicitous prose came from Alston. In October, she told him there was no hope for recovery. "I do not say it in a moment of depression, but with all my reason about me. I am endeavoring to resign myself with cheerfulness; and you, also, my husband, must summon up your fortitude to bear with a sick wife the rest of her life."[70] In November, Theo and little Aaron Burr Alston finally returned to South Carolina.

De Witt Clinton, meanwhile, refused to tone down his attacks, even after advice had been given that sufficient distrust had been created against Burr to prevent his renomination and that anything further would only injure the party. Gallatin told Jefferson that the New York "schism disgusts many Republicans." Continuing his loyalty to Burr, the Secretary of the Treasury also stated that such attacks had been "fomented by the Federalists."[71] Troup, contemptuous of Burr's silence and attributing it to a continuing attempt to pose as a supporter of the Administration, concluded that "Burr is ruined in politics as well as in fortune."[72]

By October, the anti-Burr material had become part of each issue of Cheetham's paper. Friends of Clinton were treated to nine letters that appeared over a span of more than two weeks in the columns of the *American-Citizen*. They were designed to reach those who had not read *A View of the Political Conduct of Aaron Burr*. Repetitious in theme, each letter highlighted another part of the indictment; but the objective was clarified by the very first one, which told Burr that his guilt *"ought to banish you forever from the affections of* ALL *parties, but especially the* REPUBLICANS."[73] What followed was a continuation of wholly vindictive documents. On the fifteenth of October, so much space was devoted to Burr's alleged crimes that the paper took advantage of the situation by carrying a tiny squib that stated: "We have not room today for Mr. Swartwout's note. It shall appear tomorrow—if nothing more interesting occurs."

As scurrilous as many of the intimations were, the most serious charges concerned the last presidential election. The absence of Burr's unqualified support for Jefferson, particularly through actions that had reversed his earlier declaration rejecting presidential ambitions and had obscured his true position, had aroused suspicions. Quite clearly, if judged solely on his loyalty to his party's number one candidate, Burr had failed to avoid such doubts. He had, in effect, been more loyal to himself and to his party, although the exact order can only be surmised. Moreover, by attempting to show that he had intrigued with the Federalists to defeat Jefferson, his enemies had a perfect opportunity to end for all time Burr's political prestige.

Cheetham marshaled all the charges: By falsifying Jefferson's prospects of getting votes in Rhode Island and by employing that fiction to keep Southern electors from defecting to a third candidate, Burr had actually helped to manufacture the tie. A New York elector had been induced to withhold one vote from Jefferson. Timothy Green's trip to South Carolina had really been a mission to arrange for pro-Burr electors from that state, probably in conjunction with the supporters of

Charles C. Pinckney. From Albany, where Burr and his friends had gone just before the House had balloted to break the tie, Van Ness had conducted negotiations for Burr by writing letters. One, to Representative Edward Livingston, suggested that Jefferson could not be elected and should be given up by the Republicans after the House had completed one or two ballots. Other Van Ness letters had attempted to influence New Jersey Republicans to drop Jefferson, while Davis remained in New York City to pursue a similar plan. When traveling to Trenton, Burr had had a secret meeting with David A. Ogden, a Federalist lawyer and close associate of Hamilton. Burr had assured Ogden that any success obtained through Federalist support could, as much as possible, reconcile him to Federalist policies. Furthermore, Ogden had served as Burr's liaison with other members of the opposing party.[74] Cheetham also found that Burr had cultivated an elector from New Jersey. He was Dr. Samuel Stanhope Smith, the father of Frances Ann Smith Prevost and the President of Princeton College.[75]

These charges added to smears that reached far back into Burr's career as both a state and a federal office-holder, stating every old allegation as fact without much concern for accuracy and circulated with glee by all who sensed gain from Burr's political demise. For the most part, they went unanswered, as Burr appeared too preoccupied with personal matters, particularly after the birth of Aaron Burr Alston. But Burr's defenders soon had a voice.

On October 1, while Cheetham's torrents were scoring daily, New Yorkers read the first issue of the *Morning Chronicle*. Edited by Dr. Peter Irving, the paper was *the* Burr organ. The first few issues repeated its intention to advocate "genuine Republican principles," while warning that it "will be ever ready to meet its adversaries; but it will never descend to unworthy practices, and will disdain to achieve a victory at the expence of private character."[76] Its ramparts were enforced in November with the appearance of the New York *Chronicle-Express*. The birth of both papers was actually financed by Burr, who had established Irving as editor. The papers' columns were careful to shield him from Cheetham's continuing assaults. When, for example, the *American-Citizen* asked that the anti-Burr material be copied by other papers, the *Morning-Chronicle* simply refused. Editor Irving pointed to the lack of "the substantiated *proofs* we were taught to respect" as sufficient reason for ignoring the stories.[77] Nevertheless, the *Morning-Express* gained more distinction for its use of the first published material by Peter Irving's brother, Washington, who contributed literary items under the by-line of "Jonathan Oldstyle," than for any vigorous counterattack. And the journalistic gains went to Cheetham. On November 16, the Albany *Register*, a loyal Democratic-Republican paper, came out against Burr, and most of the other Republican publications took the same position.[78]

Burr needed all the help he could get. His own behavior coupled with the accusations had deprived him of his little remaining confidence among Republicans. Those in a position to supply testimony capable of refuting some of the charges generally came forward, and the Irving papers were ready to carry the material. Timothy Green told the *Citizen*'s readers that he had gone to South Carolina for business only and not as Burr's agent.[79] Edward Livingston sent a letter to Burr testifying that the Vice President had not, "in any verbal or written communication to me," acted in any manner inconsistent with the party's desires.[80] Dr. Samuel S. Smith informed Coleman's paper that at no time prior to the voting by New Jersey's electors had Burr even discussed the subject of his own election, nor was any attempt made, through Edward Livingston or another agent, to sway his state's vote.[81] Of greater importance was David A. Ogden's version of his rendezvous with Burr.

This struck at the heart of the allegations that Burr's maneuvers had included an understanding with the Federalists. Ogden made two admissions. One was that he had gone as far as Trenton with Burr; but that, he maintained, was after they had met by chance at the stagehouse. Moreover, their conversation en route had been innocuous. Ogden also confirmed the story that members of Congress had requested him to find out how far the Republican candidate would cooperate in exchange for Federalist support. This piece of diplomacy Ogden actually discharged in New York, where, he asserted, Burr declined to make any commitment "and did neither propose nor agree to my terms." His interview was sufficiently unproductive to terminate all hopes of negotiating with him. As a result of this, Ogden had joined Hamilton in trying to persuade fellow Federalists to support Jefferson "as the less dangerous man of the two."[82]

Irving gladly printed Ogden's letter. It appeared the day after it was written, which was about as fast as journalism could operate in 1802. One week later came an editorial pointing out that Federalist hopes to negotiate with Burr and to make him the President had furnished substance for widely circulating stories. Washington Irving wrote: "the tale has been repeated with all the circumstantial additions which usually attaches to reports of this nature: till at length it has assumed that form and substance in which it has eventually been blazoned to the world."[83]

Burr had come to his own defense in a letter to his friend Governor

Joseph Bloomfield of New Jersey. The letter was a clear denial of all complicity charges. It declared that:

> You are at liberty to declare for me, that all those charges and insinuations which aver or intimate that I advised or countenanced the opposition made to Mr. Jefferson pending the late election and balloting for President; that I proposed or agreed to any terms with the federal party; that I assented to be held up in opposition to him or attempted to withdraw from him the vote or support of any Man whether in or out of Congress; that all such assertions and intimations are false and groundless.
>
>   I have not thought that calumny, unsupported by proof or even the authority of a name, could so far receive attention from the public as to require an answer or even a denial; yet if you shall imagine that any declaration from me can be necessary to remove doubts from the mind of one honest man, you may consider this letter as submitted to your discretion to publish if you shall think proper.[84]

But the most vigorous support and the harshest indictment of the entire Clintonian faction came from the pen of William Peter Van Ness. His prose reduced Cheetham's efforts to mere amateurish scribbling. Called *An Examination of the Various Charges Exhibited Against Aaron Burr* and written under the by-line of "Aristides," Van Ness offered the most comprehensive refutation of Burr's detractors. In lucid prose, he denounced the attacks as the work of those whose aim was to cost Burr the confidence of the administration." He ripped into the allegations and whispers that had been presented in lieu of evidence, particularly the position of two New York clergymen who deduced that Burr was guilty because he could not prove that he had *not* conspired with the Federalists. With his own identity hidden by the pseudonym, the author admitted that Van Ness had sent letters from Albany to move Republicans from Jefferson to Burr after the first or the second ballot. But he challenged the inevitable wisdom of following the popular choice. "The doctrine of infallibility of the people is not verified by experience," he wrote. "The political dogma, that the people can do no wrong, is as absurd, when applied to the popular sovereign of America, as to the hereditary monarch of England," he added. And while denying Burr's personal involvement, "Aristides" questioned whether a man should adhere at all costs to an indiscriminate loyalty toward his party's measures, "however unjust in themselves or dangerous to the community." Furthermore, he named others, such as Gilbert Livingston, who had also feared the consequences of holding out for Jefferson to win the election and whose inclinations had thus been for Burr to break the deadlock.

Moreover, suggested Van Ness, Jefferson himself had broken that impasse by using his patronage powers to prevent a Burr victory.[85]

As the only congressman from Delaware, Bayard could cast a crucial vote in the House. Federalist pressures had successfully moved him into Burr's column. Had he held fast, he could very likely block Jefferson's election. When he dropped Burr, unsubstantiated reports circulated that he had received assurances about political appointments and policies to be followed by Jefferson.[86] Had Burr been interested in playing this game, Van Ness reasoned, he would not have retreated to Albany that February but would, instead, have gone to Washington to compete with Jefferson in offering rewards for supporters.[87] At this point, he must have been thinking about Gallatin's letter.

His logic was reasonable. David A. Ogden had rejected any implication that Burr had been willing to cooperate with friendly Federalists. Bayard himself later wrote that "Burr had refused the offers of the Federalists," and had also observed that he could have won but "he was determined to come in as a Democrat." Later, in 1806, Burr sought to demonstrate this and obtained supporting affidavits from Samuel Smith and Bayard as part of a libel suit he had initiated against Cheetham. He was not interested at that later date in pursuing the suit. But Burr did manage to place on record statements by both men to further clear himself of having played any overt role.[88]

Yet, by 1803 Burr's standing as a Democratic-Republican had been shattered. Robert Troup noted that "Burr is ruined in politics as well as in fortune" and was also convinced that, in general, "the view of his political conduct is a just one."[89] Additional Republican newspapers, including William Duane's *Aurora*, were convinced of his guilt. Jefferson watched with an outward show of neutrality and a pious expression of regret at the internecine warfare, while, at the same time, he was convinced that Burr's treachery was quite obvious to all.[90] Before long, he and Swartwout had even lost their directorships in the Bank of Manhattan.

The movement to oust him from the bank was strong. Having actually begun toward the end of 1801, it was an extension of the political battle. One group of stockholders wrote that continuing Burr as a director "would not add a single feather to his cap or a tittle to his dignity, covered with laurels and honors of various kinds. It is not to be presumed that he is anxious to retain what to him would be a cypher."[91] As usual, Burr's personal finances had led him to indebtedness, and in 1802 he had borrowed extensively from the Manhattan coffers. So much money was involved that he could no longer tap that particular source.

That, plus the opposition from the other Republicans, kept him from being a candidate for re-election as a director during the annual December meeting. By 1803, the three remaining Federalist members were removed. The bank, so much a product of Burr's work, thus became a completely Clintonian-dominated Republican tool.

But Aaron Burr had already begun another enterprise. With John Swartwout as the organizer, in the fall of 1802 he had started a rival bank. Then began the battle to have its charter approved at Albany. Unfortunately for any undertaking associated with Burr's name, the legislators had subscribed to the growing anti-Burrite attitude. Most Republicans expressed criticism of his conduct and said he had lost their confidence. Against this tide, Swartwout worked feverishly to gather endorsements for the project from influential New York City Republicans.[92] He then appeared before the Assembly with a petition, which was finally relegated to a committee.[93] Almost all members from the city favored its acceptance, but Clintonians successfully killed the measure before it could return to the Assembly floor.[94] The Governor had noted that Swartwout's efforts were merely as a "plenepoteniary power from the party ingaged in the Measure, and they have duped some of unsuspecting friends to sign their Petition to the Legislature."[95] Consequently, Burr finally joined Robert Troup and other Federalist refugees from the Manhattan Company in the establishment of a rival called the Merchants' Bank.

During 1803, Burr's time was, as usual, preoccupied with "other matters." There are many words written to Theo about adventures with his Philadelphia "inamorata," as he called her. She was named Celeste, and she kept him busy during the romantic month of June. As fond as he was of the ladies, however, exchanging visits with Theo gave him his greatest pleasure. For such occasions enabled him to also see his little grandson. The baby's pronunciation of the word "grandfather" was the basis for Burr's calling him by the pet name of "Gampy." "If the little *gamp* could read," Burr wrote to Theo, "I should write to him volumes. I find my thoughts straying to him every hour in the day, and think more of him twenty fold than of you two together." A little later he wrote: "Dear little *gampy*; tell me a great deal about him, or I shall not value your letters."[96] Theo then obliged him with a lengthy paragraph about Gampy's latest exploits.

None of these letters tell much about political events. Burr was more inclined to discuss sex than politics with his daughter. Only when developments appeared to affect her do his letters reveal much, as when he offered her the use of Richmond Hill in the event that she should undertake a summer-long tour of the Western country. Such correspondence seems to have pleased Theo, who replied with advice on how to handle problems like his Philadelphia friend. "She called you back," Theo reminded her father. "What more could she do? I would have seen you to Japan before I should have done so much."

In October, Senator De Witt Clinton accepted an appointment to become mayor of New York City. No doubt Clinton was ambitious; and, undoubtedly, the rising young power considered becoming mayor more attractive than continuing in the Senate. Being mayor of New York was a first-rank post with important political advantages. De Witt Clinton's influence over patronage would be improved while helping his uncle keep control of the state, and he would also be closer to the source of his own political power. Just as clearly, the move symbolized the collapse of Burr as the head of a viable political machine in the city.

For Burr, then, the future looked barren. His rise had been rapid but controversial. Clinton had effectively neutralized him in New York and the Jefferson administration classified him as an opponent. Though he had been an effective president of the Senate, Vice President Burr was completing his third year in the nation's second highest office as a man virtually without political support.

CHAPTER XIV

A Morning at Weehawken

ALTHOUGH a year remained of his term as vice president, Burr was deserted by friends and enemies alike. Jefferson's popularity, based on prosperity and his much admired Louisiana Purchase, was so secure that he no longer needed Burr to carry a reluctant New York into the Republican column.

At the Republican caucus at Washington on February 25, 1804, Jefferson was nominated unanimously. Seven contestants received some votes for the vice presidency, but New York's seven-term governor, sixty-five year old George Clinton, won the nomination on the first ballot. "Mr. Burr had not one single vote, and not a word was lisped in his favor at the meeting," said an observer.[1]

The pro-Burr *Evening Post* immediately pointed out that Clinton had never been a friend of Mr. Jefferson; and had, in fact, referred to him earlier as an "accommodating trimmer in politics." But it analyzed Jefferson's motives keenly. While the President "took fair opportunity to plant the deepest thorn in the side of the Vice President," this was not his only purpose. The New York Governor represented the ruling clique in the state, the powerful and rich Clinton-Livingston axis, but personally was not a real threat to Jefferson and the Virginian succession. Election to the vice presidency might crown Clinton's career, but it would also terminate it.[2]

Early in 1804, Burr arranged for a meeting with Jefferson in order to clarify his position. The tall, freckle-faced, graying Virginian in down-at-the-heels slippers bent to listen to the small, dapper Burr. After recapitulating the events of 1800 and reasserting his sincere support of the Jefferson administration, Burr asked if Jefferson's attitude toward him had changed. Though he planned to retire from public office, the Vice President asked for some mark of favor that would indicate a continuing confidence. Jefferson answered crisply that he "never interfered directly or indirectly . . . to influence the election," and that he would continue this policy. Burr, however, would not have been surprised to read Jefferson's entry in his private journal that on their first meeting Colonel Burr's conduct "very soon inspired me with disgust."[3] Burr recognized that he had failed and there would be no presidential assistance.

Powerful enemies were overwhelming Burr, but he still had some strength in New York City: his loyal band of Burrites led by faithful lieutenants Van Ness and the Swartwouts. Though the Clinton-Livingstons were as powerful as ever, perhaps more so with De Witt Clinton now mayor of New York, the Federalists were almost defunct. As it became known that they felt themselves too weak to put up a gubernatorial candidate, Burr and company started to probe the possibilities.

John Lansing, Chancellor of the state, was the reluctant but strong Republican choice. He had no further political ambition but loyalty to the Clintons, who were responsible for his present position and who obliged him to accept in the interest of party amity. However, Lansing was not to be the only Republican candidate. At two meetings, one at the Tontine Coffee House in Albany, the other in New York City with Marinus Willett presiding, Aaron Burr was nominated as an independent contender for the office of governor.[4]

Upon hearing of Burr's nomination, Hamilton came out of retirement and shed his pose of a disappointed politician. Earlier, Burr had told Theodosia that "Hamilton is intriguing for any candidate who can have a chance of success against A. B." Even De Witt Clinton would be preferable to him, Burr added.[5]

At a Federalist meeting at Lewis' Tavern in Albany, Hamilton asked to speak on the Lansing-Burr contest. He accused Burr of using Federalism as "a ladder of his ambition" and further warned that the Colonel wished to promote "the dismemberment of the union" and to become "chief of the Northern portion." Two Burrites, eavesdropping in the next room, heard the group decide to support Burr, rejecting Hamilton's warning as personal hatred of Burr.[6]

But Lansing never became Burr's opponent. On February 18, quite unexpectedly, the Chancellor declined the nomination, refusing to state his reason. Several years later, he revealed that Clinton had demanded a commitment as to a "particular course of conduct in the administration of the government of the state."[7] Perhaps this was a convenient escape valve for a reluctant candidate, but nevertheless, it left the Republicans without a legitimate heir to Governor Clinton.

The search for a replacement netted Morgan Lewis, Chief Justice of the New York Supreme Court. Lewis' dignity and excellent family connections were lined up against Burr's dynamic personality. Hamilton stated, unhappily, that "the probability in my judgment inclines to Mr. Burr," which spurred him to a fruitless attempt to interest Rufus King in running on a Federalist ticket.[8]

The strength of the powerful Clinton-Livingston machine was either underestimated or unrecognized by the Burrites. While Colonel Burr was in Washington, it had established itself securely. But Burr had other supporters in Orange and Dutchess counties. Oliver Phelps, his running mate, expected to bring in Ontario County and other friends promised an "immence majority in the Western district."[9]

The campaign was a surprisingly bitter one. Public issues were hardly mentioned in the battle of newspapers and broadsides, but personalities and personal scandals were gleefully exhibited. No details were too ugly or distorted to restrain the generals directing the paper battles.

The Burr headquarters were located at John Street, between Nassau and William streets. Here the loyal band met with their chief, who had returned from Washington early in March. Burr participated actively in the electioneering, delivery of handbills, and making of speeches. To hear Cheetham describe it, no candidate had ever conducted himself in such an indelicate and indecent manner.

One of the new Burrite techniques was the introduction of the "degenerate" English custom of having singers to "chaunt" election songs. One was a verse product, possibly from Burr's pen, that was delivered as a broadside:

> Rise! Rise Columbians, make your stand . . .
> Entwine around the faithful band;
> The band once small, by you made great,
> Will raise the standard of the state.

> *Chorus*: Fell slander, hide your snaky crest:
>   We'll chuse the patriot we like best:
>   Burr's cause on naked truth relies,
>   And shines more brightly by Cheetham's lies.
>
>   .   .   .
>
> Avaunt, deception! Shine, bright truth!
> Aaron, who springs from Edwards' root,
> Shall rule with equal, virtuous hand,
> Columbia's free and happy land.[10]

Anti-Burrites responded with equally tasteless doggerel, such as a nasty set of verses that suggested placing the Colonel in a basket and carrying him around the countryside while the following was sung:

> Republicans won't let him rule o'er the nation:
> And, as that is the case we have now come to ask it—
> Of Governor to give him the snug little station;
> And see, we have bro't him thus far in a basket.
> Who wants little Aaron? Boo hoo![11]

The lowest nonsense level was reached with the *Poor Behrens! Poor Morgan!* broadsides which were augmented by Cheetham's daily copy. In both German and English, Burr was accused of having cheated the heir of Albright Behrens of thirty thousand dollars by withholding his inheritance, thus causing the hapless immigrant to die of a broken heart.[12] The case had occurred in 1797, and, said Burr, he had been very generous to young Behrens.[13]

Even more trivial was the case of "Poor Morgan." While Burr was in command on the Westchester lines, it was alleged that he had ordered Mr. James Morgan to be whipped with thirty-nine lashes on his bare back. This act, Cheetham said, indicated "Burr's capricious nature."[14] Letters poured into Peter Irving's *Morning Chronicle* from eyewitnesses, who said that Morgan was thought to have been a spy and, in the opinion of many, got off easy. Morgan's brother revised the account by revealing that the officer who had ordered the flogging had not been Burr. All was much ado about nothing, but it made for a fierce paper war.

Burr's alleged debauchery was another favorite theme. The Lewisites reminded the public of Burr's intrigue with the daughter of a Washington tradesman, whom he had lured to New York and then kept in Partition Street.[15] Another campaign handbill named Burr "the disgraceful debauchee who permitted an infamous prostitute to insult and embitter the dying moments of his injured wife."[16]

The "Creed of the Burrites," published in the *American-Citizen*, was even more tasteless than any of Cheetham's previous efforts. A heavy-handed reference to Jonathan Edwards and the New Lights, it read, in part:

> I believe in one Aaron Burr . . . ; I believe that Aaron Burr has done more during the late revolution to advance the liberties of America than General Washington himself; I believe that Aaron Burr is so good, pious and devout a man that after he has been Governor of the State of New York, . . . he will then be made Pope of Rome; . . . I believe that Aaron Burr is a perfect model of

chastity, piety, virtue and morality, . . . a sensible, learned, good man; I believe . . . that the governor of a state . . . need only possess such qualities as are requisite to gratify his adherents at all hazards.[17]

A political candidate in 1804 needed a strong stomach and a hard shell, but some of this abuse was softening Burr and readying him for a counterattack on the man behind it all, who, in his opinion, was not Cheetham but Alexander Hamilton. The Burr faction hit back, but in a different vein. Their campaign was directed against the dictatorship of New York by the ruling families and the excessive expenditure of funds to support them. "Plain Truth" and other broadsides estimated that the Clintons and members of the "noble families of Livingstons" had cost the state $87,500 annually.[18]

Burr said he had no family; but his opponents countered with the claim that he did, indeed, have a family. And that was composed of hungry and disappointed office-hunters, "*who like the ravenous harpies would devour the very platters on which they are fed.*" Such supporters as John Swartwout, Marshal of the District and "Prime Minister" to Burr, William Peter Van Ness, Davis, and Melancton Smith were cited.[19]

A curiosity of the campaign was the Burrite newspaper, *The Collector*, a quarto-sized semiweekly whose ten issues were limited to repetitive, uninspired satire. The editor called himself Toby Tickler, Esquire, and remains unidentified. Whether poetry or prose, it was unfortunate and the fun of pillorying De Witt Clinton must have become an expensive luxury. Clinton's problem, claimed Toby Tickler, was that he sickened at the sight of Burr's talent.[20]

Jefferson's role in this Republican Party civil war was confused, perhaps deliberately so. Burr prepared a letter in April to be sent to the President under Oliver Phelps' name. Jefferson was informed that many of Colonel Burr's supporters were loyal to the Administration and was reminded of his statement that since the contest was "a dispute in which republicans had been engaged on both sides," he would take no part in it.[21] Rufus King, however, reported hearing that Jefferson had modified his position to Phelps, and stated that "Republicans might with Equal Propriety support or vote for either candidate," with the addition that "if the Federalists took part it wd. materially alter the case and that the candidate oppsed by the Feds shd be supported by the Republicans!!!"[22]

Burr had accepted the Phelps version and had circulated handbills: "*Jefferson & Burr Against the Clinton & Livingston Combination.*" The Albany *Register* countered with Jefferson's statement that "the little band" could not be considered as "making a part of the real Republican interest." Actually, Jefferson's name was dragged through the campaign in an unauthorized manner, but for Jefferson, it served because it allowed him to preserve everyone's confidence.[23]

Cheetham devoted the entire April 24 issue of the *Citizen* to a castigation of Burr's lack of political morality. He accused him of trying to destroy both parties in order to lay the "foundation of the third upon their tomb."[24] On the eve of the election, mocked Cheetham, the desperate Vice President "did himself the honor" of inviting "twenty *gentlemen of colour*" to a ball and supper at his house.[25] Actually, a play for the Negro vote would have been a strange culmination to this bitter campaign.

The attitude toward secession in the early days of the republic differed greatly from our post-Civil War concept. All sections of the country had suffered periods of discontent with the actions of the federal government and had reconsidered seriously the wisdom of union. New England, in 1803–1804, fretted over the succession of anti-Federalist measures that culminated in the Louisiana Purchase and some of its leaders were moved to action. Timothy Pickering, former secretary of war and state under Washington, was now a senator from Massachusetts. He shared with others the fear that the Louisiana Purchase would allow Jefferson to depend on the West and South, leaving the Northeastern states to poverty and disgrace and that the country was now too big for union.[26] William Plumer, a senator from New Hampshire, carried this idea further, averring that the Purchase was unconstitutional and if the President could "*purchase* new states without the consent of the old, what was to prevent him from *selling* an old state without its consent?"[27]

For a brief moment, the Federalist members of the Eighth Congress made excessive statements; then, except for a few extremists, the rebellion faded. What was left of the plot went underground. It was unknown until two decades later.

Pickering and Roger Griswold, a Connecticut congressman whose brawl on the floor of the House with Vermont's Matthew Lyon in 1798 was still remembered, were consistently loyal to the separatist cause. Plumer, Oliver Wolcott, and Connecticut Senator Uriah Tracy, among others, hovered on the periphery of the plot.

There were varying proposals for the proper extent of the seceding area. But most argued it should range from boundaries on the Potomac River and the Hudson River, thereby limiting membership to New England and New York. The western edge would be the Susquehanna River, which would include New Jersey and Pennsylvania. A peaceable withdrawal was preferred, but if need be, General Hamilton was proposed as "the Joshua of the chosen people." It was hoped that he would attend a meeting planned for the fall of 1804 and, at that occasion, declare his support for the measure.[28] Griswold advised that the plot could be implemented by gaining control of state governments, repealing laws that ordered the election of representatives to the national congress, recalling the senators from Washington, and, finally, establishing customs collections.[29]

Burr's proposed role rested on the conspirators' recognition of New York as the key to their success. As early as 1803, Plumer had written of Burr that if he had "the reputation of as much integrity & virtue as his *good sense* actually imposes on him, we should not live under one feeble, nerveless administration of a dry dock & indissoluble salt mountain philosopher. The Vice President was joined by nature to command."[30]

Burr's candidacy provided the secessionists with a start for their plans. Griswold hoped that a combination of Federalist support, Burrites, and anti-Virginian Republicans would swing the election to the Vice President. The difficulty was that Hamilton refused to play the game this way. Burr, as leading man, would be hard enough for Hamilton to stomach, but this arrangement introduced another rival, Pickering. If he could lead a secession movement, he might emerge as the leader of the Federalist Party. Hamilton rebelled and carried many Federalists with him. Some of his motives were, undoubtedly, more sincere than jealousy. Perhaps he felt, along with George Cabot, that disunion under Burr's leadership was but the triumph of a kind of Republicanism and, therefore, no real solution.

Pickering tried to enlist other Federalists in Burr's support. He informed Rufus King that only Burr "can break your democratic phalanx" and if New York were "detached (as under his administration it would be) from the Virginia influence, the whole Union would be benefited."[31] King remained unconvinced.

Burr consistently aroused doubts from his political adherents. They feared his ambitions and his motives, but, as Griswold said, "In short I see nothing else left for us."[32] Besides, Burr had not actually committed himself. While still in Washington that March, he invited Pickering, James Hillhouse, and Plumer to one of his elegant dinners. Hillhouse ventured the suggestion that separation must soon take place. Burr answered vaguely that New England had been badly treated and that New York also had grievances that he, if elected, would allay. Plumer, who recorded the meeting, confessed himself baffled about what Burr really meant.[33]

Later, when Roger Griswold visited Burr in New York, he was cautious in his statements, but Burr was even more cautious. Burr had given the opinion that there was no middle course for the Northern states, holding that "they must be governed by Virginia, or govern Virginia."[34] Although basically unsatisfied, the Federalists had to be contented with the assumption that the defeat of Lewis would, at least, secure New York from Jeffersonian politics.

Jefferson was at no time alarmed by the reports he received about the New York election. He was a better prophet than the hopeful Federalist in Boston who proposed an election eve toast that said: "Aaron's rod: May it bloom in New York; and may federalists be still and applaud, while the greater serpent swallows the less."[35]

Burr prepared to sit out the election ordeal at his John Street headquarters. Last minute activity interrupted his letter to Theo so often that he said, "I write in a storm; an election storm." He estimated his prospect realistically, saying, "AB will have a small majority . . . *if tomorrow should be a fair day,* and not else."[36]

The New Yorkers who went to the polls, which opened at ten o'clock on the morning of April 25, voted at one of the nine polling places designated for the city's nine wards. To relieve the tedium of waiting, affluent gentlemen made bets on the outcome of the election. Odds favored the Lewisites, with majorities as high as ten thousand being estimated. If Lewis failed to win by more than five or six thousand, his friends would lose a lot of money.[37]

By April 26, Burr's hopes declined. The results of the city canvass gave him a majority of a scant one hundred votes. He managed this by winning five of the wards. On the basis of these returns, Governor Clinton predicted that the Burrites would be disappointed throughout the state. As the returns came in, the outlook for him worsened. He even lost some villages in promising areas of the Western District. "The election is lost by a great majority: *tant mieux,*" Burr wrote lightly to Theodosia. The epitaph to his last legitimate political venture was sandwiched in between news about the progress of his romance with La G. He always restrained his emotions when talking of himself, allowing the luxury of sentimentality only in matters that concerned Gampy and his mother. A week after his admitted defeat, he wrote of Gampy: "Of all earthly things I most want to see your boy. Does he yet know his letters? If no you surely must want skill, for, most certain, he can't want genius. You must tell me of all his acquirements."[38]

The official election results, which showed 30,829 for Morgan Lewis and 22,139 for Burr, were more humiliating than predicted. Lewis was the victor by a far larger majority than any other gubernatorial candidate had achieved in New York.

While the Clinton-Livingston-Lewis axis triumphed and the Jeffersonians breathed a sigh of relief, the secessionist Federalists searched for a way to save their cause. They now placed their hopes on the Boston meeting, planned for the fall, that would again solicit Hamilton's support.

However, they had reckoned without Burr. Years of calumny and spite directed at Burr now demanded payment. Burr's disappointment, coupled with the realization that repudiation by his party was definite, settled his wrath on the Federalist Hamilton rather than on the victorious Republicans. Hamilton's jealousy had been a strong obstacle in Burr's relationships with Washington and Adams. Now it had forced him out of retirement to destroy Burr's last chance. And Hamilton's loose tongue, incapable of discretion, now precipitated a final crisis.

In April of 1804, Judge John Taylor of Albany gathered a group of Federalists, among them General Hamilton, Judge Kent, and his son-in-law Charles Cooper, at his home for dinner. Inevitably, the conversation turned to the approaching gubernatorial election. Hamilton, Cooper wrote to a friend, spoke of Burr "as a dangerous man, and who ought not to be trusted. Judge Kent also expressed the same sentiment."[39] To Philip Schuyler, Cooper also wrote that "*Gen. Hamilton* and Judge *Kent* have declared in substance, that they looked upon Mr. *Burr* to be a dangerous man, and one who ought not to be trusted with the reins of government. . . . I could detail to you a still more despicable opinion which General *Hamilton* has expressed of Mr. *Burr*."[40]

The circumstances under which these letters found their way to the public were somewhat mysterious. The first letter, addressed to Andrew Brown, an Albany merchant, was, its author claimed, "Embezzled and Broken Open" while under the care of Johan J. Dietz of Bern. Therefore, instead of being delivered it was printed in the Albany *Register* of April 24, 1804.[41] The second letter, directed to Schuyler, which contained the challenging words "more despicable opinion," also found its way into print at the same time, and in the same newspaper.

These letters were not brought to Burr's attention, he claimed, until early June.[42] This statement is difficult to believe for the Schuyler-Cooper letter was reprinted as a broadside during the campaign and must have enjoyed considerable circulation. Perhaps the implications were ignored during the battle, or it was only after the despair of defeat that the sensitized Burr received the full impact of its words.

Burr's letters, at this time, gave no hint of the true state of his mind. He wrote the usual social trivia about his amours, his usual transports of enthusiasm for his grandson, and his normal directions to Theo. After one of Gampy's earlier literary efforts had charmed him, Burr wrote: "I have studied every pothook and trammel of his first literary performance, to see what rays of genius could be discovered."[43] Theo was advised to read Shakespeare, but not only for enjoyment, her father suggested. Passages that she found beautiful, absurd, or obscure should be marked. "I will do the same," Burr wrote, "and one of these days we will compare."[44] Seemingly, not the words of a man planning vengeance, but Burr was already engaged in seeking an explanation of Hamilton's conduct.

The first reaction came on June 17, when Burr sent a note to William Peter Van Ness. He urged his friend to call the following morning. When Van Ness arrived early on the eighteenth, he found that Burr wanted an explanation of Hamilton's statement contained in the April 23 Cooper-Schuyler letter. Burr told Van Ness that, urged by his friends and aware that "Genl Hamilton had at different times and upon various occasions used language and expressed opinions highly injurious to his reputation," he had prepared a note with the Cooper letter enclosed for Van Ness to deliver to Hamilton.[45]

At eleven o'clock the next morning, Van Ness presented Hamilton with Burr's note. The unfortunate newspaper clipping was enclosed. Mr. Van Ness "will point out to you that clause of the letter to which I particularly request your attention," wrote Burr. The clause in question read: "really, Sir, I could detail to you a still more despicable opinion which General *Hamilton* has expressed of Mr. *Burr*." Hamilton was then asked for "a prompt and unqualified acknowledgment or denial of the use of any expression which could warrant the assertions of Dr. Cooper."[46]

Hamilton read the note; its seriousness and unexpectedness moved him considerably. He asked for time for consideration, promising an answer that day. At 1:30 P.M., he called at the Van Ness home and, pleading the pressure of business responsibilities for the next day or two, assured Burr's friend that, by Wednesday the twentieth, he would have an answer "suitable and compatible with his feelings."[47]

As he had promised, Hamilton's reply was delivered. It was a refusal to make "the avowal or disavowal" that Burr had requested. Hamilton attempted to escape the clear accusation implicit in the words "more despicable" by asserting that this "admits of infinite shades, from very light to very dark. How am I to judge of the degree intended?" Further, the renowned lawyer hoped to pass off the comment as within the bounds "admissible between political opponents." After fifteen years of competition he stated that no "interrogation" on such a point should be necessary.[48]

Burr received the Hamilton letter on the twenty-first. His reply was dignified and precise, but adamant. "Political opposition can never absolve Gentlemen from the Necessity of a rigid adherence to all the rules of honor." Questions of syntax and grammar, he said, were irrelevant considerations. The significance lies in "Whether you have authorized their application either directly or by uttering expressions or opinions derogatory to my honor." The letter concluded with Burr's assertion that he now had "new reasons for requiring a definite reply."[49]

Burr's answer shook Hamilton. Van Ness reported that he had hoped not to have received such a letter.[50] In an attempt to arbitrate, Van Ness asked Hamilton if he could state that he had no recollection that he had used terms that could be so interpreted by Dr. Cooper because there would then be room for negotiation. With what seemed like stubborn determination not to help himself out of this unpleasant and dangerous situation, Hamilton again refused to answer Burr's letter and, furthermore, offered to put this refusal in writing. When told that this would not be necessary, Hamilton again stated that he was determined not to answer and that "Col. Burr must pursue such a course as he should deem most proper."[51]

Hamilton, realizing his predicament, consulted his friend Nathaniel Pendleton. Pendleton, a Revolutionary War veteran, was now one of the most prominent lawyers in the city; and he agreed to assist the Federalist by delivering for him the June 22 letter in which Hamilton refused to clarify Cooper's assertions but added, perhaps hopefully: "If you mean anything different admitting of greater latitude, it is requisite you should explain."[52]

Burr reacted to this direct rejection with a challenge to a duel, a course he felt had been invited by his opponent. In a verbal message carried by Van Ness, Burr accused Hamilton of "a settled and implacable malevolence; that he will never cease in his conduct towards Mr. B. to violate those courtesies of life. . . ." Burr reminded Hamilton that his own behavior to his rivals such as Jay, Adams, and himself had been "in terms of respect" with the proper regard for the individual's merits. For several years, said Burr, Hamilton had indulged in "base slanders" which he had refused to contradict and disavow. The sacrifices for the sake of harmony and the forbearance bordering on humiliation had only netted "repetition of injury." Therefore, Burr concluded, he had no other alternative, but to "announce these things to the world. . . . these things must have an end."[53]

Van Ness took the letter to the city the afternoon of June 23 and attempted to communicate with the General. Hamilton, however, was at *The Grange*, his country home, which was on the west side of Manhattan and just north of the present location of St. Nicholas Park. Van Ness wrote to him there, asking when and where he could be reached.[54]

Hamilton replied that by nine o'clock Monday morning he would be at his town house at No. 52 "Caeder" Street, where he would be glad to see him.[55]

Between June 23 and 25, the two spokesmen for the antagonists had several conversations. Pendleton tried to assert "the propriety of the ground which the General had taken."[56] He suggested that Burr write a letter asking whether the conversation Cooper had reported alluded to any "particular instance of dishonorable conduct." Hamilton would then, to the best of his recollection, state that the comments he had made were "on the political principles and views of Col. Burr and the results that might be expected from them in the event of his Election as Governor, without reference to any particular instance of past conduct, or to private character."

This was too little and too late. Burr, Van Ness reported to Pendleton, wanted reparation for the explicitly stated injuries that he had received: "a General disavowal of any intention on the part of Genl Hamilton in his various conversations to convey impressions derogatory to the character of Mr. Burr."[57] Pendleton believed that he could obtain such a declaration from his friend but, at six o'clock on June 25, when Van Ness called to receive the retraction, Pendleton admitted failure.[58]

From this point on, negotiations deteriorated rapidly. The correspondence between the seconds multiplied in quantity but accomplished no noticeable improvement in averting what seemed to be an inevitable conflict. What might have been acceptable to Burr earlier, now did not merit his attention. He and Van Ness wrote a statement of guilt and submitted it to Hamilton for his signature, but its tone was completely unacceptable. For example, the conclusion stated contritely: "I can only account for the inferences which have been drawn . . . by supposing the language I may have employed in the warmth of political discourse has been represented in a latitude entirely foreign from my sentiments or my wishes."[59]

By Tuesday, June 26, it was obvious that Hamilton had failed either to reassure Burr or to satisfy him. The two seconds were now repeating the assertions of their respective principals mechanically, well aware that no point of mutual understanding could be reached. The fatal "interview," as duels were often called in those days, had become inevitable.

A conclusive flurry of accusation and counteraccusation delayed the end briefly. Hamilton charged Burr with an attitude of predetermined hostility and the wish to extend the inquiry to his "confidential as well as his public conversations." Burr denied these motives, saying that this charge merely added "insult to injury." This extended correspondence proved only the melancholy fact that nothing was possible "except the simple Message which I shall now have the honor to deliver."[60]

At noon, the twenty-seventh of June, the challenge was brought by Van Ness to Pendleton and formally accepted. Pendleton asked for some delay because of General Hamilton's legal and personal commitments. Hamilton submitted to his opponent some "Remarks," which included his acceptance of the "alternative" and his reluctance to force his clients to seek other counsel. Van Ness refused this paper on the grounds that negotiations had been terminated once the challenge had been delivered and accepted. Nothing was left but to make final arrangements for the event. On July 3, Van Ness and Pendleton met and, after some discussion, the date was set for the morning of July 11.[61]

During this bitter exchange, both principals conducted their daily lives with an outward aplomb. Only a few friends knew anything about the crisis. Rufus King knew of the impending duel, but since Hamilton refused to discuss "the question of duel or no duel," he left New York the Friday before it was to take place. He had planned a visit to his relatives in the company of Judge Egbert Benson who, consequently, also knew of the impending event. They traveled to Jay's country home, where King told his host of Hamilton's decision. John B. Church must have realized that the pistols Hamilton had borrowed were to be used at the interview. But as far as is known, none of these men attempted to stop the proceedings.[62]

Except for Van Ness, Burr is not known to have confided in anyone. He celebrated Theo's birthday on June 23 with a gathering of more than a dozen friends at Richmond Hill for dining and dancing. "We had your picture in the dining room," he wrote his daughter, "but, as it is a profile, and would not look at us, we hung it up, and placed Natalie's at table, which laughs and talks to us." He commended her for her idea of retelling the tales of ancient mythology for children and challenged her to study natural philosophy, for "A. B. A." (which was still another way he referred to little Aaron Burr Alston) was anxious about the boy who was looking pale so early in the season. But, he said, "I like much his heroism and his gallantry."[63] All the gossip he also included hardly made him sound like a man with a potentially fatal encounter on his mind.

On July 1, his spirits seemingly as bright, he wrote about books and libraries and recommended a new publication called the Edinburgh *Review*. The weather was unseasonably cold, he reported, and went on to add that "I have now, just at sunset had a fire in my library, and am sitting near it and enjoying it, if that word be applicable to anything done in solitude. . . . Let us, therefore, drop the subject, lest it lead to another on which I have imposed silence on myself."[64]

As the day approached, both men prepared quietly and sensibly for "the last critical scene, if such it shall be."[65] Hamilton named Pendleton his executor and on July 4, the same day, wrote a farewell note to his wife, Elizabeth, to be delivered if "I shall have first terminated my earthly career." He explained his action by asserting that an avoidance was impossible "without sacrifices which would have rendered me unworthy of your esteem." Religion must be her consolation.[66]

That evening was the annual Fourth of July dinner of the Society of Cincinnati held at Fraunces Tavern. Both Burr and Hamilton were present. An eyewitness reported that the General was cheerful and sang "The Drum." Burr, in contrast, was subdued, mixing little with the company: "his countenance was that of a disappointed and mortified man." But when Hamilton sang, he raised his head and listened.[67]

On Friday, July 6, the Circuit Court closed, freeing Hamilton to fulfill his obligation. That Monday, final details were settled. They were not completely agreeable to Burr, who would have preferred an earlier date but a later hour. "What you shall do will be satisfactory to me— except an early Morning hour. I have no predilection for time," he wrote Van Ness. "From 7 to 12 is the least pleasant, but anything so we *but* get on." As to medical aid, "H - K is enough, & soon that unnecessary."[68] He referred to their mutual friend, Dr. David Hosack.

In the days before the duel, both parties prepared for the possibility of death, each in his own style. Hamilton settled his financial affairs, wrote his will, and granted John B. Church his power of attorney. The burden of a family of seven children did not make it easy for him to contemplate the elimination of its source of income.

On the eve of the duel, Hamilton committed his last political act, a death blow to the New England Confederacy and the secession movement. After referring to this "growing distaste for politics," Hamilton wrote to Theodore Sedgwick that the "dismemberment of our empire" will sacrifice positive advantages without relieving "our real disease, which is *democracy*, the poison of which by a subdivision will only be the more concentrated in each part, and consequently the more virulent."[69]

Hamilton stayed in the city his last night. Once again he wrote a letter to his "beloved Eliza," who did not know what the morrow could bring. It was ten o'clock at night. His fears and his determination almost overwhelmed him. The decision to expose his life but not to impose upon himself the guilt of taking another's was communicated to his wife.

"This must increase my hazards & redoubles my pangs for you. But you had rather I should die innocent than live guilty."[70]

At Richmond Hill, Burr, having written his will and arranged his papers, advised Theo to take charge of his private letters and burn all that could injure anyone, particularly the letters of his female correspondents. Six blue boxes, he said, contained enough information for Alston, if he thought it a worthwhile project, to "write a sketch of my life."

Burr estimated that his estate would just pay his debts, "if I should die this year." Theo, of course, was unaware of the duel. Various assignments of his belongings were made. Natalie and Dr. Eustis were each to have one of his three portraits; Bartow was to get a token. The disposition of his slaves concerned their master, too, as he arranged for the faithful Peggy to get a small lot; and, Burr advised Theo, "try to persuade her to live with you." Nancy, honest, robust, and good-tempered, was to be disposed of at Theo's discretion, but Peter, "the most intelligent and best disposed black I have ever seen," should be kept as a valet for little A. B. A.

Frederick Prevost was to receive Burr's wearing apparel, a sword or pair of pistols, and his stepfather's watch. Directions about the correspondence of specific lady friends occupied a good part of his final instructions. Clara's letters tied up in a white handkerchief in Blue Box #5 were to be handed to Mari. He had enough humor left to tell Theo that she and A. B. A. may laugh at some of the nonsense some day. Washington's seal, he wrote, "You may keep . . . for your son, or give it to whom you please."

Burr closed with these affecting words: "I am indebted to you, my dearest Theodosia, for a very great portion of the happiness which I have enjoyed in this life. You have completely satisfied all that my heart and affections had hoped or even wished. With a little more perseverance, determination, and industry, you will obtain all that my ambition or vanity had fondly imagined. Let your son have occasion to be proud that he had a mother. Adieu. Adieu."[71]

Burr sent a more businesslike letter to Alston. He told him that Van Ness and Swartwout, because they were on the spot, would be joint executors with him and Theo. Though undoubtedly Richmond Hill would cover them, he asked Alston to assume his debts. "I think, too, you would do well to retain Richmond Hill." Burr's loyal band, such men as R. Bunner, William and John Duer, J. W. Smith, John Van Ness, Yates of Albany, William T. Broome, now in Paris, were to be given "some small token of remembrance of me."

"I have called out General Hamilton, and we meet to-morrow morn-

ing. Van Ness will give you the particulars," he revealed. "If it should
be my lot to fall, . . . yet I shall live in you and your son. I commit to
you all that is most dear to me—my reputation and my daughter," he
went on to tell Alston. As a last favor, Burr asked that his son-in-law,
whatever his own feelings might be, should help Theo cultivate her
mind and acquire a critical knowledge of Latin, English, and natural
philosophy so that all this "would be poured into your son." Two
postscripts concluded the letter.

The first recommended Frederick Prevost to Alston's attention. The
second, inevitably it would seem, included this instruction: "If you can
pardon and indulge a folly, I would suggest that Madame Sansay, too
well known under the name of Leonora, has claims to my recollection.
She is now with her husband at St. Jago of Cuba."[72] The correspondence having been completed, Burr lay down upon a couch in his library
and slept soundly the remaining hours of the night.

The rules for the interview, which had been prepared by Pendleton,
were consistent with established custom. Both parties were directed to
leave the city at about five A.M., July 11. Pistols no longer than eleven
inches in the barrel were designated as the weapons, and the distance
was fixed at ten paces. When the parties had taken their positions, one of
the seconds—who would be determined by lot—would have the job of
saying loudly and distinctly, "Present." Should only one party fire, "the
opposite second will say one, two, three—fire, and he shall then fire or
lose his shot. A snap or flash is a fire."[73]

Both men knew something about duelling, of course. Besides his challenge to Monroe in 1797, at which Burr acted as peace-maker, Hamilton
had proposed a duel with General Charles Lee because of the latter's
treatment of the Commander in Chief at the Battle of Monmouth. But
the choice, by lot, had fallen to another Washington aide and Hamilton
had had to be content to serve as second. Later, a political quarrel with
Commodore Nicholson brought a challenge that was averted only at the
intervention of friends.

However, it was the tragic encounter between Hamilton's promising
young son, Philip, and George Eacker that had made duelling so abhor-
rent to him. Nevertheless, regardless of his moral and religious scruples
or his family and business responsibilities, Hamilton was not in a position to refuse Burr's challenge if he hoped to continue as a favorite for
military command. It was this consideration of "what men of the world
denominate honor" that forced him into the "peculiar necessity not to
decline the call. The ability in future to be useful, whether in resisting
mischief or effecting good in those crises of our public affairs, which
seem likely to happen, would probably be inseparable from a conform-

ity with public prejudice in this particular." Hamilton wrote this shortly before the duel, enclosing his remarks in his will, to be opened after the event, if necessary. The document also contained his decision to *"receive* and *throw away"* his first fire and perhaps also the second one, "thus giving a double opportunity to Col. Burr to pause and reflect."[74]

Burr had engaged in other duels. One had been with John B. Church. Both had emerged unharmed, although Church's bullet had ripped Burr's coat. That affair had been over Burr's involvement with the Holland Land Company.[75] A more recent duel, which was reported through family channels and never publicly revealed, developed because word of the coming Burr-Hamilton encounter had reached the ears of Samuel Bradhurst, an admirer of Hamilton and a relative by marriage of Burr's. Fancying himself as a peace-maker, Bradhurst forced an interview with Burr at Richmond Hill, a visit Burr must have received with distaste and surprise at the man's audacity. Nevertheless, the visit resulted in a challenge, although no one knows which man issued it. Bradhurst, however, was probably responsible, as he had a romantic notion that such a duel would prevent the other. So secret were the arrangements that the place, date, scene, and names of the seconds were never revealed. But it probably did take place at Weehawken, where Bradhurst sustained a sword wound in his arm or shoulder and Burr was thus freed to deal with bigger game.[76]

Before daybreak on Wednesday, July 11, 1804, the two principals, similar in age and importance if not in pedigree, headed for Weehawken in separate boats. Burr had been awakened by John Swartwout. He dressed carefully and, as usual, elegantly, in black cotton pantaloons and half boots, and a coat of bombazine. He had walked to his waiting party at the boat. From the foot of Charlton Street, John Gould rowed them across the Hudson River to the north side of the beach at Weehawken. Arriving before Hamilton, as previously agreed, Burr and Van Ness cleared the underbrush for the others.

The duelling ground at Weehawken, opposite what is now Forty-second Street, was a little ledge twenty feet above the waters of the Hudson. At water level, there was a pebbly beach with two good landing places and a high place between so the men could not observe each other. From the beach, a natural and almost regular flight of steps led up to the grassy shelf, which was about two yards wide and twelve yards long. It was the perfect size for the purpose, because the duellists were protected from interruption by the sheer cliff which rose above the ledge, making the place almost inaccessible from above. Nor could the duel be seen from the beach below.

Reverend Aaron Burr, artist unknown
(PRINCETON UNIVERSITY)

*Reverend Jonathan
Edwards, artist unknown*

*Esther Burr, detail from
a damaged painting,
artist unknown*
(COURTESY OF OLIVER
BURR JENNINGS)

OPPOSITE: *General George Washington by Rembrandt Peale.* (COURTESY OF THE NEW-YORK HISTORICAL SOCIETY, NEW YORK CITY)

BELOW LEFT: *Major General Benedict Arnold, engraving by H. B. Hall* (COURTESY OF THE NEW-YORK HISTORICAL SOCIETY, NEW YORK CITY)

BELOW RIGHT: *Major General Israel Putnam, engraved by W. Humphries after a sketch by Colonel John Trumbull* (COURTESY OF THE NEW-YORK HISTORICAL SOCIETY, NEW YORK CITY)

OPPOSITE: *Burr's daughter Theodosia by Gilbert Stuart, 1794.* (COURTESY OF OLIVER BURR JENNINGS)

BELOW: *Burr's Richmond Hill House, watercolor by Abram Hosier.* (COURTESY OF THE NEW-YORK HISTORICAL SOCIETY, NEW YORK CITY)

John Jay by Joseph Wright.
(COURTESY OF THE NEW-YORK
HISTORICAL SOCIETY, NEW YORK
CITY)

George Clinton by Ezra Ames.
(NEW YORK STATE HISTORICAL
ASSOCIATION, COOPERSTOWN,
NEW YORK)

Robert R. Livingston by John
Vanderlyn. (COURTESY OF THE
NEW-YORK HISTORICAL SOCIETY,
NEW YORK CITY)

John Adams, engraved from an
original portrait by Gilbert Stuart
(COURTESY OF THE NEW-YORK
HISTORICAL SOCIETY, NEW YORK
CITY)

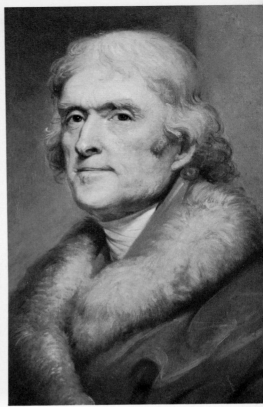

ABOVE LEFT: *James Madison,
engraved by W. H. Wilmer after a
portrait by Gilbert Stuart.*
(COURTESY OF THE NEW-YORK
HISTORICAL SOCIETY, NEW YORK
CITY)

ABOVE RIGHT: *Thomas Jefferson by
Rembrandt Peale.* (COURTESY OF
THE NEW-YORK HISTORICAL
SOCIETY, NEW YORK CITY)

OPPOSITE: *Albert Gallatin, etched
by H. B. Hall from a portrait by
Rembrandt Peale.* (COURTESY OF
THE NEW-YORK HISTORICAL
SOCIETY, NEW YORK CITY)

Chief Joseph Brant, engraved from an original painting by G. Romney (COURTESY OF THE NEW-YORK HISTORICAL SOCIETY, NEW YORK CITY)

DeWitt Clinton by John Wesley Jarvis. (COURTESY OF THE NEW-YORK HISTORICAL SOCIETY, NEW YORK CITY)

Martling's Tavern and Long Room, wash drawing by Abram Hosier (COURTESY OF THE NEW-YORK HISTORICAL SOCIETY, NEW YORK CITY)

Aaron Burr, age forty-six, by John Vanderlyn, 1809
(COURTESY OF THE NEW-YORK HISTORICAL SOCIETY, NEW YORK CITY)

Alexander Hamilton by John Trumbull
(COURTESY OF THE NEW-YORK HISTORICAL SOCIETY, NEW YORK CITY)

The duel at Weehawken by P. Meeder

ABOVE LEFT: *Jonathan Dayton by Albert Rosenthal.* (COURTESY OF THE NEW-YORK HISTORICAL SOCIETY, NEW YORK CITY)

ABOVE RIGHT: *General James Wilkinson, mezzotint by Max Rosenthal after the painting by Charles W. Peale.* (COURTESY OF THE NEW-YORK HISTORICAL SOCIETY, NEW YORK CITY)

OPPOSITE: *General Andrew Jackson, engraved by A. B. Durand after the painting by John Vanderlyn.* (COURTESY OF THE NEW-YORK HISTORICAL SOCIETY, NEW YORK CITY)

*John Marshall, engraved by
A. B. Durand after a painting
by Henry Inman.* (COUR-
TESY OF THE NEW-YORK
HISTORICAL SOCIETY, NEW
YORK CITY)

*Matthew L. Davis, artist
unknown.* (COURTESY OF
THE NEW-YORK HISTORICAL
SOCIETY, NEW YORK CITY)

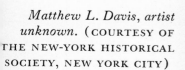

Theodosia Burr Alston, age twenty, by John Vanderlyn, 1802
(COURTESY OF THE NEW-YORK HISTORICAL SOCIETY, NEW YORK CITY)

Rebecca Smith Blodgett,
engraved by Sartain after a
painting by Gilbert Stuart
(COURTESY OF THE NEW-
YORK HISTORICAL SOCIETY,
NEW YORK CITY)

Madame Elizabeth Jumel
Burr, artist unknown
(COURTESY OF THE NEW-
YORK HISTORICAL SOCIETY,
NEW YORK CITY)

Aaron Burr by James Vandyck, 1834
(COURTESY OF THE NEW-YORK HISTORICAL SOCIETY, NEW YORK CITY)

Hamilton arrived shortly after the Colonel, at about seven A. M., in a barge carrying his second and Dr. Hosack. Their most likely debarkation was Horatio Street, three miles from Weehawken.[77] Then the opponents exchanged formal greetings as the seconds made arrangements. The distance of ten full paces was measured off and lots were cast to determine which second would give the word and make the choice of position. Pendleton won both.

The pistols were loaded in the presence of both adversaries. They were of unusual size, with a clumsy wooden stock, a barrel marked "J. Twiggs, London," almost a foot long, with a flint lock.[78] Only an X on the butt distinguished Burr's pistol from Hamilton's.[79] When the parties took their stations, Pendleton explained that he would inquire whether they were ready and, receiving an affirmative answer from both, he would say "present" and the parties could present and fire at will. Burr and Hamilton acknowledged the rules.

Pendleton had chosen the upper end of the ledge for his man, although it would not have seemed to be the best spot because of the morning sun's rays and the reflection from the river. Thus, Hamilton faced the Hudson and Burr the heights under which the duelling ground stood.[80] As the seconds withdrew the proper distance, Pendleton gave the order. Both parties took aim and fired in succession.

The eyewitnesses disagreed on precisely what had happened. That the pistols were discharged within a few seconds and that Colonel Burr's fire took effect was certain. All agreed that Hamilton fell almost immediately.[81] Later, Pendleton gave more details, which emphasized Burr's cool and determined actions. He said that the Colonel had raised his arm, took aim, and fired with an accuracy that sent his ball into the General's right side. As the ball struck, Hamilton raised himself involuntarily on his toes and turned a little to the left, at which moment his pistol went off, and he fell on his face. Pendleton and a friend, revisiting the scene the next day, found that Hamilton's ball had passed through the limb of a cedar tree at the height of twelve and one half feet from the ground and about thirteen to fourteen feet from where Hamilton had stood. It was also four feet wide of the direct line between him and Burr. The branch was cut off and brought back to the city by Church.[82]

Burr reported a different version. When Pendleton asked if the gentlemen were ready, according to Burr, Hamilton said, "Stop. In certain states of the light one requires glasses." He then levelled his pistol in different directions to try the light. Finally, he put on his spectacles and repeated the experiment several times until he was satisfied. At last, with spectacles on, he signalled that he was ready. At the command "present," he took aim and fired promptly. Burr fired two or three seconds later;

and, as Hamilton was brought down, he exclaimed, "I am a dead man." As Burr related the event about a week after the duel, he recalled that "Hamilton looked as if oppressed with the horrors of conscious guilt."

Burr questioned the accuracy of the other observers and, by the same token, his own must be accepted with some skepticism. As he himself admitted, those at the scene were "a good deal agitated and not to be in a state of mind suitable for observing with accuracy what passed." He considered Hamilton's declaration that he did not mean to injure him a "contemptible disclosure if true."[83]

When Burr saw his adversary fall, he instinctively moved toward him with a gesture of regret or concern; but, urged by Van Ness, did not speak but turned and permitted himself to be hurriedly led from the field to avoid the observation of Hosack and the bargeman who had been called to the scene. Burr was then rushed into his waiting boat, all the time protesting that he wished to return and speak to Hamilton. Van Ness, however, refused to permit such folly and, sadly, the group was rowed back to the city.[84]

Pendleton, horrified at the sight of Hamilton falling, called to Dr. Hosack, who came at once. The wounded man was half sitting on the ground. Only Pendleton's arms kept him upright. "This is a mortal wound, Doctor," he managed to say before he collapsed. Hosack, stripping his clothes away, discovered that the ball must have penetrated a vital part, which an autopsy later confirmed. The ball had struck the second and third rib, fractured it about in the middle, passed through the liver and diaphragm, and seemingly lodged in the first and second vertebrae, which splintered. About a pint of clotted blood was present in the belly cavity, probably effused from the divided vessels of the liver.[85]

He had no pulse and no respiration. Hosack advised that he be removed as quickly as possible. The anxious group of friends carried him out of the wood to the shore, where the boatman helped to convey him into the boat, still unconscious. The fresh sea winds or the application of hartshorn revived him so that he spoke feebly, complaining that his vision was poor. When he regained some sight, his eyes surveyed the boat until they lit on the case of pistols. He said, "Take care of that pistol; it is undischarged, and still cocked; it may go off and do harm;— Pendleton knows . . . that I did not intend to fire at him." He lay quiet after the exertion of speaking. But when he told Hosack that he had no feeling in his lower extremities, the doctor knew that there was no hope of survival.

As the boat approached the shore, William Bayard stood at the wharf, greatly agitated, to conduct the fallen man to his Jane Street home.

Hamilton asked that Mrs. Hamilton be sent for, but that she be told the news gradually, to "give her hope." Bayard was so touched that he burst into tears and lamentations. Hamilton remained calm and composed as he was borne gently into the house and revived with a little weak wine and water.

However, that day was one of agonizing suffering for, despite Hosack's attempts to relieve the pain in his back, it was almost unbearable. A medical colleague of Hosack's at Columbia College was consulted, but he also agreed that there was no hope of recovery. The French consul invited the surgeons from French ships lying in the harbor to look at him because of their experience with gunshot wounds. They concurred with the others.[86]

Burr went directly to Richmond Hill with Van Ness and his servant. His composure belied the morning's events. A neighbor reported that on the way there he greeted her with his usual affability. A Connecticut cousin unexpectedly called at his home at about eight o'clock. His servant, Alexis, showed the young man into the library. There, he was cordially received by the Colonel. They breakfasted together in the dining room, conversing about mutual friends. After breakfast, as the youth walked down Broadway, he imagined that passers-by were agitated until, near Wall Street, an acquaintance rushed up saying, "Colonel Burr has killed General Hamilton in a duel this morning."[87]

Burr's broker reported a similar story of how the Vice President managed to keep his self-control. About two hours after his return from the field of the battle, Burr sent for the man to discuss business. They were together about a quarter of an hour, Burr giving no hint of the early morning event. On the contrary, said the broker, he seemed cheerful and in good humor.[88]

The following day the pain had diminished, but Hamilton's symptoms were aggravated. His mind remained lucid, but he suffered terrible anxiety for the family he would leave behind. His wife was frantic with grief. He tried to soothe her with such words as, "Remember, my Eliza, you are a Christian." But even his magnificent calm broke when he was surrounded by his children, the youngest but two years old. Sadly, he asked that they be taken away.

As Hamilton lay dying, Burr wrote a note to Dr. Hosack, inquiring, in the formal third person, "for the present state of General H. and of the hopes which are entertained of his recovery."[89] Van Ness had written to Pendleton the day before to ask about his condition and to express the hope that the wound was not mortal. His concern was also for Burr, as he requested that the two seconds meet as soon as "your situation and feelings will justify it."[90]

At two o'clock on the afternoon of July 12, Hamilton died. His family, Oliver Wolcott, Dr. Hosack, Bishop Benjamin Moore, and probably the Churches were present. Moore, the second Protestant Episcopal Bishop of New York and the President of Columbia College, had administered the last rites to the dying man. He reported Hamilton as having said: "I have no ill will against Col. Burr. I met him with a fixed resolution to do him no harm. I forgive all that happened."[91]

The death of Hamilton elevated him to instant martyrdom. The press and the pulpit extolled his virtues and shouted shame and murder at Burr. The funeral for the fallen hero was arranged for Saturday, July 14. It was to be a solemn and elaborate tribute, the Common Council having voted to assume the expenses and having decreed that all the city's inhabitants suspend business for the day.

The city was draped in black as the procession arranged by the Society of the Cincinnati started out at noon from Church's house in Robertson Street. The rear of the procession did not reach its destination, Trinity Church, until two o'clock. Solemnly, it moved through streets lined with weeping citizens, past windows and housetops crowded with tearful watchers. British and French ships in the harbor fired guns during the procession and merchant ships flew their flags at half-mast.

The advanced platoon of soldiers reached the church first. They wheeled back, forming a lane and bringing their muskets to a reversed order, resting their cheeks on the butts in the customary attitude of grief. The corpse was borne through this avenue, supported by eight pallbearers. On top of the coffin lay the General's hat and sword. Directly behind, his gray horse, dressed in mourning, his master's boots and spurs reversed, was led by two black servants dressed in white, their heads covered by white turbans trimmed with black. In solemn procession, the mourners followed: the family and relations of the deceased, preceded by the clergy and the members of the Society of the Cincinnati, then the faculty and students of Columbia College, the members of the Society of Mechanics and Tradesmen, and others. They walked to the platform that had been erected in the portico of Trinity Church as muffled drums beat out a funeral dirge.

Gouverneur Morris, surrounded by Hamilton's four sons, delivered the eulogy. It was extempore and, said David Ogden, "His feelings for the loss of his friend almost prevented him from speaking at all." Some thought the oration a little disappointing, although it was well delivered in an appropriately solemn manner.

The day before, Morris had been asked to speak at the funeral. Aware of many difficulties and agitated by the deathbed scene that he had just witnessed, Morris agreed but reluctantly. However, he made clear that "in doing justice to the dead," he would not "injure the living—that Colonel Burr ought to be considered in the same light with any other man who had killed another in a duel."

Morris had another difficulty. There were many phases of Hamilton's life that would have to be omitted or passed over lightly, such as the fact that he was "a stranger of illegitimate birth"; that he was "indiscreet, vain, and opinionated"; that he was in principle "opposed to republican and attached to monarchical government"; that he was "in principle opposed to duelling, but he has fallen in a duel"; and that even his domestic life must be played down because long ago he had "foolishly published the avowal of conjugal infidelity." Even while riding to the funeral, Morris had meditated on the speech, aware that his audience's "indignation amounts almost to a frenzy already."[92]

Morris spoke of Hamilton's gallantry during the Revolution, his public service and concern for the public welfare, his professional skill and unrivalled eloquence as a lawyer. As to his death, said Morris, "I must not dwell. . . . Suffer not your indignation to lead to any act which might again offend the insulted majesty of the law."[93] He begged that anger against Burr would not give rise to violence. The oration finished, the troops who had entered the churchyard formed a column and terminated the obsequies with three volleys over the grave.

While the city and nation mourned his victim loudly and extravagantly, Burr remained in seclusion at Richmond Hill. Whatever his private thoughts, remorse, regret, or even irritation at the unfortunate outcome of the encounter, the reality presented a clear danger. The coroner of the city and county of New York had attempted to find witnesses to testify against Hamilton's slayer. But the Vice President's friends remained fiercely loyal. Matthew L. Davis, for instance, refused to answer questions about Burr and went to jail instead. The coroner was forced to adjourn for lack of evidence.

Burr blamed the intensity of the public reaction on the deliberate efforts of the Clintonians and "malignant federalists." "Thousands of absurd falsehoods are circulated with industry. The most illiberal means are practised in order to produce excitement, and, for the moment, with effect," he wrote to Joseph Alston.[94] But Burr's friends insisted that he leave town. They said that his safety depended on flight. He agreed to leave and, perhaps, travel to South Carolina.

CHAPTER XV

"The Man Who Killed Hamilton"

ARON BURR was almost a prisoner at Richmond Hill. The people of New York and New Jersey, stirred up by anti-Burr Republicans and Cheetham's editorials, accepted as a fact the notion that the duel was nothing but premeditated murder.

The newspapers filled their columns with versions of the fatal interview. The *Morning-Citizen* alleged that Burr had been sharpening his marksmanship for several years in anticipation of that day. Even a reasonable citizen such as David Ogden was taken in by "the reports in circulation." He reported that Burr had spent several hours a day for three months shooting at a mark until "he could cut a ball every time the size of a dollar at ten paces."[1]

It was said that Burr's tailor had made him, for the occasion, an extra large black silk coat that, along with his silk underwear, was guaranteed to deflect bullets.[2] But the juiciest tale concerned Madame Betsy Jumel, the new wife of the wealthy French merchant, Stephen Jumel. Rumor had it that she had been the real cause of the duel, that both men loved her, but that she preferred Burr and used Hamilton to learn his secrets and betray them to his rival. "Still more despicable"—the words that Cooper had attributed to Hamilton—referred to this personal matter, deduced a modern biographer of the lady.[3]

The public outcry was loud and unrestrained, but, privately, many prominent citizens reserved judgment. Even George Clinton, who had much to gain from Burr's fall, admitted to Senator Plumer that "Hamilton was under no obligation to have accepted Burr's challenge," and, furthermore, that the "unremitted censure and pursuit against him was by many considered as partaking of persecution."[4] The political-minded Governor weighed the effect of the duel, carefully concluding that this violent display of hostility against Burr might boomerang and make friends for him, particularly in the Southern states.

Meanwhile, Burr's friends were being hounded by the authorities with the hope that they could be pressured into making an accusation. Van Ness wrote surreptitiously to Pendleton that, because of this danger, he was hiding in Burr's unoccupied townhouse, from where he would like to arrange a meeting with Hamilton's second.[5] By the end of July, both Davis and Colonel Marinus Willett were in jail on suspicion that they had knowledge of the duel, and Van Ness and John Swartwout went into hiding. "How long this sort of persecution may endure cannot be conjectured," wrote Burr. But, he added with characteristic optimism, "The ferment, which was with so much industry excited, has subsided, and public opinion begins to take its proper course."[6]

Some of Burr's friends had been Hamilton's as well, which placed them in an ambivalent position. Commodore Thomas Truxtun, for example, assured Charles Biddle that Burr must have been justified on Hamilton's own confession. But, nonetheless, he lamented "the Death of Hamilton as much as I could the death of a brother of equal talents and worth to human society."[7]

The week after the duel, the anger and indignation of the people of New York was still rising. Burr made plans for a southern journey. At about ten o'clock in the evening of Saturday, July 21, he left Richmond Hill. Young Samuel Swartwout, John's brother, and a servant, little Peter, accompanied him to the waiting barge. As soon as its muffled passengers and their five large trunks were safely stowed aboard, the two bargemen headed the boat for Staten Island.

The barge moved up the Kill Van Kull, sailing through the night until, at sunrise, it reached Blazing Star Ferry, now Rossville, on the Staten Island Sound. By eight o'clock, the fugitives were at Bentley's Manor, near Tottenville, and at ten reached Commodore Truxtun's residence at Perth Amboy.

The Commodore was working in his study, when a servant entered to say that a gentleman wished to see him. Right behind him came Mrs. Truxtun with the news that the visitor was the Vice President. Truxtun went downstairs, where he was met by Peter, who pointed out Burr's boat laying a short distance from the shore opposite the Truxtun landing place. Truxtun welcomed his friend and ordered the boat to land. When Burr revealed that he and Swartwout had spent the night on the water and would like "a dish of good coffee," breakfast was ordered, after which Burr's companion returned to New York. Truxtun and Burr spent the day together.

Later, Truxtun used the New York *Daily Gazette* to reply to those who had criticized his aid to the fugitive Vice President. He pointed out that, as much as he regretted what had happened, "I at the same time gave him a hearty welcome, as I should have done General Hamilton had the fate of their interview been reversed."[8] William Biddle reported that the letter to the paper had a good effect in New York, but, he observed, it "has shamefully omitted to state that Mr. Burr came to his house on his earnest and repeated invitations," whereas the letter insinuated that Burr "had thrown himself uninvited and unexpected on T."[9]

The following morning, the Commodore accompanied his friend to Cranberry, a town about twenty miles away, and started him on his journey to Philadelphia. Burr was cautious, remaining incognito. Once there, he stayed with Charles Biddle and astonished the natives by the casual way he met and greeted friends and acquaintances. Many staid Philadelphians were astounded at the "unparalleled effrontery" and were further offended when the Governor visited him. When Burr was ill for a few days and his now familiar figure was absent from the scene, reports circulated that the sickness was dangerous. Cheetham lost no time in pronouncing an epitaph: "What, has the vengeance of God overtaken him so Soon?"[10]

Not only did Charles Biddle have to brave the anger of friends for harboring Burr, but there were threats that New Yorkers were coming to capture him. Since Biddle's family was safely installed at his country house, the two friends stayed together and prepared for a possible siege. "He would not have been easily taken," said Biddle.[11]

At two o'clock of the morning of August 2, the persistent New York coroner achieved a verdict of "wilful murder" against Burr, and—on evidence given by Bishop Moore—William Peter Van Ness and Nathaniel Pendleton were declared accessories to the crime. But the erratic and unpredictable public's lust for blood had already been satiated. Even Morgan Lewis called the proceedings "disgraceful, illiberal and ungentlemanly."[12] Acting immediately on the jury's verdict, an application was made to the New York governor to demand that Burr be extradited from Pennsylvania. The Colonel weighed the dangerous situation and decided to remain where he was until he could assess the enemy's strategy. "*Have no anxiety about the issue of this business*," he wrote to his son-in-law.[13]

Burr's intimate life was as unresolved as his public one. The current interest in Philadelphia was still Celeste. But she was behaving in an indecisive and timid manner that indicated, perhaps, that she was frightened by the continual "nonsense and lies" that appeared in the daily newspapers. Burr, however, was the first one to assure others that these accounts were "mere fables." Answering reports that there had been assassination attempts, he said that "those who wish me dead prefer to keep at a very respectful distance. No such attempt has been made nor will be made."[14]

Nevertheless, Burr realized that it would be best to try more congenial surroundings. By mid-August, he had completed plans to embark for St. Simon's, an island off the coast of Georgia, one mile below the town of Darien.

Before he left, he made a last attempt to resolve his courtship of Celeste. Although she seemed almost ready to accept his offer of marriage, he wrote to Theodosia that he could not delay his trip long enough to wait for her answer.[15]

Senator Pierce Butler, to whose island home Burr was sailing, was an old friend. His invitation fit in nicely with Burr's plan to go on to the Floridas. The nature of his proposed five or six week trip there, a hazardous and arduous undertaking at that time, was not revealed.

But some of Burr's activities in the spring and summer of 1804 cast light on the subject. When James Wilkinson traveled to New York in May, enroute from New Orleans, he was General-in-Chief of the United States and had just, as one of the joint commissioners, received the vast territory of Louisiana from France. A cryptic note to Burr requesting an interview with his old friend read: "To save time of which I need much and have but little, I propose to take a bed with you this night, if it may be done without observation or intrusion—Answer me, and if in the affirmative, I will be with [you] at 30' after the 8*th* Hour."[16] This mysterious summons, sent at a time when the General was at the height of his good fortune and Burr was in defeat and at loose ends, gave Wilkinson the opportunity to suggest the West as a path to restored fame and fortune. He probably described the possibility of using the frontiersmen's hatred of the Spanish as a means to oust them from the West. How far each confided in the other, what dreams they shared, what secrets Wilkinson revealed can only be conjectured. But that same spring, another former friend with westward-looking eyes, Charles Williamson, spent time with Burr. Williamson, in New York with Robert Troup to wind up the settlement of the Pulteney estate before sailing for England, had prepared a scheme for the conquest of Mexico, which he had hoped would interest the British Ministry. Burr, apparently, kept his two friends from meeting. He was sending feelers in all directions, undoubtedly keeping his own counsel at the same time.

Although all three were in Philadelphia during the summer of 1804, there is no evidence of a meeting. However, when Williamson found that Anthony Merry, the British minister, was also in town, he approached him in behalf of Burr. After the interview, Merry wrote a startling letter to his home office:

> I have just received an offer from Mr. Burr, the actual Vice-President of the United States (which situation he is about to resign) to lend his assistance to his Majesty's government in any manner in which they may think fit to employ him, particularly in endeavoring to effect a separation of the western part of the United States from that which lies between the Atlantic and the mountains, in its whole extent.

Merry added that Colonel Williamson was returning to England shortly and would relate the details. If, after considering "the profligacy of Mr. Burr's character," the government was still interested in the proposition, Merry advised that Burr "still preserves connections with some people of influence, added to his great ambition and spirit of revenge against the present Administration may possibly induce him to exert the talents and activity which he possesses with fidelity to his employers."[17]

Williamson, who had important connections in England, reached there in October. But British politics interfered with any hope of a furtherance of the Burr-Williamson scheme. Aside from competition in the same area from Francesco de Miranda, who was in London lobbying for the support of his proposal to invade South America—a scheme, incidentally, which Williamson also found intriguing—two other disasters affected Burr's hopes more directly: the death of Pitt and the impeachment of Williamson's sponsor, Lord Melville. Melville resigned, but was subsequently acquitted of charges. "The Talents," who succeeded Pitt—Lord Greenville and Charles James Fox—had to concentrate on the overthrow of Napoleon and had no time for Latin American adventures. Burr, consequently, waited in vain for some communication from Williamson. None came; perhaps because there was no good news, Williamson preferred silence.[18]

An examination of the Merry letter concerning Burr suggests a number of possibilities. Burr, perhaps, was playing a game to achieve British support for his own plans. But, the possibility that the Colonel meant precisely what Merry reported cannot be arbitrarily dismissed. The decision must wait further developments. There is corroboration that the inception of Burr's plan took place at this time. Charles Biddle reported later that his two close friends, Burr and Wilkinson, had concocted their first definite plans at his Philadelphia home during the summer of 1804.[19]

How far Burr's commitment to a far-reaching scheme of doubtful patriotism and potential treason had progressed at this stage is open to speculation. What is certain is that Burr, in September, 1804, armed with a letter from the Spanish minister, the Marquis of Casa Yrujo, was headed for St. Augustine in the Spanish-held colony of Florida. Accompanying him on his journey was Samuel Swartwout, who, at the age of twenty, was as susceptible to Burr's magnetism as the other Swartwouts.

The voyage south proved to be an escape from the censure and the hysteria of the past month. The duel was regarded in quite a different manner by the Southerners. John Randolph of Roanoke expressed their point of view aptly:

> I feel for Hamilton's immediate connections real concern; for himself, nothing; for his party and those *soi-disant* republicans who have been shedding crocodile tears over him, contempt. The first are justly punished for descending to use Burr as a tool to divide their opponents; the last are hypocrites who deify Hamilton.

Randolph criticized Hamilton's letters to Burr as obscure and equivocating, whereas he thought that Burr had an admirable style and spirit. Burr might have been cheered by these sentiments, but would have been chagrined to read further on that he had "fallen like Lucifer, never to rise again," and that his was an "irreparable defeat."[20]

While at St. Simon's, Burr retained his incognito, cautioning the Alstons to enclose their letters to Mr. Roswell King. The plantation had an idyllic setting and was wonderfully staffed for its guests' comfort. A housekeeper, cook, and chambermaid, as well as footmen, fishermen, and bargemen, were always at command. Dairies, barnyard, and fruit groves yielded every culinary delight, while the Butler cellar afforded Madeira wine, porter, and brandy. Burr was treated royally by John Cooper, the neighboring plantation owner, who sent him an assortment of French wines and a twelve month supply of orange shrub. Visitors, including a young lady from France, enlivened the stay.

The days of waiting passed pleasantly with visits to the other islands in the vicinity. One of them, called Hamilton's Bluff, had been settled fifty years before by Georgia's founder, General James Oglethorpe. For a time, it had flourished as a lovely resort for the governor and his friends. Now there were only the ruins of the formerly elegant country seats and the huts of a few shabby settlers. Little St. Simon's and several other islands around provided sport in the form of hunting and fishing.

Not only were rice birds and trout abundant, but also an exotic form of honey that abounded in the woods. Burr participated in all the sports, but had not, as yet, succeeded in providing crocodile meat for his table. He offered a reward for one, "which I mean to eat, dressed in soup, fricasses, and steaks. Oh! how you long to partake of this repast," he teased Mrs. Alston.[21]

September was hurricane time on the Atlantic Coast, and, on September 7, Burr was unable to return home after taking out a small canoe to pay a sick call on Mr. Cooper. A wind started to blow hard just as he was about to leave and gained in velocity all through the night. By noon the next day, a gale from the north had felled several outhouses and most of the trees around the house. A few hours later, part of the piazza had been carried away and some windows blown in. Then, mysteriously, the wind abated and, in ten minutes, died down completely. Burr attempted to return home during the lull but, before he had made a successful crossing, the gale rose again, this time coming from the southwest. The storm did not attain the ferocity of the previous night, but it raised the water to a flood about seven feet above high tide, inundating a great length of the coast and destroying all the rice. Most of the buildings on the lowlands were carried away, many of the slaves drowned, the roads rendered impassable, and most of the boats destroyed. No mail could arrive.

Not even the storm, however, could make the Colonel abandon his plans. On the fifteenth, having managed to get a boat, he set out for Florida. The trip was brief, only nine or ten days long, and there is no evidence to indicate whether its mission was accomplished. Burr was unable to go further south than the St. John's River, thirty miles short of St. Augustine. Theo was informed that the Florida trip was very satisfactory. "I was treated with great kindness and respect . . . and have everywhere experienced the utmost hospitality. My health has been perfect and uninterrupted."[22] No reference was made to his real reason for visiting the Spanish colony.

Continuing bad weather made the reunion with Theo an impossibility. On the return trip to Savannah, Burr arrived "in a minor hurricane" that had "upset some canoes, drowned a few negroes, unroofed some houses, and forced in a few windows," all in a few minutes. The road from the city was impassable and not a horse could be hired or purchased. Burr's disappointment was somewhat alleviated by a serenade under his window and a delegation of citizens wishing to see the Vice President.

Their good will solved his problems, for after flooding him with invitations that would have occupied Burr for months, they offered him horses to carry him to Statesburgh. If the land route proved utterly impassable, he would go by sea, a voyage of ten to twelve days. Burr wrote to tell Theodosia to "let ABA know that *gamp* is not a black man, otherwise he may be shocked at the appearance of A. B. who is now . . . Not brown but a true quadroon yellow; whether from the effects of the climate, or travelling four hundred miles in a canoe."[23]

A few happy weeks with Theo and Gampy, and then Burr had to return to Washington and reality. The weather grew colder, but not his reception from the local populace along the way. He was very surprised and pleased with the attention and acclamation. Even in Virginia, the "citadel" of Jefferson, the last place where he would have expected "open marks of hospitality and respect," everyone turned out to greet him. He wrote merrily to the Alstons about the details of "The Travels of A. Gamp, Esq. A. M., L. L. D., V. P. U. S." But real trouble was waiting for him.[24]

Although much of the violence against him had "sensibly abated" and numbers of Republicans who had been hysterical were now returning to their senses, Burr's legal position was worsening. The mills of the law were leveling vengeance, slowly but effectively. While on the road to Washington, Burr was told that he had been indicted for murder in Bergen County, New Jersey, by an ardent Federalist judge. Even more disheartening was the news that met him in Washington. Richmond Hill and its furniture had been sold for about twenty-five thousand dollars. "The library and the wine remain. They will, I think, become your property," Burr informed Alston.[25]

When Burr resumed his office as President of the Senate, many Federalists reacted with self-righteous coldness, refusing to speak to him or to visit him. It was Senator Plumer who made the virtuous observation that "in the Senate chamber, I make a very formal bow as he passes me, but hold no conversation with him."[26] And, at another time, the man from New Hampshire wrote: "What a humiliating circumstance that a man who for months had fled from justice—& who by the legal authorities is now accused of murder, should preside over the first branch of the National Legislature."[27] Mannasseh Cutler wrote that he wondered if Burr would have the audacity to take his seat in the Senate. "Can they submit to the degradation of the presidency of a man lying under the legal imputation of murder?" he asked.[28] John Quincy Adams, seemingly more in sorrow than in anger, merely noted that, although indicted in two states for his duel with Mr. Hamilton, "Mr. Burr appears and takes his seat as President of the Senate of the United States."[29]

However, the attitude of the mighty toward Burr had altered dramatically, and for excellent political reasons. Senator Plumer, who had noticed that Burr was invited to dine with the President more frequently than ever before, that Mr. Gallatin spent time with him in his lodgings, that Madison, formerly one of Hamilton's dearest friends, drove his murderer around in his carriage to visit the French minister, missed the significance of this changed attitude as did the other Federalists. The reason assigned by the Federalists to this change was that Burr had eliminated their hero. The Jeffersonians were expressing "their joy for the death of Hamilton," which manifested itself by "caressing his murderer," they deduced. Plumer even suspected the Republicans of wishing that they could retract their winter's action and re-elect the Vice President.[30]

It was quite true that Jefferson wanted Burr's good will. He had made two appointments in the new Louisiana territories that were influenced by Burr. John Bartow Prevost was made one of the territorial judges and James Brown, an intimate friend of Burr and a brother to Senator John Brown of Kentucky, was made territorial secretary. Burr's interest was equally well represented when the territorial government in the northern part of the Louisiana Territory at St. Louis was incorporated under a governor of its own, General James Wilkinson. Burr's brother-in-law, Dr. Joseph Browne, became its territorial secretary.

And the party also courted Burr's favor. The Republican senators under the leadership of William Branch Giles petitioned Governor Joseph Bloomfield of New Jersey to relieve Burr of the murder charge against him and to relieve the Senate of the embarrassment of having a presiding officer who was held up to the world as a "common murderer."[31] They reminded Bloomfield that others had engaged in duelling in his state without receiving such treatment from the courts. Governor Bloomfield, who had been a childhood friend of Burr, also received a letter from Charles Biddle and Alexander Dallas, the United States District Attorney for the Eastern District, adding their voices to the plea for the Vice President.[32]

But the New England senators, Plumer and J. Q. Adams, were wrong in attributing the official change in attitude toward Burr to Hamilton's death. The key to the mystery was Judge Samuel Chase, one of the associate justices of the Supreme Court, who was charged with high crimes and misdemeanors.

In May, 1803, just after the completion of the Louisiana Purchase, Jefferson read a newspaper article about Chase's harangue to a Baltimore jury. Chase had blasted the abolition of the offices of sixteen circuit judges and the change in the state's constitution establishing universal suffrage. "Our republican Constitution will sink into a mobocracy,—the worst of all possible governments," he thundered.[33] Jefferson determined that this excess would not go unchallenged.

It was decided that John Randolph, acting for the House of Representatives, would draw up the articles of impeachment against Chase. There were eight of them, including his withholding of legal rights from one John Fries, his conduct in several sedition trials, and the matter of the Baltimore jury.[34] The impeachment trial would take place in the Senate with Burr presiding.

The trial began in the Senate Chamber on Wednesday, January 2, 1805. The secretary read the Sergeant at Arms' report of having served the summons on Judge Chase and called for him to appear and answer them. Justice Samuel Chase, a signer of the Declaration of Independence, and since his appointment by Washington, a member of the Supreme Court of the United States, entered the chamber. Before Marshall's accession, Chase had been the most notable member of the Court. His originality, richness of expression, and grasp of political theory had set precedents that have persisted until this day. For example, his opinion in *Ware* vs. *Hylton* that asserted the supremacy of national treaties over state laws, his definition of *ex post facto* laws, his suggestion that "there are unwritten, inherent limitations on legislative powers," and his decision that the courts have no jurisdiction over crimes at common law, all showed these qualities.[35] But despite this, his inclination toward autocracy, his belief that it was the duty of a judge to guide and instruct people, had led him to this position.

Over six feet tall, with a broad and massive face, reddish brown in color, a wide brow topped by thick white hair, Chase was the epitome of dignity and strength as he bowed to the President of the Senate and the court. The contrast between the large-headed, bulky defendant and the small, elegantly attired Burr was noted by many.

An armchair had been placed for the defendant just before the senators were seated, but by order of the Vice President, it had been removed. Plumer overheard Burr say, "*Let the Judge take care to find a seat for himself.*" The Judge did request a seat and Burr, without hesitation, but in a rather formal and cold manner, permitted one to be brought. Chase sat down.[36] The Federalist papers seized on this incident, and Plumer added to the outcry against Burr's highhandedness with a story that, a few days after the event, he heard Burr say to friends in the Senate Chamber that "In Great Britain when an officer is impeached & Appears before the House of Lords—instead of having a

Chair the Accused falls on his knees & rises not till the Lord Chancellor directs him." Burr, it seemed, was deserting the pose of "plain republicanism," besides grossly overacting.[37]

Chase rose and addressed himself to the court. In his hand were several papers. He had hardly spoken a sentence before Burr interrupted him to ask if the papers were an answer to the charges. Chase replied that they were not, for his purpose that day was to beg the court for more time to prepare his case. He wished a postponement until the first day of the next session. Several times during his plea Chase was interrupted by Burr. Federalist observer Plumer thought that Burr's behavior was rude and contemptible and simply reflected his desire to ingratiate himself with the Administration.[38]

Almost a year had elapsed since John Randolph had come before the bar of the Senate to announce that, in due time, the House of Representatives would have impeachment articles prepared against Justice Chase. But the Justice was not granted equal time to prepare his defense. He was ordered to reappear on February 4 to stand trial.

Burr left Washington at the end of January to conclude a nonpolitical mission. He caused a flurry of speculation when he set off for Philadelphia. Theo, however, knew that this sally was to resolve a love affair, not a state matter. Celeste had agreed to make her final decision about their future. Burr informed Theo that the matter had ended forever, and he returned to Washington and the Chase pageant, of which he was the impresario.

While Chase worked to save his office, the Senate Chamber, under Burr's direction, was being transformed into the most elegant public room that had ever been seen in the United States. Twenty or thirty carpenters had been employed to build the seats and the new gallery needed to house the members of Congress and the guests. The decor had been inspired by the setting of the trial of Warren Hastings in Westminster Hall, London, ten years earlier.

The new gallery was built in front of the old one all around the room. The seats, covered with green cloth, rose above each other to give the effect of a theater. The chamber, crescent or half-moon shaped, had the President seated on the straight side, flanked by tiers of seats covered with scarlet cloth for the senators. Below, in front of the Vice President and Senate, were green cloth-covered boxes for the managers of the House and for Chase and his counsel. The circular part of the room had seats rising theatrically above each other, which enabled the members of the House to sit facing the Senate and the principals of the trial. To the right and left of the Vice President's chair, at the termination of the benches of the members of the court, boxes were assigned to stenographers. At the left of the manager's box was a large red morocco chair for the Speaker of the House. The permanent gallery was allotted to spectators. On the lower floor, at the left of the members of the House, was a box for foreign ministers and American dignitaries. The upper gallery was graced by some two hundred guests, and from three to four hundred stood at the back. The setting was likened by Senator Tracy to a Roman amphitheater and the temper of the observers could be compared with the curiosity that attended executions or gladiatorial combats.[39]

Burr surveyed the results of his work with great satisfaction. The setting, he thought, equalled the importance of the occasion. The Senate Chamber had become a magnificent courtroom and, in the coming days, a worthy memorial to his skill as a chairman. Early in the trial, there was much criticism and resentment of his adamant effort to maintain perfect decorum, Federalists complaining that schoolmaster Burr was admonishing his assembly of students.

And they may have had a point, after all. Included among offenses that merited reprimands, for example, were such crimes as: withdrawing from the court before the session was over, wearing a loose coat, walking between the Vice President and the Senate managers while the trial was in session, eating apples and cake at their seats, and motioning for an adjournment when it was out of order. For such violations, the individuals were scolded by Burr. Finally, one victim said: "Really, *Master Burr*, you need a ferule, or birch, to enforce your lectures on polite behavior!"[40] But these sentiments changed to admiration as the court settled down to listen to the arguments.

The House had selected its best talent to prosecute its charges, but even John Randolph of Roanoke had great shortcomings. Brilliant, original, fiery, he was also erratic and lacked the necessary legal training and skill. The other managers, Joseph Nicholson, Caesar Rodney, and the four Southerners—John Boyle of Kentucky, George Washington Campbell of Tennessee, Peter Early of Georgia, and Christopher Clark of Virginia—could not match the legal brain of a sharp and experienced lawyer like Chase.

The trial was a long one. For almost a month, the battle for the survival of the federal judiciary as a significant branch of the United States government occupied the Senate Chamber. Chase's counsel wanted the definition of impeachment narrowed to a strict interpretation of the words of the Constitution, "high crimes and misdemeanors." The managers, however, preferred a broadening of the base to include not only accusations of treason, bribery, or other high crimes, but any wrongdoing for which the Senate, using its discretion, would see fit to remove

an official. During the trial, the arguments veered back and forth, the
Senate often confused as to whether it was a court or a political forum.
It was, of course, both.

Chase's counsel included Joseph Hopkinson, Philip Barton Key, Robert Goodloe Harper, and Charles Lee. All were brilliant lawyers and
experienced politicians. But the hero was Luther Martin of Maryland, a
man who reached the peak of his career in this case.

As eccentric in his own way as Randolph, Martin argued with a flair
and a knowledge of law that completely vanquished his inadequately
trained opponent. The nearsighted Maryland lawyer, shabbily dressed,
his gray hair thin and straggling, his face mottled from too much drinking, charmed his audience as his harsh voice spun out reasonable arguments.

Rodney tried to answer the opposition on its own grounds and to
demonstrate that Chase had been technically guilty of crimes. He recognized the fear held by many that if a judge could be impeached because
of a judicial opinion, the Senate would become like the House of Lords
of that time, a court of last appeal.[41]

Burr presided zealously, demonstrating both impartiality and skill. He
asked questions of the witnesses, attempted to clear up differences,
fiercely kept order until the nervous Federalists themselves had to admire his conduct. "He conducted with the dignity and impartiality of
an angel, but with the rigor of a devil," commented the Washington
Federalist.

The trial was filled with drama and color, but the most pitiable figure
was that of John Randolph. In the interval between Chase's arraignment
and the month's postponement of his case, Randolph had been shaken by
the contention over the Yazoo lands. He came to the trial in a highly
nervous state that was aggravated by this new stress. By the time of the
closing, Randolph's behavior bordered on the irrational. He was dis-
tracted, unprepared, and forgetful. He looked ill, lost his notes, and
shrilled at the audience, his tall thin body contorted by his groans and
sobs, his penetrating eyes filled with tears. At the end, he congratulated
the Senate that this was "the last day of my sufferings and yours."[42]

On March 1, the hearing completed, the Senate convened to vote.
Both sides had misgivings. The Republicans were unsure of the necessary twenty-three votes for the two-thirds majority needed for conviction. For example, the two New Yorkers—Samuel L. Mitchill, who had
opposed impeachment, and John Smith, who had voted against the proceedings when he was a member of the House—were among the doubt-
fuls. The Senate, at the time, was composed of nine Federalists and
twenty-five Republicans, so that three Republican defectors would

mean defeat. For their part, the Federalists were almost despairing. One discouraged anti-Administration man said: "Our public . . . will be as tame as Mr. Randolph can desire. You may broil Judge Chase and eat him, or eat him raw; it shall stir up less anger or pity, than the Six Nations would show if Cornplanter or Red Jacket were refused a belt of wampum."[43]

Thirty minutes after noon on Friday, March 1, 1805, the Senate Chamber was crowded with spectators awaiting the final outcome. The Vice President, erect and dignified as usual, ordered the officers in charge to watch the spectators and seize and commit to prison anyone who should venture the smallest noise or disturbance. Consequently, a hush attended the opening of the final proceedings. At this moment, the throng was parted so that a litter upon which lay the ailing Senator Tracy could be carried down the narrow passageway. The senator, who was suffering from his final illness, insisted upon casting his vote and, after being helped from his pallet to the red-covered seat of one of the judges, remained there until the court was formally closed.

Burr rose and spoke to the members of the court, telling them to render their judgment on each article of the charges. His statement was met with the silence that had been imposed on the entire hall. The secretary, loudly and clearly, read each article of impeachment and then called individually on each senator by name and put the question to him. As the roll call proceeded for each article, the tension mounted, although the trend was fairly obvious after the fifth article was voted. After the completion of the rounds for the eighth and last article, Burr, to make doubly sure, decreed that the secretary read over the names of the senators and their answers. This procedure enabled them to correct one error.

After a short pause, Burr reported the results as follows:

Article	Guilty	Not Guilty
1	16	18
2	10	24
3	18	16
4	18	16
5	0	34
6	4	30
7	10	24
8	19	15

Burr, then, declared that since no two-thirds majority, as the Constitution requires, had found Chase guilty on any one article, Chase was acquitted, and the court adjourned.[44]

Federalists rejoiced without restraint. There was even extravagant praise for "Schoolmaster" Burr. Plumer, now charitable, found himself able to write that Burr has "certainly, on the whole, done himself, the Senate, and the nation honor by the dignified manner in which he had presided over this high & numerous Court."[45] Others commented about the Vice President's impartiality.

Jefferson was silent, concealing his disappointment. However, he never ceased to rail at the judiciary, calling it "the subtle corps of sappers and miners constantly working underground to undermine the foundations of our confederate fabric. . . . Having found from experience that impeachment is an impracticable thing, a mere scarecrow, they consider themselves secure for life."[46] Marshall and his court were the true victors, as were future courts, for they were now free to continue to strengthen the central government without fear of coercion.

Burr's silence matched the President's. Surely, however, he regarded his conduct of the proceedings as the climax of his vice-presidential career. With a flair for the dramatic, he chose to withdraw at this moment and take his formal leave of the Senate.

On the day after the trial had ended, Burr appeared in the Senate and took his seat as usual. But, at about one o'clock, he announced that he had a sore throat and had decided to say his farewell. His speech moved friend and foe to emotion. The charm of his personality was, in this instance, able to reach all. He spoke at first with affectionate sincerity, briefly outlining one or two recommendations for alterations of the Senate rules, explaining the reasons and principles involved. Then he commented on his habits and methods as their presiding officer. He was diffident but not apologetic. Aware that he may have often wounded the feelings of individual members, he assured them that it was done in the interest of the dignity of the Senate. He knew of no injuries that he had received but, he added, he was not a man to remember injuries. He admitted that, at times, he may have acted in error, but this was done advisedly, for error is often preferable to indecision. He denied that it would be arrogant for him to say that his official conduct had ignored the demands of the party, special interests, or friends.[47] His strict adherence to rules and decorum had been synonomous with retaining the dignity of the Senate and nothing that touched that dignity was trivial. "I pray you to accept my respectful acknowledgements and the assurance of my inviolable attachment to the Interest and dignity of the Senate."[48] Then he explained that he regarded the Senate as a

> sanctuary; a citadel of law, of order, of liberty: and it is here—it is here, in this exalted refuge; here, if anywhere, will resistance be made to the storms of political phrensy and the silent arts of corruption;

and if the constitution be destined to perish by the sacrilegious hands of the demagogue or the usurper, which God avert, its expiring agonies will be witnessed on this floor.

He concluded with sentiments regarding the painfulness of final separation, perhaps forever, from scenes and associations that had become familiar for many years.[49] The speech was unprepared, he wrote to tell Theo, but the response of his audience moved him as he talked. "I neither shed tears nor assumed tenderness, but tears did flow abundantly."[50] Samuel Mitchill of New York said he found the scene "one of the most affecting of my life." He also reported that a colleague had wept profusely and laid his head on his desk unable to recover from his emotion for more than a quarter of an hour.[51]

Immediately after completing his speech, the diminutive Burr descended from his chair for the last time and left the Senate Chamber. As soon as he was gone, Mr. Anderson was chosen President pro tem and a resolution of thanks to the departing President was unanimously passed. It expressed the Senate's appreciation for Burr's "impartiality, dignity, and ability" in presiding over them and it was a vote of "entire approbation of his conduct."[52]

This ceremonious exchange of mutual admiration obscured the fact that it had been Burr's painful duty to open and count the ballots that re-elected Thomas Jefferson and, in place of the incumbent Vice President, George Clinton. Of Burr's behavior on that day, wrote Mitchill, he "had learned to behave like a stoic. All the difference I discerned was that he appeared rather more carefully dressed than usual."[53]

Burr left with good wishes and noble sentiments, but the bill to grant him franking privileges for life that had been passed in the Senate, after much debate, had been postponed in the House of Representatives until the following year's session. It was never heard of again.

The Hamilton affair was still not resolved. Burr thought it best not to visit either New York or New Jersey, but prepared to travel to the friendlier and freer West. His itinerary for the summer months was extensive. The western journey would start at Fort Pitt and then proceed through the states on each side of the Ohio River. He would eventually go through St. Louis and New Orleans, and then he would return to the Atlantic coast, although he was not sure whether he would make that portion of the trip by land or by sea.

Such exciting plans were not merely a reward for years of service in the Senate, nor were they to satisfy curiosity about the wonders of the West. Burr called his trip "an operation of business which promises to render the tour both useful and agreeable."[54] He looked forward to this new phase of his career with splendid enthusiasm. If he had entertained presidential aspirations, he probably had loftier ones now. Despite his reputation for good sense and practicality, his complex make-up had sizeable streaks of adventure and romanticism. "I contemplate the tour with gayety and cheerfulness," he said.[55] But what other emotions, deeper and more portentous, rode West with him to his jumping-off place, Fort Pitt, he successfully concealed.

CHAPTER XVI

Western Adventure: Part One

BURR'S "adventure" had blurred edges from the very start. For a man of his vigor, the prospect of being disenfranchised in New York and hanged in New Jersey only spurred attempts to spread his talents elsewhere.[1] A naturally secretive man, no one was ever fully in his confidence, not even Theodosia. Besides, his motives were mixed. Money was a necessity; power, perhaps, an equally pressing need. And it seemed certain that the Republican Party had no further use for Aaron Burr.

Caution was an obsession for the former Vice President, so he had no one plan for the future but several alternate ones depending upon chance and history. Such minor ventures as the building of a canal at Louisville, a project reminiscent of the founding of the Manhattan Bank, or seeking a western congressional seat were possibilities but only if nothing more challenging developed. Actually, Burr's big plans hinged on a war with Spain which seemed imminent at the time. If the United States fought Spain, an enterprising, military-minded, popular figure such as Aaron Burr, who was prepared to move quickly and had already laid the groundwork, could capture New Orleans and then move on to Mexico. The West might follow such a leader out of the Union.

But if, by chance, no war occurred and none of the possibilities followed, Burr had an alternative. The lands he purchased on the Washita River in the Southwest could be a steppingstone to a march on Mexico. Burr had thought thus far but he needed money, men, equipment, and allies. In the winter of 1805 he had cemented his friendship with Governor Wilkinson, the Governor of the northern part of the Louisiana

Territory, and had approached England through its Minister, Anthony Merry. Spain had figured in the almost aborted Florida trip directly after the duel. The elaborate travel schedule that Burr was now following would enlarge his contacts numerically and geographically. Many in the West regarded him as a persecuted man who had suffered enough.

Although Jefferson had won adherents through the purchase of Louisiana, and the West had always been a stronghold of Republicanism, for some nothing would suffice until the hated Spanish were driven from the continent. Clearly remembered was the sixteenth of October, 1802, when the Spanish Intendant, Juan Morales, closed the port of New Orleans and forbade the right of deposit for American goods, a right that had been granted by the treaty of 1795. Even at this late date, West Florida was still in Spanish hands and so was all of Mexico.

The boundaries had been vague when Louisiana was purchased from Napoleon. Many a frontiersman, including Andrew Jackson, was anxious to define them. Spain was hated by the western settlers because she was a ruthless colonial power. In return, Spain feared the lawlessness of Americans.

Spain believed that she had been cheated by Napoleon and Talleyrand. The secret treaty negotiated at San Ildefonso by the two powers had contained provisions that the Spanish Minister, Manuel de Godoy, said the French had not honored. For one, Spain expected the French in Louisiana to serve as a buffer between New Spain and the aggressive American nation. Suddenly, after the astounding sale of Louisiana in 1803, Spain was confronted with an even more powerful rival. New Orleans, the prize that had been tossed back and forth between the two European nations, now belonged to the United States. But the Creoles were not overjoyed with their new masters, regarding them as barbarians at the gates. Burr grasped all these facts and included them in his plans.

Pittsburgh, on the site of Fort Pitt, a door to the West and jumping-off place for Burr, stood on a point of land formed by the junction of the Monongahela and Allegheny rivers, at the head of the Ohio. At that time it had four hundred dwellings and about twenty-five hundred inhabitants. Forty public houses and seventy or eighty stores served the growing population. Commercial goods had to be brought by land, 310 miles from Philadelphia, the distance Burr had just covered after nineteen days of hard riding. He had expected to meet Wilkinson and stay there until the fourth or fifth of May. However, finding that the General had not arrived but that the weather was fine and that the boat he had ordered was ready, he decided to proceed down the river. After a night's rest, he set off on a high tide with his traveling companion, Gabriel Shaw.

The ark was really a floating house, sixty feet by fourteen feet, equipped with a dining room, kitchen with fireplace, and two bedrooms. The entire structure was roofed with steps that led to the top and permitted the traveler to walk the whole length. For this elegant floating villa, Burr had paid only one hundred and thirty-three dollars; a rare bargain, he told Theo. The swift current of the Ohio River would carry the passengers downstream past the forests and small villages to their destination. No propelling force was necessary, only some dexterous poling to keep the barge off the sandbanks.

Thirty-six hours after the ark left Pittsburgh, Matthew Lyon, now a congressman from Kentucky, met Burr on the water. They lashed their boats together and floated down the river for four days. The past winter Lyon had discussed Burr's future with Wilkinson. Their first thought had been a foreign embassy for him but, they agreed, Jefferson would probably not cooperate. Lyon suggested that as soon as Burr stepped down from the vice presidency he should move to Nashville, Tennessee and practice law there until he became eligible for a congressional seat. Wilkinson called this "a heavenly thought," but when the idea was relayed to Burr, "he did not seem so much enamored of the subject." Nevertheless, the friends made tentative plans to meet on the water while they descended from Pittsburgh.[2]

Burr, in a journal of the trip with Lyon kept for his daughter's amusement, described "Wieling" as a neat, pretty little town with some fine houses and fashionable, well-dressed ladies, but not nearly as handsome or interesting as Marietta, Ohio. Some gentlemen from there met his boat and conducted him to the sites of the earthworks and parapets that had been left by antiquity. These phenomena, attributed to a prehistoric people called the Mound Builders who had a city where Marietta now stands, fascinated the Colonel, but he had no plausible explanation for them and was unsatisfied by the conjecture of others.

Curiosity attracted Burr to Blennerhassett's Island, not far from Marietta on the Ohio River, about two miles below what is now Parkersburg, West Virginia. Burr landed on the island and started to tour the property. Mr. Harman Blennerhassett was not home, but when the lady of the house heard what a distinguished guest she had, she persuaded the party to stay for dinner. Burr pleased her enormously. His courtly elegance won her confidence and she delivered a favorable report to her husband when he returned.

The island was already famous for its enchanting beauty and interesting though bizarre owners. Harman Blennerhassett was born about 1764, the son of an Irish gentleman who claimed direct descent from King Edward III of England. He had been educated at Trinity College, Dublin, after which he was admitted to the bar. The death of his elder brothers made him the heir to the family fortune and provided the means to express his eccentricities.

The arrival of the Blennerhassetts in the United States in 1796 was attributed by their friends to a wish to separate themselves from the political controversy in Ireland and to breathe fresh air. It was not until 1901 that a descendant, in an article in *Century Magazine*, revealed that Harman and Margaret Blennerhassett were uncle and niece as well as husband and wife. The pressure of the horrified family, the illegal nature of the union, and the fear that the children would find out drove them into self-imposed exile. Mrs. Blennerhassett was the daughter of Captain Robert Agnew, lieutenant governor of the Isle of Man, and Catherine Blennerhassett, Harman's elder sister.[3]

With a letter of introduction to Judge Dudley Woodbridge of Marietta, they moved to the area where they would establish themselves. In March, 1798, they purchased the island, then called Backus Isle or Isle de Belpre, for forty-five hundred dollars.

For two years workmen cleared the forest, constructed boat landings, drives, walks, the house, and the gardens. Good taste and a flair for the dramatic and romantic created the stunning effect of a palace in the wilderness. The main buildings were of wood, painted snow-white so that they gleamed in the dark green setting. A center two-story building, fifty-two feet by thirty feet, was flanked on either side by wings joined to the main house by covered porticos. The office, on the left, contained the servants' hall and kitchen; the building on the right, Blennerhassett's library and laboratory. The house itself had ten rooms.[4]

No effort had been spared to combine the glories of the natural forest setting with the refinements of a disciplined garden. The lawn, cleared for several acres, fell away from the house like a green fan-shaped carpet. Graveled walks and a carriage road from the river facilitated the approach. There was also a two-acre garden. Rare fruits and flowers grew at the rear of the house. Altogether, a hundred acres were devoted to growing crops and an orchard.[5]

The squire of the estate was six feet tall, slender, and somewhat stooped. He had a prominent forehead, a large nose, and a hesitant, serious air that partly resulted from farsightedness. He dressed in the English style, scarlet or buff-colored knee breeches, shoes with silver buckles, silk stockings, and a blue coat. He spent much of his time in the laboratory with chemical and pharmaceutical experiments. One amusing effort was an attempt to change meat into a fat that could be used instead of whale oil as a fuel for illumination. His method was to submerge large pieces of beef in a small inlet of the Ohio, which delighted the fish population.[6] All this did not keep him from also developing a reputation as a formidable classical scholar and becoming an excellent violinist and cellist. Such talents and avocations enhanced Blennerhassett's charm, but he also became a victim of his tastes. Almost his entire fortune, some sixty thousand dollars, had been spent on this island kingdom, and since Prospero tended to be unworldly in his dealings with the self-made, shrewd frontiersmen, he was having financial problems.

Mrs. Blennerhassett was an interesting contrast to her scholarly husband. She was tall, regal in bearing, fine featured, clear complexioned, with dark brown hair that was often concealed in a turban-like headdress. Riding was her passion. For this pursuit, she wore a scarlet riding dress decorated with gold lace and sparkling buttons, her hat feathered with an ostrich plume. She loved Shakespeare, and even wrote some of her own poetry.[7]

Some said that Burr drifted into this setting like the serpent into the Garden of Eden. But, in reality, when they finally met, Burr and Blennerhassett found that their positions and their needs were very similar. Both men had losses to recoup and both men dreamed of a grandiose solution that would elevate them to positions of splendor.

By May 11, Burr and Shaw arrived at Senator John Smith's home in Cincinnati, where Jonathan Dayton also awaited them. The friends had, among other matters, the Indiana Canal scheme to discuss. It was to be built at Louisville, where the rapids and falls of the Ohio made navigation at low tide impossible and portage a necessity. Louisville did not want the canal because of a possible loss of revenue, but in January of 1805 Benjamin Hovey of New York had petitioned Congress for a land grant to build a waterway. The Senate referred the matter to a committee composed of Dayton of New Jersey, Brown of Kentucky, and Smith of Ohio. Although their report was favorable to the bill, it was defeated.

However, the three senators became interested in the project and joined the original petitioners along with Burr, who had heard of the proposed project on the Senate floor. Indeed, it was one of the things that led him to the West, one of the alternate plans that were to be investigated for his future; or, perhaps, it was part of the Western scheme itself. Although it was, at this time, still in the petitioning stage, the new Indiana legislature was to meet for the first time in June, so the friends needed to consult each other on the ways and means of accomplishing their purpose. After a day's visit, Burr started out for Louisville.

The canal project did not materialize for Burr. An Indiana Canal Company *was* incorporated, and Stanley Griswold, the secretary of the Michigan Territory, wrote from Detroit to warn that great "deposits of *money* are said to be making at the *falls of the Ohio* for the *pretended* purpose of *cutting a canal* under *Aaron Burr*."[8] But although the canal was finally built, it was not built by Burr and company because too many other things kept their attention during 1805 and 1806.[9]

Although Wilkinson was supposed to have met Burr in Cincinnati at this time, as far as is known, he was not part of the canal scheme. Another missing party was John Adair, a Revolutionary War soldier and renowned Indian fighter. Wilkinson thought the two men would understand each other very well, for Adair was enthusiastically awaiting war with Spain. His fellow Kentuckians, too, he said, were "greedy after plunder as ever the old Romans were. Mexico glitters in our Eyes —the word is all we wait for."[10]

Burr had to wait for a later date to meet Adair; but Davis relates that Adair, more than any other individual, possessed Burr's confidence "in relation to his western movements." Adair always asserted that Burr's intentions were to prepare and lead an expedition into Mexico, but only if there had been the expected war with Spain.[11]

From Louisville, the ark was floated down river to the mouth of the Cumberland while Burr rode to Frankfort, Kentucky, to talk with John Brown, the third member of the triumvirate that had sponsored the waterway. From there, a short detour was made to Lexington and then, on the twenty-ninth of March, Burr galloped into Nashville.

He was received as a hero by the townspeople. Among the large numbers flocking to lionize him was Andrew Jackson. At the public dinner given for the honored former Vice President, Jackson renewed the slight acquaintance he had had with him in Philadelphia in 1797. Burr, at that time, had been a senator and had championed Tennessee's admission into the Union. Jackson recalled the marvelous dinner and the excellent wines that he had enjoyed as Burr's guest. Now, he carried the Colonel off, a willing captive, to the Hermitage, the Jackson home.

Burr stayed with the rangy frontiersman for five days. The hospitality was so good, he wrote to Theo, that he could have gladly remained for a month.[12] The exchange of ideas went well for Burr. With great skill, he exploited his host's hatred of the Spaniards, and with the certainty of war with Spain, Burr subtly insinuated that he had a secret understanding with Henry Dearborn, Jefferson's Secretary of War.[13]

Burr left Jackson on Sunday, June 2, in an open boat provided by his solicitous host. In it, he descended the Cumberland for 220 miles to his waiting area.

At Fort Massac, on the Ohio sixteen miles below Nashville, Wilkinson caught up with Burr. The two friends spent five days talking about their plans, poring over maps and discussing ways and means. When they parted, having reached their zenith of mutual confidence, Burr was provided with three letters of introduction. One, to Daniel Clark, a controversial and powerful New Orleans figure, said: "To him I refer you for many things improper to letter, and which he will not say to any other." The others were the Marquis of Casa Calvo, still a New Orleans resident, and Gilbert Leonard, a bitterly anti-Claiborne partisan, who was informed that Burr "will sent your Idiot blackguard W. C. C. C. [William C. C. Claiborne, Governor of New Orleans] to the devil."[14]

The public was told that the purpose of the Wilkinson-Burr meeting was to enable the experienced politician to advise the General on how to set up the northern part of the Louisiana Purchase. Wilkinson, therefore, marked Burr's departure with a display of favor. He and his officers fitted out the Colonel with "an elegant barge, sails, colours, and ten oars, with a sergeant and ten able, faithful hands."[15]

After an eight hundred mile voyage, Burr arrived in Natchez, a thriving town of three or four hundred houses inhabited chiefly by traders and mechanics. But the surrounding country had many wealthy and educated cotton planters, who, Burr told Theo, "live as well as yours and have generally better houses."[16] Most of the residents were native Americans who had come down the Mississippi or across from Georgia at the time of the Revolution or later. Burr was entertained with hospitality and good taste and, in return, ingratiated his hosts with his style and talked to them about his projects. His stories were aimed at their interests and prejudices and, before long, many different tales were reported in the press about the suave New Yorker and his plans for the West.

The rest of the journey to New Orleans was well within settled territory. The three hundred miles were pleasurably and profitably traversed, for each day Burr managed to dine at the house of some gentleman. His name and prominence required no letters of introduction. Whenever he heard of a gentleman "whose acquaintance or hospitalities I should desire, I send word that I am coming to see him, and have always met a most cordial reception," Burr explained. And new Burrites were thus cultivated all along the way.

New Orleans proved to be a city of enchantment. Burr found the people cheerful and living in a handsome style. Edward Livingston, his old New York friend, was his host. Livingston now lived there with his new wife, a rich and beautiful widow from Santo Domingo.

The Livingston home was his base. From it, Burr spread his activities in all directions, enabling him to sense the temper of the populace. The social whirl, the dinners at which the first toast was usually "A la Santé, Madame Alston," the curious custom the natives had of referring to the inhabitants of the United States as "Americans," were all duly reported to Theodosia.[17] However, the real reason for the visit had been suspected by M. Louis Turreau, the French minister in Washington, who wrote to tell Talleyrand that "Louisiana is thus going to be the seat of Mr. Burr's new intrigues; he is going there under the aegis of General Wilkinson. It is even asserted that he might find the means there already prepared by a certain Livingston . . . closely associated with Burr."[18]

Beneath the surface gaiety and prosperity, there was much discontent in New Orleans. Burr hoped to cultivate all elements of dissatisfaction: the Mexican Association, for example, an organization of about three hundred members that wanted to bring about the liberation or conquest of Mexico. This idea fitted perfectly into Burr's schemes, and so his following now included Daniel Clark, his supporters, and many others.

A visit to the Ursuline nuns also had political overtones. Sister Therese de St. Xavier Farjon had requested him to visit the cloister. The Bishop of New Orleans conducted him to the interview, and he was surprised at the "gayety, *wit*, and sprightliness." The promise of co-operation was also hopeful. Three Jesuit priests were assigned to Mexico as agents, as the Bishop himself had observed during his recent visit to that country that the unhappiness of the people and the priests had become very serious. And so the Bishop was enthusiastic about Burr's purpose.[19]

Promising to return in the fall, no later than October, Burr, mounted on a horse and with a servant provided by Clark, left the city amidst the "tears of regret" of many citizens. His first stop was Natchez, where he successfully publicized the reports of anti-Spanish sentiments in New Orleans. One week later, he set out on the 450 mile trek along the Natchez Trace, a route full of hardships. Once again the guest of General Jackson at the Hermitage, Burr reached Nashville on August 6. He called Jackson "one of those prompt, frank, ardent souls whom I love to meet."[20]

Meanwhile, disturbing reports were being circulated in the press, and they were being picked up by foreign ministers. Merry wrote to London that Burr's plans were meeting with great success, and also reported that a convention of all states bordering on the Mississippi and Ohio was being called with separation from the United States as a goal. Don Carlos Martinez, Marqués de Casa Yrujo, Spain's red-headed minister, however, informed his minister of state that all the talk was merely a design to get English money.[21] Rumors and speculation were thus exposing what had been secret. Burr's conversations up and down the river were beginning to be heard.

From Natchez, Burr revisited Frankfort on the last of August after a week at Lexington. John Brown lodged him magnificently; and, there, he reported the results of his New Orleans trip and arranged his plans for the next two months. His destination was St. Louis, now Wilkinson's stronghold. The 450 miles through the Indiana wilderness would be routed through Louisville, Vincennes, Kaskaskia, and so to St. Louis. The return trip would culminate in a meeting at Berkeley Springs with Theodosia. The timetable was relayed to his daughter, so he could "take measures for going by land or water to Theoville," if he had not heard from her by that time.[22]

While all this prodigious traveling was being done, the newspapers all over the country were buzzing with queries. The Lexington *Gazette* warned that Burr's movements should be watched, as his "talents for Intrigue are considered as unrivalled in America." The *Gazette of the United States* seemed particularly disturbed and, in a passage copied by many other papers, asked:

How long will it be before we shall hear of Colonel Burr being at the head of a revolutionary party on the Western Waters? Is it a fact that Colonel Burr has formed a plan to engage the adventurous and enterprising young men from the Atlantic States to Louisiana? Is it one of the inducements that an immediate convention will be called from the States bordering the Ohio and Mississippi to form a separate government? Is it another that all the public lands are to be seized and partitioned among these States, except what is reserved for the warlike friends and followers of Burr in the revolution? Is it part of the plan for the New States to grant the new lands in bounties to entire inhabitants from the Atlantic States? How soon will the forts and magazines and all the military posts at New Orleans and on the Mississippi be in the hands of Colonel Burr's revolutionary party? How soon will Colonel Burr engage in the reduction of Mexico by granting liberty to its inhabitants and seizing on its treasures aided by British ships and forces? What difficulty can there be in completing a revolution in one summer along the Western States, when they will gain the Congress' lands, will throw off the public debt, will seize their own revenues, and enjoy the plunder of Spain?[23]

The results of the Western trip were being felt in a way that was not in the plans of its directors. Daniel Clark wrote that in Texas the current story was that Burr had visited New Orleans under military escort. Clark informed Wilkinson that he had heard that the Western states were to be bribed by Spanish money to separate from the Union.[24] Clark's letter may have been an attempt to profess his innocence; but, nevertheless, all these rumors had an effect on Wilkinson that was not to be salutary for Burr, although the Brigadier casually answered Clark with a quip that called it all "the tale of a tub of Burr."[25]

Burr's St. Louis visit to Wilkinson appeared friendly and intimate. Highly encouraged by the New Orleans visit, Burr reported that part of the West and the South was ready to fight against Spain. Inquiries were made about a route to Sante Fe and Wilkinson spoke well of Burr as an enterprising man. Jackson was told by the Colonel, at their next meeting, that he and Wilkinson had crystallized the plan to attack Mexico.[26] But Wilkinson later admitted in his *Memoirs* that it was "then that the unlimited confidence I reposed in Colonel Burr, during an intimacy of many years was impaired and for the first time in my life I could not avoid feeling towards him something like distrust and suspicion." Continuing about Burr, the General added that "his altered and mysterious manner; his unexplained hints of a splendid and brilliant enterprise excited my suspicions; and although he spoke of this . . . as being countenanced by government, his usual manner and unusual reserve, would not permit him to give entire confidence to this assurance."[27] Was it that the General feared that the leak would compromise him with both his paymasters, Spain and the United States? He cooled off, but, as yet, was apparently willing to coast along until the road either became smoother or got too rough. For the time being, he concealed his doubts under a façade of good wishes and contented himself with a letter of warning about his colleague to the Secretary of the Navy.

Burr, as unaware of his old friend's changed attitude as he was of Wilkinson's role as pensioner of Spain, traveled to Vincennes, capital of the Indiana Territory, with a letter to its governor, William Henry Harrison. Written by Wilkinson, the letter said: "I will demand from your friendship a boon . . . return the bearer to the councils of our country, where his talents and abilities are all-important at the present moment."[28] There is no record of a reply from Harrison. Either Wilkinson had hoped to shed his now irksome partner in this manner or he would have liked to see Burr in this advantageous position to further the mutual cause.

Burr then returned to Washington, after a stopover with Theodosia, whose ill health had concerned him all summer.[29] At the capital, he hastened to the British Embassy, but found no reply to his petition or money, and he needed half a million dollars. Burr gave Merry a very enthusiastic report about his Western journey, stating that in every quarter of the West they were ready for the execution of his plan. Burr described the readiness for action in New Orleans as so overdue that he predicted a bloodless revolution. If Pitt would send a naval force and £110,000 to be given in the names of John Barclay of Philadelphia and Daniel Clark of New Orleans, Burr guaranteed that the revolution would start by April or May. West Florida would, of course, be included because England was at war with Spain. Burr promised an even more tempting possibility to please his potential patrons: once the Western independence was achieved, the South and East would surely separate and thus the threat of a powerful United States would be removed. It was New Orleans and not the Ohio Valley that Burr designated as the heart of the conspiracy. The invasion of Mexico was not mentioned.[30]

Burr was about to be seriously disappointed. A visit to Jefferson at the White House, during which he was cordially received, almost crushed his hopes. The success of his endeavor was contingent on war with Spain, and the President now made it clear that there would be no war. Jefferson expected Napoleon to force Spain to give up Florida. There would, of course, be a price to pay, and Congress had already been asked for an appropriation. A letter to Alston confirmed Burr's belief that there would be no war with Spain "unless we shall declare it, which is not expected. England continues a course of malevolence which will still continue and be borne. France more courteous in words; under the pressure of her own affairs."[31]

Temporarily crushed, Burr went to Philadelphia, where he met frequently with Jonathan Dayton and Dr. Erich Bollman, a useful new recruit. Bollman was a German adventurer from Hanover, who had studied medicine at Göttingen and then practiced at Karlsruhe and Paris, where he was at the time of the Revolution. He had become famous for his attempt to free Lafayette from a prison at Olmutz, Austria. Lafayette was captured and Bollman was imprisoned for eight months, after which he immigrated to America. Because of America's sentimental attachment to Lafayette, Jefferson offered him, in succession, the consulate at Rotterdam, the commercial agency at Santo Domingo, and, in late 1805, the Indian agency at Natchitoches. Apparently, Burr's offer attracted Bollman more, and the German's linguistic skills in German, French, and English, as well as his experiences in intrigue, made him a valuable addition.

Dayton's assignment, at this time, was to talk to Casa Yrujo. He revealed a hair-raising plot against the government in Washington that impressed Yrujo. It was no less than a *coup d'état*. The President, Vice President, and other high officials would be seized, the Federal arsenal and bank captured, and Burr would take over. If the *coup* failed, all the ships, except two or three that were designated as transports, would be burned while Burr and his band sailed to New Orleans with the money looted from the bank. There, he would proclaim the freedom of Louisiana and the West. The Spanish government thought the story was worth fifteen hundred dollars, with a thousand more as a later payment. But, said Yrujo, the real reason for the remuneration was that Dayton had revealed to him the plans of Francesco do Miranda.[32]

Miranda, Venezuela-born adventurer, participant in the American and French revolutions, ousted from Napoleon's France, with a formidable history of intrigue behind him, was considered by Burr more as a rival than a fellow adventurer. Inevitably, their names were linked, but interest in Miranda's schemes had lessened British interest in Burr's. Burr also disliked the fact that some of his own followers were inclined to back Miranda as well. Miranda's past association with Hamilton was an additional reason for Burr's hostility.

The Venezuelan and Burr met for the first time in Philadelphia during the last month of 1805, when Miranda was seeking and getting help for another attempt to liberate Venezuela. He planned to sail from New York publicly in the American fitted-out *Leander* on a voyage seemingly endorsed by Madison. But his expedition ended in disaster when the ship was captured by the Spaniards before it could reach its destination. After several subsequent futile attempts, Miranda was seized and died in a Spanish dungeon.

Neither Miranda nor Burr had anything kind to say about each other. Miranda blamed Burr for the betrayal of his plans to Yrujo.[33] Burr told Charles Biddle that he considered the Venezuelan "a fool, totally unqualified for such an expedition."[34] And long afterward, bristling at the suggestion that Miranda "*had taken the bread out of his mouth*," Burr responded by saying that it had been Wilkinson who had suggested the plan for an expedition, not Miranda.[35]

The only bright spot at that year's end was Blennerhassett's answer to Burr's letters. He said that he planned to either sell or lease his estate so he could straighten out his finances and that he was, therefore, looking for a new venture. The Burr enterprise seemed just the thing. Although he could not contribute large sums at this time, he completely agreed with Burr's views and would cooperate in any way possible. "I hope, Sir," he wrote, "you will feel that it flows in a conviction of your judgement and talents."[36] Burr put the letter aside to be used at a propitious time.

Until January 6, Burr stayed in Philadelphia. He was depressed because, as he wrote to General Wilkinson, "we are to have no Spanish war, except in ink and words." But his search for important associates continued. That month, William Eaton was approached as a likely prospect. Burr supposed Eaton disaffected toward the government because his claims for the cash he had advanced while United States consul at Tunis and the expenses he had incurred in the war with Tripoli had been disallowed. Eaton admitted that Burr was quite right and, later, described Burr's operating method. At first, Burr played on Eaton's dissatisfaction. Gradually, he hinted at war with Spain and the feasibility of penetrating Mexico. That plan was illustrated with maps and documents. Then, when Eaton seemed compliant, Burr "laid open his project of revolutionizing the territory west of the Allegheny; establishing an independent empire there; New Orleans to be the capital and he himself to be the chief; organizing a military force on the waters of the Mississippi and carrying conquest to Mexico."[37] At one of their several meetings, Burr proposed to make Eaton second in command, after Wilkinson.

Eaton claimed to have been so disturbed by Burr's plans that he approached the President about the wisdom of sending the Colonel out of the country, to Paris, London, or Madrid. Jefferson expressed concern about Burr's integrity. Eaton agreed that it was a cogent question, but thought that a position of honor would secure his loyalty. Jefferson would not hear of any such possibility and, instead, declared his confidence in the loyalty of the West.[38]

Eaton was of questionable character and motives. His swashbuckling and drinking made him unreliable; but he was not alone in the assertion that Burr had harbored such plans. Benjamin Stoddert, former navy secretary, called on Burr in the spring of 1806 and, after expressing criticism of Jefferson's Florida policy, was told by his host that he could send Jefferson to Monticello and execute a bloodless revolution with five hundred men because so many distinguished people were disgusted with the Administration.[39]

Another old friend, also disgruntled at the time, was approached that winter. He was Commodore Truxtun, who, during the Tripolitan War, had felt himself cheated of his command by Jefferson and so disliked him. However, Truxtun consistently turned down Burr's offers, although he referred to them as "honorable and profitable." Truxtun admitted that he advised Burr freely on the best mode of attacking Vera

Cruz and Cartagena, but refused outright to have anything to do with an expedition against Spain or Mexico that was not projected by the government. Although he was offered the command of the naval expedition and received Burr's assurances that Wilkinson and "many greater men" were involved, Truxtun refused to commit himself.[40]

Burr was sustaining resistance from some of his most important potential supporters. But he was unaware of what was to be a relentless pursuit by a self-appointed avenging fury. Joseph Hamilton Daveiss, whose brilliant performance in the important land case of *Mason* vs. *Wilson* had brought him to the attention of the Chief Justice and who later married John Marshall's sister, was now District Attorney of Kentucky. He was also an ardent Federalist, one of his chief difficulties, for seldom had a man received less support from his superiors.

Toward the end of 1805, Daveiss had information that several American citizens were pensioners of Spain, among them General James Wilkinson. Daveiss immediately relayed this shocking information to Jefferson, along with the news that an involvement with Spain was Burr's mission in New Orleans.[41] When a list of suspects followed, Jefferson must have been disturbed to read that they were solidly Republican. Included were Wilkinson, Senator Adair, Senator Smith, Burr, Governor Harrison, Henry Clay, and Harry Innes, the judge of the district court.[42] He was only partially relieved when an amended list arrived in March that exonerated Clay and a Lexington doctor.

Jefferson's first guarded reply asked for complete information. "The names are peculiarly important to prevent a misplacing of our confidence," he wrote.[43] Madison, Gallatin, and Dearborn were all informed.

This did not satisfy Daveiss, whose conviction that his suspects were fomenting the Spanish war grew daily. By spring, he had determined to investigate the activities himself as soon as the court closed. Kentucky's Secretary of State, John Rowan, told him that Burr had spent a great deal of time with Adair. Daveiss then found Cuthbert Banks of Lexington so angered by a letter from Jackson that called Burr the savior of the Western country that he had thrown the letter in the fire. He would always despise Burr, Banks asserted, but "I should like to know something about the doings of this saviour of ours."[44] Daveiss, now determined to save the government, put a note in the Lexington *Gazette* saying that Jefferson had removed him from office and submitted his letter of resignation to Madison.

In May, 1806, the peripatetic detective went to investigate in his quarry's territory. Daveiss found Wilkinson in St. Louis and talked to him about Burr. The General showed great admiration for the Colonel. At one point in the conversation, in answer to Daveiss' inquiry about

Zebulon Pike's expedition to the Southwest, the Brigadier presented a manuscript map of New Mexico and said, in a low and significant tone and manner, "had Burr been President, we would have had all this country before now."

During this period, Daveiss heard nothing from Jefferson, but continued his efforts alone. At his last interview with Wilkinson, the investigator saw the General's nerve give a little. He showed Daveiss an anonymous letter from Frankfort advising him to beware of Daveiss and his intention to extract secrets about a Spanish connection. Wilkinson laughed, said Daveiss, but "I could clearly discern through the veil of his laughter that he was thoroughly alarmed."[45]

For a couple of months, Daveiss halted his letters and reports to Washington while awaiting new sources of information. Part of the difficulty that the Attorney General encountered in his pursuit was that some of Burr's supposedly most ardent supporters denied their allegiance. Either they had cooled or they preferred to appear uninvolved because of the newspaper publicity. For example, Daniel Clark wrote to a friend disclaiming a connection with Burr, whom he called "a man of desperate fortunes, whose stay among us did not exceed a fortnight." Then Clark added: "What in God's name, have I to expect or could hope from Colonel Burr?"[46]

From January to August, 1806, Burr traveled between Philadelphia, Charleston, and Washington, trying to solidify his interests. The raising of money was crucial at this point. At Charleston, he met Theodosia and was also able to negotiate with Alston, who became his heaviest financial backer.

In early winter, the last vestiges of Burr's political influence were being felt in New York, where he dared not visit. A reconciliation was being secretly arranged between the Clintonians and the Burrites. Mayor De Witt Clinton, probably with presidential aspirations for himself, was behind the peace offer. General Theodorus Bailey, the postmaster, made an overture to Burr's lieutenant, John Swartwout. Almost daily confidential sessions between the two men followed. Many influential New York politicians of both wings of the Republican Party participated in some of the talks.[47]

Predominant in the discussion on the part of the Burrites was the interest of Aaron Burr. Matthew L. Davis expressed his loyalty to his chief in a letter to William Peter Van Ness: "I am no Clintonian; I am no Lewisite; but I am a Burrite;—& those *republicans* who are the *political friends* or *enemies* of A. B. are to calculate on my *support* or *opposition* in the same ratio as their friendship or hostility is evinced."[48] The final agreement, called the "Union," was completed on January 11. It stipulated that Burr would be recognized by them as a Republican and called for an end to newspaper attacks on him.[49] His friends, hitherto unable to obtain even one cent from the Manhattan Company, were now accommodated. A distinguished Burrite had a note discounted for nine thousand dollars on January 11, and, just five days later, an identical note was honored for the same person. Was it for Burr himself?[50]

By the next month, the secret was out. Rufus King saw the deal as a preparation for a "Bonapartean campaign at the next election, a split between De Witt Clinton and the Livingstons. Morgan Lewis, he said, "does not appear to possess a single talent for managing the corrupt party he is connected with."[51]

On February 18, Dyde's Hotel in New York was the scene of the public peace meeting. On the surface, this union supper was merry and convivial. Toasts complimenting Burr and his friends were drunk. But most Clintonians resented the implications. They interpreted the peace as the overthrow of Lewis, the rehabilitation of Burr, or some other shady maneuver. Consequently, the sick old Vice President, George Clinton, warned that it had been an unfortunate move on his nephew's part. "I am happy to hear of the predominance of the republican Interest, though I cannot say that it would add to my Pleasure if it resulted from the accession of the Burrites to the Party," wrote George Clinton.[52]

One week later, the opposition met at Martling's Long Room to protest. Those Burrites and Lewisites present carried their enmity to Clinton until his downfall.[53] The gathering, which was unusually large, numbering fifteen hundred, proceeded to renounce the meeting at Dyde's. After disavowing the earlier session, those present unanimously passed a resolution that "Aaron Burr does not & ought not to possess the confidence of the Republican party."[54]

Burr's involvement in these matters is unknown, but its effect on him was another disaster in that discouraging winter. Many opponents, including Jefferson, regarded the measure as motivated by Burr to give him importance. There had been, at the time of the reunion, some agitation by Burr's friends to return him to New York politics. For this purpose a libel suit was instituted against Cheetham to attempt to completely disprove the accusation that Burr had intrigued for the presidency in 1801. These efforts antagonized President Jefferson because some of the depositions reflected against him.[55]

At this unpropitious moment, Burr made a last attempt to conciliate Jefferson and receive some recognition from him. The meeting was reported in detail, and with acerbity, in the President's *Anas*. Burr declared that Jefferson "had always used him with politeness, but nothing more." Such treatment was unfair, complained the New Yorker, because he had always supported the Administration. When that tack failed, Burr attempted another approach, saying, darkly, that he could do much harm to Jefferson. This angered the Virginian, who answered sharply that he was afraid of no man, and although he appreciated Burr's talents, little popular confidence remained. Thoroughly rebuffed, Burr left the White House for the last time.[56]

He remained in Washington, but did little visiting and was seen by few. After his rejection by Jefferson, he reconsidered the Matthew Lyon proposal that he attempt a congressional seat from Kentucky; Senator John Brown of that state was asked for introductory letters.[57] Plumer heard the news and, as usual, made his comment: "Burr to be raised to office by the patronage of Matthew Lyon! *How are the mighty fallen!*"[58]

For the moment, the Western project looked very unpromising. Blennerhassett, whom Burr had still not met in person, was informed by letter on April 15 that the "business . . . in some degree depends on contingencies not within my control, and will not be commenced before December, if ever." Moreover, details could not be explained by letter. Hence, they should keep in touch with each other's movements for the coming season. Burr added, significantly, that there would be no war with Spain unless "we should be actually invaded."[59] The next day, Wilkinson was also informed of the postponement of the project "till December." The cipher letter gave the reasons: "Want of water in Ohio rendered movement impracticable."[60] This meant that so far there was a failure to obtain outside help from either Merry or Yrujo.[61] Wilkinson was then reminded that he had not been heard from since last October.[62]

Wilkinson at this time showed a reluctance to be associated with Burr, although he, too, was acting in an independent manner. Repeated orders from Secretary of War Dearborn calling for the ejection of the Spaniards to the west of the Sabine River had been blithely ignored. Even when orders arrived to take command of the Sabine in mid-June, the Brigadier lingered in St. Louis until August. Then, slowly, he moved toward Natchez, where he arrived on the seventh of September, 1806.

Burr needed war. Wilkinson had the opportunity to start it, and yet he deliberately delayed. Either he was afraid that Burr was not quite ready to proceed with the Mexican project or he felt some loyalty to Spain.

The foreign ministers kept the diplomatic mailbags filled with reports and speculations about Burr's activities. The French minister to the

United States reported to Talleyrand that the Administration was afraid and accepted as inevitable a division of the states which, he added, would not be bad for France because one of the resulting confederations might be friendly to France.[63]

However, Burr's two chief sources of potential foreign aid had dried up by June, 1806. Spain was uninterested; in fact, the King had made it quite clear that there would be no money available to encourage Burr's efforts.[64] Possibly Wilkinson had somehow prompted this decision. As for England, Anthony Merry received notice on June 1 that he would be replaced. The adventurers were on their own.

In May, Robert Goodloe Harper had helped Burr find a suitable lodging in Baltimore for Theodosia and little Aaron Burr Alston. She needed to escape the fever-ridden South Carolina region to try to restore her feeble health. When it became too hot in Maryland, the Alstons moved to the Pennsylvania mountains. Burr traveled back and forth between Philadelphia and their summer place.

While in Philadelphia, he was the guest of Charles Biddle, whose family was also away for the summer. The two old friends discussed Burr's project at length, but the Colonel was unable to convince Biddle that there should be a settlement of military men on the Mississippi and war with Spain. Biddle regretted later that his strong objection to Burr's plan had made him close his ears to the details. "I was sorry afterwards on his account that I had not let him proceed and heard the whole of his plan," he wrote later. "It is probable an immediate stop would have been put to it, which would have been fortunate for him." Nevertheless, Biddle insisted that Burr would not do anything to injure his country.[65]

Burr spent a lot of time that summer with General Jean Victor Moreau, who had been living in the United States since his complicity in conspiracies against the Emperor had culminated in his exile. The French soldier's experience with war and anti-government plots made him interesting to Burr.

In July, 1806, Burr made a significant purchase. He acquired the Bastrop lands on the Washita River, an area of about four hundred thousand acres. The financial arrangement, backed by Joseph Alston,[66] was five thousand dollars in cash and the assumption of a debt of thirty thousand dollars, which Colonel Charles Lynch, the holder of the claim, owed to Edward Livingston.[67] Because the title to the land was not clear, the purchase was a speculation like all the other alternatives of Burr's program. The purchase of the lands marked the end of Burr's delay and the end of the Eastern phase of the adventure.

The Western contacts were resumed, particularly with Andrew Jackson. Burr wrote to Blennerhassett that he would visit him at his island home before the twentieth of August. Samuel Swartwout and Peter Ogden of New Jersey, son of Matthias Ogden, who had died in 1791, carried the letter to Blennerhassett on their way down the river. Dr. Bollman was ordered to proceed to New Orleans.

The reluctant Wilkinson received two incendiary letters at this time. The first, from Dayton, slyly announced that Jefferson was about to replace him, allegedly yielding to public sentiment, and was going to appoint another head of the army. It was an inducement for Wilkinson to commence hostilities. "You know the rest," Dayton wrote. "*Are you ready?* Are your numerous associates ready? Wealth and Glory! Louisiana *and* Mexico!" challenged the cipher letter.[68] The second letter, Burr's, was the most notorious one of the entire conspiracy.

It was written in cipher, for Swartwout and Ogden to hand to the General. Not the only copy, as a duplicate had gone with Bollman, it outlined the plan in full. Curiously, it was written in the third person. Its opening line was of crucial importance later. Decoded, it reads as follows:

Your letter post marked 13[1] May is received I have at length obtained *funds, and have* actually commenced *The* eastern detachments from *different* points *and under different* pretence *will* rendezvous on *Ohio* 1. November.

Every thing internal *and* external favour our views. Naval protection *of England* is secured. *Truxtun* is going *to* Jamaica *to* arrange *with* the admiral there *and will* meet us *at Mississippi England a Navy* of United States ready *to* join *and* final orders are given *to my friends* and followers. *It will be a host of choice spirits. Wilkinson shall be* second *to Burr* only, *and Wilkinson shall dictate the* rank *and* promotion *of his* officers. . . . Send forthwith *an* intelligent *and* confidential friend *with whom Burr* may confer. He *shall* return immediately *with* further interes*ting* details. *This* is essential *to* concert *and* harmony *of* movement—Send *a* list *of all* persons know*n to Wilkinson*. . . .

Our project *my* dear friend is brought *to the* point so long desc*ribed*—I guarantee the result with *my* life and *honor*; with the lives *the* honor *and the* fortune of hundreds *the* best blood of our country.

Burrs plan of operation is to move down rapidly from *the* falls on fifteenth November with *the* first *500* or *1000* men in light boats now construc*ting for* that *pur*pose *to* be at *Natches* between the *5* and *15* of December there *to* meet you then to determine whether *it* will be expedient on the first instance to seize or to pass by B. R.—On

receipt of this send me *an* answer—Draw on me *for* all expence. . . .
   The govt invite *us to* glory *and* fortune. *It* remains *to be* seen
whether *we* deserve *the boons*.[69]

The flamboyantly dramatic style of the letter, more like its recipient's
than Burr's style, was either part of the design or a reflection of the
extreme excitement that Burr was feeling. There are obvious flights of
fancy in it and some downright lies, such as the exaggeration of the
promised support. The timetable might have been efficacious for Burr,
had he been able to keep it. The stated aim was clearly either Mexico or
New Orleans, for a first stop. Some of the cryptic statements would fit
either alternative, but if Natchitoches and then Mexico was the destination, why detour to Baton Rouge, which is on the road to New Orleans?
Perhaps Mobile, in Spanish Florida, was to receive the first blow. On the
other hand, three weeks would be much too short a time to revolutionize Mexico. And the letter had stated: "The people *of the* country to
which we *are* going *are* prepared *to* receive us. Their agents now *with*
me say that if *we* will protect their religion *and* will *not* subject them *to
a* foreign power that in three weeks all *will be* settled."[70] Also there is
no evidence that Mexican agents had been keeping *au courant* with the
latest sentiments there, but Burr had good friends in the Mexican Association in New Orleans among those who had been stirring up the city
for years. Also, Dr. Bollman, James Alexander, Lt. Robert Spence, and
others sailed for New Orleans. This must have been his destination.[71]

Just before leaving the East, Burr wrote a letter to Albert Gallatin
asking two pertinent questions. First, he requested any knowledge, or
any way to facilitate his acquiring it, concerning Baron Bastrop's claims
to the Washita lands. Second: "Has Wilkinson resigned or been removed from the office of Gov. of La and if so, is his successor named or
agreed on?" The Dayton letter to Wilkinson had some basis in rumor, at
least.[72]

Burr was ready to start his great adventure. Charles Willie, a German
secretary, needed to decipher Bollman's communications, and Julien de
Pestre, now Burr's chief of staff, accompanied him. His daughter and
grandson were to follow shortly; and, in October, Joseph Alston, "with
a *Corps* of worthies." In the Colonel's own words: "Burr will proceed
westward *first* August *never to return*."[73]

CHAPTER XVII

Western Adventure: Part Two

THE West was of two minds about Burr. Many supporters were still loyal, but his enemies were gaining momentum as suspicion and rumor spread. Early in the summer, a new weekly newspaper, the *Western World*, made its appearance in Kentucky. Its patron was Humphrey Marshall, a cousin and brother-in-law of John Marshall. A Federalist in a Republican state, Marshall was a scoffer at religion and the rule of the masses, as well as the wielder of a vitriolic pen. John Wood and Joseph Street were the publishers and its purpose was to expose the dealings with Spain of some important Kentuckians. The first number recalled the old Spanish conspiracy of twenty years before and attempted to link it with the Burr endeavor. Subsequent issues named those who were involved, including Aaron Burr, Jonathan Dayton, John Brown, Edward Livingston, John B. Prevost, and others. The paper's sensationalism helped boost its circulation to one thousand, a large figure in those days. Judge Benjamin Sebastian, for example, resigned from the Kentucky Court of Appeals rather than remain vulnerable to a *Western World* exposure of his continued drawing of a Spanish pension.[1]

Daveiss was still on the trail. By this time, he had revised his former theory and decided that Burr's aim was to cause a revolt of the Spanish provinces and subsequently sever the western area from the United States. Somewhat later, Daveiss wrote that his revelation to Jefferson, which included a list of suspects who were mostly Republicans, angered the President. "He saw that I now understood him," said Daveiss; "and I most faithfully believe that he hates every man on earth, who he thinks fully understands him."[2]

Daveiss was discerning. Jefferson was wary of the discrediting of Republicans, especially when most of the information that Daveiss was submitting was inadmissible as evidence in court. Daveiss told him that Burr was aiming at the young men of the area, firing them with enthusiasm for his plan. "The extensiveness of this poison among our young men" was astonishing, Madison was told.[3]

But Burr was not to be deterred from following his schedule. His long delayed meeting with Harman Blennerhassett finally took place and was mutually agreeable. They found many intellecutal interests in common. Both were admirers of Voltaire, both inclined to free-thinking, both had a love of power and prestige. Burr's dignity and pride and the promise of glory that he brought won his host to a blind devotion. Margaret Blennerhassett, already thoroughly partial to the Colonel, was also enchanted by his daughter. Theodosia stayed with the Blennerhassetts while her father went to Marietta and then down the river to gather more recruits and see about supplies.

The terms of recruitment offered the young men were twelve dollars per month, clothes, and provisions, for six months' enlistment, with a bonus of one hundred and fifty acres at the end of that time. Talented and qualified recruits were offered commissions. Thus, an independent military force was being built up regardless of Wilkinson or foreign aid.

Burr's western tour was as vigorous as the one he had accomplished the year before. His unbelievable energy made it possible for him to ride, sail, and travel through the wilderness to any destination. By August 11, he and Julien de Pestre, the Frenchman whom he now regarded as his second in command, and his German secretary rode into Chambersburg. The Alstons had been settled at Bedford Springs, Pennsylvania, where the mountain air and medicinal waters were beneficial for both of them. After a short visit, Burr rode to Pittsburgh, the hub of his activities.

All the forces were to rendezvous at Pittsburgh; Burr stayed at James O'Hara's Tavern to settle his supply problems and direct the enlistment of more recruits. Many of them were very well connected.

Fifteen miles from Pittsburgh, at Cannonsburgh, was *Morganza*, the farm of Colonel George Morgan. The sixty-three year old Colonel, an old campaigner of varied interests and activities, was well known for his studies of the Hessian fly and also for his founding of the colony of New Madrid in Spanish Louisiana. Burr informed the old man that he would like to call on him and was cordially invited to do so. At dinner, Burr spoke out eloquently but perhaps too much, revealing his belief that the West would be separated from the rest of the Union in five years, with the Alleghenies as the line of demarcation. He then said, cryptically, that great numbers are not required to accomplish great deeds: all that is necessary is a leader who can inspire confidence. To illustrate his point, he stated that New York could be taken with five hundred men and, with two hundred, Congress could be driven into the Potomac.

After dinner, Burr had a private conversation with the Colonel's son, Thomas Morgan. He asked about the boy's choice of profession. When he heard that young Morgan was a law student, he observed that our government did not encourage talent and then broached the subject of his military expedition. The young lad answered that his interest would depend on the object or cause for which the fight was being made; Burr seemed pleased with him and invited him to join his own mission.[4]

Their guest's statements upset the Morgans. Not only was it what he said, but the manner contained certain hints and insinuations that aroused Colonel Morgan's suspicions. He then summoned Presley Neville, Pennsylvania's Chief Justice, and Samuel Roberts, and told them about his encounter with Burr. Somewhat later, these two men wrote a summary of Morgan's statement to James Madison.[5]

Comfort Tyler was appointed Burr's chief commissary agent. Formerly a rich landowner from Herkimer, New York, but now penniless, Tyler had been scouting for recruits in his home area with an ample supply of cash. He wanted several hundred young men for a voyage down the Ohio, destination unknown. All were assured that there was "nothing on foot inimical to government."[6] He also was directed to have purchased and delivered on the Ohio River in November forty thousand dollars' worth of provisions.

John Wilkins, a local merchant, was ordered to provide twenty thousand barrels of flour and five thousand barrels of pork to be delivered locally or to a merchant at Natchez. A large advance was made on the contract. Either it was to be a long siege or a tremendous number of men, for the supplies were in addition to what was ordered in Marietta and other places. The quantity was sufficient for a small army, but excessive for a group of settlers on the way to the Bastrop lands.[7]

At Marietta, Burr's next stop, Dudley Woodbridge, Blennerhassett's partner, agreed to supply one hundred barrels of pork. He was a local merchant who had said that the squire of the island villa had all kinds of sense but common sense. Colonel John J. Barker was commissioned to build fifteen boats on the Muskingum at his yard six miles up the river from Marietta. The boats were to be light-weight, built like skiffs, sharp at both ends and sided up with thin weather boarding and then covered.

They were to have a shallow draft, to be able to hold forty or fifty men with their gear, and to be suitable for use upstream as well as downstream.[8] Blennerhassett took over a large part of the responsibility for getting such supplies as flour, corn meal, whiskey, and other foods. Much of the corn from which the meal was made was raised and kiln-dried on the island.[9]

After Burr's visit, Blennerhassett, quite independently, conceived the idea of writing and publishing a series of short essays in the Marietta *Gazette* under the name of "Querist." The author denied wanting to further Burr's cause; rather, he said, it was to acquaint the people of the western country with the "state of things on the Mississippi" and to explain that their choice "of an eastern or western ascendancy would determine their future prosperity." He also wished to divert attention from a Mexican expedition which, if kept secret, would have the support of the government and, if exposed, would have to be frustrated.[10]

Four issues of the *Gazette* carried "Querist" articles. They urged separation from the Atlantic states and discussed the exploitation of the West by the federal government. They said, in short, many things that Burr had said. But publishing them would seem to have been dangerous and overly provocative at this time. When Blennerhassett, under a pledge of secrecy, read the manuscript to John and Alexander Henderson, they were both horrified. On the occasion of Blennerhassett's visit to the Henderson farm, the statement was made that under Burr's auspices the separation of the Union was contemplated in nine months. Blennerhassett added that there would be no French help; but, with New Orleans secured and such stalwarts as General Eaton, Robert Goodloe Harper, Dayton, and Joseph Alston involved, Burr "could tie the President neck and heels and with three pieces of artillery and 300 sharpshooters, defend any pass in the Alleghenies." His parting advice to his host was to join the plot early and get the full benefits.[11] Instead, Henderson, the leading Federalist of Wood County, led a drive to condemn the conspiracy and provide for raising militia in case of an emergency.[12]

By mid-September, Burr was in Frankfort, Kentucky. He arrived at sunset, alone, de Pestre having gone to St. Louis to handle matters in that area. Burr would supervise activities along the Ohio. All merchandise had to be ready in October, so that it could be delivered in New Orleans by the middle or end of December, another factor suggesting that the delta city was their destination.[13]

Nashville and General Jackson received Burr in the now accustomed manner in October. Burr's news about Spanish troops camped on American soil, the jailing of United States citizens, and the removal of the stars and stripes electrified Jackson. He promptly published a proclamation in the Nashville newspaper ordering brigade commanders to place their brigades immediately on such a footing as to be able to supply their quotas on the shortest notice in preparation for governmental needs. That same government viewed this move with much concern, interpreting it as a phase of Burr's conspiracy.[14] Burr, unmindful, depended on Jackson and sent him thirty-five hundred dollars in Kentucky bank notes to pay for supplies and the construction of five large boats.

From Nashville, Burr rode back to Lexington, where he was joined by Blennerhassett and the Alstons. The group concentrated on getting money and supplies. One of the techniques was to solicit funds for the settlement of the Bastrop lands. Blennerhassett attempted a loan of eight to ten thousand dollars from the Joseph S. Lewis Company of Philadelphia for "commercial and land speculations." He asked for credit on his personal funds and offered as security "the vast estates and other property of Joseph Alston, Esq. of South Carolina . . . the son-in-law of Col. Burr."[15] Burr also informed William Wilkin, his Pittsburgh agent and merchant, that he had embarked on a "speculation of some magnitude." He enclosed a map of the settlement with his letter.[16]

Other loans were solicited, and some obtained, from the Kentucky Insurance Company, Kentucky merchants, and the firm of Ogden and Smith in New York. The figures that were circulating in the territory claimed that Burr had spent roughly two hundred thousand dollars already. A purchasing agent from Shelbyville stated that he was buying as much beef, flour, and pork as he could and paying for it in advance.[17] The private account between Burr and Blennerhassett, which was started at this time and ran to January 9, 1807, reached a total of $7,864.95.[18]

The Burr organization was preparing for action. Comfort Tyler in Pittsburgh, Davis Floyd in central Kentucky, and Patton Anderson in Tennessee were recruiting and buying.[19] Anderson had enlisted seventy-five men, including Stockly Hays, Jackson's nephew. Jackson's orders to the West Tennessee militia prompted Burr to write hopefully to Governor Harrison at Vincennes to suggest that he issue a similar order. "All reflecting men consider a war with Spain to be inevitable; in such an event, I think you would not be at ease as an idle spectator. If it should be my lot to be employed, which there is reason to expect, it would be my highest gratification to be associated with you."[20]

Burr's methods had not changed. He was still adapting his story to his listeners. Benjamin Latrobe, a prominent Philadelphia architect, received an offer of ten thousand acres of the Bastrop lands if he would help to establish the settlement. If he wished to make a surveying trip there, at the Colonel's expense, Burr would send forty or fifty men to clear the land and build cabins.[21]

But there was trouble in some crucial spots. In Cincinnati, the citizens talked about mobbing Burr. One evening, a crowd actually collected at the Colonel's tavern and played the "Rogues March" on fifes and drums. Burr refused help, saying, quite boldly, that he liked martial music.[22] Even at the hub of the conspiracy, Blennerhassett Island, opposition was organizing. Alerted by Henderson, Marietta residents were apprehensive about the news of a conspiracy, now substantiated by the building of boats on the Muskingum. They were reacting to "A fever" that is "raging . . . *the Burr* Fever." Mrs. Blennerhassett sent her gardener, Peter Taylor, to seek Burr out and to warn him. Before finding him at Lexington, Taylor went to Cincinnati and stopped at John Smith's home. When Smith heard Taylor's account of Burr's activities, he was deeply disturbed and sent a note to Burr demanding an explanation. Burr hastened to answer the letter. With an innocent air, he wrote: "If there exists any design to separate the Western from the Eastern States, I am totally ignorant of it."[23] The gardener rode into Lexington with the warning that Burr better not show his face in Marietta or he might be shot. It was the same man, Taylor, who later revealed that his master had told him about Burr's plan to crown himself as King of Mexico and have his daughter succeed him as Queen.

In Washington, the month of October brought news from the West that Jefferson could not ignore. Gideon Granger, deeply engaged in Yazoo speculations and widely believed to be involved in the Burr entanglement, heard the story of Burr's overtures to Eaton. He forwarded the information to Jefferson. The President called a cabinet meeting on October 22, the first of three, to review the problem and to plan action. Secrecy was maintained. It was, however, decided to send confidential letters to the governors of Ohio, Indiana, Mississippi, and Orleans, and to the district attorneys of Kentucky, Tennessee, and Louisiana to have Burr watched carefully and, "on his committing any overt act unequivocally to have him tried for treason, misdemeanor." His followers were to get the same treatment. Some gunboats were to be ordered up to Fort Adams to intercept any force of suspicious persons descending the river. Although the problem of Wilkinson, now generally under suspicion, was treated gingerly, recognition was made of the fact that he had disobeyed the June 11 order to descend to New Orleans and then take command at Natchitoches. He had, instead, remained in St. Louis until September.

Two days later, at the second cabinet meeting, positive action was ordered. Captains Preble and Decatur were to go to New Orleans with the *Argus*, two gunboats from New York, three from Norfolk, and two from Charleston, if Mr. Gallatin could find the money. John Graham was to be sent to Kentucky on Burr's trail, "consult Governors and arrest Burr, if he has made himself liable." Dr. Browne was to be removed. The question of Wilkinson was postponed.

The next day, when the final cabinet meeting was held, there was a decided change in the President's attitude. He told the aides that, since the latest mail from the West had contained no word of Burr's movements, this "total silence . . . proves he is committing no overt act against law." Consequently, the naval orders were rescinded and, instead, marines were to be sent to reinforce New Orleans against the Spaniards. However, Graham would replace Wilkinson as governor of Louisiana. This private eye could arrest Burr, if necessary, and alert the other governors. What changed the President's mind can only be surmised. It might have been the good offices of Dearborn being exerted for his old friend.[24]

But Wilkinson was still in a favored position. The very important letter from Burr of the twenty-second of July had been following him since August. Its bearer, Samuel Swartwout, had missed the General at St. Louis and had to follow him to the Sabine, where Wilkinson was stationed to cope with a Spanish crisis.

Spain had determined to hold a little strip of land between the Sabine and the Arroyo Hondo, an area that Wilkinson had been ordered to occupy for the United States. War seemed inevitable.

While Wilkinson awaited developments, Samuel Swartwout arrived at his camp with a letter of introduction from Jonathan Dayton. Finding Wilkinson in the company of Colonel Thomas Cushing, young Swartwout pretended that he had heard that United States troops were assembled at Natchitoches and so he had interrupted his voyage to New Orleans in order to volunteer. As soon as Cushing left the room, Swartwout handed Wilkinson the packet of letters from Burr. And for the rest of the night of October 8, Wilkinson decoded the long, provocative letter that would involve him irretrievably with the fortunes of Burr and his "host of choice spirits."[25] He had already decided to betray his friend, and this letter convinced him that there was much to be gained from playing Judas.

He had played the role before. In 1788, having been a confidant of Colonel John Connolly, who was trying to incite Americans to join the British in an attack and invasion of Louisiana, Wilkinson sold the Englishman's plans to Governor Miro. In 1790, Dr. James O'Fallon and his armed colonists, who had wanted to plant a colony on the site of present-day Vicksburg, were similarly exposed to the Spaniards. Wilkinson was the perpetrator, for cash. When George Rogers Clark planned to lead his backwoodsmen against New Orleans, Wilkinson carried the news to Carondelet, for cash.[26]

For this new betrayal, Wilkinson envisioned sundry rewards; from the Spanish, from Jefferson, with whom his stock was now low, and from the American people, whose saviour he had decided to be. Wilkinson's assertion that he had made this decision in a single night was dramatic but probably untrue. He had made the decision in St. Louis but had awaited the proper moment. The time had come; and now, once the irksome little task in hand was taken care of, the matter of Burr could be given his full attention. The letter would destroy its author. But, first, the General had to make peace with the Spanish, which also would please his peace-loving President.

Wilkinson was thoroughly aware of the fact that, in the public mind, he was deeply involved with Burr. The *Western World* and the Lexington *Gazette*, both copied all over the country, had bandied his name about freely with the chief conspirators. He, therefore, took up his glib and purple pen to proclaim his loyalty to a willing recipient. Jefferson wanted to believe that he had not been wrong in his choice of Wilkinson for so many honors.

The General's letter of October 20 was effusive and deliberately alarming. Jefferson was warned that an association reaching from New York to the Western states and territories planned to rendezvous eight to ten thousand men in New Orleans very shortly and, with the cooperation of a navy, carry on an expedition against Vera Cruz. On or before November 20, a body of these men would descend to New Orleans in light boats from the Allegheny River near the rapids of the Ohio, getting reinforcements from Tennessee. A British squadron from the West Indies might join them.[27]

The Spanish problem worked out very well for Wilkinson. He arranged with Herrera to create a neutral ground until the disputed area could be arbitrated. This freed the American general to attend to Burr, who had remained in Lexington, although the report of trouble on the island had lured its master back. The Alstons had returned to South Carolina and de Pestre was following up the Yrujo connection, telling him that the separation of the West was the real goal of the conspiracy and that the Mexican design was merely a cover-up ruse.[28]

Joseph Daveiss decided to take action. At the start of November, he applied to the Federal Court in Frankfort for a warrant to apprehend Burr on the charge of plotting to attack Mexico. Burr heard that his arrest was planned and told Blennerhassett that it was probable that "villains enough may have been found to encounter all the perjuries which may be thought necessary to gratify malice." However, he feared that this step might embarrass the Washita settlement.[29]

Harry Innes, the judge on the case, had to be convinced that he had a valid right to prosecute. Daveiss summarized his argument with the statement that Burr's buying one thousand stand of arms, engaging one thousand men to go with him for a year or more, making a new settlement, might all be innocent. But, he added, "the doing of any one of them *as a preparation* for an expedition is an offense."[30]

Burr's host was urged by his guest to write to Henry Clay, already an influential young lawyer in the new state, asking that he represent Burr in the coming hearing. Flattered that such an eminent and discerning man as Burr should choose him to handle this crisis, Clay agreed to take the assignment.

Burr arrived in Frankfort on November 7. He was wet and tired. Nevertheless, he immediately communicated with Clay and asked if his presence in court was required or expedient. On his attorney's advice, then, the Colonel appeared, voluntarily, in the court two days later.[31] Judge Innes, the importance of the case being so grave, refused to give an opinion without adequate time for deliberation. Finally, he overruled the motion of the United States attorney, Daveiss, on the grounds that the court was not invested with such power; and, if the court were, that the evidence was insufficient. The court directed that a grand jury be empaneled before which Daveiss might prefer an indictment. Further action was then postponed until November 12, to give Daveiss time to collect his witnesses.[32]

The opening of the trial was a triumph for Burr. The crowded, noisy courtroom contrasted with the calm but firm demeanor of the accused. Daveiss was somewhat flustered when he discovered that Davis Floyd, one of his chief witnesses, was absent. Another adjournment was then granted to Daveiss until December 2, when Floyd, who was at a session of the Indiana legislature, would be able to attend.

Burr took the opportunity to address the eager and curious crowd. The large audience succumbed to the charm of his presentation as he denied any intention to harm the United States in any manner and asked that there be a complete investigation. Burr told the court that, although he had business elsewhere, he would make himself available at the court's convenience. The general sentiment turned against the District Attorney, who was regarded as an alarmist.[33]

Free for the moment, Burr optimistically continued with the interrupted plans. He detoured to Lexington and then rode to Cincinnati, staying at the same tavern he had visited before. That evening, two travelers arrived in town with the story that they had passed two boats descending the Ohio. One, a large keelboat full of French muskets, the other filled with supplies and muskets; and, aboard, a French-speaking crew that told about having passed all the towns at night to avoid being seen. They also reported that Blennerhassett was soon to follow with several large boats laden with provisions.

Rumors and reports continued to fly back and forth in newspapers and in the letters of foreign ministers. None of the accounts agreed in details, but they all expressed the conviction that something serious was brewing in the West. An unfortunate loss to Burr was in Jackson's disenchantment, which occurred at this time.

A young man named Captain Fort arrived at the Hermitage with a letter of introduction and the information that he was from New York, on his way to join Burr. He passed the night and the following day talking boldly of the Burr project to divide the Union. Jackson sternly asked him how this was to be done. The captain had a ready answer, replying that New Orleans would be seized, Mexico conquered, and the western part of the United States would then unite with the conquered country. This deed would be accomplished by Federal troops under General Wilkinson. Jackson began to see the scheme that he was committed to in a new light, and then fired questions at the young man. Who was his source of information? Wilkinson? Fort said he was not. Was Colonel Burr in the scheme? the disturbed General asked. Fort answered that he hardly knew him and that his information was from Colonel Swartwout in New York. The pieces thus fell into place. Jackson knew that Samuel Swartwout was Burr's lieutenant and that Wilkinson was included in the plans. Captain Fort realized too late, however, that he had said too much. He hedged, attempted to explain, to modify, and to deny, but Jackson knew that he had been tricked by his hatred of Spain.

The General acted immediately. Writing a letter to his old friend Governor Claiborne in New Orleans, he said:

> Treachery is become the order of the day, put your Town in a State of Defence organize your Militia and defend your City . . .

Keep a watchful eye on our General [Wilkinson]—and beware of an attack, as well from your own Country as Spain . . . I fear there are plans on foot inimical to the Union . . . beware of the month of December—I love my Country and Government, I hate the Dons— I would delight to see Mexico reduced, but I will die before I would yield a part to the Dons or see the Union disunited. This I will write for your own eye & for your own safety, profit by it, and the Ides of March remember.[34]

But Wilkinson was on his way to the capital at New Orleans. When he found Ogden and Swartwout at Fort Adams, he behaved as if he were still friendly to Burr's plan because he wanted Burr kept in the dark about the trap that was being laid for him. On November 25, Wilkinson arrived in New Orleans. Claiborne had been alerted. Cowles Mead, secretary and acting governor of the Mississippi Territory, couched the question ably to Claiborne: "General Wilkinson is concentrating the whole military force of the United States at New Orleans. What is all this for? is it to act for you or *against* you?"[35]

The Governor could have relaxed about that particular danger; for at the same time that Wilkinson entered New Orleans, Jefferson received his Judas letter. Lieutenant Smith, heavily compensated by Wilkinson to get his October letter safely and quickly to the President, delivered it at the White House. Wilkinson was now ready to play the role of saviour of his country.

Jefferson accepted the accusations contained in the General's message. Then he issued the proclamation that was to be the beginning of the end for Burr, for as soon as it was heard in the West, Burr's support would quickly vanish. The proclamation ordered the military officer at Pittsburgh to uncover the preparations for a military enterprise against Spain. Any suspicious assembly of men descending the Ohio was to be prosecuted. The gunboats being built in the neighborhood of Marietta were to be seized. Governor Tiffin, General Jackson, and the governor of Kentucky were to alert the militia and stop armed vessels, while General Wilkinson was to prevent any attempt on New Orleans.[36]

The members of Jefferson's cabinet were detailed to carry out his orders. Dearborn directed Caesar Rodney to send out interrogatories all over the West to gather specific information about the Burr expedition. The questions were:

Do you know Aaron Burr and how long and how well?
Relate any conversations with him or his associates.
Was it a military expedition or enterprise?
What were the real objects of Aaron Burr and his associates?

Was it not their object to separate the Western States and territories of the United States from the Atlantic States, to establish by force of arms an independent government of which the said Aaron Burr was to be the Monarch or Emperor, and the capital of which was to be fixed at New Orleans?

Was the object simply to settle the Bastrop Lands?

Was Aaron Burr insolvent and from whom did he procure funds for his enterprizes?

How many associates had Burr collected, where assembled, and was there anything military about the group?

How many and where were the boats built for Burr?

Did Burr or his associates attempt to enlist you and, did you communicate with Burr and his associates?

If so, where are the original communications?

Can you relate anything else to reveal the real objects of Aaron Burr and his Associates?[37]

The replies were to be relayed promptly to the Secretary of War.

Jefferson's proclamation of November 27 did not name Burr directly. It revealed to the people that the President had knowledge of a conspiracy against Spain by American citizens, and therefore, he was "warning and enjoining all faithful citizens who have been led to participate in the sd. unlawful enterprises without due knolege or consideration to withdraw from the same without delay," or "they will answer the contrary at their peril." All authorities were to be vigilant and all "good and faithful" citizens of the United States should assist in bringing offenders to justice.[38]

Burr was in Louisville the day that Jefferson's message was issued. That very morning, he had learned that the United States Attorney had begun his prosecution. Clay was again consulted and asked to delay his journey to Washington so he could handle the case. Burr assured the newly elected Senator from Kentucky that "no business is done in Congress until the New Year," and promised him liberal financial compensation for his inconvenience.[39]

Before starting for Frankfort, Burr wrote to General Harrison, denying any design to separate the Union and any connection with a foreign power. He said that his sole interest was an extensive speculation in association with a number of the Governor's intimate friends.[40] Even as he wrote, preparations for the expedition were continuing, and Spanish sources were claiming that December 5 was to be the starting date and Marietta would be the place. Despite the glow of publicity that now seemed centered on the scheme, its leader was confident.

When word of the proclamation reached Washington, some were shocked. Others were incredulous. Senator Plumer, for one, could not understand Burr's entanglement with Eaton, and noted that "Burr is capable of much wickedness—but not so much folly."

The expedition had not yet been launched, but its potential impact had already been shattered. With the help of Wilkinson's defection, Burr would find that he had underestimated the loyalty of the West and had also misread the political division. But it was too late to stop.

CHAPTER XVIII

Western Adventure: Part Three

M ANY of the participants in Burr's western scheme were totally
unaware of its design. For example, when Silas Brown, a
young clerk from Onondaga County, New York, was approached by Comfort Tyler in August, 1806, about an expedition
being formed by General Dayton and other "men of respectability,"
Brown joined them. He knew almost nothing about the details, except
that it was some kind of commercial and agricultural enterprise and
that, until December, he would be assigned to Pittsburgh. Tyler, who
was Burr's western New York agent, had obviously done his job well
in this instance. Brown wrote letters to his uncle that denied the existence of any reasons to suspect that the enterprise was dishonorable
or hostile to the government. Burr's name had not even been mentioned
to him.[1]

Burr returned to Frankfort the last day of November. Since Davis
Floyd was now in Kentucky, Daveiss asked that a grand jury be called.
December 2 was set for the hearing. General Adair, who had been
accused by Thomas Read of having advised him to join an expedition
against Spain, was also indicted at this time. However, Adair was acquitted of the charge.

On December 5, Burr appeared in court to answer the charge of
having organized an expedition against Mexico. Henry Clay was representing him once again but only after Burr had assured him that he was
innocent of any design against the government or any of its territories
and that his activities had the approbation of the Administration.[2]
Henry Clay was now a Senator.

During the trial, Burr allowed his counsel to do all of the pleading. He remained silent and resigned, giving the impression of a gentleman enduring the delay of his plans because of the actions of a whimsical court. Clay, adopting a similar tone, used Daveiss as his chief target. That individual, whose reputation was sinking, heard Clay accuse him by saying: "You have heard of the screws and tortures made use of in the dens of despotism to extort confessions; of the dark conclaves and caucuses for the purpose of twisting some incoherent expression into evidence of guilt. Is not the project of the attorney of the United States a similar object of terror?"[3]

The packed court seemed to agree. Daveiss, furious, blamed the general hostility toward him on republicanism and the "Espaniolized Kentuckians." Fearing that Burr's rising popularity would prejudice the verdict, he tried to have his presence in the court declared superfluous, but Burr's attorneys protested that move successfully. Among the witnesses called were Street and Wood with the files of the *Western World*. Wood admitted that the allegations made against Burr in the paper had been based on gossip, rumor, and conjecture.[4]

After the brief trial, the grand jury delivered a written report stating that they were "happy to inform the Court that no violent disturbance of the Public Tranquility or breach of the laws has come to their knowledge."[5] The acquittal pleased the crowd and Burr and Adair were free.

That night, a grand ball was given in Burr's honor. The disgruntled Daveiss attempted a counter ball, but it was a dismal failure. Thereupon, Daveiss himself decided to abandon any further pursuit. His explanation was that "Mr. Burr would succeed in the first instance, and it would only cost the lives of a few thousand men, divided between the sword and climate to reinstate us."[6]

The proclamation, already known in the East, caused various reactions. Vice President Clinton, disturbed about Burr's excellent credit standing, sought to find out what were his sources for men and money in New York. He hoped both to curb his predecessor's activities and to strike a blow against the Federalists. The British minister, however, regarded the document in a different light. He remarked that there must be a strong proof of conspiracy and a great importance for Jefferson, "who has always pursued a temporizing line of conduct, in domestic politics," to take vigorous action.[7] Burr's friend Truxtun was shocked by the proclamation, even sending Jefferson a plan of counteraction to be used in case of "any serious design" against the states.[8] The President, on the other hand, had good reasons to be satisfied with his decision to publicize the matter, certain that as soon as the people realized that the government had not "connived at the enterprise," Burr would be "completely deserted."[9]

On the day of Burr's acquittal in Frankfort, about thirty men, among them Silas Brown and Comfort Tyler, assembled at Beaver to descend the river. Tyler informed them that he could not reveal all the details until they saw their chief, but that the expedition was destined ultimately against Mexico. First, however, they would go up the Red River and make a settlement. Everyone, he assured them, would have an equal share in the profits. A last chance was given to anyone who wished to return home—with all expenses paid.[10]

The little fleet of four boats and thirty-two men made the voyage down the Ohio River without a halt and arrived at Blennerhassett Island on the eighth of December. All hands stayed overnight on the island. Brown reported that he saw no sign of military preparations or military stores. Everyone was at liberty to pass to and from the island, and no guard was stationed.[11]

On the eleventh, Silas Brown traveled six miles up the Muskingum from Marietta to give orders for fifteen of Blennerhassett's boats to be sent to the island. When he returned very late that night, he found that preparations were going on for departure. Earlier, news had reached Blennerhassett that the Kanhawa Militia and Wood County mobs were planning to raid the island in the morning and capture Tyler's force. About one o'clock all were aboard but Mrs. Blennerhassett, who was to follow with the children.

The entire state of Ohio seemed to be roused. Judge Return Jonathan Meigs, designated the governor of Ohio's agent, authorized the arrest of Blennerhassett and the impounding of all his bateaux and equipment.[12] A militia company was ordered raised at Marietta, at the expense of the United States, to arrest and examine all who might be descending the Ohio.[13]

The hasty departure of the master and his guests was closely followed by the arrival of the Wood County Militia. When it was discovered that the place had been deserted, a party rode to Point Pleasant to intercept the flotilla, but they failed because the sentinels were either drunk or asleep while the fugitives floated past them. The troops that remained on the island caroused all night, damaging some of the property, although Mrs. Blennerhassett was still at home. In despair, she wrote to tell Dudley Woodbridge that she was without transportation to join her husband because the boat designed for her and the children had been seized.[14]

The flotilla moved quickly to evade the militia. All hands rowed furiously to get a two-day jump on their pursuers. Most progress was made at night. By the sixteenth, they had joined Davis Floyd and his boats at Jeffersonville. Tyler took some of Floyd's forty muskets aboard and they separated again to attract less attention. Varying reports from observers set the number of men on the river at that time at from three hundred to one thousand. One source said that an amazing number of Yankees were arriving on every stage asking for the rendezvous of Comfort Tyler.[15]

Daveiss observed the flotilla at Louisville and reported a total of sixteen oars, eight flatboats, and six keels. There were stories that the boats had fired many volleys of small arms and that the blast of a fieldpiece had been heard. At Clarksville, where the boats stopped to allow Blennerhassett to change boats, a group of citizens visited the party. One man asked Blennerhassett why there were no women or children aboard. He answered that the inclement weather made it impractical to transport them at this time. A witness saw a box lifted on board. From its shape, it looked as if it contained muskets.[16]

For some days, heavy rain and wind impeded their progress, but, otherwise, the voyage was uneventful. On the twenty-fourth, a message from Burr ordered the boats to continue the trip. He said that he would join them at the mouth of the Cumberland River.[17]

After the Kentucky trial, Burr and Adair remained in Frankfort for a few days; there, a message from Dr. Bollman in New Orleans was delivered. It said that the time had come to ready the volunteers.[18] A call at the Hermitage was a near disaster. Jackson was not there when Burr and Adair arrived, but Mrs. Jackson's coolness and failure to invite them to stay was an indication that something was wrong. Jackson made a formal call on them at the inn where they were staying. The General had made sure to bring along a witness. Captain Fort's indiscreet talk in November had created so much suspicion in the General's mind that Burr, finally, had to produce a blank commission signed by Jefferson before Jackson could be appeased. Partially convinced, Jackson released the two boats that he had ordered for Burr and allowed Stockly Hays, Rachel Jackson's young nephew bound for school in New Orleans, to accompany them.[19]

Numerous delays kept Burr from meeting the flotilla, but he remained optimistic, ordering more corn and farming implements. Finally, Blennerhassett got word that Burr would meet them, without fail, on Sunday, December 23.

Meanwhile, General Wilkinson had taken his position against Burr and would spare no effort to prove conclusively that he was on the side of the angels. William Dearborn's orders at the end of November that were an implementation of Jefferson's proclamation reminded Wilkinson that the "old stories" being published in Kentucky were reawakening suspicions that he was associated with Burr. Nevertheless, Wilkinson was ordered to withdraw from the frontier, if possible, and take his troops to where they could stop any enterprise, either against New Orleans or elsewhere.[20]

This was the go-ahead signal for which Wilkinson was hoping. He now had complete authorization to establish his role as saviour of the West. With this in mind, he wrote Governor Claiborne that the city of New Orleans was in such danger that martial law must be declared at once over the community, ports, and precincts lest the cause be lost.[21] Burr, said Wilkinson, would be in Natchez by December 15 with five hundred men and that many more would join him. Meanwhile, Silas Dinsmoor, a former agent of the Choctaw Indians, was employed by Wilkinson to attempt to arrest and carry off Burr and the other leaders. Dinsmoor would receive five thousand dollars if he succeeded; all expenses if he failed.[22]

On November 25, Wilkinson arrived at New Orleans and set up a flurry of activity that was to give the impression that a major attack was expected. Fortifications were repaired, a floating battery at the mouth of the river was to be prepared, and the city fully armed. This martial fuss was augmented by an attempt to make some money from his patrons, the Spanish. A dispatch was sent, in duplicate, to Governor Folch, one copy to Mobile and one to Pensacola, whichever place he happened to be. The Governor of Florida was informed that Wilkinson would protect Spain's territory from the United States citizens, who threatened Baton Rouge and had ulterior designs against Mexico.[23]

Before reaching New Orleans, Wilkinson had sent his aide-de-camp, Walter Burling, to Mexico City. Ostensibly, he was there to buy horses and mules, but his real purpose was to carry a letter from his general to Viceroy Iturriguray describing the embryo revolution in the United States and the design of the revolutionaries on Mexico. The reimbursement he asked for was refused because the Viceroy was short of funds and already knew of the project. Burling returned with only the Spaniard's good wishes.[24]

Complete power over the city of New Orleans was Wilkinson's aim. He pressed Claiborne to disregard any consideration other than the public safety, strongly urging the suspension of *habeas corpus*. But Claiborne refused to do this without the consent of the territorial legislature. Nevertheless, the Governor convened the members of the Chamber of Commerce to listen to Wilkinson's proposals. He asked for money to equip soldiers in order to protect their city from the onslaught of Burr and his forces. Apparently convinced by Wilkinson's exaggerated eloquence, the officials approved an embargo. No vessel was to leave the port without orders from Wilkinson or Claiborne.[25] The city fathers were warned that New Orleans was full of Burrites.

By the tenth, the troops from Natchitoches arrived. Added to the regulars from Fort Stoddert, they swelled the numbers available to meet the flotilla. Completely established, bristling with power, Wilkinson acted under his own authority and made several military arrests. Erich Bollman, Peter Ogden, and Samuel Swartwout were seized, their papers confiscated, and counsel denied to them. To avoid their rescue or a reaction from the citizenry, Wilkinson had Swartwout and Bollman spirited away to a ship in the harbor, which immediately set sail for Washington.

When Bollman sought his release through a writ of *habeas corpus*, Wilkinson arrived in court in full regalia and declared that he alone realized the danger to this country and was ready to rescue it, menaced as it was "by a band of traitors associated with Aaron Burr whose accomplices stretch from New York to this city."[26] By the end of December, using the same argument, he demanded that seamen be impressed to protect New Orleans. Claiborne was under constant fire for refusing to take the danger seriously enough. The cauldron had to be constantly stirred, and for this, Wilkinson needed the President's assistance.

Jefferson outlined to Claiborne the complicated plans that the War Department had devised to stop Burr. By the time the flotilla reached Natchez and New Orleans, the whole force of the United States would be ready for them. The navy was alerted to intercept and, if necessary, destroy Burr's boats; and the commanding officers of outposts along the river, such as Fort Adams, received similar orders.[27]

Some residents of New Orleans questioned the consternation as mid-December passed and still no flotilla appeared; no Colonel Burr, no army, and no invasion. General Wilkinson's sincerity was doubted by Cowles Mead, who warned Claiborne that if he stopped Burr, Wilkinson would remain loyal, but if Burr escaped with two thousand men, the General might switch sides again.[28]

In Washington, tension increased. Far from the center of action, the President had to wait until news came, belatedly, from the West. He awaited impatiently for any message about Burr's proposed general rendezvous that was supposed to take place at Louisville on December 15.

He expected, if the force had not been adequately stopped, to lay the matter before Congress, ask for an immediate appropriation for naval equipment, and order out twenty thousand militia from the Western states.[29] George Clinton was asked to check on information that a large force had sailed from New York to New Orleans to join Burr.[30]

Unaware of the extent of the operation against them, the flotilla reached Shawneetown, about twelve miles from the Wabash, and halted for five days to await Burr. Burr had left with some men, some horses, and two boats, but once again failed to meet the flotilla. Instead, he sent Stockly Hays ahead to report his change of plans. While the flotilla was at Shawneetown, articles of agreement providing for the settlement of the Bastrop lands and for military service, in case of war with Spain, were signed. On Christmas morning, the flotilla left Shawneetown. Rough water separated the boats and made their planned landing impossible. They finally managed to land about a mile below Burr, who sent orders via Hays to Blennerhassett. All of the flotilla was to attempt to leave early in the morning. "A gun will be fired as a signal for moving. All is well, very well, at this garrison," Burr's message read.[31]

The count of boats at this rendezvous was eleven, Burr's two, Comfort Tyler's four, Floyd's two, and two others, one of which was commanded by Blennerhassett. There was also one supply boat. Fifteen craft had been abandoned on the Muskingum River; three that Jackson had ordered were at Clover Bottom.[32] There were varying estimates on the numbers of men on the river at the time. Silas Brown reported that the whole body, including all those with Burr, did not exceed one hundred.[33]

Just before evening on the twenty-ninth, the small fleet beached about a mile below Fort Massac. Captain Daniel Bissell, who had received a letter from Burr announcing his arrival, sent Sergeant Jacob Dunbaugh to welcome the Colonel and offer assistance. Later, he granted the Sergeant a twenty-day leave to accompany the flotilla down the river. It was reported by one of Davis Floyd's men that, at this time, rifles, muskets, and other arms were distributed to them.[34] On December 31, they reached the waters of the Mississippi and, on New Year's Day, landed at New Madrid, where some new recruits were signed on at a salary of $12.50 per month plus one hundred acres of land. They were told that they would first go to New Orleans and then to the Bastrop lands.[35]

The President's proclamation was now speeding across the West. Jackson was shocked into immediate action. He sent a messenger to warn Captain Bissell at Fort Massac that, if a flotilla appeared, he was to capture it and send back a full report on its numbers and equipment. Bissell reported that the boats had left, but that he had only seen ten craft and there was nothing on board "that would even suffer a conjecture more than that he was a man bound to market."[36]

At Chickasaw Bluffs, now Memphis, its commanding officer was surprised by the arrival of the Burr entourage. Young Lieutenant James Jackson knew nothing about Jefferson's proclamation and so was agreeable to the requests made by his father's friend. One of the soldiers was given a furlough to accompany the flotilla; a messenger was sent to Colonel James McKee, a former United States agent to the Choctaw Indians, to raise men among the tribes; some arms were repaired, five hundred musket balls run, and thirty pounds of lead and three tomahawks purchased from the public store. Jackson was so excited about the expedition that he resigned his commission and returned home to raise a company for Burr. Richer by $150 in bills on the Kentucky bank, and a draft of five hundred dollars on John Smith of Cincinnati, the Lieutenant left the fort with the conviction that his venture had the promised assistance of Eaton, the army, the navy, and ten thousand stand of arms.[37] Burr was in desperate need of recruits now because Blennerhassett had not provided nearly enough.

On board his keelboat again with twelve men, Burr appointed officers and drilled the men. His boat led the others and touched shore in Bayou Pierre, thirty miles above Natchez in Mississippi Territory. Cowles Mead and Claiborne had roused the area against the expedition by proclamation, but Burr countered by issuing a public announcement inviting his fellow citizens to visit him and hear his explanation, "presuming that when my views are understood, they will receive the countenance of all good men."[38]

But terrible news was awaiting Burr. When he arrived at the house of Judge Peter Bryan Bruin at Bayou Pierre on January 10, he was shown a copy of the Natchez *Messenger* of the sixth. In it were two documents fatal to his enterprise: the President's proclamation and the Burr-Wilkinson cipher letter.[39] The Administration had been alerted, the local authorities were now in arms against him, and Wilkinson, he realized fully, had betrayed him. He knew, however, that it was too late to turn back.

The next day, Blennerhassett's boats arrived at Bayou Pierre to join Burr's party and to rest for a few days. They were met by a party of militia that took positions in the woods not far from where the flotilla was beached. Observing this, Blennerhassett ordered the boats to push off during the night. They then landed four miles away on the Louisiana

shore. There, Burr and Blennerhassett met and talked about their prospects. Burr concealed the certainty of their danger and sent Blennerhassett away "well satisfied."[40]

Burr remained at Bayou Pierre for three days. He was visited, finally,
by Cowles Mead's aide-de-camp, who arranged a meeting with the Governor. Burr's safety and person was assured in exchange for his promise
that his men would not attempt either to escape or to attack at this time.
At the interview, Burr agreed to submit to the civil authorities of the
Mississippi Territory and to surrender any military accoutrements that
could be found on the boats. A committee was formed to carry out the
task of inspecting their craft.

As arranged, Burr rode to the town of Washington, the capital of the
Territory, and went before Judge Rodney, who bound him over until
the grand jury could act. Colonel Benijah Osmun and Lyman Harding
served as sureties.

As arranged, the authorities came aboard the Burr fleet. They inven-
toried the boats, but found only rifles, because Burr had ordered holes
bored in the sides of his boat from which forty muskets with bayonets
were suspended under water until the end of the inspection. The boats
then pushed off and put on shore at the Pettit Gulf on the Louisiana
shore. Major Jacob Flaharty and his party, pointedly, set up immediately opposite on the other side, so Blennerhassett decided to remove the
boats up the river. The Major visited the Irishman and professed
friendly intentions while informing him that his regiment would join
them. Actually, Flaharty was marking time until his orders would come
through to start making arrests.[41]

On January 22, Comfort Tyler was taken from his boats by an
escort of militia and carried thirty miles away to Washington. Some
members of the expedition had already been examined there and ordered
to testify in behalf of the United States against Burr, whose trial was
scheduled for the first Monday in February.[42] Tyler protested his
innocence, insisting that his sole intention was to explore the country
and remove his family there. He said that the standing of the men who
represented the leadership and the advantages furnished had induced
him to gather fifteen or twenty men to meet with Colonel Burr and
embark at the mouth of the Cumberland. He had been amazed to find
hundreds under arms meet Burr, along with about fifty "unarmed de-
fenseless and peaceable fellow citizens of whom I have the misfortune to
be one."[43]

While his trial was pending, Burr was the guest of Colonel Osmun,
one of a group of wealthy planters in the area friendly to Burr. Osmun, a
Federalist and a bachelor, had been an officer on the Jersey line. Major

Isaac Guion, another officer who lived nearby, was also convinced of Burr's innocence and agreed with the sentiments of the Mississippi *Messenger* that Burr was being hounded and persecuted. "We see him always submissive to law, and friendly to our Territories and their inhabitants," they stated.[44] These loyal friends made the waiting period more tolerable for him, although he was well aware that the end of his romantic project was near.

Preparations in New Orleans intensified after the Jefferson proclamation. Wilkinson pushed aside all opposition, including Claiborne. The Governor disapproved of Wilkinson's methods, but believed that the British fleet was ready to assist Burr and, therefore, was afraid to curtail the General's activities entirely.[45] Jefferson knew very well at this time, as did Wilkinson, that Burr's project was all but defeated and that his strength had been grossly exaggerated. Nevertheless, he wrote, "Go on . . . with your works for the defence of New Orleans because they will always be useful, only looking to what should be permanent rather than means merely temporary. You may expect further information as we receive it, and though I expect it will be such as will place us at our ease, yet we must not place ourselves so until it be certain, but act on the possibility that the resources of our enemy may be greater and deeper than we are yet informed."[46]

Wilkinson kept Spanish governors Folch and Morales advised. He suggested that they transfer their whole disposable force to Baton Rouge, which Jefferson figured would be the first point of Burr's attack. Wilkinson wrote that if Burr succeeded there, it would be a prelude to an attack upon New Orleans, Mobile, or Pensacola. The slaves would furnish him as large a force as he could want. The purpose of this communication was to suggest concerted action with the Spanish to repel Burr and to reap a joint reward from both grateful countries.[47] The City Council was persuaded by Wilkinson to order that every person entering New Orleans should be detained twenty-four hours and fully identify himself. Captains of boats and hotel-keepers had to present lists of their passengers or guests under penalty of fines. Many citizens, such as the judge of the court of the County of New Orleans, were outraged by such infringements upon their personal liberty. The judge, in fact, adjourned the court in protest and was subsequently arrested by Wilkinson's order.[48]

When the Louisiana territorial legislature met in its regular session on January 12, it refused the Governor's request to suspend *habeas corpus*. Instead, it sent a memorial to the Congress of the United States with protests against the outrages of the Governor and his accomplice, the General.[49] But Burr would not have been satisfied by the extent of the action taken, for he needed a declaration of independence from Louisiana so that it would join him.

On January 24, at two in the afternoon, General John Adair rode into New Orleans. He was alone, but unafraid because he thought that the city would soon be in Burr's hands. Adair had been traveling through Indian country, visiting settlements above Mobile and Pascagoula bays, areas settled by American farmers who hated the Spaniards. While there, he had seen a New Orleans newspaper reference to Wilkinson's presence in the city, which he interpreted to mean that the General had taken that place. So, traveling by canoe, he headed for the port on the delta.

Judge Prevost called on Adair at Madame Fourage's boardinghouse and informed him that Burr was expected in three days. Prevost then proceeded to a coffeehouse, where he announced Adair's arrival to some friends. Wilkinson, upon hearing the news, sent a detachment of troops to Adair's hotel. The surprised man was violently torn from his dinner, paraded through the streets, and then confined in a barracks, where he was denied a writ of *habeas corpus*. While there, an Irishman imprisoned for debt, hearing that the distinguished General was secreted in the next room, sang to the tune of *Robin Adair*:

> Ye are welcome to Orleans,
>   Johnny Adair
> Ye are welcome to Orleans,
>   Johnny Adair!
> How does little Aaron do?—
> And Irish Blanny too?
> Why didn't they come with you,
>   Johnny Adair?[50]

The next day, despite his plea of illness, Adair was taken on a schooner twenty-five miles down river, and was then put ashore in a swamp and housed in a tent until he was shipped to Baltimore. On the schooner *Thatcher*, which took twenty-five days to reach its destination, he suffered from sciatica, seasickness, the inclemency of the weather, and poor accommodations. When arrested, he had been denied the right to take his medicine with him or to give directions concerning his horses, for which he had paid seven hundred dollars in Kentucky. While on the *Thatcher*, he was not allowed pen or paper, but a stranger on board provided him with them so he could write to Henry Clay.[51]

Wilkinson supplied a constant stream of news to the President. One particularly choice tidbit Jefferson immediately relayed to Governor Charles Pinckney of South Carolina. It asserted that Joseph Alston was engaged in his father-in-law's enterprise, had attempted to enlist others from the state of South Carolina, and had endorsed, for a considerable amount, "the bills which have enabled Col. Burr to prepare his treason."[52]

In the middle of January, Claiborne received a report that Burr had committed suicide, but he gave it little credit.[53] Burr's arrest was known to Claiborne, but he wrote to Secretary of State Madison that he believed Burr would be acquitted and would continue undisturbed "in this remote & exposed quarter his wicked Intrigues against the Government of his Country."[54]

Wilkinson, however, could not allow this prediction to come true. He had decided to sacrifice Burr and he wanted to make an end of the matter and reap his reward. So, on January 28, he dispatched a party to take Burr and carry him to New Orleans as soon as his trial was over. The trial was scheduled for February 4.

In Washington, gossiping and speculating on Burr's chances was a favorite pastime. Samuel Mitchill had heard that Wilkinson had turned down Burr's offer of one hundred thousand dollars to join him.[55] Henry Clay, worried about the official attitude toward his former client, hoped that he would not be censured for his own role in the case. Benjamin Rush revealed that Burr had once told him that, after he had established the independence of the Western states, he would turn Congress out of doors and hang Tom Jefferson.[56]

On the twenty-second of January, the President acted decisively. He sent a message to Congress with a half-hour report on the history of the conspiracy. It was fully documented.[57] Jefferson withheld names and details, however, because he said that much of his report was based on conjecture, opinion, and restricted information. But he did mention Aaron Burr as "the principal actor, whose guilt is placed beyond question." His design, stated the President, has two distinct objectives to be carried out jointly or separately, either one first, depending on the circumstances. One was the severance of the Union at the Allegheny Mountains, the other an attack on Mexico. The third objective, a cover for the other two, was the settlement of the Bastrop lands, which would serve as a retreat if the other plans failed. Jefferson enumerated the orders that he had sent throughout the Western states and to New Orleans to stem Burr's tide. Favorable mention was made of the excellent cooperation by the officials and citizens of the West.

The message, doing exactly as it was designed to do, alarmed Congress. The Senate proposed and passed a bill suspending *habeas corpus* for a limited time so that the culprits involved in the rebellion could be comfortably secured. Only James Bayard voted against it. Such an act, he declared, "leaves our persons subject to the whim and caprice of Judges." He also felt that holding Bollman and Swartwout as involuntary witnesses would violate the Fifth Amendment by forcing them to testify against themselves. Furthermore, Bayard stated that Burr "would prefer instant death to a trial before your Judiciary tribunal. He will never submit to such a process." William Branch Giles and John Quincy Adams agreed that there was a rebellion in existence and that, as Adams expressed it, though the writ of *habeas corpus* is the great palladium of our rights "in common and ordinary cases," on "extraordinary occasions," its temporary suspension is equally essential to the preservation of the government.

Bayard answered that to act from emotion rather than reason would form a dangerous precedent for free men. Though he did believe that Burr had contemplated rebellion, he saw no evidence of an overt act. The debate on the bill continued for four hours, behind closed doors. One of its most ardent supporters was John Quincy Adams. Samuel Smith, suspected of being a devotee of Burr, and Burr's erstwhile attorney, Henry Clay, both voted for the bill.

Samuel Smith carried the bill to the House on January 26 with the request that they act on it immediately and carry on their hearing behind closed doors as the Senate had done. But sentiment in the House was quite different. After the bill was read for the first time, a motion was made to reject it, and the move was sustained after a short debate.[58] Plumer regretted their action. "I admire the attachment to rights—still the errors may be fatal—a mistaken zeal for liberty—for theoretic liberty has often endangered the security of nations," he wrote.[59] A quandary that many statesmen would find familiar! Plumer commented further on man's inconsistency. He reflected that the Senate had passed a bill providing for the suspension of *habeas corpus* after a debate of one day and, after weeks of debate, postponed a bill to erect a bridge over a small stream under the pretext of gaining more information.[60]

The news that Burr's flotilla had passed Fort Massac on the last day of December, but that it was being carefully watched, partially relieved the anxious Congress. Near the end of January, Jefferson delivered a second message to Congress on Burr's progress. After he and his Attorney General, Caesar Rodney, met with the Senate committee that was composed of Adams, Giles, and Bayard to discuss the disposition of Wilkinson's prisoners in Washington, there was no final determination except the decision not to try Bollman and Swartwout in the capital.[61] The captives had applied to the District of Columbia courts for writs of *habeas corpus*, which were granted. Bollman was even granted an interview with the President. What took place was kept secret at the time but would emerge later.[62]

The communication lag kept Washington, D.C., far behind in news of what was happening in Washington, Mississippi Territory. There, Burr came before the Territorial Superior Court on February 2, as ordered. Thomas Rodney and Peter Bryan Bruin were the judges, Lyman Harding and William B. Shield, Burr's attorneys. George Poindexter, the United States attorney who examined the indictments, concluded that since the court had only appellate jurisdiction, it had no jurisdiction over the case. Furthermore, he doubted whether Burr could be legally tried in Mississippi as he had committed no offense there. Perhaps, therefore, he should be transferred to a place where he could be legally tried. Judge Rodney did not concur with this opinion, ignored it, and ordered a grand jury empaneled. When summoned, it was said to be packed with Federalists. Their partiality to Burr's cause was undisputed. Not only was he absolved on all counts, but they castigated the Mississippi Territory authorities for seizing him. Aaron Burr, they judged, had offered no resistance to civil authority. A particularly heinous infringement of personal liberty was the military arrests made without warrant in Orleans Territory. If sanctioned by the Executive, they said, such acts "must sap the vitals of our political existence and crumble this glorious fabric into the dust." The motives of the grand jury, regardless of their lofty sentiments, were unblushingly transparent. They, too, wanted to get a crack at the Spanish.[63]

After the verdict, Judge Bruin wanted Burr released; but his associate, Thomas Rodney, ordered that he be held and required to report daily. Burr protested. He alleged that his bond had been given for the duration of the trial and no longer. Secretly, Burr had been confident that this trial could result only in his acquittal.

The public believed that Burr, if acquitted, would be seized immediately. Wilkinson's emissaries only waited for word from Governor Williams to complete their mission by making the arrest. While the others remained indecisive, Judge Harry Toulmin, the third Superior Court judge, decided to act. He issued warrants for Burr, Blennerhassett, Floyd, and Ralston. But Burr had fled. Directly afterward, the chase was organized, and a reward of two thousand dollars was offered for the fugitives.[64]

Immediately after the trial, the court had permitted Burr to return to his flotilla if he promised to be back in Washington the next day. At the anchorage, he told his men that he would go, instead, in some other direction.[65] All his friends urged him to forfeit his bond and to flee for his life. However, before he left, he had a sentimental visit to make with a lady named Madeline, who had entertained him many times before; but she now rejected his offer to accompany him.[66]

The flotilla, without its leader, moved to Natchez, where it was captured and the men were arrested by the militia. The boats on the Mississippi were seized and declared off limits. On February 11, Governor Williams went to the prisoners' quarters and charged them with being confederates of Burr. He then took a small note from his pocket that, he claimed, had been found in the cap of a Negro boy apprehended near the mouth of Cole's Creek who had been captured because he was riding Colonel Burr's horse. The note, written in Burr's hand, was read to the assembly.

"If you are together, keep together and I will join you, tomorrow night; in the meantime put all your arms in perfect order. Ask the bearer no questions but tell him all you may think I wish to know . . . he does not know that this is from me or where I am."[67] It had been addressed to Comfort Tyler and Davis Floyd. But Silas Brown did not believe that Burr had written the note, and most of the others felt the same way. After this, the men were examined while the Governor and others went down to the river and searched the boats. When they returned in a few hours, the guards were dismissed, and the men were told that, since no military stores had been found, all were free and might take their property and dispose of it as they wished. Burr had already suggested that the men sell their property and go to the Bastrop lands on the Washita. Later, part of the stores were sold and the money divided. The boats brought a good sum, about seventy-five dollars each, which was much better than the usual twenty-five or thirty dollars, because they were large and of an unusual construction.[68]

The leaders of the little band were not as fortunate. Floyd, Ralston, and Blennerhassett had been committed by Judge Rodney. Blennerhassett was bound over to a court in Virginia. Floyd and Ralston asked to be tried in their home territory, Indiana, but were bound to Mississippi. Comfort Tyler was to be tried on February 15, even though Judge Toulmin believed he was innocent.[69]

Meanwhile, Burr had gone to stay with Dr. John Cummins in Bayou Pierre. While in hiding, he answered Governor Williams' offer of a reward for his capture. He said that he, Judges Rodney and Bruin, and Lyman Harding had drawn up the judicial form of his release after nearly an hour's discussion. Therefore, Williams should cancel his proclamation and acknowledge his error by public manifesto. The Governor answered that Burr could be considered only as a fugitive unless he would submit to civil authority, under which he would be protected as any other citizen.[70] The choice had been made for him. He had to attempt escape out of his country's jurisdiction, either behind the Spanish lines or, as some said, to France. All his friends were unanimous in their opinion that Burr's choice was flight or the forfeit of his life to Wilkinson's ambition.[71]

Washington opinion, as the Burr fever gripped their imaginations, was highly speculative. Those who feared involvement, as Henry Clay, denied any suspicion that Burr had plans hostile to the United States. However, former President John Adams told Dr. Rush that he had never deemed Burr a fool, but felt that he "must be an Idiot or a Lunatick" to plan such a project, if he really has. "But if his guilt is as clear as the Noon day Sun, the first Magistrate ought not to have pronounced it so before a Jury had tryed him."[72]

Jefferson, the chief apologist for General Wilkinson, admitted that he had never believed that Burr's force was formidable, but exonerated the General's exaggerations as an understandable precaution. The President reassured Wilkinson that his seizure of Swartwout and Bollman and the others, if it can be managed, "will be supported by the public opinion," and what was more important, "by Jefferson." Surprisingly, Claiborne had revised his estimate of Wilkinson. He now believed that, had Wilkinson not withdrawn his troops from Natchitoches to New Orleans, the city would probably have fallen into the hands of Burr and his adherents.[73]

Burr's friends in the East were confused and disturbed. Matthew L. Davis wrote to William Peter Van Ness that he was "totally lost in doubt & conjecture respecting Burr's movements." From the scraps of information that came through, he surmised that Burr had been betrayed but he doubted that, if captured, he could be convicted of anything more than a misdemeanor. He said, sternly, that Burr "has acted in the most weak and childish manner a great man ever did." It was a "foolish undertaking," whether directed against New Orleans or Mexico.[74]

Joseph Alston was quite shaken by Jefferson's letter to Governor Pinckney about his own involvement in the Burr scheme. He asked Albert Gallatin to give his answer to Jefferson because he would not permit his reputation to be "whispered away by *insinuations* or murdered by the licentious attacks of the Pres."[75]

An unexpected ally was John Wood, now in Washington. He had started to publish a paper called the *Atlantic World* that was friendly to Burr. Samuel Mitchill reported that the three numbers in print by February 13 intended to "demonstrate the purity of his character, the innocence of his conduct, and the patriotism of his soul. A wonderful task! like washing the Ethiopian white."[76]

Wilkinson was feeding Jefferson with material against Burr and the prisoners now in Washington. Burr's letters were sent on, duly authenticated, with the key and the cipher fully explained. Complaints accompanied every communication, from a rumor that Burr planned to kill him as soon as the trial was over, to the usual grousing about the ingratitude of the citizens of New Orleans, whom he had saved from "the horrors of civil commotion."[77] Jefferson received all the letters patiently. He was interested in the General's view of Burr. His former colleague, said Wilkinson, would make some desperate attempt to recoup his ill fortune, such as a filibuster against the Spaniards in Florida, or "he must seek the grave as his only resort."[78]

Popular opinion in Washington was turning against the vain and haughty Wilkinson. News of the humiliating treatment given to Bollman, Swartwout, and the others caused public indignation. Plumer declared that the President should strip him of his offices. He also quoted Thomas Randolph's statement that Wilkinson must be removed or his father-in-law's administration must fall.

The trials of Wilkinson's victims took place in the District at this time. James Alexander was released for lack of evidence, and the Supreme Court discharged Bollman and Swartwout from prison. John Marshall asserted that there was no evidence of crime, no part of the crime had been committed in Washington, and Wilkinson had no right to send the defendants there.[79] General Adair and Ogden had been brought before Judge Joseph Nicholson and immediately released for want of proof of any kind against them. All five of the accused were now at large. But the major malefactor remained to be snared.

After saying farewell to Madeline, Burr mounted a fast horse and, with Major Robert Ashley at his side, fled to safety behind the Spanish lines. The proud, elegant Colonel was disguised as a river boatman in an old blanket coat with a leather strap across it from which dangled a tin cup and a scalping knife. A broken down white hat almost completely obscuring his face, completed his attire. The planned route through the wilderness had to be changed because heavy rains had so swollen the streams that they were impossible to ford.

The two odd-looking strangers rode into Wakefield under a full moon. Ashley inquired of Nicholas Perkins, the registrar of the land office, how to reach the house of Major John Hinson, with whom the travelers expected to stay. Perkins advised them against attempting the trip because of the swollen streams and Hinson's absence from home. But the pair rode in that direction.

Highly suspicious, Perkins reported his encounter to Sheriff Theodore Brightwell. The two decided to ride over to Hinson's. Perkins looked at the pair in Mrs. Hinson's kitchen, and he was convinced that the quiet one was Burr. He immediately rode to Fort Stoddert to report his suspicion to Lieutenant Edmund Gaines. The next morning, Perkins and Gaines and a small troop rode toward the Hinson house. On the way, they met Burr, alone, riding in the direction of the ferry that crossed the river. On the far side, one road led to Pensacola, the other, by way of Creek country, to Georgia. Gaines stopped Burr, who said that he was not subject to military arrest but allowed himself to be taken to Fort Stoddert.[80]

Once there, Burr was an amiable and charming captive, consoling Gaines' fever-stricken brother and playing chess with his wife. But, privately, he was tormented by disappointment and apprehension about the future. "The details of the prosecutions against me cannot now be given—they are beyond all example and in defiance of all law. Please communicate this to my friends in New York," he wrote to Charles Biddle.[81] Finally, on March 5, Burr embarked on the first lap of his journey to Richmond, where his trial would be held.

Lieutenant Gaines was glad to see the last of Burr. With Ashley at large, stirring up the countryside, he was in constant fear of a rescue attempt. "I am convinced if Burr had remained here a week longer," Gaines wrote to Wilkinson, "the consequences would have been of the most serious nature." He quoted Burr as having said, privately, that "my great offense and the only one laid to my charge was a design to give you the Floridas."[82]

Great precautions were taken to insure Burr's safe delivery to his accusers in the East. Nicholas Perkins, a stalwart, unimaginative, and, it was hoped, unsusceptible frontiersman, was engaged, with six others, to conduct him on the thousand mile trip to Richmond. The first day, the band tracked thirty miles on the narrow Indian trace to the Oconee River. Burr was treated with respect, housed in the only tent at night, and furnished with tea, coffee, and wine. His needs took precedence and his dignity was maintained. Although he was allowed to keep his knife and pistols, the horses were belled and hobbled each night when they were staked out to graze. With all their consideration for him, Burr found the trip rough and hard because swollen streams and rivers impeded them all the way.

Upon reaching South Carolina, Theodosia's home and a place always partial to Burr, Perkins redoubled his vigilance. Two men rode in front of the prisoner, two behind. Until then, the remarkable control that the former Vice President had displayed amazed even his rugged captors. But here his nerve faltered. Perhaps it was the realization that soon his public sacrifice by Jefferson would be a reality. Perhaps it was his proximity to his beloved little family. Whatever the cause, as he passed a small tavern before which a crowd was gathered to listen to the music and dancing inside, Burr threw himself from his horse and cried loudly: "I am Aaron Burr, under military arrest, and claim the protection of the civil authorities." Before the merrymakers could respond, Perkins, a pistol in each hand, ordered the Colonel to remount. "I will not," Burr remonstrated. Perkins dropped his pistols, seized the little man by the waist and forcibly replaced him on his horse. The guard closed in, one seizing the bridle and the others hustling the prisoner, now surrounded by them, from the village.

They stopped a mile out of town. All were visibly shaken. Perkins, who told the story later, said that Burr was in a torrent of tears, but so was the man leading his horse. This spectacle of fallen greatness touched them all and made Perkins fear for the loyalty of his men. To ensure his mission, he sent the others ahead while he rode to town and bought a gig. The next morning, Burr was placed in the carriage and carried in it the rest of the way to Richmond. The President had made an accurate estimate: that Burr would arrive on the twenty-sixth, traveling eastward at the rate of thirty miles per day.[83]

The adventure was over. Not one of the alternatives Burr had carefully prepared had been achieved. Many of his followers were in prison or discredited. Those innocents who had followed blindly to better their lives by settling in the Bastrop lands were stranded in the West. One of them, Silas Brown, wrote six months later: "It is an unfortunate circumstance that I came to this country with Col. Burr. In the Expedition I have lost nearly 500 dollars, $150 of which was cash in hand. As Burr was looked upon as a tyrant, a traitor and murderer, I am exposed to, and do meet with the frowns and cool treatment of some of the inhabitants of this Territory, merely because they say I am a Burrite and ought not to be encouraged in the County."[84] Aaron Burr, instead of the crown that he had sought, found only disgrace and the prospect of a trial for treason.

CHAPTER XIX

Trial at Richmond

"AARON BURR—may his treachery to his country exalt him to the scaffold, and hemp be his escort to the republic of Dust and ashes."[1] In the spring of 1807, this toast epitomized public feeling about their former Vice President. He tried to derive some solace from reflections on classical parallels. "Was there in Greece or Rome a man of virtue and independence, and supposed to possess great talents, who was not the object of vindictive and unrelenting persecution?" he wrote to Theodosia. His suggestion that Theo distract herself by collecting such instances and turning them into an essay for his pleasure only added to her distress. Her father's dream of empire had been shared by Theodosia. She never questioned Burr's ability, judgment, or flights of fancy. This confidence had transferred itself to Joseph Alston, who had invested heavily in his father-in-law's project. News of Burr's capture concerned Theo deeply. She made plans to join him as soon as possible.[2]

On March 26, Burr and his posse were deposited at the Eagle Tavern on Main Street in Richmond. The weary prisoner remained there until he was turned over to the authorities. On Monday morning, Burr was conducted by Major Scott, Marshal of the District of Virginia, and two deputies to a secluded room in the tavern, where Chief Justice John Marshall awaited him. Since the Supreme Court had no appellate judges at the time, its members each took a circuit. Marshall was assigned to Virginia. Thus, ironically, Jefferson's enemy was to preside at the treason trial because the Jeffersonians had repealed the Judiciary Act of 1801.

Burr and Marshall were well acquainted from the days when Burr had been a senator and Marshall a member of the House. More recently they had both been deeply concerned over the Chase trial. A distinguished pair of opponents, the Chief Justice, the senior by one year, was a tall, slender, gray-haired man with a majestic head; the prisoner, small, neat, perfectly groomed, impeccably dressed in a black waistcoat and powdered hair, and with large, unbelievably brilliant black eyes.

At the preliminary examination, George Hay, the prosecuting attorney, charged Burr with treason and high misdemeanor and asked for an adjournment to the capital. Burr was committed to five thousand dollars bail and ordered to appear the next morning.

When the chief actors arrived in the small courtroom the following day, the crowd of spectators that milled around made another adjournment necessary, this time to the hall of the House of Delegates. A large but shabby room, it was soon filled all the way back to the sandboxes that had been placed there to receive the wads of chewed-up tobacco.

Cyrus Griffin, Judge of the District of Virginia, sat on the bench with Marshall, but was a silent partner. The prosecution was carried mainly by Hay, who was a son-in-law of James Monroe. He had Jefferson's blessing and his advice but, unfortunately, had limited talent and a brilliant opposition. The District Attorney, Caesar Rodney, attended the trial only briefly, so Hay's support came from thirty-five year old William Wirt, a blond, blue-eyed giant with a smooth tongue. The third member of the triumvirate was Gordon MacRae, Virginia's Lieutenant Governor, a lawyer of respectable ability but with a heavy-handed wit and an inclination toward sharpness.

Gathered around Burr was an impressive quartet of formidable legal talent. The moving force behind the defense was undoubtedly Burr, who spoke up in his own cause often during the trial, but each one of his defenders had impressive talents. The leader of this team was the elderly, eminent former Attorney General and Washington's Secretary of State, Edmund Randolph. He had been Virginia's Attorney General and Governor as well. Of more extraordinary skill, talent, and originality, however, was Virginia's leading legal light, John Wickham, a scion of Long Island Tories. The third member, Luther Martin, was a friend of Burr's. Although coarse, loud, and often drunk, he was unmatched for his legal learning. Benjamin Botts, the youngest link in the chain, brought verve and courage to strengthen the defense.

The challenge was worthy of its defenders. The charges against Burr were twofold: First, high misdemeanor for launching a military expedition against the dominions of the King of Spain, with whom the United States was at peace. Second, an act of treason for attempting to take

New Orleans, make it the seat of his dominion and the capital of his empire, revolutionize the territory attached to it, and separate the Western from the Atlantic states. The defendant was on trial for his life and, in the minds of many, already condemned.

The arguments of Burr's lawyers took three days. They contended that there had been no overt act of treason and that there had been no legal justification to carry Burr to the city of Richmond. As Burr put it: "Mr. Wilkinson alarmed the president and the president alarmed the people of Ohio."[3]

Marshall had strong doubts as to the validity of the treason charge. He observed that several months had elapsed since the event had occurred, and in that time, affidavits establishing the allegation that a body of troops had been assembled on the Ohio should have been obtained. Therefore, he decided to leave the decision concerning treason to the grand jury and commit Burr only on a charge of misdemeanor. Since the charge was bailable, ten thousand dollars was demanded, which Burr said was excessive because the government had seized his property and he was without funds. The court persisted, and finally, five friends came forward with the money. The prisoner was then free until the next circuit court on May 22.

Jefferson was very agitated when he heard that Marshall had not pressed the treason charge. Once again, he deplored the predominance of Federalism in the judiciary. Marshall's move, he said, was purely political and, he hoped, would be so judged by the public. His analysis of Burr was confirmed. "I never, indeed thought him an honest, frank-dealing man, but considered him as a crooked gun, or other perverted machine, whose aim or stroke you could never be sure of," Jefferson wrote in his journal.[4]

Caesar Rodney was ordered to spare no effort to obtain the necessary anti-Burr affidavits from the West. Jefferson fussed feverishly over the disposition of the case throughout the trial. Whether in Washington or Monticello, he wanted full reports from Hay and the others. He gave advice, suggested procedures, and planned strategy either through his own communications with Rodney and Hay or through Madison.

During this interval, a fashionable party on Shockoe Hill, Richmond's most elegant residential area, enabled the acid-penned editor of the Richmond *Enquirer* to accuse the Chief Justice of gross impropriety. John Wickham, he reported, entertained both Marshall and Burr at a large dinner. However, Marshall, a neighbor and chess partner of Wickham's, had been unaware that Burr was to be one of the guests. When he found out, he felt it was too late to refuse the invitation. Instead, he went to the dinner, sat as far away as possible from the defendant, and left directly after dinner. It was an embarrassing situation from which a graceful exit was impossible. The Administration faction made the most of it.

After the Wickham party, Burr paid no visits and received very few. He "lies here entirely dormant," remarked Hay. The preparation of his case absorbed most of his time. Money was a constant problem. He watched the large sums that the government was spending on his prosecution and said, "If I were possessed of the same means, I could not only foil the prosecutors, but render them ridiculous and infamous."[5] Burr never minimized the grim possible outcome of the trial, but he wanted as many of his friends as possible to be with him. William Peter Van Ness and his brother John, Peter Townsend, and many others planned to be at Richmond.[6]

The city was crowded beyond its capacity. The inns and taverns could not accommodate all the visitors, so hundreds camped under trees along the river or lived in their covered wagons. Among those who battled to get into the courtroom were the famous, the curious, and the bloodthirsty. The seriousness of the crime, the station of the prisoner, and the prospect of a hanging were irresistible possibilities for what was, in a sense, free entertainment. All the players gave excellent performances and, said some observers, were so aware of the audience that they turned to the crowded courtroom so that the eager spectators lost not a word of their eloquent pleading. Among the newspaper reporters was Washington Irving, a lawyer by profession and a writer by choice. A distaste for Jeffersonian equalitarian policies and a recollection of his early literary efforts for his brother's Burrite sheet, *The Morning Chronicle*, in 1802, compelled him to author pro-Burr letters during the trial.

The trial opened with the presentation of the panel that had been summoned to serve on the grand jury. Burr took part in the selection of the jurors, disputing many of them. William Branch Giles, who had been in favor of suspending *habeas corpus* at the height of the Burr fever, immediately agreed to withdraw. Wilson Cary Nichols who, said Burr, "has entertained a bitter personal animosity against me; and therefore I cannot expect from him the pure impartiality of mind which is necessary to a correct decision," was withdrawn.[7] But as the examination continued, it seemed that there was hardly a man without strong preconceptions about Burr's guilt. Even John Randolph, at first, asked to be excused because of an already formed opinion but then relented because he believed that his mind was open enough to listen to the evidence. Finally the jurors, with Randolph selected as foreman, were sworn in. Burr was not pleased with them, but it was the best that he could do.[8]

Richmond was host to at least forty witnesses. One of the most notable was Commodore Truxtun, who described the day's routine as follows: "I dine every day at half past four, rise at eight from dinner and am at an evening party at half past eight and in bed at twelve—up at six—go to court at ten, adjourn at three."[9] From the Governor down, he was entertained by representatives of both parties.

A future notable, General Andrew Jackson of Tennessee, caused comment with his assertion that, to his knowledge, Wilkinson was still a pensioner of Spain and would not dare show his face. Burr liked to tell, long afterward, of Jackson's partisanship for him, describing the future president atop the steps of a corner grocery store denouncing Jefferson for crushing the expedition and its leader.[10]

The absence of General Wilkinson from the trial and the uncertainty of when he would arrive caused frequent adjournments and postponements. These were received with irritation by the defense, which declared that Burr had been hounded by the government in a manner that could set a pattern for governmental oppression of any of its citizens. Burr, said his counsel, has been dragged bodily from one end of the country to the other by military force. Now that he is ready for trial, he is informed that the evidence against him is not yet sufficient.[11] Burr blamed Jefferson. He said that "our president's a lawyer, and a great one, too. He certainly ought to know what it is that constitutes war. Six months ago, he proclaimed that there was a civil war; and yet, for six months have they been hunting for it, and still cannot find one spot where it existed. There was, to be sure, a most terrible war in the newspapers, but no where else."[12] Furthermore, Burr asked the court to consider his inconvenience if he were to be committed for treason. He would have to remain until the next term, a period of six months, "until they could find out this war."[13]

On May 26, Chief Justice Marshall delivered his opinion on the treason charge. He conceded that the motion must be heard, but ordered that the defendant be tried by the laws of his country and the testimony exhibited against him, "not by public feelings."[14]

Since Wilkinson had not yet arrived, the prosecution called Peter Taylor, Blennerhassett's English gardener, and Jacob Albright, a Dutchman who had worked as a laborer on Blennerhassett Island. They were both illiterate, confused, and fantastic. Taylor repeated his statement that Burr meant to take Mexico and be crowned king; Albright gibbered of silver mines in Mexico. Neither went down well with the court.

The next day, Luther Martin appeared, girded for battle but doomed to disappointment because there was no point in continuing the examination until the chief witness arrived. Burr was ordered to give ten thousand dollars bail until that day. Martin, a contributor of twenty-five hundred, said that he was glad to have the opportunity to give public proof of his confidence in Colonel Burr's honor.[15]

"Still waiting for Wilkinson, and no certain accounts of his approach," wrote Burr to his daughter on June 3. "The grand jury, the witnesses, and the country grow impatient."[16] After all concerned bickered about the General's tardiness, the court was adjourned until the ninth of June.

Burr caused a tremendous sensation when, at the court's session, he asked that a subpoena be issued to the President of the United States, ordering his personal appearance with certain papers, including the letter from Wilkinson to Jefferson of October 21, 1806, and the army and navy orders that referred to him. Both sets of papers were essential to his case, said Burr, because the "government have attempted to infer certain intentions on my part, from certain transactions," and the military orders were to "destroy my person and my property in descending the Mississippi."[17]

Jefferson, who was informed of Burr's request in one of Hay's regular letters, answered politely that it is "the necessary right of the President of the U.S., to decide, independently of all other authority, what papers coming to him as President, the public interests permit to be communicated & to whom." However, he said, all of the papers relevant to the Burr case had been forwarded to Caesar Rodney in Richmond. "But, as I do not recollect the whole contents of that letter, I must beg leave to devolve on you the exercise of that discretion which it would be my right & duty to exercise by withholding the communication of any parts of the letter, which are not directly material for the purposes of justice." As to the copies of military orders, Jefferson refused to submit the entire body indiscriminately, but he might produce a specific order if it is "proper for communication."[18] Jefferson's answer was the beginning of extensive debate on the President's position relative to a private citizen's demand for papers that might mean his life.

Jefferson pointed out that the request that he attend the Richmond trial, in person, would set a precedent that might expose him to a series of subpoenas to attend other trials at places perhaps as far as the Mississippi Territory. Such a situation could leave the country without an executive branch. If the judiciary may subject the executive to its commands, even to imprisonment if he be disobedient, it could keep the President "constantly trudging from north to south & east to west," and could effectively withdraw him entirely from his constitutional duties, an infringement of the separation of powers that requires each branch of government to be independent from the others.[19]

Martin rejected the President's point of view, partly because he was still outraged by Jefferson's avowal, months before, that there was no doubt of Burr's guilt. "He has assumed to himself the knowledge of the Supreme Being himself, and pretended to search the heart of my highly respected friend. He has proclaimed him a traitor in the face of that country, which has rewarded him. He has let slip the dogs of war, the hell hounds of persecution to hunt down my friend," Martin stated.[20]

The prosecution took the position that the letter in question was not important, although Burr's counsel based its case on Wilkinson's credulity. Mr. Wickham exclaimed: "Surely General Wilkinson is not so much immaculate as the government." Witness his tyrannical behavior at New Orleans, which was solely to secure the conviction of Burr. In Wilkinson's guilt lay Burr's exoneration, he believed, and vice versa. Others agreed with him. If Colonel Burr is found innocent, "as sure as man is man, storms and tempest will cover the western glory of General Wilkinson, and gather darkness all around him," Randolph prophesied.[21] Burr quietly explained that he wished the papers, not to detract from the President's power, but to prove his own innocence. Therefore, he trusted that they would be delivered with no delay.

On June 13, Marshall delivered his opinion on this sensitive subject. "General principles, then, and general practice are in favour of the right of every accused person, so soon as his case is in court, to prepare for his defense, and to receive the aid of the process of the court to compel the attendance of his witnesses."[22] There is nothing in the Constitution that exempts the President from a subpoena. However, Marshall said, if the President's duties required his full time, he could submit the papers instead of appearing in court. The tempering of the decision on the subpoena issue enabled the Chief Justice to avoid a direct challenge from the President that, at first, seemed inevitable. It was one of several gambits that appeared political rather than legal and that earned Marshall the accusation that, in this case, he had succumbed to his political prejudices. However, what seemed most important to Marshall was that, unlike Great Britain, where the monarch can never be a subject, in the United States, the President is "elected from the mass of the people" and after serving his term "returns to the mass of the people again." Thus, he is subject to quite different requests.[23]

This matter settled, the calling of the witnesses was resumed. A drama, unexpected and surprising, accompanied the appearance of Dr. Erich Bollman. It had been developing since the Doctor's arrival, in custody, early in January. Mr. Hay told the court that Bollman had made a full communication to the government of the plans, designs, and views of Aaron Burr. Consequently, the President provided Hay with a pardon for him which had already been offered but which he had hesitated to take. Hay held the pardon, meaningfully, in his hand as he assured the witness that it would exonerate him completely from all legal blame. Mr. Hay declared: "In the presence of this court I offer this pardon to him, and if he refuses, I shall deposit it with the clerk for his use. Will you [he said to Bollman] accept this pardon?" "No. I will not, sir," replied the other man. Martin clarified the refusal, stating that the witness had wished "this opportunity of publicly rejecting this pardon."[24]

Hay was confounded, for he had acted on Jefferson's instructions. The President seems to have behaved insincerely, for, although Bollman was promised that his conversations with Jefferson would be confidential, Hay received a letter from the President saying that if Bollman "prevaricated grossly, shew the paper to him, and ask if it is not his handwriting & confront him by its contents. I enclose you some other letters of Bollman to me . . . to prove by similitude of hand that the paper I enclosed . . . was of his handwriting."[25]

Hay insisted that Bollman was a "pardoned man." After angry exchanges and a seeming disinclination on the part of Marshall to declare whether he was legally pardoned or not, Dr. Bollman was sent to the grand jury. Burr's comment was: "Poor Bollman is placed in a most awkward predicament."[26]

That same day, Wilkinson arrived in Richmond. The long anticipated confrontation between the defendant and the star witness took place on Monday, June 15. Some said that Wilkinson's countenance was calm, dignified, and commanding, while Burr's was one of "haughty contempt." But the literary eye of Washington Irving reported the encounter fully.

Wilkinson strutted into court, and took his stand in a parallel line with Burr on his right hand. Here he stood for a moment swelling like a turkey-cock, and bracing himself up for the encounter of Burr's eye. The latter did not take any notice of him until the judge directed the clerk to swear Gen. Wilkinson; at the mention of the name Burr turned his head, looked him full in the face with one of his piercing regards, swept his eye over his whole person from head to foot, as if to scan its dimensions, and then coolly resumed his former position, and went on conversing with his counsel as tranquilly as ever. The whole look was over in an instant; but it was an admirable one. There was no appearance of study or constraint in it;

no affectation of disdain or defiance; a slight expression of contempt played over his countenance, such as you would show on regarding any person to whom you were indifferent, but whom you considered mean and contemptible. Wilkinson did not remain in court many minutes.[27]

Jefferson continued to mastermind the trial. Almost every mail carried instructions to Hay. If Wilkinson's letter cannot be found, the General must have a copy or can remember its contents.[28] If Dr. Bollman refuses to accept his pardon, commit him for treason or misdemeanor. When Burr is convicted, his accomplices must also be arrested. Luther Martin, referred to by the President as "an unprincipled & impudent federal bull-dog," must be put down.[29]

In court, Burr's attorneys hammered away against the favored-witness treatment that Wilkinson was receiving. They did not see why "the tinsel ornaments of military grandeur" should entitle the wearer to any more respect than any other man. Martin said that, since Wilkinson had everything at stake, he would go to all lengths to hang Burr.[30] To counteract this, the defense introduced a motion accusing Wilkinson of rifling post offices and seizing private papers to use them against Burr or to deprive him of material that he needed to prepare his defense. It was further charged that he had attempted bribery and was guilty of intimidation and false arrest.

About two o'clock in the afternoon, while Mr. Botts was speaking, the grand jury entered. John Randolph, the foreman, stated to the court that they had agreed on an indictment of Aaron Burr for treason and misdemeanor and the same for Harman Blennerhassett.

Burr received the blow with unbelievable calm and dignity. That the verdict had been based in large part on perjured evidence and "the odious and constitutional doctrine of *constructive treason,*" or so he believed, strengthened him. The basis of the indictments, he wrote to Theodosia, was that Colonel Tyler with twenty or thirty men stopped at Blennerhassett's Island on the way down the Ohio and, although unarmed and with no military organization, intended to take temporary possession of New Orleans and then march on to Mexico. Since their intent was treasonable, war had been levied on Blennerhassett's Island, "by construction." Although Burr was in Frankfort on his way to Tennessee at the time, he was by construction of law present on the island and had levied war there. Theodosia was told, "I beg and expect it of you that you will conduct yourself as becomes my daughter, and that you manifest no signs of weakness or alarm."[31]

Luther Martin was furious. He wrote about the "painful news" to Joseph Alston, but reassured him that he would never leave Burr "until his Trial is at an end. Never, I believe did any Government thirst more for the Blood of a victim than our enlightened . . . philanthropic Government for the Blood of my friend." Martin confidently declared that Burr would be acquitted but, in the meantime, though he has many friends in Richmond, "it would be most pleasing, most consolatory to him, could you visit Richmond."[32]

Ironically, on that same day, the Alstons had written to Blennerhassett that, after the Richmond trial was over, which they were "persuaded cannot but be favorable, Col. Burr will be with us." Alston denied the reports that he had denounced his father-in-law, or that there was a "show" of animosity between them. The financial settlement between them must wait, Alston wrote, because the total failure of his crops caused by an autumn storm had left him temporarily out of funds.[33]

The following day, the court resumed its debate on Wilkinson until it was again interrupted by the entrance of Randolph and the jury. They requested the Burr-Wilkinson cipher letter of May 13, which, they said, was necessary for their inquiries. Burr's stand was puzzling. He not only refused, but, in spite of Hay's assertion that General Wilkinson was amenable to an exposure of their entire correspondence, declared that he had "put the letter out of my hands, with the express view, that it should not be used improperly against anyone. I wished, sir, to disable any person, even myself, from laying it before the grand jury. General Wilkinson knew this fact."[34] Whom was he protecting, or was it a mutual protection pact? Whatever may be the truth, it is a portion of significant evidence that has never been seen.

Later that day, the grand jury reported that they had found the following persons guilty of treason on Blennerhassett's Island on December 13: Jonathan Dayton; John Brown, of Ohio; Comfort Tyler; Israel Smith; and Davis Floyd. The information of twenty-nine witnesses had provided the damaging testimony. Jackson heard that the grand jury had divided eight to nine on the question of whether Wilkinson should be prosecuted for treason but, he added, "It is no longer doubted now, but he is as guilty as any."[35]

On June 26, Benjamin Botts asked that Burr be removed from the public jail to a comfortable and convenient place. Not only were the conditions in the prison miserable, but the distinguished prisoner was deprived of the comfort of a room to himself or a place where his attorneys could consult with him. The court ordered that Burr be confined to the front room of Luther Martin's house. The shutters to the windows were to be secured by bars, the door by a strong bar of padlock; seven men, to be lodged in the adjoining unfinished house, would guard him.

Under all these circumstances, Burr appeared "cheerful" and with "no alteration visible in his countenance."[36] Not even when he rose in court to say "I have been furnished with a copy of the indictment; I have perused it, and I am ready to plead not guilty to it," did his demeanor change.[37]

The next day, Wilkinson was exonerated from the charges against him because, said Marshall, the General could not control the actions of the civil magistrates and it did not appear that it was his purpose to violate the laws. Wilkinson received the decision as a welcome cessation to persecution. He confided to Jefferson, "I feel myself between Scylla and Charybdis. The jury would dishonor me for failing in my duty, and Burr and his conspirators for performing it."[38]

The date of Burr's trial was set for August 3, 1807, in the city of Richmond. Resenting his comfortable quarters and the slight expense to the state that it entailed, the prosecution insisted that, in the interim, the prisoner be held in a public jail. The Governor of Virginia cooperated by readying a suitable apartment on the third floor of the state penitentiary. Burr's tongue-in-cheek comment was that it was kind of the Governor to provide him with such airy and healthy rooms, but that the distance of fifteen miles from his lawyers might constitute a hardship for them. Actually, the former Vice President enjoyed the attentions and consideration of a considerable retinue of friends. Servants arrived continually with messages, notes, inquiries, oranges, lemons, pineapples, raspberries, apricots, butter, ice, etc., from well-wishers. Like an imprisoned prince, he held court for friends and acquaintances of both sexes. The rules were very loose; no clearance had to be obtained for the visitors and no spy was present. Burr recounted these details, attested to by others, and humorously invited his daughter to share his quarters. "If you come I can give you a bedroom and parlour on this floor." And he warned, "no agitations, no complaints, no fears or anxieties on the road, or I renounce thee." Despite his lightness of tone, he wanted his family to be with him, so that there be "an independent and discerning witness to my conduct and to that of the government." That was only part of his reason, for he thought that, while present, Theodosia would suffer less solicitude and, no matter what the outcome, would see that, as he assured her, "I may be immured in dungeons chained, murdered in legal form, but I cannot be humiliated or disgraced." Some friends prepared and furnished a house for Theodosia that was only a few steps from Burr's.[39]

His trial was exciting so much interest throughout the nation that Napoleon's doings were hardly to be found in the press. The court was subject to much criticism because Marshall's rulings were eliminating

British statutes and common law rapidly. There was speculation that Burr might be legally acquitted, but the nation strongly suspected that he had had evil intent and Wilkinson's behavior in New Orleans was generally frowned upon. For a while it was questionable whether "the court is trying Burr or Burr the President," wrote a spectator to Albert Gallatin.[40] That Burr often had the upper hand at this critical hour caused Dr. Rush to agree with John Adams that, should Burr be acquitted, he may yet become president.[41] His unfailing spirits and courage disarmed many and only intensified the admiration of his supporters. Washington Irving wrote that "the cup of bitterness has been administered to him with unsparing hand. But he did not quail."[42] Erich Bollman reported to Theodosia that her father's conduct "was so dignified and great—You never would have felt more proud to be his daughter." When the grand jury brought in the indictments, "not a feature in his countenance changed"; and it was he who recovered first and broke the stunned silence by asking his attorney, Benjamin Botts, to continue with his argument. Several times he dominated the trial with a quiet eloquence that made him the first and the commanding man in court.[43]

Witnesses converged on the city for the great trial. Jefferson had spared neither money nor effort to assure the government's position. Blennerhassett had been arrested on July 14 in Lexington, Kentucky. The Hendersons, Dudley Woodbridge, and many others less well known were taken to Richmond on subpoenas. Jonathan Dayton, who expected to exonerate himself from the charge of having been on Blennerhassett's Island, a place that he had never seen, left Elizabeth Town on Independence Day. He accused John Randolph of persecuting him because of his vote in the Chase trial.[44]

Again drawing a capacity crowd of spectators, the court opened on Monday, August 3. The preceding Saturday, Burr had been moved from his prison to his apartment near the Swan Tavern. More than one hundred witnesses had been called, but the case was not destined to begin on schedule because the choosing of a jury obstructed progress for fourteen days. It was incredibly difficult to find twelve men without opinions on Burr's guilt. Marshall, in desperation, finally ruled that "as large a portion of impartiality as possible" would have to suffice.[45] Burr participated in the chore of weeding out the undesirables with infinite patience, but the patience of all was wearing thin. On August 27, more from despair and exhaustion than conviction, a jury was accepted and sworn in. The foreman was Edward Carrington, Marshall's brother-in-law.

The day before the trial was resumed, the Alstons arrived. They stayed with Burr at Luther Martin's, making a brave and united family front. Martin succumbed heavily to Theodosia's great charm. Richmond citizens whispered about it with evident amusement. About the same time, Blennerhassett, under arrest, also arrived. His wife had remained at Natchez to be the recipient of many letters and an extensive journal kept for her by her attentive husband. She wrote to him frequently to tender such excellent family advice as: "consider your want of practise at the bar, and spare not the fee of a lawyer." But Burr had forestalled her because, upon hearing of his associate's arrival in town, he had sent Joseph Alston to call on him and to deliver tea, sugar, and cake from Theo. Edmund Randolph, who offered his services gratis, assured him that the prosecution for treason had become ridiculous and that no one would be hanged nor would the misdemeanor indictment stick.[46]

William Eaton had come to town and had set it on its ears, strutting about the streets dressed like a gypsy in various stages of inebriation. His multicolored garments, tied with a Turkish sash, were topped by a tremendous hat. Bystanders were overwhelmed as he approached them drunkenly to regale them with tales of his sorrows. Even before he was called on the witness stand, he was "despised by the Federalists, mistrusted by the Democrats."[47]

While the witnesses were being interviewed, Blennerhassett was brought to court. This was the first time that he and Burr had met since their winter parting at Cole's Creek. The Colonel went over to him and cordially shook him by the hand. The two displayed only the demeanor of gentlemen who had met at other times, perhaps, in more congenial surroundings but who, nevertheless, were pleased to see one another.

Blennerhassett was puzzled, as were all of Burr's friends, by the contradictions of Burr's complex personality. That Theodosia should be required to attend her father's trial disturbed the tender-hearted gentleman just as Burr's sexual indiscretions offended him. He could not restrain a wry comment as to Burr's latest amour, wondering whether she was able to pass his keepers as invisibly as Jupiter evaded the guards of Danae.[48]

Finally, the preliminaries settled, the prisoner stood as the clerk read the charge. Aaron Burr, "not having the fear of God before his eyes, nor weighing the duty of his said allegiance, but being moved and seduced by the instigation of the devil, wickedly devising and intending the peace and tranquility of the United States to disturb; and to stir, move, excite insurrection, rebellion and war against the United States; on the tenth day of December, in the year of Christ one thousand eight hundred and six, at a certain place called and known by the name of Blennerhassett's Island, in the county of Wood, and district of Virginia . . ." and so on, read the indictment.

The strategy of the defense revealed itself early. They claimed that an overt act must be proved before the case could continue. The court was reminded that this was not Great Britain, where just compassing the death of the king could be regarded as treason. Therefore, "would it not be absurd to go into evidence to *shew* that the *act* was committed with treasonable *intent*, without any testimony to prove that the act was committed at all?"[49] Witnesses were being brought from afar to prove Burr's declaration, but until an act of war shall have been proved, "these declarations are utterly inadmissible against him."[50] Wickham and company argued this point at length until Marshall allowed the government four days to prepare an answer.

General Eaton was the first witness called. He could only attest to Burr's treasonable intentions by retelling the story of his interviews with the Colonel in the winter of 1805–1806. Truxtun testified next, staunchly insisting that Burr's designs in Mexico were contingent on war with Spain. At this time, Truxtun was incensed at General Wilkinson, who had compromised him, by warning Sir Eyre Coote, Governor of Jamaica, not to help him aid Burr. At the time, Truxtun was in the United States and had not left it in years. The idea that he was on the high seas sailing to take over the port of New Orleans with foreign help was only in the imagination of his erstwhile friend, Wilkinson. Truxtun told Charles Biddle that he found the General's actions unforgiveable and would not speak to him. The Commodore's censure of Burr was somewhat milder, although he admitted that he could never again "hold Mr. Burr in the estimation I once did or ever make a companion of him."[51]

The defense built its case upon several points that Mr. Wickham attempted to establish. First, Burr had been in Kentucky, a great distance from Blennerhassett's Island at the time of committing the act charged in the indictment. And before he can be put on his defense, there must be some evidence to prove to the court that Blennerhassett, "the principal offender," is guilty. As for the charge that Blennerhassett and some of those with him "were in possession of arms," in the west "every man has a gun." The act of levying war must be "an act of force and of public notoriety exhibited before the world."[52] The overt act, Wickham reminded the court, was the one act of hostility against General Tupper. Jacob Allbright had testified that Tupper laid his hands on Blennerhassett in the name of the commonwealth and that, immediately, seven or eight muskets were pointed at him by the men on the island with Blennerhassett. But Tupper had no warrant with him and so Blennerhassett had every right to resist his authority. Besides, Allbright had testified previously that those who had leveled their guns at Tupper were not serious and that there had been no actual firing.[53]

To answer Wickham, Hay called Israel Miller, who had been with Comfort Tyler, to prove an overt act. However, Burr's sharp questioning forced Miller to admit that he had seen only one man running bullets at the time of the episode on the island. Edmund Randolph then took up the argument. He pronounced that Burr had been deprived of his constitutional rights and had been submitted to a trial in a locality where his good character among his neighbors could not aid him, and the jury's knowledge of the witnesses would be unavailing. Hay, overwhelmed by this long barrage, again asked for a postponement to prepare his response. The tedious, long trial was beginning to take its toll of Hay's stamina. A former Maryland congressman, who acted as Burr's amanuensis at this time, quoted Hay as having said: "Would that I could only hang upon a gate, and have a little negro to swing me to and fro all day. The law's delay—the special pleadings of the bar, its interminable controversies, have worn out and exhausted me. I shan't be able to hang Burr, but will be content to hang myself on a gate!"[54]

On August 22, the indictment against Blennerhassett was read, but as there was an error in it, the court postponed his arraignment. The prosecution now attempted to tighten its case. Burr was described as "the first mover of the plot," and the statement was made that "he planned it, he matured it, he contrived the doing of the overt acts, which others have done. He was the *Alpha* and the *Omega* of this treasonable scheme, the very body and soul, the very life of this treason."[55] Then pathos shook the prosecutor's voice as he said: "What must be the guilt of that man who is now lodged in gaol, to that of the poor ignorant man who was enlisted into his services with some prospect of benefiting himself and family?" He pointed out that each man played his own part in the conspiracy, at Beaver, at Blennerhassett's Island, in Kentucky, in New Orleans. All, in the eyes of the law, were present at each overt act committed.[56]

Mr. Wirt continued with this theme. He said that one cannot ignore the "aspiring elevated genius" who devises a plot and only punish the "mere instrument" who applies the force. Since Burr was present in the theater of action that extended from Beaver to New Orleans, Blennerhassett Island was not the object of the conspiracy; it was the West and the separation of the Union. "The object was not an *island* but a *kingdom*. Therefore Burr was a principal."[57] Wirt immortalized himself with a flight of fancy that was to become a familiar exercise in elocution for future generations:

Who is Blennerhassett? A native of Ireland, a man of letters, who fled from the storms of his own country, to find quiet in ours . . . Possessing himself of a beautiful island in the Ohio, he rears upon it a palace and decorates it with every romantic embellishment of fancy . . . Blessed also with a lovely wife and children, into the midst of all this peace, this innocent simplicity and this tranquility, this feast of the mind, this pure banquet of the heart, the destroyer comes; he comes to change this paradise into a hell. Yet the flowers do not wither at his approach . . . he soon finds his way to their hearts, with his rank, his brilliant conversation, the seductive and fascinating power of his address . . . Blennerhassett is poisoned by Burr's ambition. In a short time the whole man is changed, and every object of his former life is relinquished. His imagination has been dazzled by visions of diadems, of stars and garters and titles of nobility. His enchanted island is destined soon to relapse into wilderness . . . Let Aaron Burr then not shrink from the high destination which he has courted, and having already ruined Blennerhassett in fortune, character and happiness forever, let him not attempt to finish the tragedy by thrusting that ill-fated man between himself and punishment.[58]

To follow such eloquence as Wirt's speech—"manufactured of tropes and figures," as Botts put it—was to descend from Mount Olympus to the earth. Botts pointed out that "acts on the island were not acts of war; no war could be found in Mississippi or Kentucky. There was no bloody battle. There was no bloody war. The energy of a despised and traduced government prevented that tragical consequence."[59] Botts reflected lengthily on the danger of tyranny if a president of the United States should assume the prerogative of the King of England and by persecuting the citizens who opposed his tyranny, complete his usurpation.[60]

Rhetoric and erudition wearied the listeners in the last few days before Marshall delivered his decision. Luther Martin achieved the peak of sentiment when he spoke of Theodosia:

If our joint efforts shall be successful in wiping away the tears of filial piety, in healing the deep wounds inflicted on the breast of the child, by the envenomed shafts of hatred hurled at the heart of the father—if our efforts shall succeed in preserving youth, innocence, elegance and merit from a life of unutterable misery, from despair, from distraction—it will be to me the greatest pleasure. What dear delight will my heart enjoy! How ineffable, how supreme will be my bliss![61]

In Wickham's summary of the case for the defense, he said: "I have with pain heard it said that such are the public prejudices against Colonel Burr, that a jury, even should they be satisfied of his innocence, must have considerable firmness of mind to pronounce him *not guilty*."[62]

On Monday, August 31, Chief Justice Marshall delivered one of the longest opinions he ever wrote. It took three hours to read and covered forty-four printed pages. Closely reasoned, thoroughly prepared, exhaustively annotated with learned references to principles laid down by such authorities as Coke, Hale, Foster, and Blackstone, the importance of its pronouncements reached much further than the lives of Burr and Blennerhassett. It determined the nature of treason for the youthful American republic and thereafter, at the same time stirring up controversy that questioned the probity of the two giants, Jefferson and Marshall.

After complimenting both sides on their eloquence which, he said, indicated strong convictions, Marshall commenced his argument. It has been admitted by all concerned that the prisoner was not present when the alleged overt act was committed on the island. Thus it has been moved that since no man can be convicted of treason who was not present when the war was levied, no man can be charged with the overt acts of others until those overt acts have been proved. These are constitutional questions of "infinite moment" to citizens of the United States and require and deserve deliberate consideration.[63]

What is levying war and who may be said to levy it? Are persons not in arms but taking part in the rebellion levying war?[64] In prosecuting a war, said Marshall, there are necessary and varied military parts that may not be bearing arms but are essential to the levying of war. Such persons are committing treason. But not those who only counsel and advise war or engage in conspiracy but fail to do their part.[65]

Marshall progressed freely up to this point in his argument. Then he reached his own interpretation of treason in *ex parte Bollmann and ex parte Swartwout*. In that decision, he had stated that those who do not bear arms may yet be guilty of treason. Is this in direct conflict with his position in the Burr trial? Not if, in the reading of the case, it is accepted that Marshall requires that a man be "playing a part" in the action whether that action be on the scene or remote from it.[66]

In this case, the fact of levying war is the moot question. That a conspiracy was entered into is not treason. Though not all of the alleged seven thousand men said to have been converging on New Orleans had to assemble together, there must be an appearance of force. Also, it is necessary that the indictment specify a specific place or circumstance in which the prisoner was levying war. The place is necessary to show the jurisdiction of the court and the nature of the act is necessary to the prisoner in the preparation of his defense. He cannot be expected to come to court prepared to defend every act of his life that might be challenged.

Marshall then dealt with the principle of constructive presence. It is possible, for example, if a rebellion stretched through every state in the Union, that no one, not even the rebel chief, could be at all places at once, yet he might, perhaps, be considered as present. Therefore, was Aaron Burr legally present at the levying of war at Blennerhassett's Island? The entire evidence shows him not to have been physically present at that event.

If procurement of the assemblage is the part of the overt act that the defendant is being accused of, this too must be proved by two witnesses and it must have been committed within the district. Though such activity may be a secret act, it still must be proved in the proper manner. The difficulty of proving a fact does not justify conviction without proof.[67]

The court has the opinion that there is no testimony whatever which proved that the accused was actually or constructively present when the assemblage took place; the contrary is clear. If proof of procurement is admitted to establish a charge of actual presence, it can only be by the operation of the common law upon the statute and not admissible in this country. Furthermore, the legal guilt of the assemblage on Blennerhassett's Island must be proved before he who advised it can be called a traitor.

Behind the legal reasoning was a full realization that the trial was being conducted on another, strictly political level. Just as in the Chase trial, not only the prisoner but also his judges were on trial. Marshall alluded to this in veiled but obvious references. "Much has been said in the course of the argument on points on which the court feels no inclination to comment," he said, but they must receive some notice. "That this court dares not usurp power is most true," he wrote and added:

> That this court dares not shrink from its duty is not less true. No man is desirous of placing himself in a disagreeable situation. No man is desirous of becoming the peculiar subject of calumny. No man, might he let the bitter cup pass from him without self reproach, would drain it to the bottom. But if he have no choice in the case, if there be no alternative presented to him but a dereliction of duty or the opprobrium of those who are denominated the world, he merits the contempt as well as the indignation of his country who can hesitate which to embrace.[68]

In conclusion, no testimony relative to the conduct or declarations of the prisoner elsewhere and subsequent to the transaction on Blennerhassett's Island can be admitted, because such evidence is merely corroborative and incompetent to prove an overt act itself. It is irrelevant until there is proof of an overt act by two witnesses.[69]

There has been much discussion about Marshall's motivation in deciding this case. The length and intricacy of the argument, in contrast to his usual clarity, the uncharacteristic reliance on many and varied authorities, and, finally, his seeming reversal of his own words in the Bollman and Swartwout case of so short a time previous, have exposed him to the accusation that his decision had political overtones, that the Chief Justice used this opportunity to bulwark the court and to strike a blow at Jefferson. But there is no real evidence for these contentions. Jefferson would not have changed his mind about Marshall or the court had Burr been convicted. Marshall, it would seem, had nothing to gain from either position. Burr believed that he had been treated shabbily by the Chief Justice and that the opinion "was a sacrifice of principle to conciliate Jack Cade."[70] Nevertheless, whatever Marshall's motives and Jefferson's ire, for Burr the decision meant freedom.

After the jury was charged, George Hay arose to ask for time to consider Marshall's words. He was allowed a night's reflection, which netted him no further inspiration in the way of evidence or argument, and so he informed the court. The jury retired and, in a brief period of time, returned. Colonel Carrington read the verdict: "We of the jury say that Aaron Burr is not proved to be guilty under this indictment by any evidence submitted to us. We therefore find him not guilty."

The implication in the words of the verdict was obvious and was called "unusual, informal, and irregular" by Burr and his attorneys. Burr wanted the jury to be sent back to alter it or the court to correct it. Hay, on the contrary, found the verdict substantially one of acquittal and recognized no limitation on the jury's right to present it in this way. Carrington agreed to alter the reading, but the court settled the dispute. The verdict would remain as found by the jury, but the record on the entry would be "not guilty." The prisoner was acquitted but not completely safe from further prosecution. Hay spoke the last words. He would press the indictment for misdemeanor, and he would send Burr to Kentucky, where the overt act was said to have occurred. After Botts took care of Blennerhassett's interests, the involvement of General Dayton in the gathering on the island was argued by John Wickham. By affidavit, it was shown that Dayton could not have been on Blennerhassett's Island in December of 1806 because he had not been away from his home in Elizabeth Town for more than seven or eight consecutive days in the past few years. Dayton was then excused from the treason charge, but held in ten thousand dollars' bail to answer the charge of misdemeanor.[71]

Theodosia was greatly relieved by the verdict, but not completely pleased. Its phrasing seemed to her a continuation of the persecution that her father had been suffering. Blennerhassett also had mixed emotions. "I was little revived by the news," he wrote. "I have yet many other trials to pass." Only Burr, who had been the support of his friends rather than the reverse when any new set-back threatened his cause, reacted positively. The Irishman described him as looking fifty percent better "than I have ever seen him," and with "a command of tone and firmness of manner he did not appear to me to possess before the verdict of Tuesday."[72]

CHAPTER XX

European Interlude

THOUGH the wish of Burr's enemies to hang him had not been fulfilled, America had become too small to conceal him and too indifferent to further his dreams. He looked, instead, to the Old World to raise his crumbled castles in the air. Departure only awaited the completion of the trials.

"Am I to be pursued from place to place?" he asked; "from district to district for the same act? . . . Is an act or a supposed crime to be cut into halves or quarters or tenths, so as to authorize as many prosecutions as malice may suggest? . . . a man could be prosecuted without end." The weary weeks of the misdemeanor trial and the hearing for commitment to Ohio and Kentucky had been dragging on.[1] Some said that after Burr's acquittals for treason and misdemeanor, Marshall listened to a multitude of witnesses at the hearing as though to expiate his partiality to Burr in the earlier trials.

By the end of September, Richmond was a burdensome place. Though he was showered by gifts of food and flowers, pitied by the ladies, and admired for his display of fortitude, his patience was waning. During the summer, after his release from prison, Burr and Theodosia had taken long, leisurely walks in the long summer nights. Strolling arm and arm, talking animatedly, the devoted pair had become a familiar sight on the city's streets. But this pleasant time was shortened because Alston was needed on his South Carolina plantation. So Theodosia and the little boy left Burr sadly but dutifully. Blennerhassett, who had been released from prison on the same day that the Alstons left, carped that Theo's husband had departed without settling their accounts.[2]

Jefferson was behind Burr's additional trials. He wanted Burr hunted down and the Chief Justice dishonored. If a reform of the judiciary could be effected, even his anger at being threatened with a subpoena might be abated. In his next Annual Message to Congress, he said, referring to the trial, that: "You will be enabled to judge whether the defect was in the testimony, in the law, or in the administration of the law; and wherever it shall be found, the legislature alone can apply or originate the remedy."[3] Giles of Virginia dutifully introduced into the Senate a bill to incorporate the Bollman and Swartwout case and extend the treason penalty to those who aided in treasonable acts although they were not actually present when the act was committed. The bill passed the Senate but failed in the House. And, by this time, Jefferson was so distressed by the pressure of foreign affairs that the project of impeaching Marshall was abandoned.

It was Wilkinson, dazzling the court in all his martial splendor, who became the star performer of the final hearing. At the same time, however, he revealed himself as a villain. He was forced to hand over the cipher used in the controversial letters, to confess responsibility for the seizing of Bollman and Swartwout, and to admit that he had concealed his connection with Burr from the New Orleans legislature. His revelations failed to clear Burr; they did, however, succeed in keeping him under a suspicion until he was exonerated in 1812.

Among the witnesses against Wilkinson was a Major Bruff, who had commanded the St. Louis garrison when the General had arrived as the Governor of the Louisiana Territory. Bruff had incurred Wilkinson's displeasure and sustained charges because he had failed to display enthusiasm over the General's half-revealed, shady scheme. November 16, 1806, was supposed to be the start of the expedition, Bruff said, and recalled that he had been surprised when that day had not revealed the "knights of the sun and lords of Mexico among the chiefs of those chosen spirits." Burr examined Major Thomas Power, a Spanish subject and officer, who was to prove that Wilkinson had been and still was a pensioner of Spain. The fact that it was Burr and not Wilkinson who was on trial prevented that subject from being pursued at the time.[4] Very much later, in 1809, through the efforts of Daniel Clark, whose *Proofs of the Corruption of James Wilkinson* had been published, damning evidence of Wilkinson's dealings with Spain was revealed. But the Court of Inquiry was, fortunately for the General, composed of three of his juniors, and he was acquitted. In 1811, however, his protector, Jefferson, was no longer President and a court-martial was ordered to try him. The harried man lined up witnesses and spent a fortune defending himself. James Madison, whose chore it was to review the six hundred pages of testimony that came out of the hearing, wearily approved the verdict of "not guilty." He was not convinced of Wilkinson's innocence, but full evidence against him was unavailable.

By October 20, 1807, the team of Jefferson and Hay gave up. Marshall ruled that the object of the Burr expedition had been Mexico and, therefore, exonerated Burr and Blennerhassett from the treason charge but committed both men to trial in Ohio for misdemeanor. Though the trial was set for January 4, it was understood that the charges would be dropped. The charges against Dayton and the others who had been indicted at the trial were also dropped. Blennerhassett thought that Marshall had failed to commit Burr and himself for treason "not because we had none in our hearts, but because we did none with our hands."[5]

Aaron Burr was free. The last month of the trial had been particularly miserable because of a persistent stomach ailment and an inflamed eye. Time and Blennerhassett's concoctions had cured him. Blennerhassett took all the credit, and in return, Burr promised his amateur physician a restoration of their fortune in the guise of an English alliance. The recent naval incident in which a British ship, the *Leopard*, had violated American territorial waters had worsened relations between the two countries. Burr reasoned that now the British should be amenable to a revival of his plan to involve them in the conquest of Mexico. If Blennerhassett would write letters of introduction to his distinguished English friends and relations, there should be fruitful results. The Irishman promised the letters in the hope of getting his money back. He had no taste for further adventures, wishing only for relief from his creditors.

Blennerhassett Island, that demi-paradise, lay vandalized by the public and flooded by the Ohio. The magnificent estate, while being used by a lessee for the cultivation of hemp, had been set afire by some drunken, careless slaves. Margaret Blennerhassett wrote its epitaph.

> The black'ning fire has swept throughout her halls,
> The winds fly whistling o'er them, and the wave
> No more, in spring-floods, o'er the sand-beach crawls,
> But furious drowns in one o'erwhelming grave,
> Thy hallowed haunts, it watered as a slave.
> Drive on, destructive flood! and ne'er again
> On that devoted isle let man remain.[6]

Except for some brief success raising cotton in Claiborne County near Gillespie, Mississippi, until the War of 1812 spoiled the market, Blennerhassett's later life was spent hopelessly pursuing his lost fortune and honor. He migrated to Canada and then to his native Ireland until, finally, he retired to the Island of Guernsey, where he died in 1831.

When Burr, Blennerhassett, Samuel Swartwout, and Luther Martin appeared in Washington shortly after the Richmond trial, Jefferson itched to have the quartet arrested. The first two he wanted to send to Kentucky to be tried for treason, the others to Maryland to be tried for misdemeanor.[7] But presidential power did not reach that far, and the friends stayed in the capital unmolested.

Misfortune had soured Blennerhassett's outlook. He was receptive to rumors that Burr had retained some of the money that had passed through his hands for his own use and was waspish about Martin's generosity to the Colonel, which he attributed to an infatuation with Theodosia.

Burr stayed with friends in Georgetown, unsuccessfully attempting to interest them in a renewal of his scheme to settle the Bastrop lands. He then went to Baltimore, where he joined Luther Martin, Blennerhassett, and Comfort Tyler. They had numerous mysterious conferences, at which they discussed money, of course, and, perhaps, future plans.

Interestingly, General Wilkinson also turned up in Baltimore. He was mightily injured because John Wickham refused to engage in a duel with him. He accused Wickham of charging him with felony, perjury, and forgery in open court. A friend commented that Wilkinson "failed to bring Mr. Wickham's courage to the *sticking* point."[8]

Burr remained in Baltimore at the French Hotel on Gay Street, making few public appearances but exciting the curiosity of both friends and enemies. One evening, while the four friends were dining, a Democratic printer drew up a city regiment outside their window and played the "Rogue's March." Luther Martin was furious, but Burr, remaining calm, said: "These excesses of indecency always recoil on those who entertain them."[9]

But the printer was not finished. He circulated satirical handbills, one of which read:

Awful!!! The public are hereby notified that four 'choice spirits' are this afternoon at 3 o'clock to be marshaled for execution by the hangman, on Gallows Hill in consequence of the sentence pronounced against them by the unanimous voice of every honest man in the community. The respective crimes for which they suffer are thus stated on the record: first, Chief Justice M. for a repetition of his XYZ tricks, which are said to be much aggravated by his *felonious* capers in open court, on the plea of irrelevancy; second, His Quid Majesty, charged with the trifling fault of wishing to divide the Union and farm *Baron* Bastrop's grant; thirdly B-, the chemist, convicted of conspiring to destroy the tone of the public Fiddle; fourthly and lastly, but not least, *Lawyer* Brandy-Bottle, for a false, scandalous, malicious *Prophecy*, that before six months 'Aaron Burr would divide the Union.' N. B. The execution of accomplices is postponed for a future day.[10]

When Blennerhassett heard about the mob's intentions through one of Luther Martin's students, he hurried to Burr's lodgings to warn him. He found the Colonel aware of the news and packing his things quickly to catch the mailcoach for Philadelphia. Baltimore's mayor sent a guard to conduct an angered and chagrined Burr and Samuel Swartwout safely to the stage offices, where a small group of well-wishers had gathered to speed them on their way.

In time, the mob passed through town carrying effigies of Marshall, Burr, Blennerhassett, and Martin. Thwarted by the unavailability of live victims, they contented themselves with throwing bricks at Luther Martin's windows while playing the "Rogue's March." The public was roundly condemnatory of these excesses, wrote Martin, and the culprits, upon reflection, were thoroughly ashamed of themselves.[11]

When he arrived in Philadelphia, Burr retired to his French boardinghouse but was plagued by creditors. Charles Biddle, much concerned about his friend, described Burr as pale, dejected, and almost continually depressed. Biddle feared that Burr might try to take his own life and, he said, "to have found he had could hardly have given me more pain than I have sometimes felt on seeing him in this melancholy situation."[12]

Late in November, the final interview between Burr and Blennerhassett took place. Blennerhassett was completely disenchanted with "this American Chesterfield." He complained bitterly that Burr treated him "not as a faithful associate, ruined by my past connection with him, but rather as an importunate creditor invading his leisure or his purse with a questionable account."[13]

About the first of January, 1808, Blennerhassett arrived in Marietta, stayed a few days, and then departed secretly at midnight in a closed boat that had been waiting for him. It was rumored that Burr was hidden in town or somewhere near, but no one saw him. Neither appeared at the circuit court then meeting to try their case and no action was taken, so the official pursuit was ended.[14]

Throughout the winter and the spring of 1808, Burr lived quietly, almost secretly, in Philadelphia and New York. He constantly feared arrest because the charges against him had not been lifted. The United States offered him nothing. His political career was ended. The practice of the law was not feasible. But, truthfully, Europe had more to offer than self-imposed exile. The scheme to win the independence of Mexico that Burr referred to in his correspondence as X was foremost in his mind. Somehow he expected to be able to sell the plan to England or to France.

Samuel Swartwout, ever faithful, harbored Burr in his own house and helped him to see and communicate with his daughter. Theodosia had come North to lighten her father's departure and to spend the little remaining time with him. She, too, was concealed, but not in the same residence. Under the pseudonym of Anne and using the third person in his letters, Burr arranged their clandestine meetings. "Make haste to gather strength for the occasion; your efforts in the later interviews were wonderful, and God grant that they may not have exhausted you." With such words of praise and encouragement, the fond father hoped to prepare her for the June separation.[15]

Theodosia had been ill all of that year of 1808. In January, she had suffered from rheumatic fever. She had no sooner recovered from that when a fall had injured her spine, leaving a severe paralysis that kept her in bed for three months. In April, a physician tried his best; but his prescription consisted of "daily doses of steel dissolved in vitriolic acid and Peruvian bark mixed with Eanell Alba; and twice a week, the addition of Aloes and Rhubarb."[16] His treatment, however, induced a violent reaction and a vitamin deficiency from the rigid diet gave her a sore mouth, which was combated by drinking strawberry juice.[17] While in New York, Dr. David Hosack took her off the vegetable diet and prescribed bottled Ballston water.

By the first of June, Burr left the city. He occupied his time visiting his friends on Long Island and Staten Island. To further confound his enemies, Theo was instructed to insert a paragraph in the newspapers as soon as Burr departed. It said that Burr, one Frenchman, and two Americans had passed through a "certain place" on their way to Canada.[18]

Theo went to Ballston Springs as soon as her father was out of New York. There she soaked her body and drank the mineral waters. But her symptoms remained unrelieved while her nervous complaints increased. Her memory faltered; she suffered from a sense of stupor and displayed frequent fits of hysteria. She complained of "headaches forever, shooting pains like fire dart through . . . [my] eyes with a sensation of heaviness or weight as if it would drop off. There is constantly a taste of blood in the mouth; sometimes a little bleeding at the nose."[19] The uncertainty of her father's future only added to the dismal picture.

Under the name of H. E. Edwards, Burr sailed out of New York on June 6, on the packet *Clarissa Ann*, bound for England, with Halifax, Nova Scotia, as its first stop. Sixty dollars had obtained Burr's passage under his mother's maiden name. On the thirteenth, the ship reached Halifax, where the fugitive was met by George Prevost, who gave him letters of introduction to family friends and relatives in England, and a passport identifying "Mr. Edwards" as the bearer of dispatches to Lord Castlereagh.[20]

An uneventful and easy voyage delivered the former Vice President safely at Falmouth. Three days later, he was in London to set his plans in motion. England was to have the first opportunity to participate in X. But fatal ill-timing was to make that country as unreceptive as its enemy, Napoleonic France. Burr arrived on the same day that Joseph Bonaparte made his entrance into Madrid as its unwelcome monarch. Napoleon was now committed to the preservation of Spain's empire. England was equally committed to Spain's empire because she immediately became the champion of the deposed King and sent an army to the Peninsula to fight for Spanish legitimacy. Burr's plans served neither country. Once again, he was the progenitor of a lost cause.

Burr refused to admit defeat. The uncertainty of diplomacy, he reasoned, might result in some shift of policy that could benefit his scheme. And so, as planned, John Reeves of the Foreign Office received the brave declaration of Aaron Burr, "forty and upward," who stated as his purpose and his credentials that "I am known personally to Lord Mulgrave and Mr. Canning to whom the motives of my visit have been declared. These reasons have long been known to Lord Melville." The address given was 30 Craven Street, London. A gratuitous postscript, whose meaning would be revealed at a later date, stated: "The undersigned was born within the King's allegiance and his parents British subjects."[21]

While on his European journey, Burr kept a faithful daily journal for his daughter. He designed it as a partial record, an outline, that would recall events so that the theme could be developed more fully when he saw Theodosia. Part of the journal was kept in cipher with numbers assigned to words and personages, such as X to designate the Mexican project, 60 to refer to himself, and 64 to his grandson.[22] The most puzzling entries concern Burr's sexual encounters with an endless succession of prostitutes. Details such as the price paid and the degree of satisfaction obtained from each adventure arouse both wonder at his excessive appetite that sometimes drove him to seek satisfaction rather than such necessities as food and fuel, and disgust that such details were recorded for his daughter. The entries were often in French, the word *muse*, meaning the rutting of animals, serving as a euphemism. In a futile effort to escape the clear reality of Burr's words, an admiring biographer attempted to explain away the sordid details as a ruse by Burr. If the journal fell into enemy hands, the author would then appear as a lecherous old man rather than as a dangerous conspirator. But why should one propensity exclude the other? Demonstrably, the evidence of many Burr letters has revealed him as a constant cavalier with ladies of all types. The question that is most persistent, then, is why the need for such frankness to Theodosia? The entries sometimes display regret and even despair over his addiction. In Denmark, after a number of consecutive entries recording "recontres," Burr wrote: "How unnecessary and How silly! Sat up till 1 last evening, being a little out of humor with one Gamp; made some pious resolutions."[23] Since confession is good for the soul, or so it is said, perhaps the purpose of the revelations to Theodosia was just that.

In August of 1808, with her father in Europe, Theodosia left Ballston Springs and returned to New York. This time, Dr. Hosack recommended "a course of mercury," but Theo hesitated. She wrote to Dr. William Eustis, Burr's old friend who had recently been appointed by President Jefferson to succeed Dearborn as Secretary of War. To Eustis, Theodosia sent a detailed description of her condition, one that was written mostly in the third person, as though she could stand back and view her illness objectively. She told him that another doctor, a Frenchman, had advised "frequent warm baths and a strict diet." This, too, she had abandoned because the diet had aggravated her sore mouth. She switched to a diet of weak rennet whey, which relieved the soreness but left a hollow stomach.[24] Whatever Dr. Eustis was able to suggest, it did not cure Theo. All during her father's absence, Theo remained a very sick woman.

Burr passed his time in England variously. While the progress of his scheme met with delay and almost complete frustration, he enjoyed a pleasant round of lionization and an equally pleasant excursion into the contemporary literary circle. His friendship with Jeremy Bentham was, perhaps, Burr's happiest souvenir of his years abroad.

Bentham's works were among Burr's favorites. When he met the writer's French translator at a dinner party, he asked him to arrange a meeting with the philosopher himself. Bentham had expressed himself unfavorably about Hamilton's "murderer,"[25] but, nevertheless, agreed to see Burr. The two became good friends. Burr loved Bentham's simplicity and his interest in Theodosia. Upon seeing her picture, the Englishman exclaimed: "Dear little creature. Let her take care."[26] The friendship progressed so rapidly that Burr was lodged at Bentham's home in Queen's Square Place and frequently visited Barrow Green, the philosopher's country place. Throughout the years abroad, Burr extolled the virtues of the sixty year old gentleman whose works on philosophy, law, and government, he claimed, were unappreciated in America by all except himself and Albert Gallatin. "He is, indeed, the most perfect model that I have seen or imagined of moral and intellectual excellence. He is the most intimate friend I have in this country, and my constant associate," he wrote to Alston.[27] And Theodosia received copies of all Bentham's works, including those published only in French. She offered to translate those into English.

The Prevost relatives and others feted him throughout the fall season. He had entré into Holland House, then a center for some of the most brilliant minds in the country. A visit to Charles Lamb was recorded. "He is a writer; and lives with a maiden sister, also literaire, in a fourth story."

Turnevelli, a fashionable sculptor, was engaged to do a mask as a surprise for Theodosia. This "very unpleasant ceremoney" left a purplish mark on Burr's nose that caused a dent in his social activity until the "nasology" healed. The sculpture, Burr wrote, was hideous and though supposed to please Theodosia, it made her father look, not like Voltaire—as the sculptor claimed—but a deformity.

The days were spent pleasantly enough. Shopping for Gampy and Theo, card playing, dinners, and visits took up most of the time, but the primary purpose for Burr's presence in England made no progress. As a diversion, Samuel Swartwout, who was visiting in England, came up with a scheme to smuggle cotton bagging, then forbidden by United States law, into New Orleans. He estimated that a six hundred percent profit could be made.[28]

Don Castello, a mysterious Spaniard in Burr's confidence, was in contact with Castlereagh and Spain, but his maneuvering produced no results either. Jefferson's sneer that Burr had claimed that the British government offered him two million dollars as soon as he could raise "an ensign of rebellion as big as a pocket handkerchief" was heartbreakingly untrue.[29] Burr was ready to seek his fortune elsewhere, perhaps the Mediterranean, but he found that Reeves could not provide him with a passport.

To solve the problem, Burr took Reeves' advice and claimed the privilege of a British subject as a birthright which he had the right to resume. But the government rejected this interpretation as, in the opinion of the Lord Chancellor, monstrous and doubtful. Burr was forever an alien.[30]

News from home was distressing. Theodosia, suffering from a recurrence of her chronic ailment, missed her father painfully and was in no condition to accept the collapse of his cherished plans. She grieved for him. "X is abandoned! This certainly was inevitable but I cannot part with what has so long lain near my heart, and not feel some regret, some sorrow. No doubt there are many other roads to happiness, but this appeared so perfectly suitable to you, so complete a remuneration for all the past."[31]

Burr spoke about Theodosia's illness to physicians and friends, all of whom agreed that she should join her father in England. General Sir Samuel Bentham offered to take little Gampy home with him to be educated with his children. The frantic father wrote to Alston offering to pay Theodosia's passage and expenses. He said, "It is probable that her fate will be determined within six or eight months. If she survives, I shall return with her to the United States."[32] But Alston received these suggestions of help coolly. The demands of the Richmond trial seemed to have stretched his loyalty and his patience. However, by spring, Theodosia felt better and returned to South Carolina. Burr, who had taught his daughter her sense of duty, now scolded her for having acquiesced and criticized Alston for failing to keep his marital promise to care for her.

By December, there was still no promise of a passport. Visits to Oxford and other places near London, encounters with women, more sleep than he had enjoyed since having been a lad of fourteen, did not bring him any closer to X. A brief side-trip to Edinburgh, where he called on Walter Scott and was entertained by the aristocracy, was shortened by a message from Don Castello that demanded his presence in London. But nothing developed after the hurried trip back to the capital. The winter was empty of constructive developments and Burr's status was as unresolved as on the day he had landed.

"Gampillus," little Aaron Burr Alston, was continually in Burr's thoughts along with his mother, "Gampassa." Burr bought trinkets that he thought would please the little boy and started a coin collection for him. While at Gravesend, he wrote to tell the child that "this silly thing is the best I can get in this dirty place for my boy. You and Gampassa may puzzle at it for a month. . . . I wish you would beat that cross little mother of your's for me. The great ugly thing, she never writes me a word about you, no more than if you were a dead dog—beat her I say and tell her its for Gampus."[33]

On the morning of April 4, Burr felt uneasy. Impulsively, he packed his clothes and belongings and prepared to seek a new lodging. His premonition proved correct when, at one o'clock, four coarse-looking men burst into his room with a warrant from Lord Liverpool, the British Minister, to seize him with his papers. All loose articles were thrown into a sack, a coach was called, and, unceremoniously, all of them set out for the Alien Office.

When they reached the door, Burr refused to go in. He sat freezing in the coach while his attendants delivered a note to John Reeves. The message told of his arrest and said, "I wait in a coach at the door . . . step to the door to save me the vexation of going in."[34] An hour elapsed as Burr shivered in the coach. He wrote another note, which Reeves answered in person, although he could do nothing but advise patience. After another half hour, orders came to go with a Mr. Hughes to his house at 31 Stafford Place.

Once again a prisoner, now under the name of Mr. Kirby, Burr sought some amusement to relieve his confinement in the small house. His jailer's household, consisting of a pretty young wife and a small child with a cough that kept Burr up at night, had to adjust to the prisoner's demands. He required Hughes to play chess with him during the day and whist after supper. "Mr. Kirby" was finally discharged after a few days with an apology from Lord Liverpool, which Burr answered via Reeves with a lengthy, brazen memorandum. He demanded several passports for his own use and his companions, and assurances that no restraint would be placed on his movements until he could effect a return to the United States.

While waiting for these documents, Burr wrote a short summary of his one hundred and twenty page report, filed with the Foreign Office, that presented his argument that an American born before the separation from the Mother Country who had resolved to settle in the kingdom was entitled, under law, to do so. The rights of a natural-born subject, Burr argued, are indelible because the King's treaty of independence with the American colonies does not extend to the colonists personally. While in America, their British character is suspended but can be resumed with full enjoyment when the individual re-enters British dominions.[35] This remarkable document was not regarded seriously, possibly even by its author. However, friends of Burr were surprised at the Ministry's bad treatment of the former Vice President and attributed it to some secret enemy. Burr identified that enemy as Jefferson.

The passports arrived, but before boarding the *Diana* for Sweden and freedom, Burr received a nervously scrawled note from Reeves, who referred to Mr. George Canning, the British Foreign Secretary, as no longer useful while it bade farewell with obviously mixed emotions. "If this is the last I am to hear of you, I wish you a good voyage." A cryptic message on the other side read: "I beg of you to return me the manuscript."[32]

The voyage across the choppy North Sea was so rough that Burr kept to his cabin fighting seasickness for most of the crossing. But, in time for the landing, his health and appetite recovered. The quiet harbor looked inviting. Mary Wollstonecraft's observations on Sweden, his reading of the past few days, had aroused his curiosity and interest.

A minor disaster marked the landing. With money already tight, Burr discovered that his trunk with all of his belongings was missing. But, by May 6, everything was in order again. Hosack had arrived from England, the trunk had been found, and the two friends were traveling to Stockholm in the company of a Mr. Hedboom, an English-speaking Swede.

Though X was not furthered during these months and his life had no real direction, Burr enjoyed the friendly atmosphere of Stockholm, freedom from oppression by the civil authorities, and inexpensive costs. He was admitted to the Casino of Nobles, an elegant hotel where Swedish aristocracy met to enjoy good food, an excellent library, and a superb view. Burr was presented at court. Baron Muncks, his sponsor, rehearsed him in the ceremony. "You would have laughed to see Gamp with his sword and immense three-cornered hat," he wrote to Theodosia.

On June 20, Coronation Day, Burr saw Charles XIII, elderly uncle of the deposed and erratic Gustavus Adolphus IV, crowned in the cathedral.

Sir Augustus John Foster, then a young *charge d'affairs* from England, described Burr at this time and accused him of a fresh conspiracy. When the two, who had been slightly acquainted in Washington, met at the Casino of Nobles, Burr immediately informed his young friend that he had been ordered out of England by the British government at the request of the Americans and, therefore, was perhaps not a healthy person with whom to be seen. Foster observed enough of Burr to note that he "was a little man, well mannered and rather agreeable but looked mysterious and unquiet, his dark eyes glancing perpetually and rapidly from right and left. He was I believe ready for any enterprize that might better his fortunes."

The current "enterprize," Foster related, involved a visit to the Castle of Gripsholm, where the deposed King and his family were confined. Burr asked to see the young prince, but his manner made the authorities suspicious that he conveyed some royalist escape plot. They rudely marched him away.[37] This was, possibly, an apocryphal story, remembered in retrospect, such as frequently followed in the wake of Burr. Nevertheless, that he was well connected in Sweden, and that he was desperate enough to engage in such an adventure makes this tale another tantalizing possibility.

Visits to ruins, studies of law, social amusements, art galleries, sight-seeing, and amorous adventures occupied the Swedish months. Cut off from news of Theodosia—because letters were directed through England—Burr imagined all sorts of catastrophes. He even fancied that the well-loved picture of his daughter had faded and grown pale: an omen. Sensibly, he stifled his morbid flight of fancy and took the portrait to be cleaned and restored by Breda, Sweden's foremost painter.

The quaint local customs entertained Burr while they provided copy for his journal. He was, however, more annoyed than amused by the widespread habit of entering a room without knocking, no matter what might be going on and threatened to blow out the brains of a faithful old servant named Anna if she did not learn to knock. A pretty sixteen year old "girl coachman" caught his eye. But these diversions failed to solve the money problem. He wrote: "My first business this morning was to determine whether or not Gamp might dejeuné; found that he could not." The newspapers had been discussing his presence in the country, though "what is said about me I have neither heard nor inquired," he recorded. Since Burr's primary purpose, which was to await answers to the letters he had written to the United States, had been defeated by the British post, it became urgent for him to go to the Continent, where his mail would reach him through other channels. Denmark accepted his Swedish passport, so he planned to travel by passage boat from Helsingborg in Sweden to Helsingor on the opposite coast in Denmark.

"A letter, a letter, a letter!" delivered by a tall, meagre man, who came in and asked for him, made Burr happy on October 11. The news was two months old, but it was so welcome that he "could have kissed the fellow."[38] Burr, of course, understood fully the danger of the written word. He cautioned a friend that there would be no danger as long as he avoided all references to politics.[39]

The Swedish interlude had been both enjoyable and instructive. The wonderful honesty of the people was a phenomenon that he studied so that he could detect the secret. He sought the answer in their laws and their social and municipal institutions, particularly in the judiciary. He could conclude only that it was a country that excelled in the protection of personal liberty and in which "the violation of it is punished with so much certainty and promptitude" and where "civil justice is administered with so much despatch and expence." Nor did its wonderful people spare themselves in demonstrations of kindness and attention.[40]

Although Denmark was Burr's destination, he would have preferred Russia. Overtures had been made from Gottenberg to the Russian minister, Count Romanzoff. Unfortunately, they had been ill-timed, for the hostile John Quincy Adams was then in that country on a mission and had endorsed the Russian refusal of a passport. The American government preferred to keep its little exile running, and Russia would not issue a passport unless sanctioned by his country's representative.[41]

Burr crossed over to Denmark in an open boat that was met, about a hundred yards from shore, by a Danish boat flying a flag of truce. Before proceeding to Copenhagen, he visited Hamlet's unmarked tomb at Elsinore Castle.

Denmark offered cheap living and some interesting ancient and historic sites. Gampy's growing coin collection caused Burr some amused embarrassment as the rumor spread that he was a distinguished numismatist, and so he was invited to inspect several famous collections. But the tired exile was often homesick and found it difficult to keep up his flagging spirits. Theodosia's picture, which had become a talisman and almost an obsession, hung in whatever quarters her father lodged. He was quite out of humor if it was not extravagantly admired. "Let me see, how you are now employed?" he daydreamed as he sat in a bouncing carriage with the picture precariously balanced on his lap. "Probably at breakfast with Gampy asking you an hundred of questions about —God knows!"[42] As he packed to leave Denmark for the next stage of his travels, Germany, he wrote to Theodosia: "Done, even the picture . . . I bid you *bon soir* a dozen times before I shut you up in that dark case, I can never do it without regret. It seems as if I were burying you *alive*."[43]

Burr's foreign hosts were friendly and hospitable, but the Americans he met on his travels were often suspicious. He lamented what "a lot of rascals they must be to make war on one whom they do not know; no one who never did harm or wished harm to a human being."[44] The press was uniformly hostile, even in Paris, which he planned to make his next destination. Since Napoleon had been selected to be the recipient of X in its most mature form, this latest news made letter writing depressing. Burr hated to write the truth because he felt it could accomplish nothing except be "afflicting to my friends."

In November, he arrived at Altona, a small city on the north side of the Elbe. Its gates extended to the territory of the great German city of Hamburg. As unobtrusively as possible, he moved into a quiet residence, hoping to obtain a passport to France from Louis de Bourienne, Napoleon's former private secretary, now the French minister at Hamburg.

De Bourienne had already been informed that Burr was at Altona because the Parisian police had ordered that he be watched carefully, and if he should go to Hamburg, he should be apprehended at the first false move. The French minister ignored the instructions, for Burr's behavior was excessively prudent. He kept little company and was seldom spoken of. Consequently, instead of arresting him, de Bourienne procured him a passport for Paris that was to be picked up at Frankfort.

Burr's activities while at Altona were limited by a raging toothache. Though the offending molar was dosed with camphor and opium, it continued to torment him until the tooth and jaw were terribly swollen. What complicated his suffering even more was a bite "by a venemous animal on Friday last." The bitten lip was given in a "paroxysm of great good humor," Burr confided to his journal, which identified the "animal" as two-legged and female. The next ten days were miserable as the afflictions got "worse and worse," although a lady dentist extracted the tooth quickly and very well. Neither fasting, the time-honored Burr remedy, nor boiled figs in milk, relieved the pain. The only activity he managed to perform was the filling out of a passport application, which stated that curiosity and amusement were his motives for visiting Paris and requested that the document be at Mayence in a month. For references, he gave the Comte de Volney, M. D'Hauterive, and other Frenchmen who had known him personally in the United States and would be able to recognize his handwriting.[45]

During most of December, Burr traveled through Germany. At Göttingen, he was told of Napoleon's divorce and of his consent to Mexico's independence and that of the other Spanish colonies. All Burr could say was: "Now; why the devil didn't he tell me of this two years ago?"

The tiny intellectual center of Europe, Weimar, entertained Burr for five glittering days. He dined with the Duke, patron of the arts, and met Princess Caroline and the others in the royal entourage. The poet Christoph Wieland, Wilhelm von Humboldt, Schopenhauer's brother, and even Goethe himself were introduced to him. Then, although he was committed to many appointments, Burr was forced to flee from the most "critical danger of my life"—La Baronne De Reizenstein, a beautiful noblewoman who had captivated him so completely that he said, "I have been, as you know, in a pretty many dilemmas and jeopardies but in no one that called for so much effort and determination." Though hard hit by *l'amour*, he was not willing to see his hopes and projects "blasted and abandoned" because of a "sorceress."[46]

The tour continued throughout Germany. Even the local royalty was intrigued by the former Vice President of the United States. Every incident of his career, Burr found, was known by his hosts: duels, treason, speeches, gallantries. His reputation enhanced his interest and to his distinguished new friends, his charm and grace made him even more attractive. Burr flourished in this admiring atmosphere, but need for money and, even more basic for him, lust for power and fame, drove

him to pursue the elusive X. Reports of his activities in England had
reached the President. In his own country, it was generally accepted
that he had proposed its dismemberment in the event of a war with
England. When this gambit had failed, it was reported, he would submit
his treasonable proposal to France.[47]

At Frankfort, Burr repeated his social pattern, but bad news from
Mayence, indicating that the prospect of a Parisian passport was unfa-
vorable, convinced him that he better go there to straighten the matter
out personally. D'Hauterive, of the Department of External Affairs,
whom Burr had known in America, his most important contact in Napoleonic France, had proved to have been an obstacle rather than an aid.
Four letters had been sent to him with no response. As Burr suspected,
they had not simply miscarried. The letters had been received and had
been referred in a memorandum to Champigny, Duke de Cadore, Minister for External Affairs, which said that he "did not wish to facilitate
the trip to France of Colonel Burr" because his political actions had
been "diametrically opposed to the profession of attachment to France"
that he had pretended in the United States. Since his recent activity in
Louisiana and subsequent flight from his country, D'Hauterive judged,
"the sojourn of Colonel Burr in France is a sojourn of disquiet and
defiance for the American government," and could destroy friendship
between us.[48] Somehow, this negative report did not have the expected
result because Burr's passport arrived in time to improve his mood,
which was so absorbed with X matters that, he said, "I am very bad
company and unsocial."[49]

Paris promised to the over-optimistic Burr another opportunity to
bring his plans to fruition. Lodged in a moderately large room, two
flights up, Burr sent out feelers for the best way to approach the Emperor. Shortage of funds was a chronic source of anxiety. The city
streets, covered with snow and ice, only added to the dismal picture, for
Burr found that, without his title, stripped of his former glory, the great
names of France did not find him as appealing as they had when they
were *émigrés* and he was the squire of Richmond Hill. The Duke de
Cadore, Volney, and others all afforded either discouraging refusal to
his plans or avoided him. Talleyrand, a frequent guest at Burr's New
York estate, snubbed him harshly when Burr requested an interview. A
message from the eminent French statesman carried the message that
"General Hamilton's likeness always hangs over my mantle." So Burr
never made a second call. Continual rejection hurt. When he heard that
the artist John Vanderlyn, his protégé, was in Paris but had not sought
him out, he asked: "Is it possible that he, too, can have turned rascal?"

But Vanderlyn had simply been without his patron's correct address; presently, there was a happy reunion. And Burr was soon able to write to Theo about the artist's prize picture, *Marius in the Ruins of Carthage*, saying, "I see nothing in that line to exceed it."[50]

The ladies, as always, found Burr a delightful companion. A good deal of his time was taken up with a Madame Paschaud, whom he described as about the size and form of Dolley Madison, but ten years younger, black-haired, black-eyed, and with a healthy complexion.

The winter and spring of 1810 were occupied with petitions and travel. A memorial that Burr had prepared for Napoleon was approved by the Duke d'Alberg and did finally reach him. However, by mid-July, Burr confided to his journal that he despaired of success and might as well go back home. But a passport was refused. Madame Paschaud cooled and joined her husband in Geneva. Money was so desperate a problem that Burr approached Edward Griswold, an expatriated American lawyer, for six hundred to one thousand dollars to tide him over until he received his passport. Griswold was asked to forward the money to Vanderlyn, but, under no circumstance, was he to use Burr's name, lest John Armstrong, the American minister, who had been one of the lawyers for the state at the Richmond trial, would take his revenge by obstructing Burr's passport.

The journal was carefully silent about its author's significant activities during the winter of 1810. A lengthy entry recounted his audience with the Duke de Rovigo, Minister of Police, but failed to mention that his predecessor, Joseph Fouche, Duke of Otranto, had known Burr's plans and, some said, had been dismissed from his post because he had been the recipient of the memorial Burr had written upon his arrival in Paris. M. Roux, one of the Duke's chiefs of Division, who had been assigned to act as liaison between Burr and Fouche, filed two versions of the Burr interviews, both in the French Archives. One is a rough draft of the conversations, the other an elaborate unsigned version that clerks had prepared for Napoleon. Roux, commenting about the rough draft, said: "I thought I could perceive in all the conversation which I have just related to Your Excellency that the independence of Florida was the point to which he held fastest."[51] In the official report, however, Burr's random comments are organized, categorized, and, probably, subjected to Roux' interpretation. Every possible variation of the southwestern scheme—Florida, New Mexico, Mexico, Louisiana—is unrolled to intrigue his listeners, a technique that was reminiscent of his great adventure. Roux said that Burr suggested that if Louisiana and Mexico did not suit the Emperor, perhaps Jamaica would be an acceptable target. The

Duke de Cadore, Minister of Foreign Affairs, however, saw through the Jamaica offer. He wrote to Napoleon that such notions were "pure chimera, which he puts forward here to enhance his credit."[52]

News of these conversations leaked out because, eighteen months later, an anonymous letter, in which Burr's grandiose scheme was unfolded, reached President Madison. The *American-Citizen* said that Burr had offered himself as a peace-maker between France and England. The two powers would then turn their joint efforts to the conquest of the United States, or at least the Eastern states, which were portrayed as eager to return to their Mother Country and be free from Virginian domination. The informant made the interesting observation that the Emperor, commenting upon the part concerning the separation of the states, said: "They all admit it is inevitable sooner or later."[53]

Burr knew by March, 1810, that there was "no reason to believe my business advances, or that I shall do anything here." The French minister in Washington was also issuing warnings against him. He wrote that Burr was crazed by a zest for "money, intrigue, and fame," and that "he will plot wherever he is." But he doubted that the American still had "the necessary boldness to execute his plans."[54] Washington gossip and the attitude of many Americans in Paris and elsewhere endorsed this view.

Waiting for audiences and for the good offices of his important friends was both time-consuming and costly. Although Griswold rescued Burr from desperate poverty more than once, the wretched exile did not see how he could manage. Bizarre ideas for business ventures such as a process for vinegar making that he saw as applicable for bringing water to Charleston sapped his energies. "My affairs are quite stagnant," Burr recorded for Theodosia. "I have no other prospects but that of starving in Paris." The city was cold, his chimney smoked, and the only glimmer of hope, now, was a new gander in Holland Land Company speculation.

By the fall of 1810, it was obvious that the chief obstacle to Burr's passport was American and not French. Jonathan Russell of Rhode Island, *charge d'affairs* in Paris, who had been a frequent visitor at Burr's table, wrote self-righteously that the man who "evades and offended the laws of his country abandons for a time the right of their protection." Furthermore, Russell maintained, he "has a claim to no other passport than one which will enable him to surrender himself for trial, for the offense with which he stands charged."[55] The American colony in Paris was advised to ostracize Burr, and masters of vessels were ordered to refuse to carry letters or packages for him.[56]

Gampy's trinkets had to be traded in for food money. More valuable items were pawned with the hope that the new Holland Company venture would prove lucrative. Ironically, while Burr was enduring his starving-time, American papers were reporting that Napoleon had granted the little traitor a two thousand pound pension. Actually, Burr was subsisting on bouillon and potatoes for dinner, having forfeited sugar and tea as beyond his income. "Foggy, misty, drizzling days," marked by torpor and deprivation and no news from Amsterdam about the Holland Company or from officialdom about the passport, dampened Burr's spirit.

The new year, 1811, continued the hopeless routine and monotonous disappointments. Jonathan Russell continued his relentless persecution by cutting Burr off from communication with home. "Any letter to you would be opened," Burr wrote to Theodosia. His state was still *sans sous*. On February 16, his Holland Company speculation ruined, he recorded: "Anniversary of my happy advent in this holy city."

Finally, in March, the reluctant American legation granted him his passport and, through a powerful new friend, the Duke de Bassano, he was able to arrange a release by France. But the red tape unraveling through the bureaus snarled and the passport was lost. While a new one was being prepared, Burr arranged a trip to Amsterdam to attempt the recovery of some money from the Holland Land Company directors. He failed, however, because they refused to see him. But the journey did afford a meeting with a Captain Coombes, master of the *Vigilant*, a vessel bound for the United States. The Captain was agreeable and enthusiastic about his prospective passenger, whose cabin he offered to fit out in any manner Burr wished. Since the ship would not sail at once, there was time for Burr to return to Paris to collect his things.

At the Hotel de Normandie in Paris, some mail from Theodosia relieved her father. "My dear T., how well you write!" he noted. "You must write a book. . . . Gampillo's letters are all lost. A greater loss to me than the works of Menander or Tacitus." Bad news came, too. Aaron Burr Reeves, Sally's son, was dead. The little family circle had now become very small, for Sally had died before Burr's accession to the vice presidency.[57]

Theodosia had been giving much thought to her father's return home. Much as she would have preferred him to be with her in South Carolina, she felt that it would be best for him to surprise his friends in New York City before cabals could be formed and measures taken to discourage his supporters. In the city, he would be, at least, in the midst of his "tenth legion." *"If the worst comes I will leave everything to suffer with you,"* she promised.

Theodosia had not been idle in his behalf. In 1809, she had written to

Dolley Madison to seek a removal of "the prosecution now existing against Aaron Burr." The First Lady was asked, as an old friend, not to send the answer, if there be one, to *The Oaks* because Alston did not know of his wife's plea, but to her brother, Frederick Prevost. Wrote Theodosia:

> To whatever fate Mr. Madison may doom this application, I trust it will be treated with delicacy . . . If it be an error, attribute it to the indiscreet zeal of a daughter whose soul sinks at the gloomy prospect of a long and indefinite separation from a father almost adored, and who can leave unattempted nothing which offers the slightest hope of procuring his redress. What indeed would I not risk once more to see him, to hang upon him, to place my child on his knee."[58]

Two years later, she asked Gallatin for an enlightened opinion "whether Burr's return would subject him to any further prosecution from any branch of the government."[59] Burr learned, at this time, of Blennerhassett's threat to blackmail Alston if he failed to pay him his debt of fifteen thousand dollars. Blennerhassett said that he would publish a memoir revealing the Alstons' involvements in Burr's designs upon Mexico. The report stated that Alston had paid ten thousand dollars to stop the publication.[60] But Theodosia did not write this news to her father.

Passport delays resumed, so Burr could use what little money he had buying books and pretty seals for Theodosia and ABA. Though friends exerted their good will, time passed until it was too late for the amiable Captain Coombes. Finally, the Duke de Bassano applied the necessary pressure to force a passport from a reluctant Jonathan Russell. The tool was a lady of interest to the American minister. Burr received his passport promptly, at last, and left Paris on July 20, 1811.[61]

When he reached Amsterdam, Burr was overjoyed to find that Coombes had not sailed. But the Captain's attitude had changed. "Fear somebody had put the devil into him," Burr commented. Suddenly, Coombes demanded a huge sum of money or he would go off without him. "Alas, poor Gamp," some more of his treasures had to be sold to meet the avarice of the now hostile sea captain.

Vanderlyn had supervised the shipment of Burr's effects, but he had failed to execute the promised enamel of Theodosia. His patron had hoped that John would return to the states with him, especially as constant delays moved the sailing date further into September.

Actually, Burr had fitted out his cabin so comfortably that the uncertainty and boredom of the waiting were somewhat mitigated. While at anchor at Helder, two carpenters had been employed to build shelves for the three hundred volumes accumulated during the European trip. A handy table that let down for reading and writing, with places for candlesticks, made Burr's cabin the envy of the other passengers.[62]

But all these elaborate preparations were in vain because, once at sea, the vessel was captured by the British and brought into Yarmouth. The Captain ran out of provisions while his ship lay at anchor, so the passengers were forced to go ashore as the courts were deciding the fate of the *Vigilant*. Burr observed that England looked fresher and neater to him after the Continent.

Back in London, the social round was resumed. The Godwins were particularly attentive and were the only British friends permitted to know of Burr's financial straits. Books, watches, and trinkets were sold ruthlessly to defray the expenses of his furnished room. Reading occupied much of his day, and he was particularly interested in Milton's *Tracts on Divorce*.

Don Castello was still in London. The two men spent Christmas Eve together over porter and cheese and discussed South American revolutions. The Spaniard's nephew was actively engaged in one taking place on the borders of Peru. How Burr envied him!

The possibility of war between the United States and Great Britain worried Burr. He feared that he would never get home. Reeves was working hard to obtain a passport—but, so far, no success. Peter Irving paid a brief visit, bringing the latest news from New York, but made no offer to help.

The *Vigilant*, which had passed its trial and had been acquitted, was declared out of bounds to Burr by the United States consuls at London and Yarmouth, and its captain was worried that, if he carried the former Vice President, he would incur the displeasure of the government.[63]

"If Gampillo's coins don't bring money, Gamp must fast and freeze, too, coal out," Burr recorded in February. To top the misery of his situation, a toothache and swollen jaw tortured him for weeks until the abscess broke. The Godwins took care of him and included him in their family group, which contained a bevy of lively daughters, whom he called "les goddesses."

On March 13, a Captain Potter agreed to carry Burr back to America under the name of Adolphus Arnot. Reeves had managed the passport and, at the last minute, the passage money, too.

Now that the reality of returning to his native land faced him, Burr faltered. If his reception by Americans in Europe was an indication of what he might expect at home, he knew that he faced "the most implacable malice."[64] However, he had no regrets at leaving England. "I hope never to visit the country again," he wrote, "unless at the head of fifty thousand men. I shake the dust off my feet; adieu, John Bull! *Insula inhospitalibus!*"[65] The Continent was regarded with equal harshness. "Europe's fast, very fast barbarizing," he declared, "retrograding with rapid strides to the darkest ages of intellectual and moral degradation . . . *The science of tyranny was in its infancy—it is now matured.*"[66] Napoleon had failed him, and so was titled the destroyer of European culture.

Burr had revised his theory about imminent war. He believed that "J. Madison & Co." were too like "a bevy of boarding-house misses" to declare war.[67] M. Arnot, alias Burr, convinced the British officers who examined his papers that he was French, although he thought that Captain Nichols, the American who was second in command of the ship, had penetrated his disguise.

The voyage was reasonably calm and uneventful, enlivened only by seasickness, some playful bands of porpoises, and a view of ice islands. As Cape Ann lighthouse was sighted, Burr decided that he would maintain his incognito as they prepared to disembark. On May 4, Burr, a lonely figure, watched the happiness of the others, conscious that all were festive, "except Gamp. Why should he rejoice?" On board, in full view of the familiar city of Boston, he wrote letters to Theodosia and Samuel Swartwout. Apprehensive of the future, he said: "My enemies, I see, are not at their ease."[68]

CHAPTER XXI

The Voyage of the Patriot

S ELF-PITY was not characteristic of Aaron Burr. Yet, the frustrations and despair of being a penniless outcast, forced to travel
disguised as "Mr. A. Arnot," emerge from his own account of
the days before he returned to New York and renewed his law practice.
There was little dignity in earning thirty-two dollars by selling a
portion of his library while still aboard the *Aurora*, the boat that returned him to America. Or, for that matter, in living in fear of exposure
while passing as Arnot. Being identified might bring the reimposi-
tion of suspended federal prosecutions by a hostile Madison administration. His letter to the younger Swartwout, sent upon his arrival in
Boston, covered still another concern; for Burr needed to inquire
whether he could land in New York without some outstanding creditors
jailing him for debt. A favorable response from Swartwout, therefore,
had to precede any further move.

He was still Mr. Arnot when he found a room in an ordinary
boarding-house that a sea captain's widow operated near the waterfront.
The place was cheap. It was also fine for keeping out of sight as he
awaited Swartwout's reply. Until he got word to proceed and while he
attempted to raise more money, it had to serve as home. The thirty-two
dollars accumulated aboard the *Aurora* would not go very far, particularly if Swartwout failed to signal early clearance to New York. And
even then, passage via a sloop to his home city would cost twenty
dollars. Other sources had to be found.

One that seemed promising was a wealthy former Princeton classmate
named Mason, who had been with Burr during the Richmond trial, had

sympathized with him, and had fulminated at what he had regarded as
the outrages committed in the name of justice. Yet, when Burr sent the
man a note announcing his presence in Boston and requested an interview, the wealthy merchant could only offer an evasive, timid reply. He
explained that he dared not see Burr alone because public opinion had
become so inflamed. When Burr then tried to have Mason extend, instead, an advance of money upon some of his rare and valuable books,
the rejection came with the excuse that "he had retired from the mercantile business, and it was therefore inconvenient for him to make
advances."[1]

Finally, after he had been in Boston over three weeks, he managed to
obtain an appointment to see President Kirkland of Harvard. This gentleman helped Burr by paying him forty dollars for the acquisition by
the university of some of the former Vice President's French diction-
aries. At last, he had enough money to book passage for New York.

Even the correspondence with Swartwout was not without anxiety.
When no word had come from his friend after a wait of nearly two
weeks, Burr wrote again, this time taking care to post the letter himself.
But two days later, Swartwout's response arrived. The letter gave assurances that old friends were still loyal and that sympathy had softened
ancient enemies. There was, after all, no further reason to destroy Burr's
political position. Disassociation was the only judicious posture for a
politician. Where money was involved, however, nothing had changed.
Two outstanding creditors were as implacable as ever.

But Burr had had enough of playing "Mr. Arnot" in Boston and
decided to risk the consequences of returning to New York. Meanwhile,
Swartwout had written to such people as John Wickham, who reported
the dismissal of some suits. Other accounts brought assurances that the
Administration had become preoccupied with more pressing matters,
such as declaring war against Great Britain that June. Wickham expressed the feelings of friends when he wrote that he was "glad to hear
that after so many sufferings Col. Burr has the prospect of being restored to his country & of being permitted again to employ his talents
with advantage."[2] Burr arrived in New York on June 8, and nearly
three weeks later, the newspapers announced his reappearance as an
attorney-at-law.

The announcement worked wonders. It swept the city and caused a
commotion, which was fine, for he needed such an impact to build up a
new practice. The only money he had for a start was ten dollars from a
loan. Even the law library he used represented a generous act. Robert
Troup, a close friend of earlier days and later a sharp Federalist critic,
had retired from his own practice and had given Burr temporary use of

his books. Thus re-established, the fifty-six year old lawyer earned two thousand dollars in legal fees during the first twelve days of his comeback.[3] Seeing Theodosia and ten year old Gampy again was his next goal.

The hope of brighter days was suddenly smashed. In June, disaster struck. The little boy died. "I have lost a boy," wrote Theo. "My child is gone forever. He expired on the 30th of June. My head is not now sufficiently collected to say anything further. May Heaven, by other blessings, make you some amends for the noble grandson you have lost."[4] Alston followed with a letter saying he could not "conceal from you that life is a burden, which, heavy as it is, we shall both support, if not with dignity, at least with decency and firmness. Theodosia has endured all that a human being could endure; but her admirable mind will triumph. She supports herself in a manner worthy of your daughter."[5] Little imagination is needed to understand the impact of the news upon Burr. He had already lost his wife, his dearest friend Matt Ogden, then his sister Sally; and, while still in Europe, his nephew Aaron Burr Reeve. Yet, in many ways, ABA's death was the most tragic of all.

By November, it was decided that Theodosia should join her father in New York for their first reunion after more than four years of separation. As he had done so many times before, Burr turned to Timothy Green to fulfill a mission. Green, a layman with some knowledge of medicine, was induced to go to South Carolina to escort Burr's sick and heartbroken daughter back to New York. When Green arrived at Charleston on November 28, 1812, Alston seemed hurt that his father-in-law had apparently shown so little confidence in his ability to provide for Theo's safety. In truth, Alston was unable to accompany her himself, for he was then serving as governor of South Carolina; in addition, war with Great Britain and his additional duty as a general of the militia also confined him. He did, however, tell Green that he could have sent one of his brothers. Green's explanation was that Burr had been motivated only by consideration for Theo's health. The retired lawyer also explained that he would wait until Alston brought her to Georgetown, a port at the head of Winyah Bay north of Charleston. From there, a speedy schooner named the *Patriot*, a vessel that had only recently engaged in privateering, would sail to New York. All was set for departure on December 30, and expectations were that the schooner with the sick young woman would reach the northern city only five or six days later. A Captain Overstocks was in command with an experienced New York pilot named Coon as the sailing-master.

Alston went on board with Theo and did not leave until about noon, when the schooner reached the sand bar at the mouth of Winyah Bay.

From there, Theodosia and Timothy Green headed toward the hazards of the Atlantic Ocean, dangers that were even greater because of the presence of a British blockade. Anticipating this additional difficulty, Alston had given Captain Overstocks a letter to solicit courtesy for his sick wife from any intercepting enemy. Having thus attempted to protect her, Governor Alston could do nothing more than await word of his wife's arrival at New York.

"Another mail, and still no letter!" wrote an anguished Alston after two weeks had gone by. "I hear, too, rumours of a gale off Cape Hatteras at the beginning of the month! The state of my mind is dreadful."[6]

In New York, Burr waited. Day after day, from his office at 9 Nassau Street, he wandered down to the tip of Manhattan Island. Standing on a pier, he stared anxiously across the Bay and toward the open sea. A British blockade squadron was just off-shore, near Sandy Hook. The town was tense. "You would scarcely recognize our old peaceful city," Washington Irving reported. "Nothing is talked of but armies, navies, battles, etc."[7] As Burr scanned the waters that flowed from the sea through the Narrows, he thought of enemy ships, pirates, storms—and hoped. Finally, he received a letter from Alston that concluded with: "I may no longer have a wife."[8]

And Aaron Burr had no daughter. Providence had not even left Theodosia. All the waiting and watching were merely the pathetic motions of a helpless father. Alston later sent word that the authorities at Bermuda and Nassau had, indeed, confirmed that a violent storm had swept along the coast in early January, with the distinct probability that the small schooner had never gone beyond Cape Hatteras.[9] No proof that this had, in fact, been the fate of the *Patriot* could ever be obtained. Not a soul on the ship was ever heard from again.

The legendary qualities of Burr and his devotion to Theo, as well as the mysterious disappearance, were bound to provoke rumors, conjecture, and mere gossip for many years. Stories circulated about pirates who stopped the schooner and forced the lovely Mrs. Alston to walk the plank. Burr himself believed that there was a strong possibility—at least the boat's owner had told him so—that neither the officers nor the crew had ever planned to reach New York, but had gone off on a voyage of piracy. For him, the story perpetuated the hope that she had been deposited "on shore in some West-indian Island or on some part of South America" and that his Theodosia might still be alive.[10] But others had different ideas.

One story was flavored by a strong dose of Burr's reputation. A correspondent informed one South Carolina newspaper of his passion for the wife of the *Patriot*'s captain. To keep the seaman from thwarting his designs, the story went, "Burr corrupted his sailors to mutiny and destroy him." Unfortunately, because the plan could not be carried out until the ship's return voyage to New York, Mrs. Alston became a victim of her father's scheme. "Her fate was an awful retribution upon her abandoned father," concluded the writer. Thus, the evil Burr had unwittingly planned his own daughter's murder, and poetic justice had been done.[11]

Other stories, less fantastic, continued to appear. There was a sailor in Texas who confessed on his deathbed that he had been a member of the crew that had murdered Theodosia. He had mutinied with the rest of the men, who murdered all the officers and passengers. He even claimed that the lady had been the last person to walk the plank, and recalled her look of despair, and that she died "in the greatest agony of mind." A similar story came from a dying mendicant in Michigan. There were long accounts of visits to Nag's Head, on a sandbar just north of Hatteras Island, to inspect the oil portrait of a stately young woman that had been taken from a grounded pilot boat near Kitty Hawk. Many thought it bore a close resemblance to Theo. Any less fanciful critic, however, would regard the likeness as entirely imaginary, for the painting reveals none of the sensitivity or soft features of Burr's child. The storm must be blamed for her tragedy.

CHAPTER XXII

The Private Gentleman

O LD age, shrinking resources, and the antipathy of former friends burdened Burr's later years. But he was determined to live game and, if necessary, as he advised a complaining lady, die game. The sprightly, keen-eyed, wizened old gentleman of the James Van Dyke portrait, eyeglasses perched on his forehead, was a familiar sight in New York. Dressed in a blue waistcoat, hair thickly powdered, graceful and courtly in manner, he would walk down the street, dignifiedly keeping to himself.

Burr had resumed the practice of the law with great success. Sometimes a judge would show hostility to him but he became accustomed to that kind of slight. When Henry Clay met him in court and refused to take his hand, Burr was humbled. Nevertheless, as always, he merely bowed and withdrew quietly.[1]

Joseph Alston did not long survive his double tragedy. He was very ill in late 1814 and then suffered a relapse in November, 1815, which kept him from following his father-in-law's advice to nominate Andrew Jackson for the presidency. Burr wrote to Alston, "Exhibit yourself then, and emerge from this state of nullity. You owe it to yourself, you owe it to me, you owe it to your country, you owe it to the memory of the dead."[2]

When Alston received the letter, he was too feeble and only, as he said, "the miserable remnant of myself." His illness was emotional as well as physical, a dying of the spirit, as he told Burr. "I feel too much alone, too entirely unconnected with the world, to take much interest in anything."[3] In September, 1816, Burr heard from his brother that the unhappy Governor of South Carolina was dead and had included a clause in his will excusing Burr's debts.

The Governor was buried at *The Oaks* next to his small son. On the tombstone, Theodosia's name was inscribed as the disconsolate mother who perished at sea a few months after her ten year old son's death.[4]

Misfortune had made Burr compassionate rather than embittered. He was generous to those whose misery touched him. Luther Martin, for example, strong-willed and alcoholic, spent his last few years, sick and impoverished, as a pensioner in Burr's home.

Reversal of fortune, a common malady in these individualistic days, often impoverished the formerly respected and comfortable. Burr responded quickly to requests for money, when he had it, and, sometimes, when he did not. Funds that were earmarked for the payment of long-standing debts would somehow escape for purchase of wood for a freezing little family. Frequent letters of gratitude can be found among Burr's papers. A gentleman wrote: "It is past my means of expression to thank you sufficiently for the favor you have deigned to grant me in the real time of need. . . . I hope my future endeavors to obtain a living notwithstanding the ailment I patiently endure, may shew how far I invited such kindness."[5] A lady, full of sorrows, wrote: "my greatest illness, at present is a light purse. . . . I entreat of you; have the compassion to send me a trifle, if only sufficient to purchase a pair of shoes, that I may feel I have once more the use of my feet."[6]

When years and a practiced eccentricity had overtaken Burr, his handling of money, if the stories of his contemporaries can be believed, became bizarre indeed. The chamber in lower New York that served as his home and his office had a large, cluttered library table in the center of the room. An empty space was made in its center and into that was poured the proceeds of Burr's law practice. As the creditors and the needy came to make claims on the pile, which was sometimes large and sometimes small, Burr would scoop up an appropriate sum and hand it to the supplicant. When all the money was gone, all had to wait until the trough was refilled.[7]

Theodosia and Gampy could never be replaced, but the feeling for the young and helpless made Burr take on the responsibility for countless wards of both sexes. The education of young people added interest to his declining years, as he followed their progress and conferred with their teachers. Some of them were—or might have been—his natural children. Charles Burdett, for example, was educated at Hartwick Seminary near Cooperstown, New York, under the direction of Ernest Hazelins, a pedagogue who kept his pupil busy with a most ambitious program. "In Latin he reads Horace and Livy; in Greek he continues

Xenophon; in French he reads an extract from Gil Blas. I keep him at home as busy as possible; he has still a volatile mind but he continues to improve," wrote the schoolmaster to Burr.[8]

Burdett later became a novelist. In a memoir written in retrospect, he described a portion of Burr's life at this time. The Selden Mansion, a stately double-brick house surrounded by trees and bushes, situated in the upper part of Washington Street in Albany, housed three of Burr's charges for a number of years in the mid-1820's. It was Charles' home as well as that of the Eden sisters, Rebecca and Elizabeth. The Eden case, one of Burr's longest and most renowned, a litigation that Alexander Hamilton had pronounced hopeless, concerned the property of a New York City brewer named Medcef Eden. While Burr achieved the piece by piece return of the property to the surviving Edens, he became the legal guardian of the little girls. Their charm and youthful grace recalled Theo and his devotion was rewarded by their love and exuberant affection. Mrs. Eden apparently acted as Burr's housekeeper, for when the recurring yellow fever epidemic struck New York particularly hard in 1822, she reported the death of one of Burr's clerks and expressed her determination to leave the plague-ridden city for Manhattanville.[9]

Elizabeth and Rebecca both studied with Mr. James O'Shammusy, a first-rate classical and mathematics scholar. Burr was as certain as ever that a girl's education should fit her for "any position, any sphere," and to be equal to any circumstances. Astronomy and navigation found their way into this curious curriculum, along with modern languages, music, and outdoor exercises. When Burr came to Albany, he was pleased to hear Rebecca recite a portion of Homer's *Iliad* and Elizabeth read the *Aeneid* to him.

But, in 1828, Elizabeth Eden married Isidore Guillet, an attractive, well-educated Frenchman, who carried her off to France; and, the following year, Rebecca became the wife of John Lyde Wilson, an ex-governor of South Carolina, and went to live in Charleston. His gay little adopted daughters were no longer around to amuse Burr with their chatter or to read to him from his law books. They no longer needed him to direct their education. The dwindling circle made him restless, ready for the wiles of the "artful syren," a twenty year old beauty who "knew his weakness and exploited it fully." She "harassed him daily with clamorous demands for money," reviving Burr's reputation for dalliance with women.[10]

But was his interest ever suspended? An extensive, extant correspondence with Rebecca Blodgett, a former Philadelphia socialite with whom Burr had been well acquainted in the past, acquired a renewed interest. Now a widow, she wrote to Burr that he must disentangle her property from the complicated litigation in which it was involved. In 1815, when the correspondence began, the Blodgett children were young, their mother sentimental and provocative to their attorney. When he failed to write or visit, she wrote playfully, "If I did not love you more than all the rest of the world I shou'd be more inclined to give you a blow on the face than a kiss"; and, later, "It was a bad thing to spend a *short* time with me—I am restless."[11] As time went on, her financial difficulties multiplied.

In 1823, Burr was asked to take John Adams Blodgett, Rebecca's son, into his law office. The final available letters reveal Rebecca in very straitened circumstances, living in one room, often cold and hungry. Apparently, Burr was not successful in resolving Mrs. Blodgett's financial tangle because her last letter reads: "In bloom of youth—generally thought gay, unthinking, romantic & visionary & without *common sense* . . . my heart has never been estranged from you." There is a marked thread of respect for Burr's talents and person throughout the correspondence and a sense of gratitude for such services as he had performed.[12]

As he grew older, Burr's fortunes diminished. William Seward, then a state senator, visited him in 1831 at the Merchant's Exchange. Burr's lodgings, he said, were at the top of a dirty, narrow staircase. In this small room with two beds, Seward was shocked by Burr's appearance: an almost dwarflike little man with a few straggly gray hairs and coarse cotton clothing. Only his keen, sparkling, penetrating eyes retained the spirit of youth.[13] However, his residence there was only temporary because he planned to buy a place on Duane Street, east of Broadway, a grand three-story house that was cheap because it adjoined the public furnace. That was inconvenient, Burr admitted, "for when the wind is Eastwardly the smoke and ashes are an annoyance."[14]

Very few echoes of the past reached him. His letters were free of famous correspondents. Many of them were dead, it is true, but most preferred to ignore their fallen friend. A comment from the *Memoirs* of John Quincy Adams has been interpreted to bear out the contemporary rumors that Martin Van Buren was Burr's natural son. With this in mind, Adams wrote, "Mr. Van Buren paid me a morning visit . . . [he] is now the great electioneering manager for General Jackson . . . He is now acting over the part in the affairs of the union which Aaron Burr performed in 1799 and 1800; and there is much resemblance of character, manners, and even person between the two men." Then Adams added: "Van Buren has now every prospect of success in his present movements, and he will avoid the rock upon which Burr afterwards split."[15]

Indirectly, Jackson's victory benefited Burr. The hawk-faced General could not recognize his former friend, but despite his having paid heavily in adverse publicity for his past association with Burr, he rewarded some of Burr's stalwarts. Samuel Swartwout was made Collector of the Port of New York—a post he left in disgrace a number of years later.

Europeans, less critical, mellowed by centuries of experience with broken fortunes, treated Burr more kindly. When the Duke of Saxe Weimar visited the United States, he called on Burr and was undeterred by his modest quarters. Jose Alvarez de Toleda, probably the same gentleman whom Burr knew in New Orleans, offered him the management of the Mexican revolution in 1816.

The Colonel did not accept, but he had a continuing interest in such matters.[16] Some mysterious letters regarding a proposed expedition to New Granada, as Colombia was then called, revealed the involvement of seasoned and ardent revolutionaries. A John Alderson was Burr's contact. He wrote to Burr, "Now Sir, I am to ask you what can be done with you? What do you advise . . . What are the preliminary steps to be taken? and in fine what are your views on the whole—I am requested to desire you to answer me immediately if possible. . . ."[17] The old conspirator was tired, however. And, even if he did extend advice, the revolution never materialized because of funds. However, the Republic of Venezuela recognized Burr's services when, in 1819, it granted him a commission to "legally exert himself in favor of the emancipation of Venezuela and New Granada, and all other countries of South America and Mexico now contending against the arbitrary and oppressive powers of Spain, without in any manner giving offense to friendly or neutral powers. . . ."[18]

As Burr watched the former Spanish possessions gain their freedom, he realized that the failure of his endeavor had been, in part, the fact that not all the ingredients necessary to make a great undertaking successful were present for him. The man and the place were right, but the time was awry. When Texas achieved her independence, Burr exclaimed to a friend, "There! You see? I was right! I was only thirty years too soon. What was treason in me thirty years ago, is patriotism now."[19]

For the most part, now, the past lay quietly buried. Friends mentioned it cautiously, if at all, avoiding talk of the duel, the conspiracy, or the trial. But sometimes Burr would speak of the giants he had known, usually not in a complimentary manner. George Washington was labeled dull but well-intentioned; Jefferson, a plain farmer whose egalitarian ideas were harmful. Of Wilkinson, he had only harsh words.[20] The unfortunate episodes in his past no longer plagued him. He could speak of them without self-consciousness and even with humor. A favorite project, to write a "true" version of the Revolutionary War, was often mentioned but never seriously considered. Burr was well aware that the chief figures had already been assigned their positions in history, and though he contested their stations, he accepted the official judgments. In a like manner, he accepted the slander that was directed toward him. He had determined never to answer his tormentors, although he did say, "Slander has slain more than the sword."[21]

Of all the varied incidents in these later years, Burr's second marriage to Madame Elizabeth Jumel was surely the most bizarre, bordering on the ludicrous. She was born in 1775, in Providence, Rhode Island, the daughter of Phoebe Kelley and John Bowen, a sailor. Her early life was unfortunate and dissolute. It is known that she had a son, George Washington Bowen, whom she abandoned. Her entrance into the upper levels of society was roundabout. A sea captain, much taken with her charms, carried her off to France, where, apparently, she acquired some polish. Upon her return to the United States, now known as Eliza Brown, she went on the stage. Stephen Jumel saw her and wanted her.

He was a Frenchman who had escaped from Haiti in 1795 at the time of the Black uprisings, but knowing the wine business and with excellent connections, he was able to recoup and expand his lost fortune by beating the embargo. He was successful in evading the law, but not Eliza. They lived together in Jumel's elegant Whitehall Street house, where the lady was furnished with every luxury except a wedding band and the acceptance of New York society. By feigning a fatal illness, she finally managed to marry him, but society was less sentimental. In 1810, as a consolation prize, the devoted husband bought her the Roger Morris house on Harlem Heights, the same one that had been used by Washington during the Revolution. The white-pillared mansion with rolling lawns that allowed a superb view of the river was refurbished and restored lavishly. Five more years passed and still no callers. Admitting defeat, the Jumels went to France, where charm, beauty, and money substituted for family and respectability.

Madame Jumel enjoyed a great success. She spent freely, and with a diabolical cleverness managed to extract a power-of-attorney from her husband. While he remained in France, she returned to the United States. M. Jumel became friends with Joseph Bonaparte, and with Louis Napoleon was said to have fathered the plan to bring Napoleon to the United States after Waterloo. Madame, meanwhile, gained complete control of her husband's fortune, displaying a natural aptitude for shrewd finance. After his return to the United States, Jumel died in 1832 as a result of a fall from a wagon. His widow, fifty-seven years old, was wealthy and ambitious.

Nelson Chase, the husband of an illegitimate cousin of Madame Jumel, a law clerk in Burr's office, claimed the credit for introducing his employer to the notorious lady while she was at the office on a business matter. However, it does not seem credible that the city's most sensational siren should have been a stranger to Burr. Her name had, on occasion, been mentioned with Hamilton's along with other famous men. Gossip insisted that the two had been acquaintances. Nevertheless, the eccentric and, by many reports, unpleasant woman was chosen to be Burr's second wife.

Whatever Burr's motive—money, the house, disgust with his modest way of life, or simply the human desire to be taken care of in his old age—the match turned out to be a failure. The "Madame of the Heights," as Burr termed her after the deluge, never proved tractable. In every way, she was a startling contrast to Theodosia Prevost.[22]

The ill-matched pair was married by the Reverend David Bogart on July 1, 1833, at the mansion. Burr surprised the lady with the clergyman so that she could not refuse him. However, Madame Burr rallied in time to order a good dinner complete with wine from Monsieur Jumel's cellar.

In the lady's yellow carriage, Colonel and Mrs. Aaron Burr toured Connecticut, visiting with the Edwardses and combining some business with pleasure. Perhaps Eliza looked forward to having the famous attorney care for her property. She had, however, not bargained for his methods.

While at Hartford, Burr convinced his wife to sell her shares in a local bridge and, instead, invest her money in real estate. The sale was quick and the proceeds found their way into his pocket. Without informing his wife, Burr used the money for a favorite scheme: the settlement of a colony of Germans in Texas. Again, his timing was unfortunate. Although the settlement of Texas eventually became a lucrative enterprise, this project proved a disaster because the settlers balked at the last minute, and besides, the title to the property was not clear. Burr hoped to bury the mistake, but he had not reckoned on the shrewd Madame, who demanded an explanation. The coolness that ensued set the pattern for estrangement and reconciliation that marked the rest of their brief relationship. She regarded him, now, as a man of many speculations but without the Midas touch and visualized the gradual dissolution of her fortune. He had his pride to consider and often sulked alone at his city office.

By June, 1834, the marriage had broken up and only the details of the divorce remained to be completed. Burr's remarkable vitality had begun to ebb even before the final separation. Toward the end of 1833, while on lower Broadway, near the old City Hotel, Burr suffered his first stroke. He was driven to his office in Nassau Street and carried away to Fort Washington to be cared for by his remorseful estranged wife. He recovered his restlessness as quickly as his health and, in a few months, was back in the city busying himself with his affairs, legal and otherwise.

New York was titillated by the adventures of the elderly Burrs. William Dunlap reported that when he met Madame Burr on the street in June, 1834, and inquired about her husband's health, she answered, "Oh, I don't see him anymore." She then described the inroads that had been made into her fortune: thirteen thousand dollars, a new carriage, and a pair of horses. Dunlap expressed the view of many New Yorkers when he said, "What confidence can be placed in the words of such a woman it is hard to say, but Burr's marrying her makes anything told of him credible."[23]

Madame Burr filed for a divorce on July 12, 1834. Her lawyer was named Alexander Hamilton. She charged a number of infidelities and specifically named Jane McManus of Jersey City. The divorce was granted in July, with the stipulation that Eliza Burr may lawfully remarry at any time, but that Aaron Burr could not marry again until she was dead.[24] She lived on for many years, getting richer and more disagreeable.

A second stroke in 1835 left Burr paralyzed and completely dependent. An old friend, identified as Mrs. Joshua Webb, who had a boardinghouse on Broadway, near Bowling Green, cared for him, until her house was sold in June of 1836. Some decision had to be made about the dying man. Judge Ogden Edwards wanted his cousin near him, and so it was arranged that he be housed in Port Richmond, Staten Island, at Winant's Hotel.

Burr was carried on a litter to the steamboat, which discharged him at his new quarters near the boatdock. At first, the sea air seemed to revive him, and although Dr. Hosack had predicted in early June that he had but a short time to live, the improvement was marked. It was a temporary final surge of well-being. By summer's end, he was sinking visibly and rapidly.

Burr's last moments have been described by many friends and enemies. Matthew L. Davis reported that when the Colonel was near death in June, he questioned him on the Western scheme and on the accusation that he had planned to sunder the Union. Impatiently, Burr answered his literary executor. "No, I would as soon have thought of taking possession of the moon, and informing my friends that I intended to divide it among them!"[25]

A pathetic little story, perhaps apocryphal, relates that shortly before he died, as he lay propped up on pillows so that he could view the ships at anchor in the water, he said, "Ah, if I could only see her [Theodosia] coming to me over the water there, as they said she walked into it from the ladder." He wept as he spoke.[26]

A Reformed Dutch clergyman, the Reverend Dr. P. J. Van Pelt, attended Burr daily during the last few days of his life. He received the clergyman graciously, listened to his ministrations with interest, and thanked him for his prayers. He did not, however, request, nor was he given, the holy sacrament. The final hours were calm and painless and he was, or seemed to be, in full possession of his faculties. When asked if he expected salvation, his answer, discreet but filled with emotion, was, "On that subject I am coy," meaning, according to his spiritual adviser, that he was cautious and not fully confident. His last audible word was, as he looked at his spectacles as they lay in his attendant's hands, "Madame." Probably he was saying that he meant them for Mrs. Webb. For a few hours more, he breathed softly until, at two in the afternoon, he slipped unresisting and quietly out of life.

In the parlor of Winant's Hotel, Reverend Van Pelt conducted a brief service that was attended by assembled family and friends. Among those present were the Swartwouts, Davis, and a number of Edwards relatives. As was his wish, he was to be buried in Princeton, near his parents.

Burr's body traveled to Amboy aboard a boat, then by rail to Heightstown, where it was met by a funeral cortege that completed the journey to Princeton. Until the interment, he lay in state in the college chapel.

On the afternoon of September 16, at half past three o'clock, the students of Princeton College and Seminary gathered to pay final tribute to the third Vice President of the United States. The Ninetieth Psalm was followed by a prayer delivered by Reverend Van Pelt. Dr. James Carnahan, the president of the college, delivered a funeral address on the text, 1 Cor. VII:31: "And they that use the world, as not abusing it; for the fashion of this world passeth away." After the service, the pallbearers, military men, and friends formed the procession on the green that accompanied Colonel Burr to the churchyard. Military honors were accorded by the Mercer Guards, who played martial music and fired over the grave.

The Cliosophic Society was out in full numbers to pay its respects to one of its earliest members, whose interest in them had been maintained throughout the years. They were directed to "follow his remains to the grave as mourners," and "To wear crape on the left arm for the space of thirty days."[27] Alfred Edwards, a relative, had a modest stone erected at Burr's grave twenty years later. On it was incised a simple epitaph:

Aaron Burr
Born February 6, 1756
Died September 14, 1836
A Colonel in the Army of the Revolution
Vice President of the United States 1801 to 1805

NOTES

Chapter I

1. Rev. Aaron Burr to Rev. Joseph Bellamy, September 26, 1752, Hartford Theological Seminary.
2. Joseph Shippen, Jr., to his father, July 6, 1752, New Jersey Historical Society.
3. *Ibid.*, August 1, 1752.
4. William K. Bixby (ed.), *The Private Journal of Aaron Burr*, Vol. I (Rochester, New York, 1903), p. 465.
5. Charles Burr Todd, *Reverend Aaron Burr* (New York, 1879), p. 66.
6. Matthew L. Davis, *Memoirs of Aaron Burr*, Vol. I (New York, 1847), p. 18.
7. Typescript of manuscript letter no. 154 in Doddridge Correspondence, vol. 4, Library of New College, London, England, in Burr Additional Papers, Princeton University Library.
8. Rev. Aaron Burr to Rev. Joseph Stennett, November 9, 174[?], Simon Gratz Collection, Historical Society of Pennsylvania.
9. Minutes of Trustees of The College of New Jersey, vol. 1, pp. 13–16, Burr Additional Papers, Princeton.
10. Charles F. Pidgin, *Theodosia* (Boston, 1907), pp. 78–79.
11. Varnum L. Collins, *Princeton* (New York, 1914), pp. 39–41.
12. Rev. Aaron Burr to William Hogg, December 3, 1775, Burr Additional Papers, Princeton.
13. Ola E. Winslow, *Jonathan Edwards* (New York, 1961), p. 19.
14. *Ibid.*, p. 25.
15. A Reprint of the Worcester Edition, *The Works of President Edwards*, Vol. I (New York, 1857), p. 632.
16. Dumas Malone (ed.), *Dictionary of American Biography*, Vol. VI (New York, 1935–1958), p. 35.
17. Josephine Fisher, "The Journal of Esther Burr," *The New England Quarterly*, Vol. 3, p. 300.
18. *Ibid.*, p. 299.
19. *Ibid.*, p. 312.
20. *Ibid.*, p. 313.
21. *Ibid.*, p. 303.
22. *Ibid.*, p. 305.
23. Jonathan F. Stearns, *Historical Discourses Relating to the First Presbyterian Church in Newark* (New York, 1853), p. 182.
24. Fisher, "Esther Burr," 314–315.

25. James Parton, *The Life and Times of Aaron Burr*, Vol. I (New York, 1858), p. 47.

26. Esther Burr to Jonathan Edwards, November 2, 1754, A. B. Jennings Collection, Yale.

27. *Works of President Edwards*, Vol. I, pp. 48–50.

28. *Ibid.*, Vol. I, p. 51.

Chapter II

1. Parton, *Burr*, Vol. I, pp. 52–53.

2. *Ibid.*, p. 54.

3. "On Dancing," Duer Collection, Historical Society of Pennsylvania.

4. "On Style," Simon Gratz Collection, Historical Society of Pennsylvania.

5. Jacob Beam, *The American Whig Society* (Princeton, 1933), pp. 46 and 67.

6. Davis, *Memoirs*, Vol. I, p. 28.

7. Lyman Butterfield (ed.), *Letters of Benjamin Rush*, Vol. II (Princeton, 1951), p. 938.

8. Elizabeth De W. Root, "Joseph Bellamy and Theological Education," *Hartford Seminary Foundation Bulletin*, Vol. 24, p. 34.

9. Burr to Mrs. Reeve, January 17, 1774, Park Family Papers, Yale University.

10. *Ibid.*

Chapter III

1. Burr to Ogden, February 26, 1775, Simon Gratz Collection, Historical Society of Pennsylvania.

2. Davis, *Memoirs*, Vol. I, p. 49.

3. William T. Hutchinson and William M. E. Rachal (eds.), *The Papers of James Madison*, Vol. I (Chicago, 1962–   ), p. 158.

4. Peter Force (ed.), *American Archives*, Vol. II (Fourth Series; Washington, 1837–1853), p. 1689.

5. George Washington to Lewis Morris, August 4, 1775, C. P. G. Fuller Collection, Princeton.

6. Burr to Mrs. Reeve, September 18, 1775, Park Family Papers, Yale.

7. *Ibid.*, September 24, 1775.

8. *Ibid.*

9. Arnold to Enos, October 15 and 17, 1775, *Maine Historical Society Collections* (Series One; Portland, Maine, 1831), Vol. II, p. 363; Kenneth Roberts (ed.), *March to Quebec* (Garden City, New York, 1942), pp. 75, 205.

10. Roberts, *March*, pp. 55, 438.

11. Matthias Ogden, "Journal of Matthias Ogden," *New Jersey Historical Society Proceedings* (New Series), Vol. 13, p. 27.

12. *Ibid.*, p. 29.

13. Arnold to Montgomery and Washington, November 20, 1775, *Maine Historical Society Collections*, Vol. I, p. 380.

14. Burr to Timothy Edwards, November 22, 1775, newspaper clipping, New York Public Library.
15. Burr to Mrs. Reeve, February 2, 1776, Henry E. Huntington Library, San Marino, California.
16. Davis, *Memoirs*, Vol. I, pp. 67–69; Parton, *Burr*, Vol. I, pp. 71–72.
17. Arnold to Richard Montgomery, November 30, 1775, *Maine Historical Society Collections*, Vol. I, p. 386.
18. Roberts, *March*, pp. 185, 363, 227; Force, *Archives*, Fourth Series, Vol. IV, p. 248.
19. Isaac Leake, *Memoir of the Life and Times of John Lamb* (Albany, New York, 1850), pp. 125–126.
20. John Codman, *Arnold's Expedition to Quebec* (New York, 1902), pp. 197–198; Davis, *Memoirs*, Vol. I, pp. 69–70.
21. Force, *Archives*, Fourth Series, Vol. IV, p. 296.
22. William Dunlap, *Diary of William Dunlap*, Vol. III (New York, 1929–1931), p. 737.
23. Force, *Archives*, Fourth Series, Vol. IV, p. 479; Roberts, *March*, p. 103.
24. Daniel Morgan, "An Autobiography," *The Historical Magazine of America*, Vol. IX (Second Series; June, 1871), p. 380.
25. Roberts, *March*, p. 103; Force, *Archives*, Fourth Series, Vol. IV, p. 481.
26. Rev. Gardner Spring to Matthew L. Davis, October 23, 1838; Parton, *Burr*, Vol. I, p. 76.
27. Roberts, *March*, p. 387.
28. Everett S. Brown (ed.), *William Plumer's Memorandum of Proceedings in the United States Senate, 1803–1807* (New York, 1923), p. 612.
29. Charles Francis Adams, "Davis's Memoirs and Journal of Burr," *The North American Review* (July, 1839), p. 165.
30. Tapping Reeve to Burr, January 27, 1776, American Antiquarian Society, Worcester, Massachusetts.

Chapter IV

1. Davis, *Memoirs*, Vol. I, p. 78.
2. Christopher Ward, *The War of the Revolution*, Vol. I (New York, 1952), p. 197.
3. Burr to Mrs. Reeve, May 26, 1776, Yale University Library.
4. Force, *Archives*, Fourth Series, Vol. V, p. 967.
5. Douglas Southall Freeman, *George Washington: A Biography*, Vol. IV, (6 vols.; New York, 1948–1954), pp. 635–637.
6. Force, *Archives*, Fourth Series, Vol. V, p. 1043.
7. Burr to Mrs. Reeve, July 1, 1776, Park Family Collection, Yale.
8. Margaret Moncrieffe, *Memoirs of Mrs. Coghlan* (New York, 1795), pp. 42–43.
9. *Ibid.*, p. 48.
10. Matthias Ogden to Burr, July 26, 1776, Dreer Collection, Historical Society of Pennsylvania.
11. Davis, *Memoirs*, Vol. I, p. 94.

12. Samuel L. Knapp, *The Life of Colonel Burr* (New York, 1835), p. 39.
13. Davis, *Memoirs*, Vol. I, p. 98.
14. *Ibid.*, p. 99.
15. Davis, *Memoirs*, Vol. I, pp. 103–106; Benjamin Silliman to Edward de Lancey, January 22, 1876, Museum of the City of New York; Thomas Jones, *History of New York During the Revolutionary War* (New York, 1879), Vol. I, pp. 608–611.
16. Stokes, *Iconography*, Vol. V, p. 1022.
17. Davis, *Memoirs*, Vol. I, pp. 107–108.
18. Knapp, *Burr*, p. 42.
19. Burr to Mrs. Reeve, October 27, 1776, Penniman Collection, Yale.
20. Anonymous to Mr. Bird, February 23, 1863, Litchfield Historical Society, Litchfield, Connecticut.
21. Frederick W. Seward (ed.), *Autobiography of William H. Seward* (3 vols.; New York, 1877–1891), Vol. I, p. 98.
22. Davis, *Memoirs*, Vol. I, p. 109.
23. *Ibid.*, p. 112.
24. Adrian C. Leiby, *The Revolutionary War in the Hackensack Valley* (New Brunswick, New Jersey, 1962), p. 138.
25. Henry Steele Commager and Richard B. Morris (eds.), *The Spirit of 'Seventy-Six*, Vol. I (Indianapolis and New York, 1958), p. 651.
26. George Weedon, *Valley Forge Orderly Book* (New York, 1902), p. 191.
27. John C. Miller, *Triumph of Freedom, 1775–1783* (Boston, 1948), p. 225.
28. Davis, *Memoirs*, Vol. I, pp. 119–120; Knapp, *Burr*, p. 48.
29. Ward, *Revolution*, Vol. II, p. 573.
30. William Malcolm to Burr, June 16, 1778, American Antiquarian Society Library.
31. Ward, *Revolution*, Vol. II, p. 578.
32. William S. Stryker, *The Battle of Monmouth* (Princeton, 1927), p. 211.
33. Davis, *Memoirs*, Vol. I, p. 135.
34. Lord Stirling to Burr, July 6, 1778, American Antiquarian Society Library.
35. Rupert Hughes, *George Washington*, Vol. III (New York, 1926–1930), p. 408.
36. Robert H. Harrison to Burr, August 1, 1778, Morristown National Historical Park.
37. Robert Benson to Burr, August 2, 1775, C. P. G. Fuller Collection, Princeton.
38. Burr to George Clinton, August 19, 1778, New-York Historical Society Library.
39. Davis, *Memoirs*, Vol. I, p. 137.
40. George F. Scheer (ed.), *Private Yankee Doodle* (New York, 1963), p. 138.
41. Davis, *Memoirs*, Vol. I, p. 142.
42. Aaron Burr, "Orderly Book," January 21, 1779, New-York Historical Society Library.
43. *Ibid.*, February 11, 1779.
44. *Ibid.*, February 14, 1779.

45. McDougall to Burr, January 15, 1779, American Antiquarian Society Library.
46. Richard Platt to Burr, January 20, 1779, Simon Gratz Collection, Historical Society of Pennsylvania.
47. Davis, *Memoirs*, Vol. I, p. 151.
48. Charles Burdett, *The Beautiful Spy* (Philadelphia, 1865), pp. 406–407.
49. Burr to Washington, February 25, 1779, Additional Burr Papers, Princeton.
50. Davis, *Memoirs*, Vol. I, p. 168.
51. *Ibid.*
52. Burr to Mrs. Reeve, April 25, 1779, newspaper clipping, New York Public Library; Washington to Theodosia Prevost, May 19, 1779, American Antiquarian Society Library.
53. DS, February 5, 1833, Marietta College Library.

Chapter V

1. Mrs. Theodore Sedgwick to Burr, August 3, 1779, Park Family Collection, Yale.
2. Davis, *Memoirs*, Vol. I, p. 187.
3. *Ibid.*, p. 194.
4. Burr to William Paterson, February 14, 1780, Simon Gratz Collection, Historical Society of Pennsylvania.
5. Peter Colt to Burr, August 12, 1780, Simon Gratz Collection, Historical Society of Pennsylvania.
6. Thaddeus Burr to Burr, August 12, 1780, Burr Miscellaneous Mss, New York Public Library.
7. Willard N. Wallace, *Traitorous Hero: The Life and Fortunes of Benedict Arnold* (New York, 1954), pp. 252–255.
8. Davis, *Memoirs*, Vol. I, pp. 224–225.
9. *Ibid.*, p. 231.
10. Catherine Bartow to Burr, December 30, 1781, Simon Gratz Collection, Historical Society of Pennsylvania.
11. Davis, *Memoirs*, Vol. I, p. 235.
12. Burr to Tapping Reeve, n. d., Park Family Collection, Yale.
13. William Kent, *Memoirs and Letters of James Kent* (Boston, 1898), pp. 31–32.
14. Davis, *Memoirs*, Vol. II, pp. 14–15.
15. C. H. Truax, *History of the Bench and Bar of New York*, Vol. I (New York, 1897), pp. 273–274.
16. William A. Duer, *Reminiscences of an Old Yorker* (New York, 1867), p. 24.

Chapter VI

1. Parton, *Burr*, Vol. I, p. 169.
2. Davis, *Memoirs*, Vol. II, p. 43.
3. James Cheetham, *A View of the Political Conduct of Aaron Burr* (New York, 1802), p. 9.

4. *Journal of the Assembly*, State of New York, Eighth Session, October 12, 1784, p. 3.
5. *Ibid.*, February 15, 1785, p. 39; Charles Tillinghast to Hugh Hughes, February 26, 1785, John Lamb Papers, Box 4, New-York Historical Society.
6. *Journal of the Assembly*, State of New York, February 25, 1785, pp. 53–54.
7. Burr to Richard Oliver, July 29, 1788, New York State Library.
8. Davis, *Memoirs*, Vol. I, p. 286; Parton, *Burr*, Vol. I, p. 172.
9. Mrs. Burr to Burr, n. d., Simon Gratz Collection, Historical Society of Pennsylvania.
10. Theodosia Burr to Burr, July 16, 1791, A. B. Jennings Collection, Yale.
11. Davis, *Memoirs*, Vol. I, p. 253.
12. *Ibid.*, pp. 262 and 266.
13. *Ibid.*, p. 268.
14. *Ibid.*, p. 276.
15. Burr to Frederick Prevost, February 22, 1789, H. E. Huntington Library, San Marino, California.
16. Mrs. Burr to Tapping Reeve, March 20, 1789, A. B. Jennings Collection, Yale.
17. Parton, *Burr*, Vol. I, p. 170.
18. George Dangerfield, *Chancellor Robert R. Livingston of New York, 1746–1813* (New York, 1960), p. 245.
19. Burr to Theodore Sedgwick, January 20, 1791, Massachusetts Historical Society Library; *Journal of the Assembly*, State of New York, January 19, 1791.
20. Harold C. Syrett (ed.), *The Papers of Alexander Hamilton*, Vol. VII (New York, 1961–   ), p. 445.
21. *Ibid.*, pp. 442–443.
22. Burr to [?], April 2, 1793, Burr Miscellaneous Papers, New York Public Library.
23. Burr to Rush, August 20, 1793, A. B. Jennings Collection, Yale.
24. Davis, *Memoirs*, Vol. I, p. 367.
25. Mrs. Burr to the Reeves, n. d., Park Collection, Yale.
26. Burr to Edwards, May 24, 1794, Knollenberg Collection, Yale.

Chapter VII

1. Parton, *Burr*, Vol. I, p. 179.
2. Burr to Sedgwick, February 3, 1791, Sedgwick Papers, Massachusetts Historical Society.
3. Davis, *Memoirs*, Vol. I, p. 306.
4. Dumas Malone, *Jefferson and the Rights of Man* (Boston, 1951), pp. 359–360.
5. *Ibid.*, p. 362.
6. John C. Hamilton, *History of the Republic as Traced in the Writings of Alexander Hamilton*, Vol. IV (New York, 1857–1860), p. 506.
7. Irving Brant, *James Madison: Father of the Constitution, 1787–1800* (Indianapolis and New York, 1950), p. 339.
8. Dangerfield, *Livingston*, p. 255.

9. Burr to Pierpont Edwards, June 10, 1791, Massachusetts Historical Society.
10. Philip M. Marsh, "The Jefferson-Madison Vacation," *Pennsylvania Magazine of History and Biography*, Vol. 71, p. 71.
11. Malone, *Jefferson*, p. 362.
12. Davis, *Memoirs*, Vol. I, p. 303.
13. *Ibid.*, p. 304.
14. *Ibid.*, p. 311.
15. Burr to [?], March 13, 1792, The National Archives, Record Group No. 59.
16. Annals of Congress, Second Congress, First Session, p. 25.
17. *Ibid.*, p. 89.
18. Malone, *Jefferson*, p. 402.
19. Charles R. King (ed.), *The Life and Correspondence of Rufus King*, Vol. I (New York, 1894), p. 421.
20. Samuel F. Bemis, *Jay's Treaty*, rev. ed. (New Haven, 1962), p. 84.
21. Burr to Sedgwick, February 17, 1791, Sedgwick Papers, Massachusetts Historical Society.
22. Aaron Ogden to Nelson Chase, January 20, 1834, Burr Papers, New-York Historical Society.
23. Benjamin D. Silliman to Edward de Lancey, January 22, 1876, Museum of the City of New York; Parton, *Burr*, Vol. I, p. 185.
24. Jefferson to Burr, January 20, 1793, American Antiquarian Society.
25. John C. Hamilton (ed.), *The Works of Alexander Hamilton*, Vol. V (New York, 1850–1851), p. 494.
26. New York *Journal and Patriotic Register*, February 22, 1792.
27. Worthington C. Ford (ed.), *Correspondence and Journals of Samuel Blachley Webb*, Vol. III (New York, 1893–1894), p. 175.
28. Hamilton, *Works*, Vol. V, p. 495.
29. Hamilton, *History*, Vol. V, pp. 24–25.
30. *Ibid.*, p. 25.
31. Jabez D. Hammond, *The History of Political Parties in the State of New York*, Vol. I (Buffalo, 1850), p. 56.
32. New York *Journal and Patriotic Register*, February 15 and 18, 1792.
33. *Ibid.*, March 7, 1792.
34. Peter Van Gaasbeek to Burr, March 28, 1792, Van Gaasbeek Papers, folder 2974, Old Senate House Museum, Kingston.
35. Hammond, *Political Parties*, Vol. I, p. 63.
36. *Ibid.*, pp. 64–66.
37. Parton, *Burr*, Vol. I, p. 189.
38. Davis, *Memoirs*, Vol. I, pp. 336–337.
39. *Ibid.*, p. 338.
40. Hamilton, *History*, Vol. V, p. 515.
41. Sedgwick to Strong, August 27, 1792, Bellamy Papers, Hartford Theological Seminary.
42. Burr to Tapping Reeve, n.d., Penniman Collection, Yale.
43. Davis, *Memoirs*, Vol. I, p. 357.
44. E. Wilder Spaulding, *His Excellency George Clinton* (New York, 1938), p. 203.

45. Davis, *Memoirs*, Vol. I, pp. 339–341.
46. Hoffman to Peter Van Schaack, June 26, 1792, Nicholas Low Mss, New-York Historical Society Library.
47. Frank Monaghan, *John Jay* (Indianapolis and New York, 1935), p. 336.
48. Davis, *Memoirs*, Vol. I, p. 355.
49. Monaghan, *Jay*, p. 335.
50. James A. Frost, *Life on the Upper Susquehanna, 1783–1860* (New York, 1951), p. 44.
51. Sedgwick to Burr, September 9, 1791, Simon Gratz Collection, Historical Society of Pennsylvania.
52. Beckley to Madison, September 2, 1792, Madison Papers, New York Public Library.
53. Rush to Burr, September 24, 1792, American Antiquarian Society.
54. Hamilton, *Works*, Vol. V, p. 526.
55. *Ibid.*
56. *Ibid.*, p. 527.
57. *Ibid.*, p. 529.
58. Spaulding, *Clinton*, p. 206.
59. Nathan Schachner, *Aaron Burr* (New York, 1937), p. 114.
60. Noble E. Cunningham, Jr., *The Jeffersonian Republicans* (Chapel Hill, North Carolina, 1957), p. 46.
61. *Ibid.*
62. Burr to Nicholson, October 7, 1792, Burr Papers, New York Public Library.
63. George Gibbs, *Memoirs of the Administrations of Washington and John Adams*, Vol. I (New York, 1846), p. 80.
64. Hamilton, *Works*, Vol. V, p. 532.
65. William P. Cresson, *James Monroe* (Chapel Hill, North Carolina, 1946), p. 117.
66. Cunningham, *Jeffersonian Republicans*, p. 48.
67. Beckley to Madison, October 17, 1792, Madison Papers, New York Public Library.
68. Schachner, *Burr*, pp. 119–120.
69. Beckley to Madison, October 17, 1792, Madison Papers, New York Public Library.
70. Davis, *Memoirs*, Vol. I, p. 358.
71. Gibbs, *Memoirs*, Vol. I, pp. 379–380.

Chapter VIII

1. Luss Ms, Burr Additional Papers, Princeton.
2. Rebecca Blodgett to Burr, August 18, 1814, Burr Papers, New-York Historical Society.
3. *Ibid.*, June 2, 1817.
4. *Ibid.*, November 18, 1816.
5. *Ibid.*, December 28, 1823.
6. Power of Attorney, Marietta College Library, Marietta, Ohio.
7. Burr to Edwards, May 24, 1794, Burr Folder, Secretary's Office, Princeton University.

8. Davis, *Memoirs*, Vol. I, p. 362.
9. *Ibid.*, pp. 361–362.
10. Burr to Theodosia Burr, March 21, 1794, A. B. Jennings Collection, Yale.
11. *Ibid.*, January 16, 1793.
12. Davis, *Memoirs*, Vol. I, p. 365.
13. Burr to Theodosia Burr, December 19, 1793, A. B. Jennings Collection, Yale.
14. Davis, *Memoirs*, Vol. I, p. 401.
15. *Ibid.*, p. 293.
16. *Ibid.*, pp. 293–294.
17. *Ibid.*, p. 300.
18. *Ibid.*, pp. 317–318.
19. *Ibid.*, p. 314.
20. Dorothy Valentine Smith, "An Intercourse of the Heart," *New-York Historical Society Quarterly*, Vol. 37, p. 42.
21. Burr to Mrs. Payne, May 8, 1795, Burr Papers, Princeton.
22. Brant, *Madison*, p. 406.
23. Stokes, *Iconography*, Vol. V, p. 1324.
24. Davis, *Memoirs*, Vol. I, p. 390.
25. *Ibid.*, p. 392.
26. Richard Bayley, *An Account of the Epidemic Fever Which Prevailed in the City of New York During Part of the Summer and Fall of 1795* (New York, 1796), p. 58.
27. Theodosia Burr to John Bartow Prevost, November 13, 1795, New-York Historical Society Library.

Chapter IX

1. Stokes, *Iconography*, Vol. V, p. 1217.
2. *Ibid.*
3. Tammany Membership List, Tammania of Edwin P. Kilroe, Columbia University.
4. Edwin P. Kilroe, *St. Tammany and the Origin of the Society of the Tammany* (New York, 1913), p. 140.
5. *Ibid.*, p. 194.
6. *Ibid.*, p. 193.
7. Eugene P. Link, *Democratic-Republican Societies, 1790–1800* (New York, 1942), pp. 13–14.
8. *Ibid.*, p. 12.
9. Cf. Harry Ammon, "The Genêt Mission and the Development of American Political Parties," *The Journal of American History*, Vol. 52, pp. 725–741.
10. *Annals of Congress*, Third Congress, First Session, pp. 32 and 38.
11. Henry Adams, *Life of Albert Gallatin* (New York, 1943), p. 121.
12. Raymond Walters, Jr., *Albert Gallatin* (New York, 1957), p. 61.
13. Davis, *Memoirs*, Vol. I, p. 407.
14. Walters, *Gallatin*, p. 61.
15. Bemis, *Jay's Treaty*, p. 4.

16. Nathan Schachner, *Alexander Hamilton* (New York, 1946), p. 330.
17. Davis, *Memoirs*, Vol. I, pp. 407–408.
18. Stanislaus M. Hamilton, *Writings of James Monroe*, Vol. I (New York, 1898–1903), p. 295.
19. *Ibid.*, p. 296.
20. *Ibid.*, pp. 299–300.
21. De Alva Stanwood Alexander, *A Political History of the State of New York*, Vol. I (New York, 1906), p. 65.
22. King, *Rufus King*, Vol. I, p. 581.
23. *Ibid.*, p. 584.
24. Van Gaasbeek to Ebenezer Foote, January 26, 1795, A. B. Jennings Collection, Yale.
25. Cheetham, *Political Conduct*, p. 21.
26. Samuel A. Barker to Foote, February 9, 1795, A. B. Jennings Collection, Yale.
27. *Ibid.*, February 22, 1795.
28. King, *Rufus King*, Vol. 2, p. 7.
29. Broadus Mitchell, *Alexander Hamilton: The National Adventure, 1788–1804* (New York, 1962), p. 342.
30. Bemis, *Jay's Treaty*, p. 400.
31. *Ibid.*, p. 273.
32. *Ibid.*, p. 274.
33. *Annals of Congress*, Third Congress, Tenth Session, p. 858.
34. Adams, *Gallatin*, p. 151.
35. Hamilton, *Works*, Vol. VI, p. 6.
36. *Annals of Congress*, Third Congress, Tenth Session, pp. 860–861.
37. Dumas Malone, *Jefferson and the Ordeal of Liberty* (Boston, 1962), p. 277.
38. Cunningham, *Jeffersonian Republicans*, p. 87.
39. *Ibid.*
40. Manning J. Dauer, *The Adams Federalists* (Boston, 1953), p. 95.
41. *Ibid.*, pp. 101–102; Page Smith, *John Adams*, Vol. II (New York, 1962), p. 902.
42. Dayton to Sedgwick, November 12, 1796, Hamilton Papers, Library of Congress.
43. *Ibid.*, November 13, 1796.
44. Sedgwick to Dayton, November 19, 1796, Hamilton Papers, Library of Congress.
45. *Ibid.*
46. Beckley to Madison, October 15, 1796, Madison Papers, New York Public Library.
47. Smith, *Adams*, Vol. II, p. 901.
48. Burr to Edwards, November 22, 1796, Burr Papers, New York Public Library.
49. Smith to Izard, May 18, 1796, *American Historical Review*, Vol. 14, p. 780.
50. *Ibid.*, November 8, 1796, p. 785.
51. Beckley to Madison, June 20, 1796, Madison Papers, New York Public Library.

52. Lyman H. Butterfield (ed.), *Diary and Autobiography of John Adams*, Vol. III (Cambridge, Massachusetts, 1961), p. 229.
53. Gibbs, *Memoirs*, Vol. I, p. 387.
54. Hamilton, *Works*, Vol. VI, p. 188.
55. Stephen G. Kurtz, *The Presidency of John Adams* (New York, 1961), p. 128.

Chapter X

1. Hammond, *Political Parties*, Vol. I, pp. 60–61.
2. Green to Burr, August 21, 1794, C. P. G. Fuller Collection, Princeton.
3. Liston to Grenville, November 1, 1797, Adams Transcripts, British State Papers, Library of Congress.
4. H. C. Allen, *Great Britain and the United States* (London, 1954), p. 302.
5. W. L. Morton, *The Kingdom of Canada* (Toronto, 1963), p. 191; William Kingsford, *The History of Canada*, Vol. IX (Toronto, 1894), pp. 441–442.
6. Samuel F. Bemis, "Relations Between the Vermont Separatists and Great Britain, 1789–1791," *American Historical Review*, Vol. 21, pp. 547–560.
7. Morton, *Canada*, pp. 195–196.
8. Kingsford, *Canada*, Vol. VII, p. 453.
9. Lamb Papers, Box 6, New-York Historical Society.
10. Burr to Witbeck, September 5, 1796, C. P. G. Fuller Collection, Princeton.
11. William L. Stone, *Life of Joseph Brant*, Vol. II (Albany, New York, 1864), p. 398.
12. Burr to de la Roche, February 28, 1797, A. B. Jennings Collection, Yale.
13. Stone, *Brant*, Vol. II, p. 456.
14. *Ibid.*, p. 458.
15. *Ibid.*, p. 455.
16. *Ibid.*
17. Burr to Lamb, April 19, 1797, Lamb Papers, Box 6, New-York Historical Society.
18. Burr to Eustis, April 21, 1797, Massachusetts Historical Society.
19. Burr to Phelps, December 16, 1796, Phelps-Gorham Papers, New York State Library.
20. *Ibid.*, December 23, 1796.
21. *Ibid.*, December 29, 1796 and January 5, 1797.
22. John B. Prevost to Burr, May 11, 1797, *The Vineland Historical Magazine*, Vol. 19, p. 119.
23. *Annals of Congress*, Tenth Session, pp. 860–861.
24. Hamilton, *Works*, Vol. VI, p. 521.
25. Hamilton to Rutledge, January 4, 1801, Edward Carey Gardiner Collection, Historical Society of Pennsylvania.
26. Paul D. Evans, *The Holland Land Company* (Buffalo, 1924), pp. 6–7.
27. Schachner, *Aaron Burr*, p. 155.
28. *Ibid.*, p. 156.

29. Leake, *Lamb*, pp. 353–355.
30. Lamb to Burr, March 29, 1797, Lamb Papers, Box 6, New-York Historical Society.
31. Burr to Pierpont Edwards, April 19, 1797, Knollenberg Collection, Yale; Burr to Lamb, April 19, 1797, Lamb Papers, Box 6, New-York Historical Society.
32. Burr to Lamb, June 7, 1797, Burr Papers, New York Public Library.
33. Indenture of Sale, June 17, 1797, American Antiquarian Society; Burr to Pierpont Edwards, May 5, 1798, Pierpont Morgan Library.
34. *Greenleaf's Journal & Patriotic Register*, April 26, 1797; *The Time-Piece and Literary Companion*, May 5 and 8, 1797.
35. Burr to Green, December 4, 1797, C. P. G. Fuller Collection, Princeton.
36. Evans, *Holland Company*, p. 209.
37. *Ibid.*, p. 212.
38. Burr to Lamb, January 12, 1798, Lamb Papers, Box 6, New-York Historical Society.
39. *Journal of the Assembly*, State of New York, February 7, 1798, p. 112.
40. *Ibid.*, February 20, 1798, p. 145.
41. Evans, *Holland Company*, p. 210.
42. Burr to Phelps, April 4, 1798, Phelps-Gorham Papers, New York State Library; *Laws of the State of New York*, Twenty-first Session, Chapter 72.
43. Davis, *Memoirs*, Vol. I, p. 419.
44. Schachner, *Aaron Burr*, p. 158.
45. Burr to Monroe, August 13, 1797, Henry E. Huntington Library, San Marino, California.
46. Monroe to Burr, December 1, 1797, Morristown National Historical Park.
47. Schachner, *Aaron Burr*, p. 158.
48. Hamilton to John Rutledge, January 4, 1801, Edward Carey Gardiner Collection, Historical Society of Pennsylvania.
49. *Ibid.*

Chapter XI

1. Tammania Membership List, Kilroe Collection, Columbia University.
2. Peter Paulson, "The Tammany Society and the Jeffersonian Movement in New York City," *New York History*, Vol. 34, p. 79.
3. H. A. Washington (ed.), *Works of Jefferson*, Vol. IX (New York, 1853–1854), p. 207.
4. Jefferson to Burr, June 17, 1797, Jefferson Papers, Library of Congress.
5. Burr to Jefferson, June 21, 1797, Jefferson Papers, Library of Congress.
6. Burr to Eustis, June 12, 1797, Massachusetts Historical Society.
7. Albert J. Beveridge, *The Life of John Marshall*, Vol. II (Boston and New York, 1916), p. 336.
8. *Journal of the Assembly*, State of New York, March 19, 1798, p. 246.
9. *Ibid.*, p. 312.
10. Paul L. Ford (ed.), *The Journals of Hugh Gaine, Printer*, Vol. II (New York, 1902), p. 194.

11. Theodosia Burr to Prevost, January 13, 1799, Burr Papers, New-York Historical Society.
12. *Ibid.*
13. *Greenleaf's Journal & Patriotic Register*, May 5, 1798.
14. Don C. Sowers, *The Financial History of New York State* (New York, 1914), pp. 114–115.
15. Cheetham, *Political Conduct*, p. 29.
16. Gibbs, *Memoirs*, Vol. II, p. 71.
17. Hamilton to Jay, February 12, 1799, C. P. G. Fuller Collection, Princeton.
18. Burr to Stevens, August 8, 1798, Stevens Papers, New-York Historical Society.
19. *Journal of the Assembly*, State of New York, August 10, 1798, p. 9.
20. *Ibid.*, p. 13.
21. *Ibid.*, p. 15.
22. *Ibid.*, p. 18.
23. *Ibid.*, p. 22.
24. Burr to Stevens, August 17, 1798, Stevens Papers, New-York Historical Society.
25. Edward A. Wyatt, IV, "John Daly Burk, Patriot, Playwright, Historian," *Southern Sketches*, 1st Series, No. 7 (Charlottesville, Virginia, 1936), p. 10.
26. James Morton Smith, *Freedom's Fetters* (Ithaca, New York, 1956), p. 210.
27. Joseph I. Shulim, *John Daly Burk* (Philadelphia, 1964), p. 30.
28. King, *Rufus King*, Vol. II, pp. 364 and 432.
29. Smith, *Freedom's Fetters*, p. 213.
30. Paul L. Ford (ed.), *The Writings of Thomas Jefferson*, Vol. VII (New York, 1892–1899), p. 310.
31. Henry Cabot Lodge (ed.), *The Works of Alexander Hamilton*, Vol. X (New York, 1904), p. 330.
32. New York *Commercial Advertiser*, January 31, 1799.
33. *Ibid.*, April 29, 1799.
34. John C. Miller, *Crisis in Freedom* (Boston, 1951), p. 179.
35. *Journal of the Assembly*, State of New York, February 16, 1799, pp. 120–123.
36. Ford, *Gaine*, Vol. II, p. 203.
37. Joseph A. Scoville, *The Old Merchants of New York City*, Vol. II (New York, 1885), p. 69.
38. *Minutes of the Common Council of the City of New York, 1793–1801* (New York, 1917), p. 464; Stokes, *Iconography*, Vol. V, p. 1356.
39. John Duffy, "An Account of the Epidemic Fevers That Prevailed in the City of New York from 1791 to 1822," *New-York Historical Society Quarterly*, Vol. 50, p. 348.
40. New York *Time Piece*, May 17, 1797.
41. Duffy, "Epidemic Fevers," p. 334.
42. King, *Rufus King*, Vol. II, p. 428.
43. *Ibid.*, p. 429.
44. New York *Commercial Advertiser*, September 5, 1798.

45. Nelson M. Blake, *Water for the Cities* (Syracuse, New York, 1956), p. 47; Beatrice Reubens, "Burr, Hamilton and the Manhattan Company," *Political Science Quarterly*, Vol. 72, p. 583.
46. Reubens, "Manhattan Company," Vol. 72, p. 584.
47. Blake, *Water*, p. 47.
48. *Minutes of the Common Council*, pp. 497–498.
49. Reubens, "Manhattan Company," Vol. 72, p. 584; *Minutes of the Common Council*, p. 515; New York *Commerical Advertiser*, February 11, 1799.
50. Reubens, "Manhattan Company," Vol. 72, p. 585.
51. *Minutes of the Common Council*, Vol. II, p. 514.
52. Reubens, "Manhattan Company," Vol. 72, p. 592.
53. *Ibid.*, pp. 593–594.
54. *Ibid.*, pp. 596–597.
55. *Ibid.*, p. 598.
56. Blake, *Water*, p. 51.
57. New York *Commercial Advertiser*, April 29, 1799.
58. King, *Rufus King*, Vol. II, pp. 597–598.
59. Stokes, *Iconography*, Vol. V, p. 1370.
60. New York *Commercial Advertiser*, May 22, 1799.
61. King to Troup, May 29, 1799, King Papers, New-York Historical Society.
62. Browne to Burr, July 7, 1799, Simon Gratz Collection, Historical Society of Pennsylvania.
63. Troup to King, December 12, 1799, King Papers, New York Public Library.
64. Stokes, *Iconography*, Vol. V, p. 1367.

Chapter XII

1. Ford, *Writings of Jefferson*, Vol. VII, p. 402.
2. *Ibid.*
3. Adams, *Gallatin*, p. 239.
4. New York *Commercial Advertiser*, February 15, 1799.
5. Smith, *Freedom's Fetters*, p. 394.
6. Alexander, *Political History*, Vol. I, p. 89.
7. *Ibid.*
8. Hammond, *Political Parties*, Vol. I, p. 134.
9. King, *Rufus King*, Vol. III, p. 171.
10. Ford, *Jefferson's Writings*, Vol. VII, p. 433.
11. Adams, *Gallatin*, p. 233.
12. *Ibid.*
13. Schachner, *Aaron Burr*, p. 170.
14. Adams, *Gallatin*, p. 236.
15. New York *American-Citizen*, April 29, 1801; Edwin P. Kilroe, "Tammania," Columbia University.
16. New York *American-Citizen*, April 28, 1800.
17. Davis, *Memoirs*, Vol. II, p. 56.
18. Mordecai Myers, *Reminiscences, 1780–1814* (Washington, 1900), p. 11.
19. Davis, *Memoirs*, Vol. II, p. 58.

20. *Ibid.*
21. Schachner, *Aaron Burr*, p. 172.
22. Myers, *Reminiscences*, p. 11.
23. Adams, *Gallatin*, p. 234.
24. Myers, *Reminiscences*, p. 12.
25. Davis, *Memoirs*, Vol. II, pp. 16–17.
26. Reubens, "Manhattan Company," Vol. 73, p. 122.
27. Adams, *Gallatin*, p. 233.
28. New York *Daily Advertiser*, April 28, 1800.
29. New York *American-Citizen*, May 1, 1800.
30. Dawson to Monroe, May 4, 1800, Monroe Papers, New York Public Library.
31. Albany *Register*, May 30, 1800.
32. Burr to Jefferson (received May 5, 1800), Henry E. Huntington Library, San Marino, California.
33. Davis to Gallatin, May 5, 1800, Gallatin Papers, New-York Historical Society.
34. Lodge, *Works*, Vol. X, p. 371.
35. Schachner, *Aaron Burr*, p. 178.
36. Adams, *Gallatin*, pp. 239–240.
37. *Ibid.*, pp. 241 and 243.
38. Clinton to De Witt Clinton, December 13, 1803, and Statement by James Nicholson, December 26, 1803, Clinton Papers, Columbia University.
39. *Ibid.*
40. Clinton to De Witt Clinton, December 13, 1803, Clinton Papers, Columbia University.
41. Adams, *Gallatin*, p. 243.
42. Burr to Eustis, August 10, 1800, Massachusetts Historical Society.
43. Lodge, *Works of Hamilton*, Vol. X, p. 387.
44. Hamilton, *Works of Hamilton*, Vol. VI, p. 454.
45. *Ibid.*, p. 445.
46. Burr to Robert R. Livingston, September 7, 1800, Livingston Papers, New-York Historical Society.
47. *Ibid.*, September 24, 1800.
48. Burr to Taylor, October 23, 1800, Massachusetts Historical Society; Burr to Edwards, November 18, 1800, A. B. Jennings Collection, Yale.
49. Hamilton, *Works of Hamilton*, Vol. VI, p. 453.
50. Gelston to Madison, October 9, 1800, A. B. Jennings Collection, Yale.
51. Burr to Madison, October 9, 1800, A. B. Jennings Collection, Yale.
52. Irving Brant, *James Madison: Secretary of State, 1800–1809* (Indianapolis and New York, 1953), p. 24.
53. Hammond, *Political Parties*, Vol. I, p. 148; King, *Rufus King*, Vol. III, p. 331.
54. Brant, *Madison: Secretary of State*, p. 24.
55. Jefferson to Madison, November 9, 1800, Presidential Papers, Library of Congress.
56. Gelston to Madison, November 21, 1800, Presidential Papers, Library of Congress.

57. *Ibid.*

58. Madison to Jefferson, January 14, 1824, Presidential Papers, Library of Congress.

59. Burr to Jefferson, December 23, 1800, Jefferson Papers, Library of Congress.

60. Burr to Edwards, November 18, 1800, A. B. Jennings Collection, Yale.

61. Burr to Edwards, November 29 and December 1, 1800, Burr Papers, New York Public Library.

62. Freneau to Jefferson, December 2, 1800, Jefferson Papers, Library of Congress.

63. Alston to Theodosia Burr, December 26, 1800, American Antiquarian Society.

64. Jefferson to Burr, December 15, 1800, Jefferson Papers, Library of Congress.

65. Burr to Smith, December 16, 1800, Henry E. Huntington Library, San Marino, California.

66. Burr to Smith, December 17, 1800, Smith Papers, University of Virginia.

67. Ford, *Jefferson's Writings*, Vol. VII, p. 470.

68. Hamilton, *Works of Hamilton*, Vol. VI, p. 499.

69. Gibbs, *Memoirs*, Vol. II, pp. 458–460.

70. Dawson to Madison, December 18, 1800, Presidential Papers, Library of Congress.

71. Ford, *Jefferson's Writings*, Vol. VII, p. 470.

72. Hamilton, *Works of Hamilton*, Vol. VI, pp. 493–494.

73. New York *American-Citizen*, January 10, 1801.

74. Samuel Eliot Morison, *The Life and Letters of Harrison Gray Otis, Federalist, 1765–1848*, Vol. I (Boston, 1913), p. 212.

75. Morton Borden, "James A. Bayard," Unpublished Columbia University Ph.D. Dissertation, 1953.

76. King, *Rufus King*, Vol. III, p. 358.

77. Hamilton, *Works of Hamilton*, Vol. VI, p. 514.

78. Burr to Jefferson, December 23, 1800, Jefferson Papers, Library of Congress.

79. Borden, "Bayard," p. 148.

80. Schachner, *Aaron Burr*, p. 197.

81. John S. Pancake, "Aaron Burr: Would-Be Usurper," *William and Mary Quarterly*, Vol. VIII (April, 1951), p. 210.

82. Davis, *Memoirs*, Vol. II, p. 113.

83. Burr to Smith, December 29, 1800, Henry E. Huntington Library, San Marino, California.

84. Borden, "Bayard," p. 158.

85. King, *Rufus King*, Vol. III, p. 366.

86. Albert A. Lipscomb and A. E. Bergh (eds.), *The Writings of Thomas Jefferson*, Vol. I (Washington, 1903), pp. 442–443.

87. Adams, *Gallatin*, p. 256.

88. New York *Gazette and General Advertiser*, January 20 and February 21, 1801.

89. Ford, *Jefferson's Writings*, Vol. IX, p. 485.

90. Livingston to Davis, February 5, 1801, American Antiquarian Society.
91. AD, Journal of Benjamin Betterton Howell, New-York Historical Society.
92. *Ibid.*
93. Burr to Gallatin, February 12, 1801, Gallatin Papers, New-York Historical Society.
94. Burr to Livingston, February 16, 1801, Burr Papers, New York State Library.
95. Burr to Jefferson, February 12, 1801, Jefferson Papers, Library of Congress.
96. Adams, *Gallatin*, pp. 261–262.
97. New York *American-Citizen*, February 16 and 18, 1801.
98. Beckley to Gallatin, February 15, 1801, Gallatin Papers, New-York Historical Society.
99. Morton Borden, *The Federalism of James A. Bayard* (New York, 1955), p. 91.
100. *Ibid.*, p. 93.
101. Schachner, *Aaron Burr*, p. 207.
102. Plumer to Henry Dearborn, June 1, 1801, Plumer Papers, Library of Congress.

Chapter XIII

1. Constance McLaughlin Green, *Washington: Village and Capital, 1800–1878* (Princeton, New Jersey, 1962), p. 3.
2. Burr to Gallatin, February 25, 1801, Gallatin Papers, New-York Historical Society.
3. Green, *Washington*, p. 23.
4. Henry Adams, *History of the United States*, Vol. I (New York, 1962), p. 186.
5. Davis, *Memoirs*, Vol. II, pp. 162–163.
6. *American Historical Review*, Vol. III, p. 290.
7. Burr to Smith, May 19, 1801, Henry E. Huntington Library, San Marino, California.
8. Davis, *Memoirs*, Vol. II, p. 148.
9. Burr to Eustis, April 25 and 28, 1801, Massachusetts Historical Society.
10. Davis, *Memoirs*, Vol. II, p. 150.
11. Burr to Smith, April 4, 1801, Henry E. Huntington Library, San Marino, California.
12. *Ibid.*, April 11, 1801.
13. Burr to Livingston, April 20, 1801, Livingston Papers, New-York Historical Society.
14. Burr to Gallatin, April 21, 1801, Gallatin Papers, New-York Historical Society.
15. Davis, *Memoirs*, Vol. II, p. 149.
16. Burr to Eustis, May 13, 1801, Massachusetts Historical Society.
17. Noble E. Cunningham, Jr., *The Jeffersonian Republicans in Power* (Chapel Hill, North Carolina, 1963), p. 39.
18. Burr to Eustis, April 28, 1801, Massachusetts Historical Society.

19. *Ibid.*, May 13, 1801.
20. Ford, *Jefferson's Writings*, Vol. VIII, p. 53.
21. Howard Lee McBain, *De Witt Clinton and the Origin of the Spoils System in New York* (New York, 1907), p. 129.
22. Burr to Gallatin, June 28, 1801, Gallatin Papers, New-York Historical Society.
23. Davis, *Memoirs*, Vol. II, p. 155.
24. McBain, *De Witt Clinton*, pp. 132–133.
25. Cf. Schachner, *Aaron Burr*, p. 217.
26. Clinton to Madison, September 3, 1801, Gallatin Papers, New-York Historical Society.
27. Adams, *Gallatin*, p. 286.
28. Jefferson to Gallatin, September 18, 1801, Gallatin Papers, New-York Historical Society.
29. Alvin Kass, *Politics in New York State, 1800–1830* (Syracuse, New York, 1965), p. 14.
30. Davis, *Memoirs*, Vol. II, p. 156.
31. *Ibid.*, p. 160.
32. William P. Cutler and J. P. Cutler (eds.), *Life, Journals, Correspondence of Reverend Manasseh Cutler*, Vol. II (Cincinnati, 1888), p. 48.
33. Kathryn Turner, "Federalist Policy and the Judiciary Act of 1801," *William and Mary Quarterly*, Third Series, Vol. XXII (January, 1965), pp. 3–32.
34. *Annals of Congress*, Seventh Congress, First Session, pp. 147 and 150.
35. Burr to Bidwell, February 1, 1802, Harvard University Library.
36. Davis, *Memoirs*, Vol. II, p. 171.
37. Alexander J. Dallas to Burr, February 3, 1802, American Antiquarian Society.
38. Anne Cary Morris (ed.), *The Diary and Letters of Gouverneur Morris*, Vol. II (New York, 1888), pp. 426–427.
39. Cheetham to Jefferson, December 10, 1801, *Massachusetts Historical Society Proceedings*, Third Series, Vol. 61 (April, 1907), pp. 49–51.
40. John Wood, *The Suppressed History of the Administration of John Adams* (Philadelphia, 1846), pp. 26–27.
41. Davis, *Memoirs*, Vol. II, p. 183.
42. James Cheetham, *A Narrative of the Suppression by Col. Burr of the History of the Administration of John Adams* (New York, 1802), p. 21.
43. Davis, *Memoirs*, Vol. II, p. 167.
44. Cheetham, *A Narrative*, p. 34.
45. Schachner, *Aaron Burr*, p. 227.
46. J. P. Van Ness to W. P. Van Ness, April 2, 1802, Van Ness Papers, New York Public Library.
47. New York *American-Citizen*, April 28, 1802.
48. *Ibid.*, May 24, 1802.
49. J. P. Van Ness to W. P. Van Ness, April 2, 1802, Van Ness Papers, New York Public Library.
50. King, *Rufus King*, Vol. IV, p. 103.

51. Davis, *Memoirs*, Vol. II, p. 178.

52. *Ibid.*, p. 184.

53. Theodosia B. Alston to Frances Prevost, March 24, 1802, Burr Papers, New-York Historical Society.

54. Davis, *Memoirs*, Vol. II, p. 196.

55. Joseph Alston to T. B. Alston, August 22, 1802, Simon Gratz Collection, Historical Society of Pennsylvania.

56. Dr. Theodore B. Russell to C. P. G. Fuller, February 20, 1952, C. P. G. Fuller Collection, Princeton.

57. King, *Rufus King*, Vol. IV, p. 121.

58. New York *American-Citizen*, May 26, 1802.

59. New York *Evening Post*, May 27, 1802.

60. King, *Rufus King*, Vol. IV, pp. 135–136.

61. Cheetham, *A Narrative*, pp. 9–10.

62. Cheetham, *Political Conduct*, p. 102.

63. Alexander, *Political History*, Vol. I, p. 127.

64. Dorothea Bobbé, *De Witt Clinton* (Port Washington, New York, 1962), p. 92.

65. Davis, *Memoirs*, Vol. II, p. 209.

66. Alston to Theodosia B. Alston, July 26, 1802, Simon Gratz Collection, Historical Society of Pennsylvania.

67. *Ibid.*

68. *Ibid.*, August 13, 1802.

69. *Ibid.*, August 22, 1802.

70. Davis, *Memoirs*, Vol. II, p. 213.

71. Cunningham, *Republicans in Power*, p. 207.

72. King, *Rufus King*, Vol. IV, p. 160.

73. New York *American-Citizen*, September 30, 1802.

74. *Ibid.*, October 9, 11, 12, and 14, 1802.

75. Cheetham, *Political Conduct*, p. 45.

76. New York *Morning Chronicle*, October 1, 1802.

77. *Ibid.*, October 14, 1802.

78. Hammond, *Political Parties*, Vol. I, p. 190.

79. New York *American-Citizen*, October 14, 1802.

80. New York *Chronicle-Express*, May 2, 1803.

81. Davis, *Memoirs*, Vol. II, p. 90.

82. New York *Chronicle-Express*, November 25, 1802.

83. *Ibid.*, December 2, 1802.

84. Burr to Bloomfield, September 21, 1802, Massachusetts Historical Society.

85. William Peter Van Ness, *An Examination of the Various Charges Exhibited Against Aaron Burr . . . by Aristides* (Philadelphia, 1803), pp. 22, 25, 34, and 40.

86. Borden, *Bayard*, pp. 92–95.

87. Van Ness, *An Examination*, p. 34.

88. Schachner, *Aaron Burr*, pp. 233–234; Borden, *Bayard*, p. 85.

89. King, *Rufus King*, Vol. IV, pp. 160–161.

90. Cunningham, *Republicans in Power*, p. 207.

91. Reubens, "Manhattan Company," Vol. 73, p. 119.
92. Swartwout to W. P. Van Ness, February 9, 1803, Van Ness Papers, New York Public Library.
93. George Clinton to De Witt Clinton, February 16, 1803, De Witt Clinton Papers, Columbia University.
94. Swartwout to Van Ness, February 23, 1803, Van Ness Papers, New York Public Library.
95. George Clinton to De Witt Clinton, February 16, 1803, De Witt Clinton Papers, Columbia University.
96. Davis, *Memoirs*, Vol. II, pp. 245–246.

Chapter XIV

1. Joseph Crowinshield to Barnabas Bidwell, February 26, 1804, Simon Gratz Collection, Massachusetts Historical Society.
2. New York *Evening Post*, March 2, 1804.
3. Lipscomb and Bergh, *Jefferson's Writings*, Vol. I, pp. 443–448.
4. New York *Morning Chronicle*, February 21 and 23, 1804.
5. Davis, *Memoirs*, Vol. II, p. 277.
6. Hammond, *Political Parties*, Vol. I, p. 208.
7. *Ibid.*, p. 241.
8. Hamilton, *Writings of Hamilton*, Vol. VI, p. 560.
9. William Kettaltas to Burr, February 27, 1804, Phelps-Gorham Papers, New York State Library.
10. Broadside, New York Public Library.
11. New York *American-Citizen*, April 7, 1804.
12. "Poor Behrens!" Broadside, New York Public Library.
13. "Behrens Lie Detected," Handbill, April, 1804, New York Public Library.
14. New York *American-Citizen*, April 7, 1804.
15. Broadside, 1804, New York Public Library.
16. Campaign poster, Burr-Lewis, 1804, New York Public Library.
17. New York *American-Citizen*, March 30, 1804.
18. "Plain Truth," Broadside, New York Public Library.
19. "Answer to Plain Truth," Broadside, New York Public Library.
20. *The Corrector*, March 31, 1804.
21. Oliver Phelps to Jefferson, April 10, 1804, Phelps-Gorham Papers, New York State Library.
22. King, *Rufus King*, Vol. IV, p. 357.
23. Cunningham, *Republicans in Power*, p. 211; Broadside, New York Public Library.
24. New York *American-Citizen*, April 24, 1804.
25. *Ibid.*, April 28, 1804.
26. H. P. Prentiss, *Timothy Pickering as the Leader of New England Federalism, 1800–1815* (Salem, Massachusetts, 1934), p. 24.
27. Lynn W. Turner, *William Plumer of New Hampshire* (Chapel Hill, North Carolina, 1962), pp. 112–113.
28. J. Q. Adams to William Plumer, December 21, 1828, Morristown National Historical Park.

29. Turner, *Plumer*, p. 135.
30. *Ibid.*, p. 96.
31. King, *Rufus King*, Vol. IV, pp. 365–366.
32. Henry Adams (ed.), *Documents Relating to New-England Federalism, 1800–1815* (Boston, 1905), p. 357.
33. Turner, *Plumer*, p. 141.
34. Adams, *Federalism*, p. 358.
35. New York *Evening Post*, April 30, 1804.
36. Davis, *Memoirs*, Vol. II, p. 284.
37. New York *Morning Chronicle*, April 28, 1804.
38. Davis, *Memoirs*, Vol. II, p. 287.
39. Harold C. Syrett and Jean G. Cooke (eds.), *Interview in Weehawken* (Middletown, Connecticut, 1960), p. 45.
40. *Ibid.*, pp. 45–48.
41. *Ibid.*
42. Davis, *Memoirs*, Vol. II, p. 294.
43. Davis, *Memoirs*, Vol. II, p. 288.
44. *Ibid.*, pp. 287–288.
45. "William Van Ness's Story," *New York History*, Vol. 27, p. 492.
46. Burr to Hamilton, June 18, 1804, Pendleton Papers, New-York Historical Society.
47. Davis, *Memoirs*, Vol. III, p. 295.
48. Davis, *Memoirs*, Vol. II, pp. 295–297.
49. Syrett and Cooke, *Interview*, pp. 56–58.
50. Davis, *Memoirs*, Vol. II, pp. 298–299.
51. Syrett and Cooke, *Interview*, p. 60.
52. Hamilton to Burr, June 22, 1804, Pendleton Papers, New-York Historical Society.
53. Syrett and Cooke, *Interview*, pp. 68–69.
54. Van Ness to Hamilton, June 23, 1804, New-York Historical Society.
55. Syrett and Cooke, *Interview*, p. 73.
56. *Ibid.*, p. 74.
57. Nathaniel Pendleton's Account, June 25, 1804, Pendleton Papers, New-York Historical Society.
58. Syrett and Cooke, *Interview*, p. 83.
59. *Ibid.*, p. 85.
60. Van Ness to Pendleton, June 27, 1804, Pendleton Papers, New-York Historical Society.
61. Syrett and Cooke, *Interview*, p. 109.
62. Timothy Pickering to William Coleman, July 1, 1825, Pickering Papers, Massachusetts Historical Society.
63. Davis, *Memoirs*, Vol. II, p. 290.
64. *Ibid.*, p. 291.
65. Hamilton to Pendleton, July 4, 1804, Pendleton Papers, New-York Historical Society.
66. Syrett and Cooke, *Interview*, p. 111.
67. New York *American-Citizen*, August 8, 1804.
68. Syrett and Cooke, *Interview*, p. 114.

69. Hamilton, *Writings of Hamilton*, Vol. VI, p. 568.
70. Syrett and Cooke, *Interview*, pp. 132–133.
71. Davis, *Memoirs*, Vol. II, pp. 322–324.
72. *Ibid.*, pp. 324–326.
73. Pendleton's Statement of Regulations, July 10, 1804, Pendleton Papers, New-York Historical Society.
74. Syrett and Cooke, *Interview*, pp. 99–102.
75. Broadus Mitchell, *Alexander Hamilton, The National Adventure, 1788–1804* (New York, 1962), p. 764.
76. A. Maunsell Broadhurst, *My Forefathers* (London, 1910), pp. 63–66.
77. Mitchell, *National Adventure*, pp. 533–534.
78. Newspaper clipping, Princeton University Library.
79. Newspaper clipping, New York Public Library.
80. Parton, *Burr*, Vol. I, pp. 354–355.
81. Syrett and Cooke, *Interview*, p. 141.
82. *Ibid.*, p. 153.
83. Biddle, *Autobiography*, pp. 404–405.
84. Syrett and Cooke, *Interview*, p. 154.
85. *Ibid.*, p. 160.
86. *Ibid.*, pp. 161–164.
87. Parton, *Burr*, Vol. II, p. 13.
88. New York *Evening Post*, July 30, 1804.
89. Syrett and Cooke, *Interview*, p. 143.
90. Van Ness to Pendleton, Pendleton Papers, New-York Historical Society.
91. William Coleman, *Death of Alexander Hamilton* (Boston, 1904), p. 52.
92. Morris (ed.), *Letters of Gouverneur Morris*, Vol. II, pp. 456–458.
93. Coleman, *Hamilton*, p. 47.
94. Davis, *Memoirs*, Vol. II, p. 327.

Chapter XV

1. David Ogden to William Meredith, July 31, 1804, Meredith Papers, Historical Society of Pennsylvania.
2. New York *American-Citizen*, August 7, 1804.
3. William Cary Duncan, *The Amazing Madame Jumel* (New York, 1935), pp. 114–132.
4. Brown, *Plumer's Memorandum*, p. 451.
5. William Peter Van Ness to Nathaniel Pendleton, July 16, 1804, Pendleton Papers, New-York Historical Society.
6. Davis, *Memoirs*, Vol. II, p. 329.
7. Biddle, *Autobiography*, p. 406.
8. New York *Daily Gazette*, August 9, 1804.
9. William Biddle to Nicholas Biddle, August 16, 1804, Autograph Collection, Historical Society of Pennsylvania.
10. Parton, *Burr*, Vol. II, p. 18.
11. Biddle, *Autobiography*, p. 304.
12. Davis, *Memoirs*, Vol. II, p. 329.
13. *Ibid.*, p. 330.

14. *Ibid.*, p. 331.
15. *Ibid.*, p. 332.
16. Thomas Robson Hay, "Charles Williamson and the Burr Conspiracy," *Journal of Southern History*, Vol. 11 (May, 1936), p. 181.
17. Adams, *History*, Vol. II, p. 395.
18. Hay, "Williamson," pp. 189–190.
19. Thomas P. Abernethy, *The Burr Conspiracy* (New York, 1954), p. 15.
20. Henry Adams, *John Randolph* (New York, 1961), p. 83.
21. Davis, *Memoirs*, Vol. II, p. 338.
22. *Ibid.*, p. 343.
23. *Ibid.*, p. 345.
24. *Ibid.*, p. 348.
25. *Ibid.*, p. 349.
26. William Plumer, Jr., *Life of William Plumer* (Boston, 1856), pp. 329–330.
27. Brown, *Plumer's Memorandum*, pp. 203–204.
28. Cutler, *Life of Cutler*, Vol. II, pp. 175–176.
29. Charles F. Adams (ed.), *Memoirs of John Quincy Adams*, Vol. I (Philadelphia, 1874–1877), pp. 314–315.
30. Brown, *Plumer's Memorandum*, p. 185.
31. Davis, *Memoirs*, Vol. II, p. 360.
32. *Ibid.*, p. 353.
33. *Annals of Congress*, Eighth Congress, Second Session, p. 674.
34. Adams, *History*, Vol. II, p. 150.
35. Malone, *Dictionary of American Biography*, Vol. II, pp. 34–37.
36. Brown, *Plumer's Memorandum*, pp. 236–238.
37. *Ibid.*, p. 244.
38. *Ibid.*, p. 239.
39. Uriah Tracy to Gould, February 4, 1805, Pierpont Morgan Library; *Annals of Congress*, Eighth Congress, Second Session, p. 99.
40. Brown, *Plumer's Memorandum*, pp. 282–285.
41. Adams, *History*, Vol. II, p. 235.
42. *Ibid.*, pp. 236–237.
43. Beveridge, *Marshall*, Vol. III, p. 174.
44. Davis, *Memoirs*, Vol. II, p. 358; *Annals of Congress*, Eighth Congress, Second Session, p. 663.
45. Brown, *Plumer's Memorandum*, pp. 309–310.
46. Adams, *History*, Vol. II, p. 243.
47. *Annals of Congress*, Eighth Congress, Second Session, p. 71.
48. Burr Mss, Massachusetts Historical Society.
49. *Annals of Congress*, Eighth Congress, Second Session, p. 71.
50. Davis, *Memoirs*, Vol. II, p. 360.
51. Samuel L. Mitchill, "Letters from Washington, 1801–1813," *Harper's Magazine*, Vol. 58, p. 750.
52. *Annals of Congress*, Eighth Congress, Second Session, p. 72.
53. Mitchill, "Letters," p. 749.
54. Davis, *Memoirs*, Vol. II, p. 359.
55. *Ibid.*, p. 367.

Chapter XVI

1. Davis, *Memoirs*, Vol. II, p. 365.
2. Parton, *Burr*, Vol. II, p. 35.
3. Typescript, Mrs. William H. Wolf, Campus Martius Museum, Marietta, Ohio.
4. William H. Safford, *The Life of Harman Blennerhassett* (Chillicothe, Ohio, 1850), p. 37.
5. *Ibid.*
6. *Ibid.*, p. 42.
7. Safford, *Blennerhassett*, pp. 46–47.
8. Griswold to Elijah Boardman, October 10, 1806, Photostat, Miscellaneous Mss, New-York Historical Society.
9. Schachner, *Aaron Burr*, p. 299.
10. J. R. Jacobs, *Tarnished Warrior* (Indianapolis and New York, 1938), p. 214.
11. Davis, *Memoirs*, Vol. II, p. 380.
12. *Ibid.*, p. 370.
13. James, *Jackson*, p. 110.
14. Abernethy, *Conspiracy*, p. 28.
15. Davis, *Memoirs*, Vol. II, p. 370.
16. *Ibid.*
17. *Ibid.*, p. 372.
18. Abernethy, *Conspiracy*, p. 24.
19. Davis, *Memoirs*, Vol. II, p. 382.
20. *Ibid.*, p. 372.
21. Walter F. McCaleb, *The Aaron Burr Conspiracy* (New York, 1903), p. 39.
22. Davis, *Memoirs*, Vol. II, p. 374.
23. McCaleb, *Burr Conspiracy*, p. 36.
24. Adams, *History*, Vol. III, p. 224.
25. Parton, *Burr*, Vol. II, p. 49.
26. Abernethy, *Conspiracy*, p. 32.
27. James Wilkinson, *Memoirs*, Vol. II (Washington, 1811), p. 301.
28. Parton, *Burr*, Vol. II, p. 50.
29. Davis, *Memoirs*, Vol. II, p. 375.
30. Adams, *History*, Vol. III, p. 232.
31. Davis, *Memoirs*, Vol. II, p. 375.
32. McCaleb, *Burr Conspiracy*, p. 55; Abernethy, *Conspiracy*, p. 40.
33. Abernethy, *Conspiracy*, p. 38.
34. Biddle, *Autobiography*, p. 314.
35. Parton, *Burr*, Vol. II, p. 57.
36. William H. Safford, *Blennerhassett Papers* (Cincinnati, 1864), p. 118.
37. David Robertson, *Reports of the Trials of Colonel Aaron Burr*, Vol. I (Philadelphia, 1808), pp. 473–485.
38. *Ibid.*
39. Abernethy, *Conspiracy*, p. 42.
40. Robertson, *Trial*, Vol. I, pp. 485–491.
41. Joseph H. Daveiss, "A View of the President's Conduct Concerning the

Conspiracy of 1806," *Quarterly Publication of the Historical and Philosophical Society of Ohio*, Vol. 12 (1917), p. 69.

42. *Ibid.*, p. 75.
43. *Ibid.*, p. 77; Ford, *Jefferson's Writings*, Vol. VIII, p. 424.
44. Daveiss, "A View . . . ," p. 85.
45. *Ibid.*, pp. 89–90.
46. Daniel Clark, *Proofs of the Corruption of General James Wilkinson* (Philadelphia, 1809), p. 126.
47. Anonymous, *Letters of Marcus* (New York, 1806), p. 4.
48. Davis to Van Ness, May 28, 1806, Davis Papers, New-York Historical Society.
49. *Marcus*, pp. 5–6.
50. *Ibid.*, p. 6.
51. King, *Rufus King*, Vol. IV, pp. 494–495.
52. George Clinton to De Witt Clinton, 1806, Clinton Papers, Columbia University Library.
53. *Marcus*, p. 14; Alexander, *Political History*, Vol. I, p. 152.
54. Brown, *Plumer's Memorandum*, p. 441.
55. Parton, *Burr*, Vol. II, p. 53.
56. Lipscomb and Bergh, *Jefferson's Writings*, Vol. I, pp. 448–453.
57. Beveridge, *Marshall*, Vol. III, p. 292.
58. Brown, *Plumer's Memorandum*, p. 477.
59. Safford, *Blennerhassett*, p. 67.
60. Parton, *Burr*, Vol. II, p. 55.
61. McCaleb, *Burr Conspiracy*, p. 63.
62. Parton, *Burr*, Vol. II, p. 55.
63. Adams, *History*, Vol. III, p. 227.
64. *Ibid.*, p. 249.
65. Biddle, *Autobiography*, pp. 313–314.
66. Parton, *Burr*, Vol. II, p. 59.
67. Abernethy, *Conspiracy*, p. 74.
68. Dayton to Wilkinson, July 24, 1806, University of Virginia.
69. Burr to Wilkinson, July 29, 1806, University of Virginia.
70. *Ibid.*
71. Abernethy, *Conspiracy*, p. 60; McCaleb, *Burr Conspiracy*, p. 76.
72. Burr to Gallatin, July 31, 1806, Gallatin Papers, New-York Historical Society.
73. Burr to Wilkinson, July 29, 1806, University of Virginia.

Chapter XVII

1. McCaleb, *Burr Conspiracy*, pp. 172–174.
2. Daveiss, "A View . . . ," p. 92.
3. *Ibid.*, p. 93.
4. Robertson, *Trials*, Vol. I, pp. 505–506.
5. Nevill and Roberts to Madison, October 7, 1806, Burr Conspiracy Papers, Library of Congress.
6. Brant, *Madison*, pp. 344–345.
7. Unsigned letter to Jefferson, n. d., Burr Papers, Library of Congress.

8. AD, Campus Martius Museum, Marietta, Ohio.

9. Safford, *Blennerhassett*, p. 74.

10. *Ibid.*, pp. 228–230.

11. Deposition of Alexander Henderson, Campus Martius Museum, Marietta, Ohio.

12. Safford, *Blennerhassett*, p. 230.

13. Abernethy, *Conspiracy*, p. 70.

14. Adams, *History*, Vol. III, p. 258.

15. Safford, *Blennerhassett Papers*, p. 142.

16. Burr to Wilkinson, n. d., Burr Papers, New York Public Library; Walter F. McCaleb, *New Light on Aaron Burr* (Austin, Texas, 1963), p. 78.

17. Abernethy, *Conspiracy*, p. 73.

18. AD, Henry E. Huntington Library, San Marino, California.

19. Abernethy, *Conspiracy*, p. 72.

20. Clark, *Proofs*, p. 17.

21. Burr to B. H. Latrobe, October 26, 1806, Burr Papers, New York Public Library.

22. William Eaton to Madison and Morris Belknap to Jim Danielson, October 11, 1806, Burr Conspiracy Papers, Library of Congress.

23. McCaleb, *Burr Conspiracy*, p. 89.

24. Lipscomb and Bergh, *Jefferson's Writings*, Vol. I, pp. 458–462.

25. Parton, *Burr*, Vol. II, p. 275.

26. Jacobs, *Tarnished Warrior*, p. 135; Isaac Cox, Jr., *The West Florida Controversy* (New York, 1918), p. 23.

27. Wilkinson to Jefferson, October 20, 1806, Burr Conspiracy Papers, Library of Congress.

28. McCaleb, *Burr Conspiracy*, pp. 90–91.

29. Safford, *Blennerhassett Papers*, p. 154.

30. Daveiss to Innes, November 6, 1806, Harry Innes Papers, Library of Congress.

31. James F. Hopkins (ed.), *The Papers of Henry Clay*, Vol. I (Lexington, Kentucky, 1959–1963), p. 253.

32. *Ibid.*

33. Parton, *Burr*, Vol. II, p. 71.

34. Dunbar Rowland (ed.), *Official Letterbooks of W. C. C. C. Claiborne, 1801–1816*, Vol. IV (Jackson, Mississippi, 1917), pp. 53–54.

35. *Ibid.*

36. Lipscomb and Bergh, *Jefferson's Writings*, Vol. I, pp. 463–465.

37. AD, Campus Martius Museum, Marietta, Ohio.

38. Ford, *Jefferson's Writings*, Vol. X, pp. 301–302.

39. Hopkins, *Clay*, Vol. I, p. 256.

40. Clark, *Proofs*, p. 17.

Chapter XVIII

1. Silas Brown, *Letters to Ephraim Brown from Silas Brown* (Mansfield, Ohio, 1916?), pp. 15–18.

2. Hopkins, *Clay*, Vol. I, pp. 256–257.

3. *The Western World* (Frankfort, Kentucky), December 18, 1806.

4. McCaleb, *Burr Conspiracy*, p. 191.
5. Samuel Wilson, "The Court Proceedings of 1806 in Kentucky Against Aaron Burr and John Adair," *The Filson Club History Quarterly*, Vol. 10, p. 40.
6. Daveiss, "A View . . . ," p. 103.
7. McCaleb, *Burr Conspiracy*, p. 199.
8. Truxton to Jefferson, December 4, 1806, Jefferson Papers, Library of Congress.
9. Ford, *Jefferson's Writings*, Vol. X, p. 322.
10. Report of James Knox, n. d., Burr Papers, Library of Congress; Brown, *Letters*, p. 19.
11. *Ibid.*
12. Meigs to Buell, December 10, 1806, Campus Martius Museum, Marietta, Ohio.
13. Tiffin to Buell, December 14, 1806, *Ibid.*
14. Margaret Blennerhassett to Dudley Woodbridge, December 12, 1806, Typescript manuscript, Marietta, Ohio.
15. Abernethy, *Conspiracy*, p. 247.
16. Daveiss, "A View . . . ," p. 104.
17. Safford, *Blennerhassett Papers*, p. 185.
18. Abernethy, *Conspiracy*, p. 100.
19. *Ibid.*, p. 112.
20. Dearborn to Wilkinson, November 29, 1806, Rush Papers, Historical Society of Pennsylvania.
21. Rowland, *Letterbooks*, Vol. IV, p. 46.
22. Wilkinson to Dinsmoor, n. d., Burr Conspiracy Papers, Library of Congress.
23. Jacobs, *Tarnished Warrior*, p. 233.
24. McCaleb, *Burr Conspiracy*, p. 167; Jacobs, *Tarnished Warrior*, p. 234.
25. McCaleb, *Burr Conspiracy*, p. 227.
26. *Ibid.*, p. 217.
27. Jefferson to John Shaw, n. d., Burr Conspiracy Papers, Library of Congress.
28. McCaleb. *Burr Conspiracy*, pp. 226–227.
29. Ford, *Jefferson's Writings*, Vol. X, p. 331.
30. Henry Dearborn to Clinton, December 22, 1806, Clinton Papers, Columbia University Library.
31. Safford, *Blennerhassett Papers*, p. 186.
32. Brown, *Letters*, p. 8; Abernethy, *Conspiracy*, p. 113.
33. Brown, *Letters*, p. 20.
34. Abernethy, *Conspiracy*, pp. 114–115.
35. *Ibid.*, p. 115.
36. James Parton, *Andrew Jackson*, Vol. I (New York, 1860), p. 324.
37. Abernethy, *Conspiracy*, p. 117.
38. Parton, *Burr*, Vol. II, p. 88.
39. *Ibid.*
40. Safford, *Blennerhassett Papers*, p. 188.
41. *Ibid.*
42. *Ibid.*, p. 189.

43. Comfort Tyler to Horatio Stark, January 23, 1807, Burr Conspiracy Papers, Library of Congress.
44. McCaleb, *Burr Conspiracy*, p. 271; Abernethy, *Conspiracy*, p. 211.
45. Rowland, *Letterbooks*, Vol. IV, p. 79.
46. Ford, *Jefferson's Writings*, Vol. X, p. 334.
47. McCaleb, *New Light*, p. 52.
48. McCaleb, *Burr Conspiracy*, p. 231.
49. *Ibid.*, p. 233.
50. Safford, *Blennerhassett*, p. 129.
51. Brown, *Plumer's Memorandum*, p. 615.
52. Ford, *Jefferson's Writings*, Vol. X, p. 346.
53. Rowland, *Letterbooks*, Vol. IV, pp. 99–100.
54. *Ibid.*, p. 115.
55. Mitchill, "Letters from Washington," Vol. 58, p. 751.
56. Butterfield, *Rush*, Vol. II, p. 936.
57. Adams, *Memoirs*, Vol. I, p. 444.
58. *Ibid.*, p. 446; Brown, *Plumer's Memorandum*, pp. 588–591.
59. *Ibid.*, p. 592.
60. *Ibid.*, p. 596.
61. Ford, *Jefferson's Writings*, Vol. X, p. 356; Adams, *Memoirs*, Vol. I, p. 449.
62. Brown, *Plumer's Memorandum*, p. 590.
63. J. F. H. Claiborne, *Mississippi as a Province, Territory and State* (Jackson, Mississippi, 1880), pp. 283–284.
64. Harry Toulmin to P. P. Schuyler, February 7, 1807, Burr Conspiracy Papers, Library of Congress.
65. Brown, *Letters*, p. 8.
66. Claiborne, *Mississippi*, pp. 287–288.
67. Brown, *Letters*, pp. 8–9.
68. *Ibid.*, p. 9; Safford, *Blennerhassett Papers*, p. 206.
69. McCaleb, *Burr Conspiracy*, p. 186.
70. Williams to Burr, n. d., Burr Conspiracy Papers, Library of Congress.
71. McCaleb, *Burr Conspiracy*, p. 282.
72. Beveridge, *Marshall*, Vol. III, p. 338.
73. Claiborne to Madison, February 6, 1807, Burr Conspiracy Papers, Library of Congress.
74. Davis to Van Ness, February 11, 1807, New-York Historical Society.
75. Joseph Alston to Albert Gallatin, February 12, 1807, Gallatin Papers, New-York Historical Society.
76. Mitchill, "Letters from Washington," Vol. 58, p. 751.
77. Wilkinson to Jefferson, February 13, 1807, Burr Conspiracy Papers, Library of Congress.
78. *Burr's Conspiracy Exposed and General Wilkinson Vindicated Against the Slander of his Enemies on That Important Occasion* (Washington City, 1811), p. 101.
79. Brown, *Plumer's Memorandum*, p. 619.
80. McCaleb, *Burr Conspiracy*, p. 279.
81. Biddle, *Autobiography*, p. 316.
82. McCaleb, *Burr Conspiracy*, p. 279.

83. Jefferson to Caesar Rodney, March 22, 1807, Henry E. Huntington Library, San Marino, California.
84. Brown, *Letters*, p. 11.

Chapter XIX

1. Parton, *Burr*, Vol. XXI, p. 127.
2. Davis, *Memoirs*, Vol. II, p. 405.
3. Robertson, *Trials*, Vol. I, p. 7.
4. Ford, *Jefferson's Writings*, Vol. X, p. 387.
5. Davis, *Memoirs*, Vol. II, p. 406.
6. Burr to Comfort Tyler, April 14, 1807, Henry E. Huntington Library, San Marino, California. Burr to William Peter Van Ness, April 26, 1807, Campus Martius Museum, Marietta, Ohio.
7. Robertson, *Trials*, Vol. I, p. 41.
8. *Ibid.*, p. 44.
9. Biddle, *Autobiography*, p. 409; William Cabell Bruce, *John Randolph of Roanoke, 1773–1833*, Vol. I (New York, 1922), p. 301.
10. Parton, *Burr*, Vol. II, p. 107.
11. Robertson, *Trials*, Vol. I, pp. 57–58.
12. *Ibid.*, p. 78.
13. *Ibid.*
14. *Ibid.*, p. 81.
15. *Ibid.*, p. 106.
16. Davis, *Memoirs*, Vol. II, p. 406.
17. Robertson, *Trials*, Vol. I, p. 114.
18. Ford, *Jefferson's Writings*, Vol. X, pp. 398–399.
19. *Ibid.*, p. 404.
20. Robertson, *Trials*, Vol. I, p. 128.
21. *Ibid.*, p. 156.
22. *Ibid.*, p. 178.
23. *Ibid.*, p. 181.
24. *Ibid.*, p. 191.
25. Ford, *Jefferson's Writings*, Vol. X, pp. 395–396.
26. Davis, *Memoirs*, Vol. II, p. 407.
27. Parton, *Burr*, Vol. II, p. 373.
28. Ford, *Jefferson's Writings*, Vol. X, p. 406.
29. *Ibid.*, p. 403.
30. Robertson, *Trials*, Vol. I, p. 252.
31. Davis, *Memoirs*, Vol. II, p. 408.
32. Luther Martin to Joseph Alston, June 26, 1807, American Antiquarian Society.
33. Safford, *Blennerhassett Papers*, pp. 255–257.
34. Robertson, *Trials*, Vol. I, p. 329.
35. Jackson to Thomas M. Bayley, June 27, 1807, Henry E. Huntington Library, San Marino, California.
36. *Ibid.*
37. Robertson, *Trials*, Vol. I, p. 351.
38. McCaleb, *Burr Conspiracy*, p. 336.

39. Davis, *Memoirs*, Vol. II, p. 410.
40. Nathaniel Bacon to Albert Gallatin, June 30, 1807, Gallatin Papers, New-York Historical Society.
41. Butterfield, *Rush*, Vol. II, p. 951.
42. Beveridge, *Marshall*, Vol. III, p. 474.
43. Erich Bollman to Theodosia Alston, July 27, 1807, Simon Gratz Collection, Historical Society of Pennsylvania.
44. Jonathan Dayton to A. J. Dallas, July 4, 1807, Henry E. Huntington Library, San Marino, California.
45. Robertson, *Trials*, Vol. I, p. 370.
46. Safford, *Blennerhassett Papers*, p. 274.
47. *Ibid.*, p. 316.
48. *Ibid.*, p. 320.
49. Robertson, *Trials*, Vol. I, p. 461.
50. *Ibid.*, p. 464.
51. Thomas Truxtun to Charles Biddle, July 11, 1807, Henry E. Huntington Library, San Marino, California.
52. Robertson, *Trials*, Vol. I, pp. 582 and 587.
53. *Ibid.*, p. 594.
54. Parton, *Burr*, Vol. II, p. 131.
55. Robertson, *Trials*, Vol. II, p. 39.
56. *Ibid.*, p. 49.
57. *Ibid.*, p. 81.
58. *Ibid.*, pp. 81 and 96–98.
59. *Ibid.*, p. 123.
60. *Ibid.*, p. 139.
61. *Ibid.*, p. 262.
62. *Ibid.*, p. 377.
63. *Ibid.*, p. 401.
64. *Ibid.*, p. 403.
65. *Ibid.*, p. 405.
66. Robert K. Faulkner, "John Marshall and the Burr Trial," *The Journal of American History*, Vol. LIII, pp. 2 and 255.
67. Robertson, *Trials*, Vol. II, p. 437.
68. *Ibid.*, pp. 444–445.
69. *Ibid.*
70. Davis, *Memoirs*, Vol. II, p. 412.
71. Robertson, *Trials*, Vol. II, p. 448.
72. Safford, *Blennerhassett Papers*, p. 386.

Chapter XX

1. Robertson, *Trials*, Vol. II, pp. 488 and 499.
2. Safford, *Blennerhassett Papers*, p. 395.
3. Carl B. Swisher, *American Constitutional Development* (Boston, 1943), p. 130.
4. Jacobs, *Tarnished Warrior*, p. 241.
5. Safford, *Blennerhassett Papers*, p. 461.
6. *Ibid.*, p. 197.

7. Jefferson to Caesar Rodney, October 28, 1807, Simon Gratz Collection, Historical Society of Pennsylvania.

8. George Poindexter to Thomas Rodney, October 31, 1807, Simon Gratz Collection, Historical Society of Pennsylvania.

9. Safford, *Blennerhassett Papers*, p. 476.

10. *Ibid.*, p. 481.

11. *Ibid.*

12. Biddle, *Autobiography*, p. 323.

13. Safford, *Blennerhassett Papers*, p. 504.

14. B. Ruggles to Eleanor Peters, January 20, 1808, Typescript Collection, Mrs. Josephine Phillips, Marietta, Ohio.

15. Parton, *Burr*, Vol. II, p. 163.

16. Theodosia B. Alston to Dr. William Eustis, October 3, 1808, C.P.G. Fuller Collection, Princeton.

17. *Ibid.*

18. Parton, *Burr*, Vol. II, p. 164.

19. Theodosia B. Alston, to Dr. William Eustis, October 3, 1808, C.P.G. Fuller Collection, Princeton.

20. Parton, *Burr*, Vol. II, p. 164.

21. William K. Bixby (ed.), *The Private Journal of Aaron Burr*, Vol. I (Rochester, New York, 1903), p. 3.

22. Parton, *Burr*, Vol. II, p. 379.

23. Bixby, *Journal*, Vol. I, p. 253.

24. Theodosia B. Alston to Dr. William Eustis, October 3, 1808, C.P.G. Fuller Collection, Princeton.

25. Parton, *Burr*, Vol. II, p. 169.

26. *Ibid.*

27. *Ibid.*, p. 171.

28. *Ibid.*, p. 174.

29. *Ibid.*, p. 166.

30. Bixby, *Journal*, Vol. I, p. 20.

31. Davis, *Journal*, Vol. I, p. 72.

32. *Ibid.*, pp. 83–84.

33. Autograph catalogue clipping in Secretary's Office, Princeton University.

34. Bixby, *Journal*, Vol. I, p. 95.

35. Unsigned letter, April 16, 1809, Simon Gratz Collection, Historical Society of Pennsylvania.

36. John Reeve to Aaron Burr, April 24, 1809, Dreer Collection, Historical Society of Pennsylvania.

37. Richard Beale Davis (ed.), *Jeffersonian America* (San Marino, California, 1954), pp. 282–283.

38. Bixby, *Journal*, Vol. I, p. 243.

39. Davis, *Journal*, Vol. I, pp. 310–311.

40. Henry Gahn to Theodosia B. Alston, September 18, 1809, Simon Gratz Collection, Historical Society of Pennsylvania.

41. Adams, *Memoirs*, Vol. II, p. 67.

42. Bixby, *Journal*, Vol. I, p. 263.

43. *Ibid.*, p. 267.

44. *Ibid.*, p. 274.

45. *Ibid.*, p. 301.
46. *Ibid.*, pp. 357–358.
47. Brant, *Madison*, Vol. V, p. 180.
48. McCaleb, *New Light*, p. 136.
49. Bixby, *Journal*, Vol. I, p. 410.
50. *Ibid.*, pp. 419–420.
51. McCaleb, *New Light*, p. 139.
52. *Ibid.*, p. 140.
53. Unsigned letter to James Madison, Madison Papers, New York Public Library.
54. McCaleb, *New Light*, p. 145.
55. Bixby, *Journal*, Vol. II, p. 39n.
56. *Ibid.*, p. 28.
57. *Ibid.*, p. 199.
58. Parton, *Burr*, Vol. II, p. 394.
59. *Ibid.*, p. 392.
60. Safford, *Blennerhassett Papers*, p. 537.
61. Bixby, *Journal*, Vol. II, p. 229n.
62. *Ibid.*, Vol. II, p. 267.
63. *Ibid.*, p. 310n.
64. *Ibid.*, p. 396.
65. *Ibid.*, p. 401.
66. Parton, *Burr*, Vol. II, p. 226.
67. Bixby, *Journal*, Vol. II, p. 402.
68. *Ibid.*, p. 432.

Chapter XXI

1. Parton, *Burr*, Vol. II, pp. 239–240.
2. Schachner, *Aaron Burr*, p. 496.
3. *Ibid.*, p. 496.
4. Parton, *Burr*, Vol. II, p. 246.
5. Davis, *Memoirs*, Vol. II, p. 426.
6. Davis, *Memoirs*, Vol. II, p. 428.
7. Stokes, *Iconography*, Vol. V, p. 1557.
8. Davis, *Memoirs*, Vol. II, p. 429.
9. *Ibid.*, p. 430.
10. Burr to unknown, March 29, 1813, Wetmore Papers, Yale.
11. Newspaper clippings, New York Public Library.

Chapter XXII

1. George D. Prentice, *Henry Clay* (Hartford, Connecticut, 1831), p. 34.
2. Davis, *Memoirs*, Vol. II, pp. 434–436.
3. *Ibid.*, p. 437.
4. Charles Felton Pidgin, *Theodosia* (Boston, 1907), p. 356.
5. Samuel Bradstreet to Aaron Burr, March 29, 1824, Simon Gratz Collection, Historical Society of Pennsylvania.
6. S. Philipps to Aaron Burr, March 30, 1824, Simon Gratz Collection, Historical Society of Pennsylvania.

7. Parton, *Burr*, Vol. II, p. 278.
8. Ernest Hazelins to Burr, January 14, 1825, Burr Papers, New-York Historical Society.
9. Rachel Eden to Burr, Burr Papers, New-York Historical Society.
10. Charles Burdett, "Reminiscences," Newspaper clipping, New York Public Library.
11. Rebecca Blodgett to Burr, March 11, 1818, July 21, 1815, Burr Papers, New-York Historical Society.
12. *Ibid.*, December 28, 1823.
13. Seward, *Seward*, Vol. I, pp. 169–170.
14. Burr to Mrs. Catherine Hawes, April 13, 1831, Burr Papers, New York Public Library.
15. Adams, *Memoirs*, Vol. VII, p. 272.
16. Davis, *Memoirs*, Vol. II, p. 443.
17. John Alderson to Burr, November [?], 1817, Burr Papers, New-York Historical Society.
18. Davis, *Memoirs*, Vol. II, p. 445.
19. Parton, *Burr*, Vol. II, p. 319.
20. *Ibid.*, p. 262.
21. *Ibid.*, p. 276.
22. Burr to Nelson Chase, January 20, 1834, C.P.G. Fuller Collection, Princeton.
23. William Dunlap, *Diary*, Vol. III (New York, 1929–1931), p. 796.
24. Eliza Burr *vs.* Aaron Burr, Jumel Papers, New-York Historical Society.
25. Parton, *Burr*, Vol. II, p. 327.
26. I. K. Morris, Typescript, July 11, 1904, New-York Historical Society.
27. Davis, *Memoirs*, Vol. II, p. 449.

BIBLIOGRAPHY

Manuscripts

American Antiquarian Society
      Burr Papers
Campus Martius Museum, Marietta, Ohio
      Miscellaneous manuscripts
      Typescript, Mrs. William H. Wolf
Columbia University
      De Witt Clinton Papers
      Tammania of Edwin P. Kilroe
Connecticut Historical Society
      Burr Papers
      Jefferson Papers
      Spanish Papers
Hartford Theological Seminary
      Rev. Joseph Bellamy Papers
Harvard University
      Burr Papers
Henry E. Huntington Library
      Burr Papers
Historical Society of Pennsylvania
      Claude W. Unger Collection
      Dreer Collection
      Edward Carey Gardiner Collection
      Etting Papers
      Helena Hubbell Collection
      Mary Suydam Collection
      Meredith Papers
      Peters Papers
      Simon Gratz Collection
      Society Miscellaneous Collection
      Rush Papers
      Hazard Family Papers
Kansas State Historical Society
      Burr Papers
Library of Congress
      Adams Transcripts
      Burr Conspiracy Papers

     Burr Miscellaneous Papers
     Hamilton Papers
     Innes Papers
     Jefferson Papers
     Plumer Papers
     Presidential Papers
Litchfield Historical Society
     Miscellaneous manuscripts
Marietta College Library
     Miscellaneous manuscripts
Massachusetts Historical Society
     Eustis Papers
     Pickering Papers
     Henry W. Taft Collection
     Sedgwick Papers
Morristown National Historical Park
     Burr Papers
Museum of the City of New York
     Silliman Papers
National Archives of the United States
     Record Group No. 59
New Jersey Historical Society
     Burr Papers
New-York Historical Society
     Burr Papers
     Gallatin Papers
     Gates Papers
     Journal of Benjamin B. Howell
     John Lamb Papers
     R. R. Livingston Papers
     Nicholas Low Papers
     Rufus King Papers
     Schuyler Papers
     Stevens Papers
New York Public Library
     Burr Papers
     William Edgar Papers
     Van Ness Papers
     Madison Papers
     King Papers
     Monroe Papers
     Tammany Membership Book
     Minutes of the Mayor's Court, 1784–1804
New York State Library
     Burr Papers
     Certificate of Elections, 1799–1814
     Phelps-Gorham Papers
Pierpont Morgan Library
     Burr Papers

Princeton University
  Burr Additional Papers
  Burr Papers
  Burr Folder in Secretary's Office
  C. P. G. Fuller Collection
United States Department of State
  Letters in Relation to Burr's Conspiracy, 1806–1808
University of Missouri
  Burr Papers
University of Rochester
  Burr Papers
University of Virginia
  McGregor Collection
  Smith Papers
  Wickham Papers
Yale University
  E. A. Park Collection
  Knollenberg Collection
  Aaron Burr Columbus Papers
  Webb Family Papers
  Penniman Collection
  Wetmore Family Collection
  A. B. Jennings Collection

Printed Primary Sources

Adair, Douglass and Schutz, John A. (eds.), *Peter Oliver's Origin & Progress of the American Rebellion: A Tory View*. San Marino, California, 1961.

Adams, Charles Francis (ed.), *Memoirs of John Quincy Adams*. Philadelphia, 1874–1877. 12 vols.

Adams, Henry (ed.), *Documents Relating to New-England Federalism, 1800–1815*. Boston, 1905.

——— (ed.), *Writings of Albert Gallatin*. Philadelphia, 1879. 3 vols.

American State Papers.

Anburey, Thomas, *Travels Through the Interior Parts of America*. Boston and New York, 1923. 2 vols.

Annals of the Congress of the United States.

Arnold, Benedict, *Collections of the Maine Historical Society*, Series 1, Volume 1. Portland, Maine, 1831.

Bayley, Richard, *An Account of the Epidemic Fever which Prevailed in the City of New York During Part of the Summer and Fall of 1795*. New York, 1796.

Beecher, Lyman, *Autobiography*. New York, 1866. 2 vols.

Biddle, Charles, *Autobiography*. Philadelphia, 1883.

Brown, Everett Somerville (ed.), *William Plumer's Memorandum of Proceedings in the United States Senate, 1803–1807*. New York, 1923.

Brown, Silas, *Letters to Ephraim Brown from Silas Brown*. Mansfield, Ohio, 1916(?).

Buell, Rowena (ed.), *The Memoirs of Rufus Putnam*. Boston, 1903.

Burr, Aaron, *The Private Journal of Aaron Burr*, William K. Bixby, ed. Rochester, New York, 1903.

Butterfield, Lyman H. (ed.), *Diary and Autobiography of John Adams*. Cambridge, Massachusetts, 1961. 4 vols.

—— (ed.), *Letters of Benjamin Rush*. Princeton, New Jersey, 1951. 2 vols.

Cheetham, James, *A Letter to a Friend on the Conduct of the Adherents to Mr. Burr*. New York, 1803.

——, *A Narrative of the Suppression by Col. Burr of the History of the Administration of John Adams, late President of the United States, written by John Wood*. New York, 1802.

——, *Nine Letters on the Subject of Aaron Burr's Political Defection*. New York, 1803.

——, *A View of the Political Conduct of Aaron Burr*. New York, 1802.

Clark, Daniel, *Proofs of the Corruption of General James Wilkinson*. Philadelphia, 1809.

Coleman, William, *A Collection of the Facts and Documents Relative to the Death of Major-General Alexander Hamilton*. Boston and New York, 1904.

Commager, Henry Steele and Morris, Richard B. (eds.), *The Spirit of 'Seventy-Six*. Indianapolis and New York, 1958. 2 vols.

Cutler, William P. and Cutler, J. P. (eds.), *Life, Journals and Correspondence of Rev. Manasseh Cutler*. Cincinnati, 1888. 2 vols.

Daveiss, Joseph, "A View of the President's Conduct Concerning the Conspiracy of 1806," *Quarterly Publication of the Historical and Philosophical Society of Ohio*. Volume 12 (1917).

Davis, John, *Travels of Four and a Half Years in the United States of America During 1798, 1799, 1800, 1801, and 1802*. London, 1803.

Davis, Matthew L., *Letters of Marcus*. New York, 1806.

—— (ed.), *Memoirs of Aaron Burr*. New York, 1855. 2 vols.

Davis, Richard Beale (ed.), *Jeffersonian America: Notes on the United States of America Collected in the Years 1805, 1806, 1807 and 1811–1812 by Sir Augustus John Foster*. San Marino, California, 1954.

Donnan, Elizabeth (ed.), "James Aston Bayard, Papers from 1796–1815," *Annual Report of the American Historical Association, 1913*. Vol. 2 (1915).

Duer, William Alexander, *New York as it Was, During the Latter Part of the Last Century*. New York, 1849.

——, *Reminiscences of an Old New Yorker*. New York, 1867.

Dunbar, Rowland (ed.), *Official Letter Books of W. C. C. Claiborne*. Jackson, Mississippi, 1917. 6 vols.

Duncan, William, *The New-York Directory and Register for the Year 1794*. New York, 1794.

Dunlap, William, *Diary*. New York, 1929–1931. 3 vols.

Earle, T. and Congdon, C. T. (eds.), *Annals of the General Society of Mechanics and Tradesmen of the City of New York, 1785–1880*. New York, 1882.

Edwards, Jonathan, *The Works of President Edwards*. New York, 1857. 4 vols.

Fitzpatrick, J. C., *Writings of Washington*. Washington, 1931–1944. 39 vols.

Force, Peter, *American Archives: Fourth Series*. Washington, 1837–1853. 6 vols.

Ford, Paul L. (ed.), *The Journals of Hugh Gaine, Printer*. New York, 1902. 2 vols.

—— (ed.), *The Works of Thomas Jefferson*. New York, 1905. 12 vols.

—— (ed.), *The Writings of Thomas Jefferson*. New York, 1882–1899. 10 vols.

Ford, Worthington Chauncey, "Some Papers of Aaron Burr," *Proceedings of the American Antiquarian Society*, 29:43–128.

—— (ed.), *Correspondence and Journals of Samuel Blachley Webb*. New York, 1893–1894. 3 vols.

Gibbs, George, *Memoirs of the Administrations of Washington and John Adams*. New York, 1846. 2 vols.

Greenleaf, Thomas (ed.), *Laws Comprising the Constitution, and Acts of the Legislature of New York, 1st to the 15th Session, March 1778–April, 1792*. New York, 1792. 2 vols.

Hamilton, John C., *History of the Republic Traced in the Writings of Alexander Hamilton*. New York, 1857–1860. 6 vols.

—— (ed.), *The Works of Alexander Hamilton*. New York, 1850–1851. 7 vols.

Hamilton, Stanislaus M., *Writings of James Monroe*. New York, 1898–1903. 7 vols.

Hopkins, James F. (ed.), *The Papers of Henry Clay*. Lexington, Kentucky, 1959–1963. 3 vols.

Hough, Franklin B., *The New-York Civil List*. Albany, 1855.

Hunt, Gaillard (ed.), *First Forty Years of Washington Society, Portrayed by the Family Letters of Mrs. Samuel Harrison Smith*. New York, 1906.

—— (ed.), *The Writings of James Madison*. New York, 1906. 9 vols.

Hutchinson, William T. and Rachal, William M. E. (eds.), *The Papers of James Madison*. Chicago, 1962, 2 vols.

Kennedy, John P., *Memoirs of the Life of William Wirt*. Philadelphia, 1849.

Kent, William, *Memoirs and Letters of James Kent*. Boston, 1898.

King, Charles R. (ed.), *The Life and Correspondence of Rufus King*. New York, 1894. 6 vols.

Liscomb, A. A. and Bergh, A. E., *The Writings of Thomas Jefferson*. Washington, 1903. 20 vols.

Lodge, H. C. (ed.), *The Works of Alexander Hamilton*. New York, 1904. 12 vols.

Longworth's American Almanac and New York Register. New York, 1800.

Martineau, Harriett, *Retrospect of Western Travel*. New York, 1837. 2 vols.

Moncrieffe, Margaret, *Memoirs of Mrs. Coghlan*. New York, 1864.

Morison, Samuel Eliot, *The Life and Letters of Harrison Gray Otis, Federalist, 1765–1848*. Boston, 1913. 2 vols.

Morris, Anne Cary (ed.), *The Diary and Letters of Gouverneur Morris*. New York, 1888. 2 vols.

Myers, Mordecai, *Reminiscences, 1780 to 1814*. Washington, 1900.

New York City, *Minutes of the Common Council, 1793–1801*. New York, 1917.

New York State, *Journal of the Assembly.*

Rankin, Jeremiah Eames (ed.), *Esther Burr's Journal.* Washington, 1903.

Roberts, Kenneth (ed.), *March to Quebec: Journals of the Members of Arnold's Expedition.* Garden City, New York, 1942.

Robertson, David, *Report of the Trials of Colonel Aaron Burr.* Philadelphia, 1808. 2 vols.

Rowland, Dunbar (ed.), *Official Letter Books of W. C. C. Claiborne, 1800–1816.* Jackson, Mississippi, 1917. 4 vols.

Rutherfurd, Livingston, *Family Records and Events.* New York, 1894.

Safford, William H., *Blennerhassett Papers.* Cincinnati, 1864.

Scheer, George F. (ed.), *Private Yankee Doodle.* New York, 1963.

Seward, Frederick H. (ed.), *Autobiography of William H. Seward.* New York, 1877–1891. 3 vols.

Sparks, Jared, *Correspondence of the American Revolution.* Boston, 1853. 4 vols.

Stokes, I. N. Phelps, *The Iconography of Manhattan Island, 1498–1909.* New York, 1895–1928. 6 vols.

Street, Alfred B., *Council of Revision of the State of New York . . . and its Vetoes.* Albany, 1859.

Syrett, Harold C. and Cooke, Jean (eds.), *Interview in Weehawken.* Middletown, Connecticut, 1960.

Syrett, Harold C. (ed.), *The Papers of Alexander Hamilton.* New York, 1961– . 7 vols.

Van Doren, Mark (ed.), *Correspondence of Aaron Burr to his Daughter.* New York, 1929.

Van Ness, William P., *An Examination of the Various Charges . . . by Aristides.* Philadelphia, 1803.

Washington, H. A. (ed.), *Works of Jefferson.* New York, 1853–1854. 9 vols.

Webster, Noah, *The New York Directory for 1786.* New York, 1905.

Weed, Harriet A., *Autobiography of Thurlow Weed.* Boston, 1883.

Wilkinson, James, *Memoirs of My Own Times.* Philadelphia, 1816. 3 vols.

Wood, John, *A Correct Statement of the Various Sources from Which the History of the Administration of John Adams was Compiled and the Motives for its Suppression by Col. Burr.* New York, 1802.

———, *A Full Exposition of the Clintonian Faction and the Society of the Columbian Illuminati.* New York, 1802.

———, *The Suppressed History of the Administration of John Adams.* Philadelphia, 1846.

Newspapers

Albany *Register,* 1799–1802

The *Monitor* (Litchfield, Connecticut), 1806

The *National Intelligencer* (Washington, D. C.), 1803

New York:

> *American-Citizen,* 1800–1804
>
> *Chronicle-Express,* 1802–1803
>
> *Commercial Advertiser,* 1800–1801
>
> *Daily Advertiser,* 1788
>
> *Daily Gazette,* 1800

        Evening Post, 1802–1804
        Gazeteer, 1785
        Greenleaf's Journal & Daily Patriotic Register, 1798
        Morning-Chronicle, 1802–1803
        Morning Post, 1785
        Packet, 1785
        Spectator, 1799–1800
        Time-Piece and Literary Companion, 1798
Philadelphia *Aurora*, 1801
The *Western World* (Frankfort, Kentucky), 1806

Secondary Works and Articles

Abernethy, Thomas Perkins, "Aaron Burr at Blennerhassett Island and in
        Ohio," *History and Philosophy Society Bulletin*, 12:2–16.
————, *The Burr Conspiracy*. New York, 1954.
Adams, Charles Francis, "Davis's Memoirs and Journal of Burr," The *North
        American Review*, 49:174.
Adams, Henry, *Life of Albert Gallatin*. New York, 1943.
————, *History of the United States of America*. New York, 1962.
————, *John Randolph*. New York, 1882.
Adams, James Truslow, *Provincial Society, 1690–1763*. New York, 1927.
Alden, John, *The American Revolution*. New York, 1954.
Alexander, de Alva Stanwood, *A Political History of the State of New York*.
        New York, 1906. 3 vols.
Anthony, Katherine, *Dolly Madison*. New York, 1949.
Arnold, Isaac N., *The Life of Benedict Arnold*. Chicago, 1880.
Bancroft, George, *History of the United States*. Boston, 1834–1874. 10 vols.
Beam, Jacob, *The American Whig Society*. Princeton, 1933.
Becker, Carl L., *The History of Political Parties in the Province of New
        York, 1760–1776*. Madison, Wisconsin, 1909.
Beirne, Francis F., *Shout Treason: The Trial of Aaron Burr*. New York, 1959.
Bemis, Samuel Flagg, *Jay's Treaty*. New Haven, Connecticut, 1962.
————, "Relations Between the Vermont Separatists and Great Britain,
        1789–1791," *American Historical Review*, 21:547–560.
Benson, Adolph Burnett, "Aaron Burr in Sweden (1809)," *American
        Swedish Historical Foundation, Year Book*, 1952, 35–41.
Beveridge, Albert J., *The Life of John Marshall*. Boston and New York,
        1916. 4 vols.
Blake, Nelson M., *Water for the Cities*. Syracuse, New York, 1956.
Bliven, Bruce, *The Battle for Manhattan*. New York, 1955.
Bobbe, Dorothie, *De Witt Clinton*. Port Washington, New York, 1962.
Bogert, Frederick W., *Paramus: A Chronicle of Four Centuries*. Paramus,
        New Jersey, 1961.
Borden, Morton, *The Federalism of James A. Bayard*. New York, 1955.
Bradford, Gamaliel, *Damaged Souls*. Boston, 1923.
————, *Wives*. New York, 1925.
Bradhurst, A. Maunsell, *My Forefathers: Their History from Records and
        Traditions*. London, 1910.

Brant, Irving, *James Madison: Father of the Constitution, 1787–1800*. New York and Indianapolis, 1950.

———, *James Madison: Secretary of State, 1800–1809*. New York and Indianapolis, 1953.

Brebner, J. Bartlett, *Canada: A Modern History*. Ann Arbor, Michigan, 1960.

Bruce, William C., *John Randolph of Roanoke, 1773–1833*. New York, 1922. 2 vols.

Burdett, Charles, *The Beautiful Spy*. Philadelphia, 1865.

Burr, Jr., Samuel Engle, *Colonel Aaron Burr: The American Phoenix*. New York, 1964.

———, "In Defense of Aaron Burr," *Virginia Magazine of History*, 60:582–590.

Burt, Nathaniel, *The Perennial Philadelphians*. Boston, 1963.

Butler, M., *A History of the Commonwealth of Kentucky*. Cincinnati, 1834.

Cable, George, *The Creoles of Louisiana*. New York, 1884.

Callahan, North, *Daniel Morgan: Ranger of the Revolution*. New York, 1961.

Carter, Clarence Edwin, "The Burr-Wilkinson Intrigue in St. Louis," *Missouri Historical Society, Bulletin*, 10:447–464.

Chambers, William Nisbit, *Political Parties in a New Nation*. New York, 1963.

Channing, Edward, *A History of the United States*. New York, 1905–1925. 6 vols.

Chapin, Bradley, *The American Law of Treason*. Seattle, Washington, 1964.

Charles, Joseph, *The Origins of the American Party System*. New York and Evanston, 1961.

Chinard, Gilbert, *Thomas Jefferson*. Boston, 1939.

Claiborne, J. F. H., *Mississippi as a Province, Territory and State*. Jackson, Mississippi, 1880.

Clark, Joshua V. H., *Onandaga*. Syracuse, New York, 1849.

Cochran, Thomas C., *New York in the Confederation*. New York, 1932.

Codman, John, *Arnold's Expedition to Quebec*. New York, 1902.

Collins, Varnum Lansing, *Princeton*. New York, 1914.

Coombe, J. J., *The Trial of Aaron Burr*. Washington, D. C., 1864.

Cox, Jr., Isaac, *The West Florida Controversy*. New York, 1918.

Cresson, W. P., *James Monroe*. Chapel Hill, North Carolina, 1946.

Cunningham, Jr., Noble E., *The Jeffersonian Republicans: The Formation of Party Organization, 1789–1801*. Chapel Hill, North Carolina, 1957.

———, *The Jeffersonian Republicans in Power: Party Operations, 1801–1809*. Chapel Hill, North Carolina, 1963.

———, "John Beckley: An Early American Party Manager," *The William and Mary Quarterly*, 3rd Series, 13:40–52.

Dangerfield, George, *Chancellor Robert R. Livingston of New York, 1746–1813*. New York, 1960.

Dauer, Manning J., *The Adams Federalists*. Baltimore, 1953.

Drake, Francis S., *Life and Correspondence of Henry Knox*. Boston, 1873.

Duncan, William Cary, *The Amazing Madame Jumel*. New York, 1935.

Dunlap, William, *A History of the Rise and Progress of the Arts of Design in the United States*. Boston, 1918. 3 vols.

Edwards, William H., *Timothy and Rhoda Ogden Edwards and their Descendants*. Cincinnati, 1903.

Evans, Paul D., *The Holland Land Company*. Buffalo, 1924.

Faulkner, Robert K., "John Marshall and the Burr Trial," *Journal of American History*, 53:247–258.

Fisher, Josephine, "The Journal of Esther Burr," *The New England Quarterly*, 3:297–315.

Fisher, Samuel H., *The Litchfield Law School*. Litchfield, Connecticut, 1930.

Flick, Alexander C. (ed.), *History of the State of New York*. New York, 1934.

———, *Loyalism in New York During the American Revolution*. New York, 1901.

Fox, Dixon Ryan, *The Decline of the Aristocracy in the Politics of New York*. New York, 1918.

Freeman, Douglas Southall, *George Washington*. New York, 1948–1954. 6 vols.

French, Allen, *The First Year of the American Revolution*. Boston and New York, 1934.

Gayarre, Charles (ed.), *History of Louisiana*. New Orleans, 1903. 4 vols.

Graham, James, *The Life of General Daniel Morgan*. New York, 1856.

Green, Constance McLaughlin, *Washington: Village and Capital, 1800–1878*. Princeton, 1962.

Green, T. M., *The Spanish Conspiracy*. Cincinnati, 1891.

Groves, Joseph A., *Alstons and Allstons of North and South Carolina*. Selma, Alabama, 1902.

Hammond, Jabez D., *The History of Political Parties in the State of New York*. Buffalo, 1850. 2 vols.

Harmon, George Dewey, *Sixty Years of Indian Affairs*. Chapel Hill, North Carolina, 1941.

Hatch, Louis Clinton, *A History of the Vice-Presidency of the United States*. New York, 1934.

Hatcher, William B., *Edward Livingston*. Baton Rouge, Louisiana, 1940.

Hay, Thomas Robson and Werner, M. R., *The Admirable Trumpeter . . . General James Wilkinson*. New York, 1941.

Hay, Thomas Robson, "Charles Williamson and the Burr Conspiracy," *Journal of Southern History*, 11:181.

Hecht, Marie B. and Parmet, Herbert S., "New Light on Burr's Later Life," *The New-York Historical Society Quarterly*, 47:399–419.

Higginbotham, Dan, *Daniel Morgan: Revolutionary Rifleman*. Chapel Hill, North Carolina, 1961.

Hunt, Gaillard, "Office-Seeking During Jefferson's Administration," *American Historical Review*, 3:270–291.

Jacobs, J. R., *The Beginnings of the United States Army, 1783–1812*. Princeton, 1947.

James, Marquis, *Andrew Jackson: The Border Captain*. Indianapolis, 1933.

Jensen, Merrill, *The New Nation*. New York, 1962.

Johnston, Henry Phelps, "New York after the Revolution, 1783–1789," *Magazine of American History*, 29:305–331.

Jones, Thomas, *History of New York During the Revolutionary War*. New York, 1879. 2 vols.

Kass, Alvin, *Politics in New York State, 1800–1830*. Syracuse, 1965.

Kilbourne, Payne K., *Sketches and Chronicles of the Town of Litchfield, Connecticut*. Hartford, 1859.

Kilroe, Edwin P., *St. Tammany and the Origin of the Society of the Tammany*. New York, 1913.

Kingsford, William, *The History of Canada*. Toronto, 1894. 9 vols.

Knapp, Samuel L., *The Life of Colonel Burr*. New York, 1835.

Kurtz, Stephen G., *The Presidency of John Adams*. New York, 1961.

Leiby, Adrian C., *The Revolutionary War in the Hackensack Valley*. New Brunswick, New Jersey, 1962.

Levy, Leonard W., *Jefferson and Civil Liberties: The Darker Side*. New York, 1963.

Link, Eugene Perry, *Democrat-Republican Societies, 1790–1800*. New York, 1942.

Lodge, Henry Cabot, *Life and Letters of George Cabot*. Boston, 1878.

Lossing, Benson J., *The Life and Times of Philip Schuyler*. New York, 1860. 2 vols.

McBain, Howard Lee, *De Witt Clinton and the Origin of the Spoils System in New York*. New York, 1907.

McCaleb, Walter F., *New Light on Aaron Burr*. Austin, Texas, 1963.

MacLean, John, *History of the College of New Jersey*. Philadelphia, 1877. 2 vols.

Main, Jackson Turner, *The Antifederalists*. Chapel Hill, North Carolina, 1961.

Malone, Dumas (ed.), *Dictionary of American Biography*. New York, 1935–1958. 22 vols.

———, *Jefferson and the Ordeal of Liberty*. Boston, 1962.

———, *Jefferson and the Rights of Man*. Boston, 1951.

Marsh, Philip, "Hamilton and Monroe," *Mississippi Valley Historical Review*, 34:459–468.

———, "The Jefferson-Madison Vacation," *Pennsylvania Magazine of History and Biography*, 71:70–72.

———, "John Beckley—Mystery Man of the Early Jeffersonians," *Pennsylvania Magazine of History and Biography*, 71:54–69.

Miller, John C., *Alexander Hamilton: Portrait in Paradox*. New York, 1959.

———, *Crisis in Freedom*. Boston, 1951.

———, *Origins of the American Revolution*. Boston, 1943.

———, *Triumph of Freedom*. Boston, 1948.

Miller, Perry, *Jonathan Edwards*. New York, 1949.

———, *The New England Mind*. Boston, 1953.

Miner, Clarence E., *The Ratification of the Federal Constitution in the State of New York*. New York, 1921.

Mitchell, Broadus, *Alexander Hamilton: The National Adventure, 1788–1804*. New York, 1962.

———, *Alexander Hamilton: Youth to Maturity, 1755–1788*. New York, 1957.

Monaghan, Frank, *John Jay*. New York and Indianapolis, 1935.

Monaghan, Frank and Lowenthal, Marvin, *This Was New York, the Nation's Capital in 1789.* New York, 1943.

Myers, Gustavus, *The History of Tammany Hall.* New York, 1917.

Nevins, Allan, *The American States During and After the Revolutionary War.* New York, 1924.

Nye, Russell B., *The Cultural Life of the New Nation.* New York, 1960.

Osborn, Norris Galpin, *History of Connecticut.* New York, 1925. 5 vols.

Pancake, John S., "Aaron Burr: Would-Be Usurper," *William and Mary Quarterly*, 3rd Series, 8:204–213.

Parkes, Henry Bamford, *Jonathan Edwards.* New York, 1930.

Parton, James, *Famous Americans of Recent Times.* Boston, 1867.

———, *The Life and Times of Aaron Burr.* Boston, 1882.

Paulson, Peter, "The Tammany Society and the Jeffersonian Movement in New York City," *New York History*, 34:72–84.

Pidgin, Charles Felton, *Blennerhassett: A Romance. Boston*, 1901.

———, *Theodosia.* Boston, 1907.

Plumer, Jr., William, *The Life of William Plumer.* Boston, 1856.

Pomerantz, Sidney, *New York: An American City, 1783–1803.* New York, 1938.

Prentiss, H. P., *Timothy Pickering as the Leader of New England Federalism, 1800–1815.* Salem, Massachusetts, 1934.

Randall, Henry S., *The Life of Thomas Jefferson.* New York, 1858. 3 vols.

Reubens, Beatrice, "Burr, Hamilton and the Manhattan Company," *Political Science Quarterly*, 72:578–607 and 73:100–125.

Root, Elizabeth, "Joseph Bellamy and Theological Education," *Hartford Seminary Foundation Bulletin*, 21:34.

Sabine, Lorenzo, *Notes on Duels and Duelling.* Boston, 1855.

Safford, William H., *The Life of Harman Blennerhassett.* Chillicothe, Ohio, 1850.

Savage, Henry Lyttleton, *Nassau Hall, 1756–1956.* Princeton, 1956.

Schachner, Nathan, *Aaron Burr.* New York, 1937.

Schneider, Norris F., *Blennerhassett Island and the Burr Conspiracy.* Zanesville, Ohio, 1938.

Scoville, Joseph A., *The Old Merchants of New York City.* New York, 1885. 5 vols.

Sears, Lorenzo, *John Hancock.* Boston, 1913.

Shulim, Joseph I., *John Daly Burk: Irish Revolutionist and American Patriot.* Philadelphia, 1964.

Silliman, Benjamin, *History of the Bench and Bar of New York City.* New York, 1869.

Smith, Dorothy Valentine, "An Intercourse of the Heart: Some Little-Known Letters of Theodosia Burr," *New-York Historical Society Quarterly*, 37:41–53.

Smith, Horace W., "Descendants of the Rev. William Smith, D. D.," *Pennsylvania Magazine of History and Biography*, 4:373–382.

Smith, James Morton, *Freedom's Fetters.* Ithaca, New York, 1956.

Smith, Justin, *Arnold's March from Cambridge to Quebec.* New York, 1903.

———, *Our Struggle for the Fourteenth Colony.* New York, 1907. 2 vols.

Smith, Page, *John Adams.* New York, 1962. 2 vols.

Smith, Ray B., *Political and Governmental History of the State of New York*. Syracuse, 1922. 4 vols.

Sowers, Don C., *The Financial History of New York State*. New York, 1914.

Spaulding, E. Wilder, *His Excellency George Clinton*. New York, 1938.

————, *New York in the Critical Period*. New York, 1932.

Stearns, Jonathan F., *Historical Discourses Relating to the First Presbyterian Church in Newark*. New York, 1853.

Stillwell, John, *The History of the Burr Portraits*. New York, 1928.

Stone, William L., *Life of Joseph Brant*. Albany, 1864. 2 vols.

Stryker, William S., *The Battle of Monmouth*. Princeton, 1927.

Stuart, Isaac W., *Life of Jonathan Trumbull*. Boston, 1859.

Tarbox, Increase N., *Life of Israel Putnam*. Boston, 1876.

Thomas, Howard, *Marinus Willett, Soldier Patriot*. Prospect, New York, 1954.

Todd, Charles B., *A General History of the Burr Family*. New York, 1891.

————, *Life of Colonel Aaron Burr*. New York, 1879.

————, *Reverend Aaron Burr*. New York, 1879.

Truax, C. H., *History of the Bench and Bar of New York*. New York, 1897. 2 vols.

Turner, Kathryn, "Federalist Policy and the Judiciary Act of 1801," *William and Mary Quarterly*, 3rd Series, 22:3–32.

Turner, Lynn, *William Plumer of New Hampshire, 1759–1850*. Chapel Hill, North Carolina, 1962.

Van Der Linden, Frank, *The Turning Point*. Washington, D. C., 1962.

Van Doren, Carl, *Secret History of the American Revolution*. New York, 1941.

Van Schaack, Henry Cruger, *Life of Peter Van Schaack*. New York, 1842.

Venable, William Henry, *A Dream of Empire*. New York, 1901.

Wallace, Willard M., *Appeal to Arms*. New York, 1951.

————, *Traitorous Hero: The Life and Fortunes of Benedict Arnold*. New York, 1954.

Walters, Jr., Raymond, *Albert Gallatin*. New York, 1957.

Wandell, Samuel H. and Minnigerode, Mead, *Aaron Burr*. New York, 1927. 2 vols.

Ward, Christopher, *The War of the Revolution*. New York, 1952. 2 vols.

Warren, Charles, *The Supreme Court in United States History*. Boston, 1923. 3 vols.

Williams, Charles R., *The Cliosophic Society*. Princeton, 1916.

Wilson, James G. (ed.), *Memorial History of the City of New York*. New York, 1892–1893. 4 vols.

Winslow, Ola Elizabeth, *Jonathan Edwards*. New York, 1961.

Wrong, George M., *Canada and the American Revolution*. New York, 1935.

Wyatt, Edward A., "John Daly Burk, Patriot-Playwright-Historian," *Southern Sketches*, 1st Series, 7:8–11.

Zeichner, Oscar, *Connecticut's Years of Controversy, 1750–1776*. Williamsburg, Virginia, 1949.

INDEX